Elementary Treatise On Practical Magic:

Adaptation, Practice, Theory of Magic

with an Appendix
on the History and Bibliography of Magical
Evocation
and a Dictionary of Folk Magic,
Love Potions, etc.

---

by Papus (Dr. Gérard Encausse)

Translated by
Piers A. Vaughan

November 2017

This book is dedicated to Charles 'Chic' Cicero and Sandra Tabatha 'Tabby' Cicero, who gently but firmly led me along the path of Ceremonial Magic

ISBN 978-1-947907-02-7

Rose Circle Publications
P.O. Box 854
Bayonne, NJ 07002, U.S.A.
www.rosecirclebooks.com

TABLE OF CONTENTS

PART ONE – THEORY

PART TWO – PRACTICE

PART THREE – ADAPTATION

APPENDIX

FOREWORD

Gérard Anaclet Vincent Encausse, known throughout the occult world as Papus, was born in La Coruña, Spain at 7:00 am on 13 July 1865. He was the son of a French father, Louis Encausse, a chemist. His mother, Irene Perez, was Spanish and of Gypsy origin. While he was still a boy the family moved to Paris.

In the early 1880s Papus became a regular figure at the Bibliothèque Nationale de France and other libraries. His areas of study focused on Kabbalah, Magic, Alchemy and other occult subjects. In particular he studied the works Eliphas Lévi and Fabre d'Olivet. He was also influenced by the work and ideas of Saint-Yves d'Alveydre, Wronski and Louis-Claude de Saint-Martin. This influence is visible in the occult orders he chose to join, as well as being clear in the orders he ultimately created as his own.

In 1884, he joined Madame Blavatsky's French Theosophical Society, but resigned a year later due to the Society's emphasis on Eastern occultism.

In 1888, he founded the Ordre Kabbalistic de la Rose-Croix with Marquis Stanislas de Guaita (1861-1897), Joséphin Péladan and Oswald Wirth.

Also in 1888, he founded *L'Initiation*, which was the official magazine for the Librairie du Merveilleux which he founded with Lucien Chamel. Papus was an undisputed leader in this endeavor. In this magazine, they published papers by Stanislas de Guaita, Sédir, Péladan, Marc Haven, de Rochas, Matgioi, Barlet, Chamuel and others.

It was during this time that Encausse chose the pseudonym 'Papus' after the name of a Nyctameron spirit of Apollonius of Tyana.

In 1891, Papus and Augustin Chaboseau founded the Ordre Martiniste which owed its name to the memory of Saint-Martin and perhaps that of Martinez de Pasqually. The Order was founded for the purpose of transmitting initiations derived from Martinez de Pasqually and Louis-Claude de Saint-Martin, the Unknown Philosopher. Saint-Martin was a disciple and secretary of de Pasqually, and an Initiate of his Ordre des Chevaliers Maçons Élus Coëns de l'Univers.

In 1894, Papus became a Doctor of Medicine at the University of Paris and opened a clinic at the rue Rodin in Paris.

In Paris on 23 March 1895, Papus joined the "Ahathoor Temple" of the Order of the Golden Dawn under S.L. Mathers. His initiation was held at an Equinox Assembly and his was the first Neophyte ceremony to be performed in French. He would leave the Order a year later. A few years later Mathers changed the name of the Order to the Alpha et Omega.

F.L. Gardner's handwritten copy of Ritual Document A: General Orders states that members of the Martinist Order were in amenity with the R[osæ] R[ubeæ] et A[ureæ] C[rucis] or Second Order of the Golden Dawn "as long as they adhere to the teachings of their Founder."

Papus visited Russia three times between 1901, 1905 & 1906 and was the physician as well as an occult advisor for Tsar Nicholas II and his wife, Alexandra. In 1906 it was reported he met Rasputin. He predicted that they would be the victim of revolutionaries and in later years he warned them against Rasputin.

During World War I he served in the medical corps of the French army. In a military hospital he contracted tuberculosis and he died on 25 October 1916 in La Coragne. He was buried at Père Lachaise, rue du Repos 16 in Paris. His son, Dr. Philippe Encausse (1904-1984) was buried beside him.

I first learned of the *Traité Élémentaire de Magie Pratique* from an online auction listing. The text was a part of a very large private collection of Papus's Masonic and Martinism books, manuscripts and regalia that was being sold. The auction material included Martinism manuscripts and rituals, a large Martinism library with identifying stamps from the Ordre Martiniste and many photographs. Many of the items were sold to knowledgable buyers at prices far beyond the estimated auction values.

The *Magie Pratique* was one book I bid on but was unable to purchase. I had to wait several years until I discovered a copy in Paris. Although I am unable to read French fluently I began transcribing sections of the book and I realized the immense value of the text.

Early in 2016, I mentioned the book to Piers and he asked to see the text. After he received a copy of the book he agreed to translate it, and I am delighted that he has translated this valuable text so beautifully.

Now the ritual magic techniques of Papus can directly benefit an even greater audience than before.

Sub LVX,

Darcy Kuntz
Austin, 2017

PREFACE

In 1893, Dr. Gérard Encausse, also known by his *nomen mysticum*, Papus, wrote a book entitled *Traité Élémentaire de Magie Pratique: Adaptation, Réalisation, Théorie de la Magie,* or "Elementary Treatise of Practical Magic: Adaptation, Practice, Theory of Magic." This was the moment the general public came to meet 'Papus' for the first time.

Perhaps the most important word in the long title is *Adaptation*, for Papus makes the very important point that it isn't necessary to follow the instructions of the Grimoires slavishly, with no understanding or engagement of the intellect. He argued that modern man had neither the time to undertake the extensive and exclusive practices of old, and that many of the materials and implements required could either be purchased ready-made, or replaced with more modern substitutes. In this, he was perhaps the first public exponent of the Art to allow the ancient rituals to be *adapted* to modern use.

The book was a brave attempt to 'normalize' the esoteric world by placing it firmly in the realm of science, and Papus brought his medical knowledge to the challenge, in an attempt to show that everything which magic claimed to do was either firmly within the scientific domain, or would be in the near future. By applying his scientific methods to the study of esoteric phenomena, he hoped to make the magical arts a more respectable fiend of study.

To support this, he included extensive lessons on physiology, neural pathology and hypnotherapy. These were interwoven with discussions of magic, which were primarily based on the Grimoires, and in particular the Clavicles of King Solomon, to show that in some areas of study they were moving along similar paths. However, with hindsight the attempt fails for two reasons. Firstly, although he fills chapters with discussions on the functions of the human body, he makes little attempt to link these directly to the effects brought about by the practice of Magical Operations. Secondly, he tries to bring scientific method into the study of parapsychological phenomena, including telepathy and enchantment: but instead of demonstrating rigorous methodology, large sample populations, and repeatable results, the doctors use tiny samples (often a single person) and the controls of the experiments seem positively to encourage the subjects to lie, or at least exaggerate the symptoms to gain sympathy and attention. Yet for the high road he tries to take, Papus is not above adding phrases like 'Country' or 'Folk Magic' and 'Love Potions' to his subtitle!

That said, the book is important in the history of esoteric education for a number of reasons. It was one of the first books which brought knowledge of the Grimoires and Ceremonial Magic to the general public, rather than to a rarified group of disciples. He was also the first to try to marry esoteric studies to science, in order to make them more palatable; and indeed, his work in this field does not appear to have negatively affected his professional life. Compare this to the rather less fortunate William Wynn Westcott, a founder member of the Hermetic Order of the Golden Dawn, who was forced to resign from the Order in order to retain his position as a coroner in England.

Perhaps most importantly, it provides a fascinating insight in *fin de siècle* Paris, with its aspirations, energy, fears, and pride. We see a people galvanized with excitement, anticipating the World Fair in 1889, which would see the Eiffel Tower as a monument to man's scientific advances, the appearance of mass transportation by railroad, electric lighting, photography (all of which Papus mentions in this book), together with a burgeoning knowledge of the structure and functioning of the Microcosm – Man – as advancing strides in surgery, anesthetics, hygiene, inoculation, dissection and even early psychology expanded his understanding of how the human body works: yet as the true functioning of the brain still eluded him, there was nothing wrong with seeing the mind, soul and spirit from a rather more spiritual point of view.

Indeed, alongside all the advances in the sciences, at the same time we see an explosion in what we would term esoteric societies. In England, the Theosophical Society and the Hermetic Order of the Golden Dawn were being established, and even in English Freemasonry bodies were claiming connections with Rosicrucian and Templar forebears. In America, the Mormons had established their headquarters in Utah, Mary Baker Eddy was promoting Christian Science; and in France, there was an explosion in the number of esoteric societies, including the Ordre Martiniste, the Ordre Kabbalistique de la Rose+Croix, the Rose+Croix d'Orient, and again the Golden Dawn, to name but a few. This movement also affected religion, with the advent of Jules Doinel's resurrection of the Cathar – or Gnostic – Church; and even the world of art entertained the whims of that extraordinary gentleman, Sâr Péladan and his Salons de la Rose+Croix.

With this came the "Wars of the Magi." Everyone, it seemed, was writing books on esoteric topics, offering courses and subscriptions to magazines or correspondence courses. All were at war with one another, either because they saw their potential for profit being diluted, or because they genuinely believed the others were charlatans, and felt that they were doing the public a service by exposing them. Some fifty years later, we find Robert Ambelain making the same accusations, lamenting that many people were stealing his ideas and trying to sell them on as secret and proprietary teachings. Incidentally, we hope that one day, we can bring this fascinating author's works to the English-speaking world.

But as well as providing an intriguing view of the Paris of the 1890s, this important book stands as a milestone in the development of man's critical thinking. Compare, for example, the descriptions of science in this book with that of Louis-Claude de Saint-Martin in *Des Erreurs et de la Vérité* ('Of Errors and Truth') published 120 years earlier, in 1775. Compare Saint-Martin's belief in spontaneous generation, the dual composition of the human body, and the almost magical manner in which thunder and lightning happened, with the considerably more advanced scientific views of late 19th Century Europe. Then compare this to our present time, and be amazed by the distance which we have traveled since, in just over one Century.

We hope the reader will find this book of interest, both in the teachings it contains, and because of its important historical context, as a link between the Grimoires of the 16th and 17th Centuries and the Age of Enlightenment and beyond.

However, it is worth pointing out one final use for this book, beyond the portrait of 19th Century France. While the transcriptions of the Greater and Lesser Keys of Solomon might not be one hundred percent accurate, this is, perhaps surprisingly, the most comprehensive attempt to synthesize the entire system that I have seen. Even recent books work at translating the individual sections, without trying to produce a workable system which explains how the various parts of different books need to be used together in order to create a complete operation. The translations remain just so many unconnected books. This book, for all its faults, attempts to achieve that synthesis, and for that reason alone it deserves a place on any serious student's bookshelf.

This translation has tried to remain as close as possible to the original text, while avoiding ambiguity. Since some phrases do not translate directly, such colloquialisms have been substituted by phrases with a similar meaning in English.

The text has been supplied with extensive footnotes: Papus had a habit of writing for his times, and therefore makes many assumptions of his readers regarding current politics and history, newspapers, books and magazines, and famous characters and Orders existing in his times. Since it is unlikely any modern reader would be very familiar with these references, the footnotes are intended to provide a quick background, without forcing the reader to have to keep turning to endnotes in order to look up references. This will either delight or annoy the reader!

Again, as with any text which was written pre-emancipation, every reference is to the male sex, which is in fact odd in this context, given that the Hermetic Order of the Golden Dawn, Martinism and the Theosophical Society had both female members, and female leadership. Nevertheless, Papus used the masculine throughout, and it goes without saying that everything said applies equally to any human being.

Wherever a footnote ends with [PAPUS], this means the footnote was in the original book, to distinguish them from the current translator's comments.

As always, any errors in the text or in the translation are mine alone.

Piers A. Vaughan
November 2017

Note: So far as possible, copies of the original images have been included. This means that some will contain French words rather than English. Where the original was illegible it has been replaced with a modern version. Understand that not all the original images were of high quality.

The cover photograph is an interior of the Basilica of Notre-Dame de Fourvière, Lyon, France, and was taken by the Translator in 2010. The Basilica was completed the year after this book was published. Since Papus was a regular visitor to his Spiritual Master, Maître Philippe Nizier, who lived in Lyon at the time, the image is an appropriate homage to their mutual respect.

to anyone, for it leads neither to fortune nor official honors, and the person who follows this path, by going in this direction, must be ready to endure the three great initiatory expiations, and know how to suffer, to forebear and to die.

But whatever fate awaits him, the recipient of the Sacred Tradition mustn't fail in his mission. Up to now, the teachings of Esotericism have been hidden in the bosom of the Occult Fraternities, which have preserved them intact. The time has come to leave behind that reserve which up till now has been necessary, and expose the true worth of those pale copies and false concepts which absurd individuals or ignorant practitioners have sought to spread abroad. Now the spirit of liberty must finally vanquish clerical obscurantism and fearlessly reveal the teachings of practical magic, adapting them to the science of our age. And those who know *shouldn't fear this publication, for to most it will all seem little more than hollow dreams or alien musings, and only those worthy of mystical Adeptship will understand it and act on it. The facts of Magic are dangerous, and the words of one of our greatest contemporary Masters, Eliphas Lévi, anticipate those imprudent people who will open themselves up to madness or even death, by pursuing these studies simply because of idle curiosity. Anyone who fears suffering and privation, or who flinches in the face of death, would be better off studying sport rather than Magic; and the tutus of ballerinas would be a more appropriate spectacle for him than visions of the astral.*

Yet there is a lightweight magical experiment used by people who are easily scared, and we cannot recommend the practice of Spiritualism highly enough to people who wish to entertain themselves after dinner. It's not difficult, and it's very consoling. And it is so far from real magic, that one need never fear serious mishaps, seeing that one can always stop in time.

*

* *

At the time of the fall and transformation of the Ancient World, the Sanctuaries authorized the divulging of a part of the Mysteries: and the School of Alexandria, Gnosis and nascent Christianity called every reasonable being into Holy Communion with the Divine Word.

Now, our current times present striking similarities to the last Centuries of that Ancient World. In the West, Catholicism has taken the place of the ancient religious teachings, and the Pharisees have simply changed their title over time.

All the Schools of Philosophy are in motion, and Catholicism is on the point of death, beaten senseless by the clerical Pharisees.

At the same time the widest variety of doctrines and the most secret traditions are seeing the light of day. The Eastern Tradition represented by

Buddhism tried in vain to attract the intellectuals of this ancient continent. But then, the Schools which are the depositories of the Western Tradition were thrust into the limelight, and laid claim to the place which that nebulous Hindu mysticism had tried to invade – which incidentally is now reduced to only six disciples in France[3] – the Kabbalah has set forth its teachings; and Martinism, of more recent origin, has extended its influence and seen the number of its initiates multiply a hundredfold. Gnosis has reappeared brighter than ever; and that unanticipated movement which attracted people to Spiritualist philosophy is becoming so widespread, that industrious people are popping up everywhere, and with neither claim to tradition or understanding, are preparing to fabricate works of magic in the same way that, just a few years ago, they made up books about "Science for Everyman", and as just as tomorrow they will no doubt throw together Manuals on Witchcraft. Only one weapon is truly effective against these people: enlightenment which is as absolute as possible.

May their eccentric titles and their reputations, built on the audacity of empty affirmations and unjustified pride, fall away like so many houses of cards when they are made to explain the origins, transformations and adaptations of magical practice. Such subjects are their nemesis, since they are little more than so many pieces of wood, floating along the river.

Anyway, if analogies to the law of the Evolution of the Idea, *as expertly outlined by Charles Barlet[4], are true, none of these Schools currently which are at work can claim victory. All these attacks and all these battles have led to a breakthrough, and it is to provide help in these difficult times that we have decided to publish a summary of our works, as they currently stand, in such haste; yet knowing that we are not destined to see that Promised Land whose vision is reserved for future generations.*

Here we ask forgiveness for outlining some details about the layout of this work.

*

*   *

---

[3] He is referring to the fading of the initial enthusiasm for the Theosophical Society in France.

[4] In the original 1893 edition Papus wrote a gushing dedication to Charles Barlet, which had disappeared by the time the 1906 version was published. Similarly, with a kind of ruthlessness this dedication Barlet was removed from the front of the book, although he left the references to him in the main body of the text, probably to avoid having to do too much revising. This phrase including Barlet is also completely omitted in the 1906 version!

For six years now, we have been collecting documents and performing experiments necessary for the creation of a Treatise on Experimental Magic, which will show how all Magical Operations are in fact scientific experiments executed using forces which are still little understood, but very similar in their general laws to the most active physical forces, such as magnetism and electricity.

Preparing such a book takes a long time, and in reality, many more years were still needed to come to a proper conclusion.

However, given the multiplication of errors spread in the name of magic, and given the ridicule which a certain author, a great artist but a pitiful experimenter, has attracted to everything concerning such studies, and particularly at the pressing insistence of our friends, we have decided to publish a summary of the practical part of Occult Science, *which is as succinct and scientific as possible. This summary has no other purpose than to serve as an introduction to the excellent book "Ritual" by Eliphas Lévi, who has been reproached for not being sufficiently practical, mainly due to a lack of understanding of his work.*

The first part of our work, Theory, *shows the application of Pythagoras' and Plato's theories, and continued by Fabre d'Olivet, yet misinterpreted by all the translators, to contemporary psychology,*

The second part, Practice, *studies the possible manifestation of human abilities under the influence of various stimuli coming from outside. There you will find an essay on "intellectual hygiene" which summarizes one of the most personal parts of our research. Also, our chapter on Astrology begins to cover the purely technical part of Magic.*

With Adaptation, *we jump with both feet into purely traditional teachings. It is on this point that our experiments focus, to properly bring to light those facts on which we have been working for several years. Lack of time has obliged us to limit ourselves to manuscripts and Grimoires, and we have no illusion about the strange effect that reading some of these teachings will have on the mind of a modern person who is used to positivist theories. On the other hand, the documents provided in that chapter will be a powerful aid to the independent seeker, and help him to avoid much expense in terms of both time and money.*

Still, since we are discussing a subject which is very personal to us, we ask the reader permission to take a step back, and to introduce him to the person of Papus, whose name is taken from a doctor, a daïmon from the First Hour of the Nuctemeron *of Apollonius of Tyana. Then it will become clear who this work connects to, and who will immediately close this book, or even throw it on the fire, depending on the case.*

Concerning our profession, *we are a Doctor of Medicine in Paris, where we finished our studies, and our* occupation *is that of a student of the occult meta-sciences. The medical career was only a preparation for our occupation, for, outside of the Hospitals, we studied hypnotism at Saint-Antoine before continuing at La Charité, where, after winning the Bronze Medal for Public Assistance, we became the head of the hypnotherapy laboratory. Our evenings have been dedicated to attending mystical groups, where, for the four years our study lasted, we were able to participate in some of the most disturbing psychic phenomena which could occur. It's during this period that we were able to gather very important field notes on the degeneration of magical experimentation in the fields of Magnetism and contemporary Spiritualism. At the same time, we entered into relations with Occult Fraternities across Europe and the Orient. We aren't talking about the Theosophical Society, an association with no tradition or common teaching, which all the French writers are presently rushing to leave by every door available. We were even personally obliged to request our expulsion from that Order, but all the members of that Society learned of our decision which it had been hoped would remain secret, and for good reason. We can therefore state simply that the few serious practices that we were able to try out and verify were transmitted to us by an Eastern Society, of which Charles Barlet is the official representative for France, and in which we were a member of the lowest Grade. But all these stories won't particularly interest the reader. It's enough to know that our profession as a doctor at least assures the reader of our knowledge of physiology, and that, in any event we would point to our career and works as the sole guarantees we can offer in response to the insinuations and calumnies which have always surrounded our works in this area.*

We have no illusion as to the many imperfections of this work, which in a way is the Preface to a far more complete and voluminous work which we will published in instalments under the name 'Methodological Treatise on Practical Magic'. If we can realize our wish, this methodological *Treatise will be an encyclopedia on the subject, and will contain complete reproductions of rare books, manuscripts and Grimoires.*

Let us also add that this Elementary Treatise, *which is put together from some of the notes we have assembled over several years, was written in six months in the most diverse surroundings, across the days of our material life. Thus, the early chapters on* Theory *were written in the countryside, in the outskirts of Paris.* Practice *was written in the National Library in Paris, which is so rich in manuscripts and rare books on this topic. Finally,* Adaptation *was begun in Brussels, continued in Paris and completed in Cannes, in winter, during January. This is the reason we ask for the reader's forbearance, while affirming that every care had been taken in the composition of these materials, so unfamiliar to many of our contemporaries.*

PART ONE

THEORY

CHAPTER I – THE DEFINITION OF MAGIC

I am sure you know the story of Christopher Columbus' egg? Therefore, I won't repeat it here[5].

This story shows that, in general, nothing is harder to understand than the simplest things. However, if Magic seems so hidden and hard to understand (for those who study it seriously, that is), this is clearly due to the complications in which the student embroils himself[6] from the outset. We are known to our regular readers as an author who likes to use and even abuse images and comparisons: defect or talent, it's an inveterate habit which we will no more abandon in this book than in any of our previous ones. Similarly, we couldn't begin our study of magic better than with what might see a preposterous question: have you ever seen a Hansom cab making its way along the roads of Paris?[7] 'Why do you ask this bizarre question?', you ask. Simply because, if you have truly observed such a Hansom cab, you are in a position to be able to quickly grasp mechanics, philosophy, physiology and, above all, Magic. There you have it!

If my question – and especially my answer – seems absurd to you, it is because you don't know how to *see*. You look, but you do not observe: you passively experience sensations, yet you are not in the habit of rationalizing them, of searching out the connections between things, even those most obvious

---

[5] After Columbus' discoveries, legend has it that a group of critics suggested his finding the Americas was nothing important, and that eventually somebody would have found them. In response, Columbus challenged them to stand an egg on its end. When they failed, he tapped the end, flattening the shell, then stood it on its end. The point was, that any great discovery or brilliant invention seems simple after the fact.

[6] To state this up front: all works of the time used the masculine to denote both male and female. This was the time when most Esoteric Orders accepted both sexes (e.g. the Hermetic Order of the Golden Dawn, Sat Baha'i, Memphis-Mizraïm, etc.), and women also led these Esoteric Orders – so this was no more than a convention of the times. Indeed, even in 2017 a debate is going on in France over the fact that, even if there are 49 women in a class, if one man joins that class, the masculine form must then be used (*ils assistant à la classe* instead of *elles assistant à la classe* – they are attending the class).

[7] Remember we are talking about Paris over a century ago! To younger readers the Hansom cab was a Victorian one-horse taxi with a low center of gravity which could take corners at speed. Invented in England, it quickly spread to Paris, St. Petersburg, New York and other major cities, and was in general use until overtaken by the automobile in the 1910s. Any television episode of Sherlock Holmes will show you what they looked like!

in appearance. One day, Socrates, seeing a man laden with wood pass him in the streets of Athens, *saw* the artistic manner in which the wood had been prepared. He went to the man, spoke with him, and thus Xenophon was born. This is because Socrates saw with his mind rather than with his eyes[8].

So, if you want to study Magic, begin by clearly understanding that everything around you that makes an impression on you, all those things which act on your physical senses – in short, the visible world – are only of interest as coarse translations of the laws and concepts which are freed from these sensations when they have not only been filtered through the organs of the senses, but also digested by your brain.

What interests you in a man, if you are sincere, is not the clothing but the character, that is, how this man behaves. His clothing, and above all the way he wears them, may indeed give a fair indication of his level of education; but these are only reflections, more or less exact images of his personal nature.

Now, all physical phenomena which make an impression on our senses are only reflections – the clothes – of considerably higher principles: *of ideas*. This bronze before me is simply the clothing in which the artist has dressed his idea; this chair here is also the physical translation of the artisan's idea; and in all of Nature, a tree, an insect or a flower are material translations of a wholly ideal language, in the true sense of the word[9].

This language is unappreciated by the savant, who is only interested in the outer clothing of things, of phenomena, and who already has trouble with this concept; but poets and women understand this mysterious language better that any other, for poets and women intuitively understand universal love. Soon we will see why Magic is the science of love. For now, let us return to our Hansom cab.

A car, a horse, a driver: here is all of Philosophy, here is all of Magic, understanding of course that we must take this coarse phenomenon as an analogical model, and know how to *see*.

---

[8] Diogenes Laertius reports: "They say that Socrates met [Xenophon] in a narrow lane, and put his stick across it and prevented him from passing, asking him where all kinds of necessary things were sold. And when he had answered him, he asked him again where men were made good and virtuous. And as he did not know, he said, 'Follow me then and learn.' And from this time forth, Xenophon became a follower of Socrates." (*en.wikipedia.org/wiki/Xenophon* as of Nov 20, 2017). They became friends, and Xenophon, along with Plato, was one of those who documented the life and philosophy of Socrates.

[9] Student of the Kabbalah will recognize the concept of the Four Worlds in this statement; as readers of Plato will recognize the Parable of the Cave.

Have you noticed that if the intelligent being, the driver, wanted to move his Hansom cab without the horse, the Hansom cab wouldn't move?

Don't laugh and call me 'Callinus',[10] for if I ask this question, it is because many people imagine that Magic is the art of making Hansom cabs move without a horse or, to use slightly more elevated language, to act upon matter through will, without any intermediary.

Therefore, keep this first point in mind that, with a Hansom cab, the driver cannot move both himself and his coach without a motor, which in this case is a horse.

But have you noticed that the horse is stronger than the driver, and that nevertheless, by means of the reins, the driver uses and dominates the brute energy of the animal which he directs?

If you have noticed all this, you are already half a magician and we may confidently continue our study, but always remembering to translate your observations into a 'cerebral' language.

The driver represents intelligence and especially the will, *which governs* the entire system: in other words, the DIRECTING PRINCIPLE.

The coach represents matter, which is inert, and *which supports*: in other words, the DRIVEN PRINCIPLE[11].

The horse represents energy. Obedient to the driver and acting on the coach, the horse *moves* the entire system. It is the DRIVING PRINCIPLE, which is at the same time the INTERMEDIARY *between the coach and the driver*, and the LINK which brings together that which supports and that which governs, or links matter to will.

If you have truly grasped all this, you know how to *see* a Hansom cab, and you are close to knowing what Magic is.

You will understand, then, that the important thing to know is the art of managing the horse: how to avoid it bolting and making missteps, how to make it give its best efforts at a particular time, and how to rein it back when the road is long, and so forth.

Now, in practice the driver is human will, the horse is life, identical in its cause and effect on all senseless beings, and life is the INTERMEDIARY, the

---

[10] It appears that Papus is referring to Callinus of Ephesus, a poet of the 7th Century who is credited with inventing the elegiac couplet, which was form used by poets who were writing about topics elevated lofty than epics. Given how tangential this is to the story in hand (other than suggesting the driver pull his own coach, I guess), this would be more a comment to show off Papus' extensive reading than a particularly valid analogy!

[11] In the original text "le PRINCIPE MU": 'MU' from 'mouvoir', to move, to stir, to drive.

LINK, without which the will, indeed, cannot act on matter, any more than the driver can act on the coach if the horse is removed.

Ask your doctor what happens when your brain no longer has enough blood to allow it to function. The moment your will wants to move your body, you will suffer giddiness, bewilderment and, if this continues even for an abbreviated time, you will quickly lose consciousness. Now, anemia is the lack of activity in the blood, and this activity, this energy that the blood brings to all the organs (including the brain), call it oxygen, heat or oxyhemoglobin, only describes its external form, its clothing. Call it *vital energy*, and now you depict its true character.

So see how useful it is to observe the Hansom cabs strolling along the street, and see how our horse has become the image of blood, or rather the vital energy acting in our organism, and you will naturally realize that the coach is the image of our body and the driver the image of our will.

Now, when we become angry to the point of losing our head, the blood rises to the head, that is to say that the horse bolts, and outwits or side-tracks the driver if he doesn't have a firm grip. In this case the driver's duty is not to release the reins, but to pull on them firmly, if need be, and little by little the horse, subdued by this energy, becomes calm once more. It is the same for the human being: his driver, which is his desire, needs to act vigorously when angry, and the reins which connect the vital energy to the will must be held firm, so that the being will quickly regain his composure.

What does the driver need to gain control over an animal five times stronger than himself? A sufficiently long leather lash, a well-prepared bridle, and that is all. Yet we will see later how nervous energy, which is the means by which the will acts on the organism, has its importance in Magic: but let us not anticipate.

When one understands man's constitution in terms of the body, life and will, is one then a Magician?

Alas, no; no more than seeing how to drive makes one a driver. To be a Magician it isn't enough to know the theory, it isn't enough to learn what needs to be done in such or such treatise: he must do it himself, for it is by regularly driving more and more difficult horses that one learns how to drive.

What differentiates Magic from Occult Science in general, is that the former is a *practical* science, while the latter is, above all, theoretical. But wanting to practice Magic without understanding Occultism is like wanting to drive a locomotive without going through the requisite specialized *theoretical* education. One can imagine the result.

Now, just as the dream of a child who is given a wooden sword is to be a general without having to go through life in the barracks, the dream of the ignoramus who hears these things discussed is to command the rivers to move backwards, and the sun to go dark by means of formulas learned by heart, and all this to "show off" in front of friends, or to seduce a farm-girl in the neighboring village.

And this man is baffled when he fails miserably in his adventure! Yet what would soldiers say if the child with the wooden sword tried to give them orders? Before commanding the forces acting in a grain of wheat, learn how to command the forces acting within yourself, and remember that before you can claim a professorial chair in the Sorbonne, you must go through school, college and university faculty. If that seems to be too hard or to take too long, become an ostler[12]; for school alone, or a few months of apprenticeship, will suffice.

Magic, being a *practical* science, requires a preliminary theoretical knowledge, like all practical sciences. Thus, one can be a mechanic after passing through the School of Arts & Crafts[13], and then one is a mechanical *engineer*; or a mechanic after serving an apprenticeship and then one is an *operative* mechanic. Similarly, there are *workers* of magic in our villages who produce some interesting phenomena and bring about healings, because they have learned to do this by watching those who taught them do this. They are generally called 'witches' and are feared, wrongly in my opinion.

Alongside these magical workers, there are seekers who also understand the *theory* behind the phenomena produced. These are the magical engineers, and it is them we are primarily addressing in this current work.

Magic, being practical, is a science of application.

So, what is it that the Operator is going to apply? *His will.* This is the Directing Principle, the driver of the system.

But to what is he going to apply this will?

To matter – never! For then he would be acting like the ignoramus, like the driver who, jumping around in his seat and shouting at the top of his voice, wants to make his cab move while the horse is still in the stable. A driver acts *on a horse*, not on a cab. It is perhaps the third time that we have reiterated this truth of La Palisse[14], and we will need to repeat it many more times during the course of our exposition. One of the great merits of the Occult Sciences is having

---

[12] Someone who grooms and feeds horses, and mucks out the stables.
[13] *Arts et Métiers ParisTech* , founded in 1780, is a French engineering and research graduate school (one of the pretigious Grande Écoles), and is the equivalent of the American ivy league, or the English 'Oxbridge'. It is recognized as a leader in higher education in the fields of mechanics and industrialization.
[14] Jacques de La Palice (or Palisse) was a French nobleman of the 15th – 16th Centuries, whose poorly-worded epitaph was developed into a series of satirical songs, collected in the 18th Century by Bernard de la Monnoye who published them as a burlesque *Song of La Palice*. From the song came the French term *lapalissade*, meaning a truism.

precisely determined and established this point: that the spirit cannot act on matter directly – it acts on an intermediary, and it is this intermediary which reacts on matter.

The Operator must therefore apply his will, not directly on matter, but rather on that which incessantly modifies matter, in what Occult Science calls the Plane of Formation of the material world, the Astral Plane.

In antiquity, Magic could be defined as the application of the will on the powers of Nature, because the physical sciences reflected the framework of those times, and students of Magic learned how to manage heat, light, and also, as the story of Rabbi Yechiel under St. Louis[15] shows us, electricity.

But today this definition is too broad, and doesn't correspond to the idea of what an Occultist should do in Practical Magic.

These are indeed those powers of Nature on which the Operator must impose his will. But what are these 'powers'?

We're not talking about physical forces, as we've just seen, because the action of this sort of energy is the purview of engineers rather than practicing Occultists. But, outside of these physical forces there are hyperphysical ones, which only differ from the former in that they are produced by living beings instead of being produced by machines.

And we are not talking of the release of heat, light or even electricity produced by living beings. Again, those are entirely physical forces.

In 1854, Reichembach[16] proved that animate beings and certain magnetic bodies give out emanations in darkness which are visible to sensitives. For Reichembach, these emanations constituted the manifestation of an unknown energy which he called the OD. Since then, Dr. Dr. Luys on the one hand and Colonel de Rochas on the other have rediscovered various manifestations of this energy. But a fact now verified by hundreds of witnesses across various epochs will put us on the track of our definition.

---

[15] St. Louis was Louis IX of France (1214 – 1270). During his reign Nicholas Donin, a Jewish convert to Christianity, translated the Talmud into French, to assert that there were passages hostile to Jesus. In 1240 Rabbi Yechiel defended the Talmud, but nevertheless King Louis IX ruled that all copies of the Talmud found were to be burned. There is a legend that the Rabbi had a candle which burned without oil; also, to dissuade local hooligans from knocking on his door at night and disturbing his study, he rigged an electrical gadget to his doorknocker, so that, by pressing a button on his desk, he could administer a shock to the person knocking.

[16] Dr. Karl von Reichenbach was a renowned German polymath and inventor who, in 1939, retired from conventional science to focus on the human nervous system. Initially interested in Mesmerism, he developed his own theory of a life force which emanates from all living things and links them together, which he called the *Odic force*, or *OD*.

In India, there are human beings trained for many years in the handling of these hyperphysical energies, called *fakirs*. One experiment that these fakirs are currently undertaking, an experiment reported to me personally over a period of three years by hundreds of credible people, and which has also been described often, is as follows:

The fakir is given a seed of any kind that someone has personally selected. At the same time, he brings in small amount of soil taken from his home, and the seed is put in the soil, on the flagstones in the dining room, for example. The fakir, who is completely naked except a small loincloth, places himself about a meter from the pile of soil, sitting in the East. He fixes his gaze upon the soil, and little by little he turns pale and becomes motionless, his arms extended toward the seed. A modern hypnotist would say that he was in a cataleptic state. We also find that his body quickly cools down.

The fakir remains in this posture for an hour or two. After this time, the plant has grown to a meter or a meter and a half. If we continue the experiment, in the space of three or four hours the plant is covered with flowers, then fruit that one can eat.

And there, briefly described, is this experiment that our regular readers know well, having read it often. So, what has just happened?

The will of the fakir has put into play a power which animates a plant in only a few hours, that a year of cultivation would take to barely obtain the same result. Now, this force doesn't have many names to a man with good sense: it is called *life*.

We will not discuss whether life is the result or the cause of organic motion here. The important thing is to remember here is that the fakir's will acted on the dormant life in the plant and not only put this vital energy into motion, but also furnished elements of action which are more active than those which Nature normally provides. Has he perhaps performed a supernatural act? Not in the least. He has exaggerated, or precipitated a natural action: he has performed a magical experiment, but has produced nothing that goes against the fixed laws of Nature.

It is therefore by acting on the life of the plant that the fakir actuated the matter of this plant. But what did he use to act on the vital energy dormant in the plant? The teachings of Occult Science allow us to reply with confidence: *with his own vital energy*, that energy which he uses to produce phenomena attributed by doctors to vegetative life, the unconscious or organic life of the human being.

The point which confuses the seeker accustomed to physical forces, is that life can leave the human body and act at a distance; but even a superficial study of the facts about healing produced by our modern Mesmerists for the last fifty years, will quickly put the seeker on the path that we mention.

To give currency once more to our mania for analogies, so tiresome for the reader, let us retell our little story about carriages in terms of the fakir and his experiment.

The fakir, we know, can be compared to a Hansom cab, where his will is the driver, his vital energy the horse, and his body the carriage.

The seed is another carriage whose cab is very heavy for a poor sickly horse (the life of the plant) and whose driver, very young and still inexperienced, is currently asleep.

Now, our first carriage arrives before the second. Thinking of the suffering and the length of time that this poor horse will have to endure in order to climb up the slope, the driver-fakir is moved by pity. *He unharnesses his horse,* harnesses it to the other cab, and wakes the other driver who takes the reins. As for him, he takes the two horses by the bridle right by the bit, and encourages them along with his voice.

In no time (four hours), the slope (evolution of the plant), which would have required a long time (a year) to be climbed under normal conditions, is surmounted.

Once done, the driver-fakir leads his horse (his life) and harnesses it to his own cab (his body) which hitherto had remained in abeyance (in catalepsy) on the road.

Have you understood the action of the fakir on the plant? If yes, you are able to discern the role of life in magical experiments. From all this, it's clear that the energy on which the will acts, is life. And it is by means of that life which the human will controls, that it can act on the life of another being, be it visible *or invisible*. But let us not get ahead of ourselves.

We can already define Magic: the conscious action of the will upon life. But in our opinions this definition is not yet complete.

Will is a power found in all human beings. But how many know how to use their will properly? One must therefore not only possess will; one must also know how to put it to use, and education and training alone will permit one to obtain that result. To the previous term will we will therefore add the adjective 'trained', or better, *activated*[17], which indicates the effect of training.

On the other hand, the term 'life', or 'universal life', gives rise to many interpretations and debates, yet doesn't adequately bring to mind those connections existing between all the powers of Nature. We would suggest the term vital energy, but this term has taken on a totally human meaning. To distinguish those powers concerning the magic of physical forces, we will call them by a term which never fails to bring down the wrath of Materialist[18] Philosophers and others: LIVING FORCES. 'This term is absurd', our adversaries say. It matters little to us, for it is exact and, in our opinion, corresponds to a precise reality. We will seek to prove this later.

Bringing all these elements together, we ultimately obtain the following as a definition of Magic: MAGIC IS THE APPLICATION OF FOCUSED HUMAN WILL TO THE RAPID EVOLUTION OF THE LIVING FORCES OF NATURE.

This definition shows the entire plan on which this book is based.

First of all, we can see that the generator of the means for primordial action, will and life, which is considered to be the vehicle of will, is man.

We will therefore have to make a detailed study of the human being, particularly from the psychological point of view.

---

[17] *Dynamisée*, which can mean 'dynamic', 'active', or 'concentrated'. In most instances the words 'active' or 'activity' has been used.

[18] We should remember that, at this time (the latter end of the Enlightenment), the word 'materialist' has a slightly different meaning. It did not refer to a person who was focused on money and pleasure, but rather the philosophy behind this belief: the materialist was someone who believed that nothing exists except matter and its movements and modifications, and that there were neither any psychic phenomena nor anything outside of materiality. He was therefore an atheist. We should remember, of course, that this was as much a rebellion against the previous control exercised by the Roman Catholic faith, and many so-called 'materialists' were more likely to have been agnostic in outlook.

Thus, we will need to examine the various methods of training, once we understand the bases on which these educational methods for the human being are founded.

But once this training is complete, and once the conscious action of the will has been developed, these activities must be performed on objects which are clearly determined, and in a field of operation that is precisely delineated.

We will also consider Nature as it is understood by Magicians, and the helps and hindrances that this human energy directed by will is likely to encounter.

It is here that we will attempt to justify our strange term of *living force*, by showing how life in some cases can act as a totally physical power, following the same laws if it is materialized; and how, on the other hand, a physical power suddenly developed under the influence of vital focus can act in manifesting traces of intelligence.

It is from the result of this double play of life on physical energies and physical energies on life, that all the Operator's actions work on plants, animals, and generally on all the auxiliaries he asks Nature to apply his will, along with the application of the influences of the stars, whose emissions are considered in Magic to be living powers in the broadest sense of the word.

We make no reference to the effects produced by studies by those seekers who have already accomplished everything, and for whom science has already reached the *ne plus ultra* of possible evolution.

Though their analytical discoveries, those seekers have rendered sufficiently eminent services to humanity to have the right to be severe. Unfortunately,[19] a law of fate also requires all who appear to depart from the narrow bounds of routine be condemned to the pillory in advance.

It is to the young that I address myself: those who do not fear to affirm, to be bold, those who sense that there is something more than what they have been taught in the Universities and the Faculties. To those people I say: study carefully the explanations given by Magic, meditate upon them and only accept them under the very serious control of experimentation. You will soon be called to study *powers endowed with intelligence*, which will distance you from the studies of your current Masters, just as studying the transformation of energy distanced your Masters from the Physics of the beginning of the [18th] Century. Make it a habit therefore to look the unknown coldly in the face, under whatever aspect it presents itself, and make of it a classic phantom. As victors over clerical

---

[19] Occasionally it is necessary to add a word to make the meaning clearer. In this case I added the word 'Unfortunately'. Papus, as a doctor himself, is paying homage to scholars and scientific researchers, while pointing out that their assertions can sometimes restrict our thinking.

bigotry in former times, don't be conquered by scientific bigotry today: for this is just as dangerous beneath its liberal appearance. Be proud of your freedom, use it, and learn how to be guided by your person in everything, even in the determination of your scientific opinions.

And now, if the plan laid out above doesn't frighten you too much, turn the page and let's continue our exposé.

CHAPTER II – MAN

A SUMMARY OF HIS ANATOMICAL, PHYSIOLOGICAL & PSYCHOLOGICAL CONSTITUTION

The fundamental basis of Practical Magic, as we've stated, is the human being. Indeed, it is man who is the generator of will, without which it is impossible to act consciously on anything.

But if it's easy to pronounce this sonorous word: man, it's very difficult to really understand what this word corresponds to. For the several thousand years that this issue has been discussed, we know from the number of opinions put forward just how much this subject particularly interests all of us.

Therefore, we must begin with a study of man which must necessarily be a summary, but must also be as clear as possible. This study will have the sole aim of preparing us to see more clearly, for we shouldn't forget that we are attempting to write a very elementary treatise on Practical Magic, and not a treatise on physiology or psychology. However, we will be obliged, in the name of the constitution of the human being, to outline certain elementary principles of physiology and psychology, without which everything which follows would be obscure and incomprehensible.

What we must understand from the outset, is this word: *man*, which is a composite term under which many essentially different elements have been united, although all lead to a certain unity. When we say *man*, it is as if we are saying *Nature*, for man is as complex as Nature in its apparent simplicity. Our first task should consist of separating as best we can the elements which compose the human being; and then we can try to see the connections between these elements. Finally, we will end by considering the links between these elements and the other principles to which the human being might find himself connected.

The first difficulty which arises is in understanding precisely not what man is, but on the contrary, what he essentially isn't, all of which is nevertheless covered by his name.

Thus, in considering sleep, we can make a most important observation. Man seems to be composed of two parts, since the heart beats, the lungs inspire and expire the restorative air, the blood circulates; and yet the human being is not capable of love or hate, anger or pity, for he who normally feels these sentiments or exhibits these passions is at rest, is asleep. There is a part of the human organism which continues its functions, and another part in which the functions have stopped. Where is the true man in all this? Is it the part which sleeps, or the part which is awake?

Commonsense will lead you to reply unanimously: during sleep man is dormant. It isn't him who carries out the functions which we call organic. Not at all.

That which we call man is endowed with the faculty of feeling, or thinking and desiring. Now, this part is *dormant* during sleep, and that which remains awake is another thing which, independently of consciousness, is responsible for maintaining organic movements. Doctors call this vegetative or organic life, Philosophers generally call it unconscious: it is the automatic, almost mechanical part of the human being. Let's call it, if you will, the man-machine. But this is not true man, him who we see as being endowed with consciousness,[20] and above all with free will. We shall return to this point later on. But for now, let's take note of this fundamental distinction between the part of the human being which is susceptible to waking and sleeping, and the part which never sleeps, in a manner which endures at least until death.

But these two parts of man are closely linked during life, and this union results in a series of phenomena which it is essential to understand.

Man, once woken, can indeed show us a new aspect of his being.

Let us leave aside the purely organic and automatic side of the human being for a moment, and focus a little on the part of man we call intelligent.

Have you ever wondered why a child, which is evolving into a man, hits a piece of furniture when he bumps into it?

Have you also noticed that the *first impulse* (to use the popular expression) always leads a man who has been hit to hit back?

So, here is a German solider. He receives a slap from one of his officers, and *his first impulse* is surely to commit an outrage upon its author. The soldier's hand suppresses a violent impulse which tends towards putting this into action. This movement is almost involuntary, and occurs inevitably since what we call 'reason' is absent.

However, at the instant the soldier's hand is about to follow the inevitable impulse produced, the idea of discipline, the duty to passive obedience, and above all the counsel of war and death present themselves to his mind, and an *impulse*, conscious this time, stops the effect of the first impulse, which *hadn't been reflected on*, dead in its tracks.

One can commit an action in a thoughtless or a considered manner, thought a brutal impulse or a conscious impulse. What is that telling us?

---

[20] *Conscience* can mean both 'consciousness' and 'conscience' in French.

This seems to indicate that beyond the conscious and reasonable being, a man who weighs his decisions, there is another, someone who acts in a brusque and brutal manner. We should therefore be led to admit that alongside consciousness and will, there is a new active principle. Does this correspond to any sort of reality? Remember that we're not claiming to write a psychological treatise, which would require endless discussions and exhibits. We are only seeking to bring to our contemporaries' attention the teachings of Magic as it concerns man's constitution, and to do this, so far as possible, by making use of the very latest opinions and discoveries. This is the limit of our intentions.

Now, evidently that which impels one to render slap for slap; and that which, on the contrary, impels one to realize the consequences of the action one is going to take before committing the act, constitutes one single and same principle.

And it is very true that the man of the people, who is all impulse, begins by lashing out before reflecting, whereas the man of the world knows how to control himself, to hand out his card and establish witnesses if he was dealing with an equal in intelligence.

Later, we shall investigate the possible relations which exist between these two external manifestations of the activity called 'psychological[21]'. For now, we will avoid complicated discussions and details.

To summarize: When man sleeps, he can be divided into two parts:

1.   The automatic part, which is acting at this time;
2.   The intelligent part, which is at rest during sleep.

But when man wakes up and when he *acts*, we are led to make a new subdivision in the intelligent part, according to the effects produced, and we can determine two new modes in the human being:

Impulsive man, who obeys his *first impulse*;

Reasoning man, who reflects before acting, and whose every act is the manifestation, no longer of an idea or a sensation, but rather of a thought or a judgement.

---

[21] In the original text Papas used the word 'psychique'. Unfortunately, the term 'psychic' immediately conjures up a completely different mental image to the one it would have done just over 100 years ago. When this book was written, psychology as a named area of study was less than 20 years old, and all aspects of the human mind, whether it was being considered from the material or spiritual world, was considered part of the psychological/psychic world. To the disappointment of some readers, perhaps, this book will use the term 'psychological' rather than 'psychic' unless it is clearly referring to what we would recognize in modern parlance are dealing with 'psychic phenomena'.

In sum, we have at this point decomposed our man into three modalities:

1. Man-machine;
2. Impulsive man;
3. Man of reason.

All efforts of Magic are based on the various processes which allow the man of reason to completely supplant the impulsive man. But the idea we have of man is still very vague and somewhat metaphysical. So, let us first clearly outline these three human modalities, then begin an attentive study of each.

THE HUMAN MACHINE

The first question which comes to the mind of an observer on seeing a machine, is to ask after its purpose.

Having focused on the machine's purpose, the observer then seeks to understand its function and the key details of its construction. With regard to the description of the human machine, we will strive to follow the path indicated by our observer's questions.

We shall see presently that true man, the man of will, acts on the organism, and by means of this on the outside world, by means of certain powers placed at his disposition by this organism.

Now, the human machine creates these powers in a certain order. But it also differs from other machines which man invents in unconsciously following its own constitution; and because of this, as a machine or rather a series of machines composed of living elements, it must lead to two ends: on the one hand to supply the powers and means of action to the man of will, as we have already said; but on the other hand, to endlessly support and repair its own cogs,[22] which are used to the full extent of their actions.

To get an idea of the human organism, it is necessary to imagine three factories superposed on one other, connected by pipes and electric wires.

The bottom factory is called the 'stomach', the middle the 'chest', and the uppermost one the 'head'.

The entrance for the materials used in each of the factories is placed in the façade of the upper factory, a façade we call the *face*.

At the base of the face is the entrance to the stomach, called the *mouth*, where the aliments (primary materials to be transformed by the stomach)

---

[22] Papus if, of course, simply stretching the analogy of a machine.

undergo a first modification. They are chopped by a series of knives (incisors) after being torn apart by filed points (canines), and finally ground by grindstones (molars) placed at the back of the mouth. A liquid secretion (saliva) aids the work and produces an initial breakdown of part of the aliments (starch). From here the primary materials descend directly to the stomach factory by means of a long tube (esophagus).

In the middle of the face we see the entrance to the chest called the *nose*. Two holes, openings to the pulmonary pumps, alternately aspire and expel the air which forms the primary material on which this factory works. After being warmed in a series of special chambers constructed in the form of cones (horns), the air arrives directly in the chest by means of a long tube (trachea) which divides at its base to plunge into two pulmonary pumps.

At the top of the face we see the entrance to the head called the *eyes*. These two organs, openings to the cerebral hemispheres, receive luminous impressions, which are transformed a first time by passing through several chambers (chambers of the eye), and are then subjected to actions of the very complex organs of other machines (rods) before being sent to the central factory. Two other organs placed on the sides of the head (the ears), as well as a host of others placed on the contours of all the factories (touch sensors) assist the eyes, and put everything into relation for the centralizing factory (the head).

To fix these ideas in the mind, one can imagine the stomach factory as a hydraulic factory in which the machines are relatively large. The chest factory is a steam factory with pumps, reservoirs, motors and a large quantity of pipes. Finally, the head factory is an electrical factory with dynamos, accumulators, commutators and a prodigious quantity of conducting wires.

In the basement are the organs of excretion, charged with expelling the unused primary materials and the by-products of transformation following their use.

These three factories thus comprised give a neat enough first idea of the *human machine*. Remember that we are still there, as we continue the analogy.

Let us see what functions each of these three factories perform specifically.

In simple terms the lower factory, the stomach, creates the material of the organism. It takes various aliments from outside, masticates them and from them makes chyle. If we want to remain within the bounds of our comparison, we would say that the stomach factory makes the wheels and the material organs which support the efforts of all the machines in motion in the other factories and all the powers which are fabricated there. In this manner the stomach replaces all those cogwheels, all those pipes, and all those electrical wires after they have served for a period of time. To economize on time, in many places within the organism there are depots, reserves, organic materials ready to be utilized. These depots are called lymphatic ganglions. Lymphatic vessels unite the organism to these depots and the depots to the main center, the stomach.

The middle factory, the chest, seizes the material elements which the lower factory sends to it, and *activates* these elements through the action of inspired air. Elsewhere, the chest restores to the elements which are spread through the entire organism (the corpuscles) the energy which these elements have lost. This energy carried by the corpuscles will be the source of nervous energy. Now, the Magician must understand the principles of physiology, without which it would be impossible for him later on to apply these specific rules to the elements, and others to respiration, in order to modify the sanguine corpuscles and nervous energy. To return to the function of the chest, the two lungs inspire air and release active elements, above all oxygen, to support the vital energy which animates the whole organism. From the lungs, the sanguine liquid goes to condense a part of its energy in the heart, and from there, the blood is diffused throughout all the parts of the human being. In this manner, the chest factory adds the first active element to the material fabricated by the stomach.

The higher factory, the head, takes hold of the energy carried by the blood, and a special organ, the *cerebellum*, according to the theories of Dr. Luys[23], gives birth under its influence to a new force: nervous energy.

This nervous energy spreads throughout the ganglionic nervous system, where it condenses in the ganglions of the great sympathetic nervous system acting like true electrical accumulators; and it is from the sympathetic nervous system that *all the movements* which are produced in the human machine originate. We can now get a clear idea of the connections between these three factories, or the links which make a single unity of the three segments of the organism.

The stomach is responsible for transforming the elements, but without the chest which sends it the sanguine afflux necessary for animating its machines, and the head which sends it the nervous afflux necessary to put everything in motion, nothing would be produced. The chest and the head therefore both have specific centers of action on the stomach, which also contains, as we have said, the organs of excretion of the three centers, although the organs of entry are contained in the head.

The chest is charged with activating all the organic elements; but if the stomach doesn't continually send it new chyle to repair the material losses

---

[23] Dr. Jules Bernard Luys (1828 – 1897) was a French neurologist. As well as being a pioneer in investigating the operation of the central nervous system, he produced the first photographic atlas of the brain and nervous system. Born nearly 40 years prior to Papus the latter, who was himself a doctor, clearly held Dr. Luys in high esteem.

brought about, and if the head doesn't put them in motion via the intermediary of its nervous centers, lungs and heart, nothing will be produced.

Finally, the head (or better, the lower back part of the nervous centers with its dependents) would scarcely be able to move anything if the chest didn't furnish it with blood, the primary material of nervous energy. And let's not forget that it is the human machine, or to use a rather trivializing term, the *Man-machine*, that we have just described.

It is this part of the human being which functions during sleep, while all the rest is in repose. This is what has allowed us to describe it as if we were describing some kind of machine, though it should be pointed out, however, that it is a *living* machine, far more delicate than any other kind.

The quality of blood depends to a large measure on the quality of the chyle; and the quality of the nervous energy depends directly on the quality of the blood.

That is why a good or bad alimentary diet can modify nervous energy for better or worse and, as a result, the connections man has with the outside world, as we will see later on.

IMPULSIVE MAN

From our example of the individual who receives a slap and whose *first impulse* is to hit the person back, but who *reflects* upon the consequences of his action and nevertheless decides to continue with his first impulse, we we able to distinguish a man of first impulse, or impulsive man from a man of reflection, or a man of reason.

This distinction is of the greatest importance as much for Magic as to better understand the psychological activities to which the human being gives birth. Moreover, this distinction corresponds to an extremely important reality, which allows us to clearly understand the psychological phenomena produced by hypnotism, insanity, and to some extent by drunkenness.

The fundamental characteristic of all impulsive acts is responding almost immediately and without resistance to the incitement which preceded the action. This corresponds to what modern physiologists call a *reflex action*.

A rapid and very summarized study of the constitution of the nervous system is indispensable for understanding what a reflex action is, and what it isn't.

Remember that the human machine is composed of three superposed factories, and that all the apparatuses acting in these factories are put into motion by a special nervous system call the ganglionic nervous system or the sympathetic nervous system. This nervous system represents a series of accumulators or ganglions, either isolated, or grouped in large quantities in one of the three organic centers: head – chest – or stomach. These groups have the name of *plexus*.

But an accumulator is only a *reservoir of power* which regularizes the current but produces nothing by itself. It must be charged by means of other apparatuses which themselves produce the power without storing it. We have said something about the role of the cerebellum in this regard.

But alongside the sympathetic nervous system there exists another on which we need to focus for a moment.

A long osseous column, the spinal column, runs the whole length of the human body occupied by the three factories, the head, chest and stomach. This long column contains within it all the electrical wires which connect the factories both to one another, and the factories to the center-general, the head. These wires are called the nerve *fibers*[24].

Now, seeing that these fiber bundles carry stimuli coming from the head going to the periphery, where, going the other way around, they import stimuli coming from the periphery going to the interior, the former are called motor fibers and the latter sensory fibers[25]. One can compare them to the ascending and descending tracks of a railway. The descending one is in front (anterior fiber bundle), and the sensory or ascending one is at the back (posterior fiber bundle). Both these bundles are *white* and laid out symmetrically to the right and left, for all the organs dependent upon this nervous system are paired or symmetrical. But if you were to cut the spinal medulla crosswise, you wouldn't only find white matter, indicating the bundles; you would also find another substance at the center of the medulla, grey matter, which identifies a tiny channel indicating the center of the whole system, So, what is the role of this grey substance relative to the white substance? It has the role of a center connected to a conduit, a station connected to a railway, a telegraph station connected to telegraph wires. As we

---

[24] In the text Papus uses the term 'cords', but he was writing in the early days of neurophysiology, and what he describes are more properly called fibers now, which are collected together in bundles in the spinal cord. Indeed, the layout of the motor and sensory bundles is now known to be far more complex than simply on the right and left – but this was written over 100 years ago.

[25] We should remember that neurophysiology was still in early stages of development in the late 1800s. Indeed, it was only a few years earlier that physicians had determined there to be a difference between sensory and motor nerves (before then it was assumed that all nerves performed both functions). We can see Papus' pride in this research by the extent to which he talks about these two types of cell, notwithstanding it has little impact on the content of the rest of his book!

have said that the head factory has more in connection with electricity than any other energy, we can use the telegraph as an example.

The medulla now appears in its entirety. All around these telegraphic wires, in front are those which carry messages from the center (the motor fibers), and at the back are those which report messages back to the center (the sensory fibers). In the middle is a long wire of the auxiliary telegraphic offices. Each office has two huts: behind, the place where messages are received; in front, the place where they are sent out. The two huts are linked, not only between themselves, but also to the other huts.

What is the purpose of all these auxiliary offices? To replace the central office, the *head*, as often as possible.

So, let us lay out once more the whole of the human organism: there are three superposed factories, linked directly to each other, as we have already seen. These factories contain all that is necessary for them to work. Also, they have no *central* communication with the nervous system other than that performed by the sympathetic nervous system. That is why the head cannot *direct* the functioning of the heart nor that of the liver: it's not its domain. So, what on what does the nervous system act other than the great sympathetic system? Now we will turn our attention to this point.

To each of the three factories is attached a pair of special organs called *members*. Thus, the stomach factory has a pair of legs, the stomach factory a pair of arms, and the head factory a pair of lower jaws attached to a symmetrical organ, the larynx.

Now these pairs of members aren't operated by the same nervous system as the apparatuses working in the factories. The sympathetic nervous system governs the interior movement of blood in these members and over the respiratory changes which are produced locally there; but it has no action over the movements of the members themselves.

The medulla governs these movements when they are automatic, and the brain when they are conscious. Also, at the level of each factory, the medulla exhibits a *characteristic swelling*, a bulge from which all the fibers which go into the maxillaries or the larynx, into the arms or the legs, depending of the location of the swelling, come in or go out. Also, all the sensory points of the skin which envelop the whole organism correspond to sensory nerves which go to the medulla. For ease of description, let us add that the anterior or posterior bundles of the medulla take on the name of *nerves*, motor or sensory, when they leave the medulla and travel to the peripheral organs.

And so, each factory is divided into two very distinct parts:

1.   The central part, the machinery, on which the sympathetic nervous system acts alone;
2.   The peripheral part, the skin and the members, on which the other nervous system acts.

If we wished to draw that, we would represent it by a circle whose central part would be white to indicate no medulla or brain, and whose periphery would be colored to indicate the opposite.

What is true for each factory is also true for the whole human organism.

But let us now return to what is called the conscious nervous system.

It acts upon the periphery, as we have seen; but this can be of two types: reflex or conscious.

The figure below is going to help us understand all that.

This figure schematically represents the middle factory, the chest. In the center one sees the heart and the lungs operated by the Cardiac Plexus of the sympathetic nervous system. This plexus takes its root from the anterior part of the medulla.

At the periphery we see two types of fiber going to the Arm, the thoracic member. These fibers come both from the Brain directly, and from the Medulla.

Moreover, the Motor Neurons are centrifugal, as is indicated by the arrows. The Sensory Neurons are centripetal.

The Brain is composed of the Motor (anterior) and Sensory (posterior) parts.

The motor nerves and the sensory nerves are brought together into a single bundle on arriving at the Arm

Now let's see the passage of a sensation and a movement.

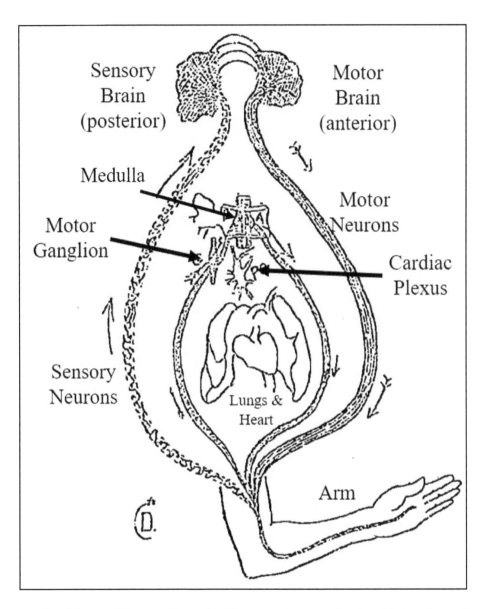

I prick myself on my fingertip. The sensation perceived at this level travels at the same time (if I am sufficiently awake and the sensation is strong enough) via the trajectory of both Sensory Neurons. Let us look at the one traveling to the Medulla first.

The sensation traveling in the nerve going to the medulla first crosses the Motor Ganglion, then arrives in the posterior medulla (the gray center), that is, in the office of the auxiliary telegraph. The employee (the nervous cell) immediately sends the electric current to his colleague in the anterior medulla. He acts via the electric wire, or along the nerve which goes from the medulla back to the muscles of the arm, *which quickly pulls back*. Here is the mechanism, perfectly understood nowadays, of a first impulse, of what is called a *reflex action*.

But under normal circumstances two phenomena take place at the same time and equally quickly. The nervous vibration also follows the route to the brain, and via the sensory nerve arrives at the sensory part of the brain, where the sensation is perceived as *pain*, that is to say where, instead of a nervous shock as in the medulla, it is *an idea* which is born. Shocked by this idea, the will acts immediately, and the order departs from the motor part of the brain, following the route along the nerve to arrive at the arm which, then, not only mechanically avoids it as in the case of a medullary reflex, but also rises into the air, and quickly throws itself backwards, such that the action of the *first impulse* finds itself singularly amplified by the *conscious* action of will.

In this case, the will acts in the same manner as the medulla. Let us return to our example of the slap to better understand the mechanism of this type of phenomena.

Let us follow the explanation on the figure below. The Prussian officer slaps a soldier at point A. Immediately, the two phenomena which we have just described are produced, and the sensation arrives in the grey center of the medulla C where it gives birth to an emotive impulse. The immediate reflex would be the movement of the larynx; but this is not the case in our example. The impulsive past of man is quickly put in motion and the two centers C and E of the medulla vibrate at the same time, since when a shock is sufficiently strong, it can make several medullary centers vibrate together.

From center E the shock is transmitted to the anterior part of the thoracic swelling of the medulla, and by F, F1, F2, the nervous movement arrives at the arm, and the medullary centers carry the arm towards the gesture to respond to the act as well as towards the individual. But the sensation has at the same time reached the posterior brain I via the direct sensory cord V.

There, the idea of pain is manifested, but at the same time the most elevated psychological centers X come into action, and the ideas of discipline, the counsel of war, of death, quickly arrive to determine *a judgement* which puts the voluntary centers into motion against the *contrary sense* of the reflexive movement.

The voluntary impulse V via the cord M arrives at the arm and acts in the sense NO, destroying the reflexive impulse F. The German soldier remains calm, having submitted to these two psychological movements which were so opposed.

Please forgive me for the naivety of these comparisons and the length of this exposition. I am persuaded that it is impossible to understand anything about magical training without all this.

To summarize, conscious and voluntary movement, either in the same or opposite sense of reflex movement, is always more powerful than the latter, and can either strongly exaggerate or prevent entirely the action of this reflex movement.

To compare this function with that of a powerful brake would be to understand only half the phenomenon. It is preferable to compare it, like d'Olivet,[26] with that of a sphere of considerable diameter in which are contained all the little spheres which represent reflexive actions.

Thus, alongside the purely mechanical part of the human machine, there exists a human mode endowed with a certain intelligence and comparable to an animal being in its appetites and its effects. This modality, which we have called *Impulsive man*, can always be subdued by true man, the man of will, but on condition that man is taught to use his will, and doesn't become a simple brute who submits to his every impulse, which so often the case.

But these impulses which can subdue man: what are they? What is their distinguishing characteristic?

Here we are obliged, once more, to ask for the reader's complete attention, because this involves questions which are normally poorly understood, and require sustained effort to grasp fully.

Everything we have said up to now, both about the constitution of the three segments (head, chest, stomach), and about the medulla and its swellings, has shown us that man is triple in nature, and that everything manifests in him under a trinitarian appearance. It is the same with his psychological constitution, and this is the stumbling block on which the majority of systems constructed by modern psychologists have failed.[27]

---

[26] Fabre d'Olivet (1767 – 1825) was an author and poet whose writings influenced many occultists, both of his time (allegedly Saint-Martin and Willermoz) and future generations (including Eliphas Lévi and Papus, among others). Vilified by the Church and Napoleon I (which was probably part of his attraction!), he studied and wrote on Hebrew, and his research of Pythagoras contributed considerably to the resurgence of interest in this philosopher, and the revival of the Neo-Platonist movement, particularly with an esoteric bias.

[27] This is a somewhat strong observation to make about a scientific area of research which had only commenced in 1880. Indeed, the proof he then goes on to provide could in no terms be described as 'scientific'!

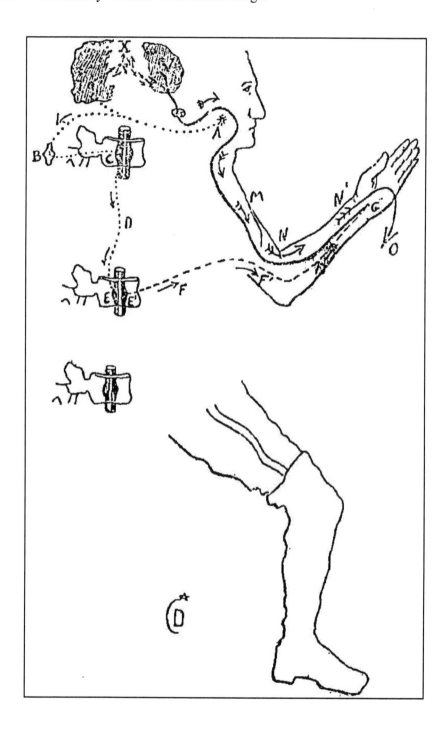

Ask yourself where you would experience a sensation of heaviness when, as a student, an examination needs to be taken? You would reply: 'in the (pit of the) *stomach*', and you would smile while thinking about the consequences produced on certain comrades by this type of psychological problem.

In contrast, at the instant of revealing your love to the object of your affection, where do you feel a specific oppression – an oppression where it feels as if your heart is going to burst? In the chest, no?

*

* *

But in the course of life, when strong anxiety or researching a difficult problem makes you thoughtful, isn't it in the head what you feel this particular oppression, which I first shown you in the abdomen, and then in the thorax? Am I not correct?

Well, this certainty which your good sense teaches you is the key to the psychology of Pythagoras and Plato, brought to light by the considerable work of one of our most eminent Masters: Fabre d'Olivet.

But this is all too natural, too simple to satisfy modern philosophers, concerned as they are with checking how long it takes for a sensation to turn into a movement with their watches. Let us return to impulsive man.

Man is triple and even three-one [28] when he is completely developed, psychologically speaking. But how many men have only developed one or two of the intellectual centers of the four [29] they possess? The first goal of Magic will be to ask the serious student, before anything else, to learn to understand his impulses and to know how to increase or to curb them, depending on the situation.

Before beginning to delve into this question, let us recall some preliminary points.

When the human being is asleep, his psychological doors, the organs of sense, are closed. In the same manner, his organs of expression are at rest. So, what are these organs of expression?

Just as man submits to the influence of the outside upon him through the organs of sense, he acts upon the outside through gaze (the eyes), speech (larynx), gesture (arms) and by walking or action (legs). These are the organs of expression. But a little thought allows us to see that, if the will can always act

---

[28] 'tri-un' – a word created by Papus.
[29] As we shall see, this refers to the passive traits of the instinctive, emotional and intellectual man, and the controlling power of reason, if it is present, over them.

on all these organs, some among them are more particularly connected to one of the centers in man.

Therefore, the eyes belong to man himself as a man of will, who uses regard as a means of expression. Notice, too, that perception is the first organ to be modified by madness, drunkenness, somnambulism, etc…

The larynx, considered as the origin of the word, appears above all in intellectual man, he who we call the psychological being, and the larynx is the organ of expression of this intellectual man[30].

The arms, considered to be the origin of gesture which, on being fixed, will become writing, belongs to the stomach, just as the arms belong to the chest.

Now, all these organs of expression can obey either the man of will, or the reflexes. We have already explained this when talking about the slap a little earlier.

When we walk straight ahead or when we follow a route we've followed each day for a long time, our will has nothing to do with this action, and the inferior reflexes act alone.

Similarly, when we work manually at a habitual occupation, our brain is free, and our hands act under the sole influence of reflexes.

Often, in a similar manner, we recite words learned by heart and known for a long time, such as prayers or similar things, without bringing our brain into the equation.

In all these examples, it is *impulsive man* who is functioning.

One trains a reflex as one trains a young animal, through habit, and some men's ideal consists of replacing themselves by their reflexes in all occupations of life. Then they say that they are happy.

The disdain people have for the lowly clerk often arises from this. This man is no longer good for anything. He has allowed his brain to fall asleep little by little, and replaced its functions with that of the medulla. He is a good and honest citizen, perhaps, but for all that he is a mollusc with a human head, an animal, a good and tranquil ox, but not a man: for a true man is a man of *determination*, and never, absolutely never, a man of *habit*. He is a brain which works actively, and not a medulla which operates passively.

Now, the greatest enemy of Magic is the impulsive man. He it is we must know how to tame, despite his protestations in every one of us, for from him all compromise and all baseness comes. He is mortal, as Plato taught us in *Timaeus*, and true man alone is immortal. He who submits the immortal to the mortal materializes himself, and through his present indolence creates an immense labor for the future. But let us proceed. Impulsive man, reflexive man, is triple. He can

---

[30] Vurgey has described the function of the larynx very well in this regard. [PAPUS]

present himself to us as sensual, as sentimental or as intellectual. But his fundamental character is that of passivity. He obeys the suggestions of his craft or other whim, but he never acts by or for himself. This is the man-machine of Condillac: this is a somnambulistic subject who is perhaps intelligent: but this is not a man.

Sensation is the sole means of entrance existing in physical man. But, having entered the organism, sensation can be transformed to a greater or lesser extent.

A purely instinctive man, a brute from among base people reacting to a sensation, can only manifest needs. In this case he is guided purely by appetites. The ideal in life is, for him, to eat, to drink, to sleep. The ultimate joy is to get drunk, and it is in this state of inebriation alone that the immediately superior sphere, that of feeling, will awaken in him a little, and this being will love, as a male can love, a female. Now, let us apply the psychological theories of our philosophy to such a man. Where is his reason? Yet, he isn't mad: his reason is simply instinct, for he is an instinctive man, but this is not really a man. Let us go on.

A man more elevated than the preceding one, a workman in the city, or perhaps an artisan in the suburbs, will develop a feeling from an emptiness. This sensation will firstly create a need, but this shock will only last a short time, and soon it becomes *a passion* which will become the pivot of the whole machine, for it is the sphere of sensation which comes into play. What can one say, then, about these words regarding shock and sphere?

When we consider man, as we are, from a psychological point of view, we can perhaps compare him to a garden planted on three stepped terraces. These terraces are named: the first is called 'instinct', the second 'feeling', the third 'intellect'. At birth, every being has seeds with which to sow his first garden, instinct. Once these seeds have been sowed, they produce wild plants which require almost no care, since, alongside the gardens, la fountain of sensation is responsible for irrigating everything.

But when the plants which are able to have grown, they produce flowers called ideas and seeds which contain the potential for germination, too.

These are the seeds which must be sown in the garden of feelings, and under the influence of the fountain of sensation, aided this time by the work of the gardener, the plants grow, less wild, although of the same nature as the preceding ones, and new abilities come and adorn the psychological garden of the human being.

When these plants produce fruits in their turn, it becomes necessary to laboriously extract the seeds and sow them in the garden of intellect where the new abilities will be born, assuming the gardener redoubles his care and attention.

Thus, there are no ideas which are innate in man, just as there are no fully-grown oaks when a forest begins to grow in a corner of Nature. But there is in man an innate seed which develops more or less according to the will of man, and this seed gives birth to a tree which Christian mythology calls the Tree of Good or Evil, for we must know how to gather and to cultivate the mystical seeds which issue from this tree.

*

*   *

Well, once again we have given currency to our obsession with comparatives; but we hope that you can now understand the expressions used by Plato or Fabre d'Olivet.

Our image of a garden has a major fault in that it presents human abilities as immobile. Now, since everything in a human being is in motion, one should imagine the garden as also being in motion, and, in this case, it is preferable to write the name of one's abilities in a circle or on a sphere which can be turned at will. This is why every sensation arriving in the human being turns or disturbs one, two or three circles, following which this human will have evolved within himself one, two or three orders of ability. And it is on this evolution that man's place in Nature depends.

Psychological evolution! That's a good topic for study for our young philosophers. By investigating this question in depth, they would probably come to rediscover Plato, which could do no harm to their progress at University. But let us return to impulsive man.

We have just quickly described the man of passion, and we have shown that the artisans in our great cities understand this type of human being well; yet a fear of being improperly understood leads us to a comparison which will perhaps clarify this question a little.

For such a man, feelings hold the most important place. Who doesn't know how much painters and also many of those employed in the manufacture of novelties[31] love emotional music, the "genre which is eminently French", comic opera and romance? The ultimate joy for these good children is love with lots of

---

[31] *Peintres en bâtiments et aussi de beaucoup d'employés du commerce des nouveautés* - this phrase seems to be a very specific reference. It is possible it was a common phrase at the turn of the 20th Century in France, but other than that no further light can be shed on the selection of these two classes of workmen.

the outdoors, a rowboat and music all around them. Women hold first place in such a brain, and the French people, emotional to a fault, are famous throughout Europe in this regard. This kind of totally passionate human being has great qualities and great faults, but is also capable of great advances through education and instruction.

We have come to the third incarnation of impulsive man: the intellectual. The first question we are often asked on this subject is as follows: How can you claim that a man can manifest intelligence outside of the action of the immortal soul? This is materialism, the abomination of destruction, etc., etc. To this I reply by sending my adversary back to the study of hypnotism or insanity, and go on my way in peace, since here we can discover a key point in the study of impulsive man.

Just as there are sensual machines like the brute we have just considered, and emotional machines like the artisan, so there are intelligent machines like the office worker.

The office worker doesn't drink; for this is a habit beneath his caste. He courts few women after middle age, since he married early and goes home on the dot. The office worker is a reasonable being, balanced, and serves as a model of the bourgeois to his children. Yet this is not a man – it's a machine.

For him sensation, having stirred up very little instinct, has been asleep for a long time. Rather disquieted by the emotional sphere, he has focused all his self-growth on the intellectual sphere. Empty reason replaces love, counting insignificant minutiae replaces music. The question of money occupies the most important place in his existence, and life's journey is marked by luminous boundaries on which he reads: 1,200 – 1,800 – 2,000 – 2,800 – 3,000 – 3,600 – 4,000 – 5,000 – Legion of Honor![32]

All of life slips away between 1,200 francs and the Legion of Honor. After this, it is the long-calculated, long-measured and weighed happiness of a house in the country with little rabbits gamboling in the yard. When the office employee remains single, which is rare, the intellectual sphere stops at retirement, as does the emotional sphere, and often the instinctive sphere takes their place; and senile decay or the correctional police end this career of disinterest, honor and cerebral sloth.

Still, this office employee is an ideas machine, created by the State for its use, very useful to society, since the abilities he has developed by dint of teachers and extra homework are more advanced than impulsive man could produce:

---

[32] Of course, he is charting the average government employee's fantasy of a career of ever-growing salary, ending at retirement with a minor honor from the government or monarch!

deduction, analysis, comparison, memory. But this is not a man in the psychological sense, and above all in the magical sense of the word. He is an organism raised to calculate, to such an extent that his preferred vice, which is this kind of being's weakness, isn't wine or women, but rather *gambling*. Now, the recent example of Inaudi[33] has shown us that a human being can be an exceptional calculator without knowing how to read or write. The motive which moves the intellectual machine of man is *number*. From that comes the obedience to the hour and even to the second seen in somnambulistic subjects, and from this the ability almost all of us have of waking up at the hour we want, by thinking strongly about it before going to sleep.

There is nothing intelligent or extraordinary when one has grasped these three modalities of impulsive man, which Pythagoras, Plato, Neoplatonists, Hermetists and Occultists of every age have always taught.

So, it is possible to let the man of determination, which is true man, be extinguished during his life, to be replaced by the passive movement of the instinctive, emotional and intellectual spheres. This is the terrible danger of administrative jobs and careers which encrust a man with inveterate habits; and neither the army nor the magistracy can escape these pernicious influences. Alongside a *trade*, which puts in motion the mechanical part of our intellectual being, it is important for all men worthy of that name to have an *occupation* which is freely chosen. One may then relax from mechanical work by doing intellectual work, and *never rest by remaining unoccupied*. You become tired, and you will wear yourself out unwillingly. Yet this is the entire secret of being happy, as Maimonides[34] revealed to us in the 12th Century.

Now that we have spoken about impulsive man, let us look at the modifications which the man of will can make to his actions, and say a few words about the constitution of this man of will himself. To end, we will return to all these points when we consider inebriation, madness and hypnotism.

---

[33] Giacomo (or Jacques) Inaudi (1867 – 1950) was an Italian shepherd who demonstrated a phenomenal gift for mental calculation. Despite being illiterate, his peculiar talent caught the attention of showmen of the time, and he travelled the world. Indeed, Camille Flammarion, the Astronomer, wrote a pamphlet about him, in which he wryly noted that, due to his fame, Inaudi at that time received a salary triple that of the Director of the Paris Observatory!

[34] Maimonides, or Rabbi Moses ben Maimon (c. 1135 – 1204) was a polyglot, being well-read in theology, philosophy and the sciences. His expertise spanned Jewish history, religion and culture, Greek philosophy and even Islamic sciences and learning. He was a very busy man, often writing his many tomes while travelling or in temporary accommodation, since he was often found in persecuted groups.

THE MAN OF REASON

Dominating all impulses, perceiving and judging them, there exists a marvelous power more or less developed in each of us: the human will, the real and true man.

The man of will can act directly on the reflexive stimuli of sensation, emotion or intellect. He can act through gaze, word, gesture and action on other men and on Nature, for he has incarnated in himself one of the three great cosmic powers of the universe.

Like the mechanic on a locomotive, who occasionally looks at the manometer which shows him the status of the engine, and sometimes looks straight ahead in order to identify the current state of the outside world, and any dangers he should avoid by opening or closing the throttle, thereby slowing or accelerating the train's movement; so the man of will, immortal man, carried by the human machine, letting the wheels of impulsive man turn, informed through the senses as to the state of the outside world and informed by the internal senses of the state of his organism, has nervous energy at his disposal, which allows him to accelerate or stop dead any psychological movement produced in him.

This man does battle with Nature as an equal: he clears the forests which cover the earth, and establishes in their place wonderful towns where the results of his imagination on his will, innumerable inventions, render the place more pleasant, but also more dangerous for men of poor character. It is this being of will who reclaims the world of matter or the world of ideas, the inventor or founder of cities, the daring explorer or the revealer of eternal truth; and he knows he must suffer, abstain and die if need be, for he commands his organism and isn't controlled by it. He is a master and not a slave. Now do we understand the distance which separates Pythagoras or Newton from an office chief, even a decorated one...? They are all called 'men' by the common crowd: yet only the first two merit that name. And now we can try to give ourselves an idea of man conceived in his completeness.

SUMMARY

Three segments, three stages, three modalities, however one wants to label them, each divided into three.

Below, anatomically, is the stomach, physiologically the factory of material, and psychologically the domain of sensation and instinct.

In the middle, anatomically, is the chest, physiologically the factory of vitality, and psychologically the domain of feelings and passion.

At the top, anatomically, is the head (the lower posterior part) extended by the medulla, physiologically the factory of nervous energy, and psychologically the domain of the intellect and passive inspiration.

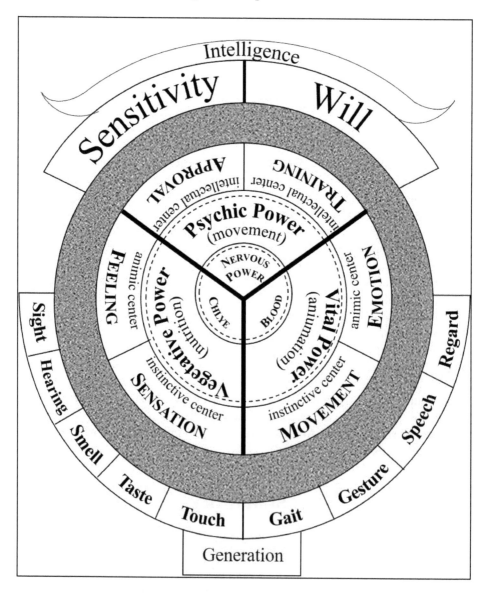

THE PSYCHOLOGICAL CONSTITUTION OF MAN
(after Louis Delfosse, the original illustrator)

Impulsive man, being able to move equally under a stimulus from above (will) or below (organism), is at the center of the figure, bathed on all sides with the nervous energy which connects this impulsive man to the man of reason above and to the physical body below. To the left in the figure is the receptive and sensory part, and to the right is the voluntary and motor part.

Above and all around these three centers, enveloping and ruling them as an angel envelops the one whom he protects with his wings in the mystical legends, is anatomically the brain with its servants the five senses, and the organs of expression, with the doorways (the entrance and exit for all that circulates in the organism. Physiologically it's the sublimating and toning center of the organic powers; and psychologically it's the domain of will and active intelligence.

CONNECTIONS BETWEEN THE MAN OF WILL AND THE IMPULSIVE BEING

Now that we have a preliminary and overall idea of this true man, this man of will, let's examine his influence on the impulsive being.

We've already considered the act of prevention exercised by the will over the impulsive centers many times. Let us continue with our analysis of this subject.

Each time a sensation affects the instinctive center, a man who is awake and in a normal condition of psychological health perceives this sensation at the same time that the reflex begins to move. Then he can bring about several different outcomes.

If the man belongs to the class of instinctive beings, or if he is in an poor psychological state, he perceives the sensation, and hands it off to the impulsive being who acts in view of satisfying his appetites, and passively perceives the new sensations of the accomplished actions. In this case the conscious center of perception, sensibility, alone has been activated, but only like a mirror which receives an image and simply registers it. There is no reaction from the superior being.

But if the man has the habit of acting on his impressions, he is not content to passively approve a sensation, and instead, at the instant it's produced, masters it and makes it submit to a specific kind of work to which we give the name of *meditation*[35].

---

[35] Note here the term *meditation* is merely being used to mean to think about, to ruminate on.

Meditation consists of the psychological digestion of an idea produced by sensation. It is also what brings abilities into play which may be more or less developed, and whose work transforms the initial idea into a thought, from which comes judgement.

Completely different results will be produced depending on whether the sensation is followed by meditation or not. Use of meditation is therefore a first requirement in the study of Magic and the use of will, and meditation is a mode of receptivity just as voluntary training is a mode of activity.

But we have barely outlined our study... We have considered sensation as only acting in its own domain, in the instinctive center. It's there that it is produced in a brute with a human face; but in a moderately developed man, other elements of action come into play.

We can think of this man, as we've seen, as three reflexive and passive centers crowned and enveloped by a conscious and active center.

The conscious being has three primordial function:

1.   He *feels*: he perceives images or ideas resulting from a shock or from the operation of each of the centers of impulsive man;
2.   He makes these ideas submit to a particular kind of digestion, a work more or less complicated depending on the psychological development of the human being who acts. In this case, we say that the man *thinks*;
3.   The result of this psychological work determines the action that conscious man is going to exercise, on the impulsive being, externally, or on himself. Here it is *will* that is put into action.

The distinction of the conscious being in these three aspects, that which feels, that which thinks and that which wishes, or sensibility, intelligence and will, will suffice to give us an idea of the principle aspects under which the fundamental unity of consciousness is presented for consideration.

Let us now return to sensation.

A sensation, once produced, can only activate the impulsive center of instinct, and we have seen what happens.

But this sensation can also reach the center which is immediately superior and affects the sphere of feeling. Then it produces two new actions:

1.   An impulsive reflex action, of sensory origin, towards the organs of expression, or *transport*;
2.   A specific action on the conscious being, who perceives not only a sensation with qualities of pleasure or pain, but a *feeling* with qualities of love or hate.

And that is not the end of the possible action of the sensation which, after being transformed into feeling, can still act as a feeling in the sphere of the intellect, which then puts it into motion and now produces:

1. An impulsive reflex action, of intellectual origin, to the organs of expression, an impulse;
2. A specific action on the conscious being, who then experiences not only a feeling, but an agreement with its quality of truth or error.

Thus, a sensation entering the organism of a man whose centers are developed is manifested to his consciousness successively as pleasure or pain, love or hate, truth or error, and at the same time produces three reflexive stimuli: appetite, emotion or education[36], which can be positive or negative, that is to say, passive or active.

The entire human being, after the sensation occurs, will either approach or distance himself from it, depending on whether the sensation is agreeable (pleasure, love, truth) or disagreeable (pain, hate, error). Let us not forget, however, that this is the *first impulse*, that the will can always modify.

So, if each of the centers expressed itself by revealing itself to us in the character of impulsivity, the conscious being, the man of will expresses himself on the contrary by always revealing his free character.

But there is a principal function exercised by the sentient being on each of the three impulsive centers: and this is *equilibrating function*, without which the gravest psychological accidents would be produced. We will now see what comprises this function.

In circuses, you have seen tight-rope walkers or rope-dancers. You will remember that the less experienced of these tight-rope walkers are provided with a long pole which they hold horizontally, and which singularly aids their practice. This pole is a purely passive instrument which only functions to provide a counterweight to the *push* which could sweep the tight-rope walker off his rope, which is the exact center line along which he has to move.

In his mind the human being also suffers a series of *pushes* which could throw him off the exact center without an equilibrating principle. So where does this principle come from?

From the harmonic connection between the two extremes, a connection such that when the tension of one of the extremes increases, the tension in the

---

[36] *Entrainement* can mean emotion, enthusiasm, rapture, impulse, training. Here the word 'education' has been selected, since this would pair well with 'truth or error' as being a learning experience (as 'pleasure or pain' relate to 'appetite'; and 'love or hate' to 'emotion').

other diminishes in proportion to that increase. This is why, when our tight-rope walker feels himself being pushed to the right, he inclines his pole to the left, and thus re-establishes his equilibrium.

All objects in equilibrium therefore assume two extremes and a middle term which serves as a pivot. In our example, the tight-rope walker is the pivot and the two extremities of the pole are the two other terms.

In the human organism, the mind and body are the extremes and the intermediary principle (life, the plastic mediator, the astral body) constitutes the pivot which transforms the whole into a balanced organism.

Now, physical as well as psychological health depends on this balance. Because of its delicacy, the human organism has often been compared to a watch, and this makes sense, since the least thing can bring about profound problems in this organism.

What we call health in the physical body is a balance, a result of many forces. Bichat considered life and death as forming the two poles, and health resulted from the equilibrium of these two contraries. Illness of the organic cells and, as a result, that of the entire human being, could result from an excess or a lack of nourishing elements. In the former case this would result in congestion; in the latter, we see anemia.

The preceding thoughts lead us to assert that everything is closely interlinked in the human organism, and that every center must be considered as being both a center of matter, a center of vital activity, and a center of psychological impulse. So, as congestion and anemia act only on the psychological being, correspondingly analogous states act on the impulsive being and the conscious being as well. In other words, there are maladies of the astral body and the spirit just as there are maladies of the person, and most of the time these maladies are caused by a disequilibrium, either due to an excess or a lack thereof.

Now, when the unconscious being acts on the three impulsive centers by means of nervous energy, it leads to a special tension in these centers which acts like a true equilibrating energy.

This is how, under the influence of this reaction to the consciousness of the true self, the lower impulsive center – or instinct – becomes *commonsense*. In the middle impulsive center, or that of emotion, the influence of the conscious being produces the marvelous equilibrium called *reason*. Finally, in the intellectual center, the true self manifests *wisdom*.

Once again, these three states, commonsense, reason and wisdom, are the result of a balance between sensibility and consciousness, and this equilibrium can be broken for many reasons. From this fact derive several psychological states which are most interesting, and very important to understand.

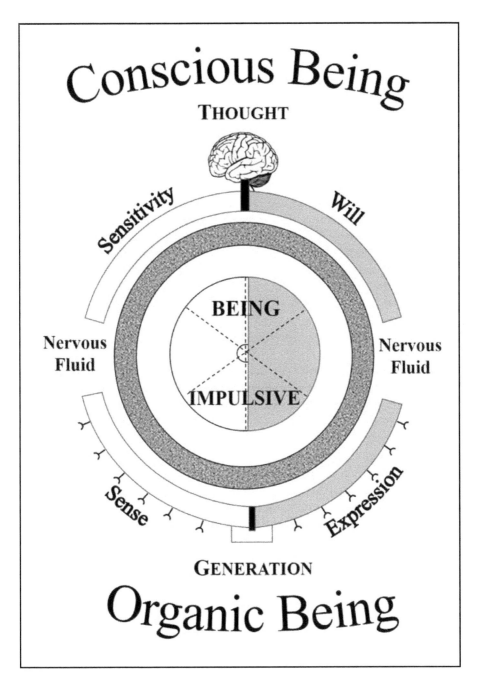

(See the Figure on the Psychological Constitution of Man for more detail)

To give a precise enough account of these states, we must now concern ourselves with the psychological powers in contact with each of our psychic elements.

The action of the external world on the mind and the mind's reaction on the external world doesn't happen directly, any more than the driver acts directly on his cab.

The organ of sense open to the external world represents matter (the cab), and spirit represents the driver; but between the two there is a physiological energy provided by the work of life: *this is nervous energy, analogous to the horse.*

The nervous energy is the link which unites the mind to the material body in both actions and reactions. This nervous energy is in fact, as we have seen, simply a sublimation of life by specific organs. The mind uses this nervous energy like a telegrapher uses electricity: it is in augmenting or diminishing the quantity of this energy at a particular point that the mind moves or stops the organs which are under its control.

Now, in this action, the nervous cell represents the telegraphic transmitter, the motor nerve attachment represents the telegraphic wire, and the motor plate of the striated muscle tissue represents the telegraphic receiver. This is for the operation of the will.

In the case of sensitivity, the opposite happens: the organ of sense is the telegraphic transmitter, the sensory nerve is the telegraphic wire, and the nervous cell the telegraphic receiver. Yet who would claim that the electrical apparatus alone sends out all the telegrams, without the telegrapher being involved? This opinion, unsupportable when it is this concisely presented, is nevertheless considered as dogma by the materialist, for whom the nervous cell is everything, absolutely everything there is. Now, do you know the great argument the Materialists use in support of such a system? It's that any change to the nervous cell corresponds to a localizable psychological change.

Yet it seems to us that any change to the telegraphic machine will be reproduced in the telegram, and that doesn't mean that the telegrapher is necessarily a myth.

A bad transmission of the telegram can be due to a number of causes:

1. The absence of the telegrapher which would stop all transmissions cold;
2. Disturbance in the equipment, be it in the transmitters or the receivers;
3. A break in the transmitting electrical wire;

4. Poor regulating of the electrical supply which serves as the intermediary between all parts of the system.

Now, analogous psychological problems could be due to:

1. The momentary absence of the action of the conscious mind (sleep, for example);
2. A disturbance of the nervous cell, or the sensory organ, or the motor transmitter;
3. A rupture of the nerve;
4. Poor circulation or defective production of the nervous fluid[37].

All this can cause a loss in equilibrium, and all this can cause mental effects which are of a long or short duration and more or less serious. But to make such a jump and say that this invalidates the existence of the soul is rather a stretch.

It's clear that without the telegraphic apparatus (the nervous cell) the mind is like the driver without a horse; without electricity (nervous energy), the mind is like a driver without reins; and in both cases, it is difficult to move. But who would say that this proves the driver doesn't exist?

Nervous Energy

Since we have been concerned with the psychological action of various elements which constitute the human being), we now see the importance physiological forces play in this action.

---

[37] This was an early time in neurophysiology, so it is not surprising to see the terms 'psychological' and 'psychic' being interchanged (as noted earlier); and also the search for how the nervous system communicates within itself and with other organs, resulted in the theory that somehow the 'fluid', which we now know is present more as a shock-absorber, was the means by which cells communicated, and that it was physically produced as nervous nourishment and used up during the day, following which man fell asleep. It is interesting to note that, while the Church was hardly supportive of science, it was keen to latch on to this concept to support its notion of 'masturbation – *bad'*, by telling the faithful that there was only a limited supply of semen and that, overindulgence led not only to tiredness and stupor, but also severely reduced the possibility of fathering good Catholic children (to say nothing of those *hairy hands*...). So, when he refers to 'force' we will normally use 'energy'; but we will retain the term 'fluid' since it is normally compared to other fluids, such as 'solar fluid', etc. In this section, *esprit* has been transalated as 'mind'.

Nervous energy is therefore the indispensable tool whose management permits the mind to act effectively on the organism, and through this on the external world.

From the preceding study, we know the various conditions in which the organic machine is controlled by use of this nervous energy. It now remains to us to see the use the mind makes of this tool which provides it with the body.

Let us remember that the human being, beyond simply being the support of the physical body, includes another element tasked with animating and moving the whole: the astral body. This astral body almost always acts in accordance with the law of reflexes, that is to say that organic irritability is the cause of almost all the movements produced and this includes the movements of the impulsive psychological being.

So, when the stomach is excited by the presence of food, the organic nervous reflex comes into play and the glands secrete gastric juices. It is the same with the impulsive centers. Once a stimulus has reached them, these centers spring into action and give birth to ideas which manifest themselves to the mind.

These centers of impulse can be stimulated by emotion. But what, from the point of view of the organic powers aroused, is an emotion?

An emotion is a special vibratory disturbance, sent from a sense organ and transmitted to the psychological center by the nervous fluid. It is under the influence of this action of the nervous fluid that the impulsive psychological center comes into play, and the idea can be born.

In the case we are considering, the disturbance of the nervous fluid is centripetal: it comes from outside and enters the organism.

But the impulsive psychological center, put in motion, can in its turn act on the nervous fluid, which is put in communication with the motor organ, and a new vibratory current, centrifugal this time – that is to say motor – is born.

In both instances, it is the same nervous fluid which is used (there aren't two types in the organism), and the direction of the current depends solely on the original of the vibratory impulse.

So, the impulsive psychological center can be put in motion either by a stimulus coming from the external world, as we have just seen, or by a stimulus coming from the conscious mind.

Thanks to the provision of the nervous fluid, which the mind always has at its disposition in a state of wakefulness, it can directly excite any psychological center it judges preferable, and this is how the mind can stop a reflex movement dead by acting directly on the center producing the reflex.

The impulsive being, in its three modifications, is thus placed between the physical body and the mind, and it submits equally to the stimuli of either one: it is content to obey the strongest stimulus. This is why a man who, little by little, loses his ability to control his impulsive centers through his will, allows these centers to submit solely to the action of the external world, and rapidly becomes a slave to his physical body, instead of being its master.

Let's remember that nervous energy is the vibratory medium which transmits all impulses, and we can now better understand the action of the mind over the body.

In a normal state, the impulsive psychological centers are maintained by the mind in a state of tension, so that they cannot act in a contrary sense. But, where the mind no longer has the necessary quantity of nervous energy available, this tension diminishes, and the psychological center begins to act in an exaggerated manner to the slightest stimulus coming from outside. Then the sensation produced as a result in the organism itself, and the idea it gives rise to as a result has no correlation to anything objective. This is what one calls a *hallucination*. The origin of this ailment, which can have very serious consequences, is not due to any illness of the mind (since the mind, being of divine essence, cannot be ill), but derives from an insufficient means of action put at the mind's disposal, which is not the same thing at all. The danger of hallucinations is that they lead the human being to make false judgements due to the absence of commonsense or reason. That is why nervous anemia is so dangerous.

But that doesn't stop the mind from having the power to represent sensations, feeling or agreements, which it can produce itself by acting on the centers ofimpulse. In this instance the mind knows it is being deceived about the true cause of its impressions, since it not only has sufficient nervous energy to continue to maintain the state of normal tension, but it also has in reserve the ability to expend energy by means of its *imagination*, which is the will's ability to represent ideas by the movement imprinted on the impulsive centers and to group them together by exercising the particular abilities of the conscious mind. Imagination is a luxury which quickly disappears at the slightest fatigue, that is to say when nervous fluid is no longer in sufficient quantity to provide a reserve for the mind's use.

All we've just said is difficult to understand, and will seem unclear to many readers. Given the length of this book, we can only provide summaries of scientific knowledge, each of which would require a large volume in itself. But the serious student who wishes to study the several preceding concepts further by adding to his reading list the *Treatise on Psychology* by Fabre d'Olivet (*État social de l'homme*, 1er vol., Préface) and Plato's *Timaeus* will, we are sure, draw precious teachings from these.

Let us summarize what we've just said: the key to studying psychological phenomena and above all their problems resides, not so much in an understanding of the organic mechanisms, as in an understanding of nervous fluid and how it is used. It is through this nervous fluid *alone* that the human mind possesses sensibility and will, and can develop them.

Essentially, the human mind resides completely in the ability to think. Sensing and commanding the organism are modalities necessitated by its presence on the material plane.

Now, all the proofs invoked to deny the existence of an immortal principle in man draw their origin from disorders in the nervous fluid. It is by confusing the telegrapher with the telegraphic equipment and the wire with electricity that materialism has pronounced on arguments which cannot survive even the most casual examination.

Having read the preceding summary, a philosopher would not be able to stop himself saying: "Look at those Occultists! Having invented the plastic mediator to unite the soul to the body, here's one who gives this plastic mediator psychological abilities, and claims by this to have solved most of the problems raised." This language has been used across the ages, and to some extent it is to reply in advance to this kind of objection that we have attempted to apply the teachings of Fabre d'Olivet on physiology and anatomy. But the facts which we must now describe will suffice to show how easily the impulsive being, activated outside of the conscious being, can give rise to certain phenomena which are somewhat inconvenient for neo-philosophers who do not want to remember the teachings…of Plato, who defended this theory of the three modalities of the impulsive being, which he called the *mortal soul*, and which he carefully distinguished from the immortal soul or conscious spirit[38].

Natural Sleep

In the state of wakefulness, the mind uses up a certain quantity of nervous fluid, and following the use – good or bad – which it makes of this deposit, it creates a man in his right senses or a brute with a human face (instinctive center), virtuous or vicious (emotional center), wise or ignorant (intellectual center). What is called "working on oneself" or "taking a decision" only requires an initial effort of will at the beginning of the activity. After this initial effort which

---

[38] Nevertheless, for all Papus' praise of Plato's *Timaeus*, let us not forget that it was in this book, too, that Plato talked about the pathological 'wandering womb', believing a woman's uterus was a living entity which migrated around the body, "blocking passages, obstructing breathing, and causing disease." This passage, together with the use of the Greek word for uterus, hystera (ὑστέρα) led to the term 'hysteria', that common diagnosis of everything female in the 18th and 19th Centuries.

puts the psychological center in motion, the will now only has to let it run its course, guiding the movement as a captain guides his ship by the rudder, in other words, by the slow emission of nervous fluid.

When the quantity of this nervous fluid diminishes at the end of a certain period of work, the mind's connections lose their intensity little by little, and the nervous fluid which gave tension to the psychological centers similarly subsides more and more.

Then the arms and legs become languid, for the individual *no longer has the strength to stay upright,* his eyes close, his sensory organs no longer function, and *natural sleep* is produced.

Sleep is caused by the progressive diminution of the quantity of nervous fluid. Then external senses and will are lost, since the relationship between the conscious mind and the organism are interrupted for a time.

It is during this sleep that the astral body, creator of the physical body, makes up the losses in the conscious nervous centers, and produces a new quantity of nervous energy.

When this quantity of nervous energy is large enough, communication between the mind and the organism is re-established, and *waking* takes place until the next period of sleep. This mechanism has been described in detail by Chardel[39] in his *Physiological Psychology* (1825), and we would refer the reader at this point to this excellent work.

What we've said about the spirit applies equally to the impulsive movements of the psychological being, which leads us to say that natural sleep is produced by a diminution of the nervous fluid in the organism.

We'll see later how alcohol and coffee allow us to replace sleep temporarily, but with the danger of a strong reaction afterwards.

Inebriation

In a normal state and in a healthy man, the mind's tension on the impulsive centers is always equal to the tension of those centers on the mind. From this we see the existence of a kind of balance, the two centers each being in equilibrium

---

[39] Casimir Chardel (1777 - 1847) was in fact a magistrate whose legal career commences in 1806. Given this fact, it may appear odd that he wrote an essay on physiological psychology. However, in those times most educated people were both polyglots, well read in the classics, and something of Renaissance men, in that they studied – and became proficient in – a number of different areas of academic study.

with the other. From this we also realize that the ability to be impulsive can easily be put into motion.

The man who gets tipsy by whatever means gives his blood a larger than usual activation. All the organs are stimulated and the centers in which the reserve of energy is condensed are also stimulated. In addition, at the commencement of an action, the mind seems more alert and the imagination functions more strongly than ever, having at its disposal a considerable excess of nervous fluid. This is the first phase, the excitable phase of the action of alcohol on the harmony of the body.

At this moment the surplus of nervous energy pours into the intellectual center and the ideas it produces are more numerous and more alive than ever. But these positive effects only last a short time. The nervous tension of the impulsive being slowly surpasses that of the conscious mind. The mind tries in vain to stop the psychological wheels set in motion, since it perceives with concern that it isn't able to do so; it doesn't have enough nervous energy at its disposal. The horse has taken off, and the driver pulls strongly at the reins, but he can only make weak attempts. Man's animal center has conquered the rational center: commonsense, reason, wisdom, all these results of the action of the mind over the impulsive being are clouded, then disappear. The human being loses all notion of equilibrium, including that of physical balance, and if he tries to walk he sways and at any moment he might fall over.

Physical equilibrium is broken by the excessive charge of nervous energy in the impulsive centers, and, at this instant an obsessive idea, generally absurd, can become the driving factor behind the actions of the drunkard, over whom the mind no longer has any control at all.

This is the second phase of phenomena, a phase during which all the bad instincts, all the mad passions now awaken, and which can lead the human being to his doom, for the reflexes are all-powerful and impulsive man is, for now, driving the entire human machine.

If the actions of the drunkard increase in intensity, all the nervous energy the mind was still using is absorbed, and the feeble tension the mind had maintained in the organism disappears. The being collapses in a heap, asleep; and if the separation of the mind with the organic centers was too quick or too complete, death ensues.

This is the third phase of this phenomenon. There is a lot in common between these symptoms, and those produced by insanity.

Hypnotism and Suggestion

We have seen that each of the three impulsive centers can be put in action, either by a vibratory nervous disturbance coming from the outside via the senses, or by a nervous disturbance coming from the inside via the mind and the cerebral nervous cells.

Now, the different procedures of hypnosis have the effect of destroying the balance which normally exists between the impulsive being and the conscious being and, acting on the nervous energy, separates the mind from the body for a period.

The purpose of this consists of vigorously exciting the impulsive being, so that the action of this impulsive being holds sway over the conscious being.

This state is accomplished by eliciting a sensation of very great intensity (for example, the turning mirrors used by Dr. Luys, a brilliant point of light, the sound of a gong) which has a considerable disturbance on the impulsive center. It then produces phenomena analogous to those derived from inebriation, and the relationship between the mind and the body is broken for a time, which causes a specific kind of sleep. Whether this sleep was obtained by a mechanical object or by suggestion, it is still the same process, since an auditory suggestion is only a more intelligent form of the sound of a gong. When this sleep is obtained, the sleeping being is completely ready to receive any kind of impulse. It is now that the Operator intervenes.

He commands the subject to perform some kind of activity. The impulsive being of the subject obeys the hypnotist just as it would obey a sensation from outside or through the stimulation of its own mind and, as a reflex action, the suggested action is executed. At this instant all that remains in the subject is the impulsive part of the human being, and we know that the very essence of the impulsive being is a total neutrality and machine-like obedience to the strongest stimulus felt. Such is the mechanism behind all suggestions made to the subject and executed during his sleep. In this case it is the conscious mind of the Operator (the Hypnotist) which acts and can obtain any action possible, including effects on the vaso-motor nerves and on organic life, for the impulsive being has all the organic life of the being under its control. This is how we, personally, have been able to obtain considerable amelioration of vascular tumors or *naevi* (congenital port-wine birthmarks) by simple suggestion, at the Hospital de la Charité, where we have been running the Laboratory of Hypnotism founded by Dr. Luys for nearly four years. This is how we have also been able to obtain stigmata and other similar phenomena through suggestion. The reader might judge the simplicity by which we present this explanation, compared with the complex explanations provided by physiologists who claim to study these facts.

But we've only spoken about suggestions while in a state of sleep. Let us say a word about suggestions executed immediately on waking up, then suggestions of a longer term, that is to say, which are executed in a more or less extended timespan (an hour to a year).

When one has given a suggestion, and wakes the subject, he is immediately aware of the impulse which he received. The impulsive being acts with all his powers, but it is the conscious being which watches over him. It is then that the subject's prior level of education acts in a significant way.

If the subject is an instinctive being, and has a habit of passively following his or her impulses, for example a working class or country girl, she will obey the behavior suggested, certainly rather astonished, but then seeking to justify her actions to her fellows.

But if the subject is a person of will, used to controlling his impulses, the suggestion will only work if his will acquiesces. I remember making vain efforts for an hour to suggest that the handkerchief of a subject from an elevated social class would fly. Once the suggestion was made, the subject woke up and his will fought long and hard against the impulse of the suggestion!

In other cases, the subject loses consciousness, but doesn't execute the suggestion; in other words, he breaks the nervous link which unites the mind to the body.

Finally, and the most common result, the subject falls back into somnambulism, going back to sleep at the precise moment of executing the suggestion.

So, as well as commanding an impulsive being to do something at that instant; one can also command him to perform an activity which he must execute later, at a fixed hour, and experience shows that the movement will be executed precisely in most cases.

It's here that the marvelous active power of an idea appears again. When we give a suggestion a time period, we sow the seed of an active creature in the impulsive center, and mark the date of its birth through our suggestion. This active creature must act from within to without: it is not therefore a sensation, since the primordial character of a sensation is on the contrary to act from the outside to the inside. It is an idea clothed by our *will* with a special active power which we bury as a seed in the impulsive being and, on the indicated day, this idea will develop its power of action and put the psychological center in motion.

Occultists and Magicians give a particular name to this type of impulsive creatures created for a time by human will: they call these active ideas *Elemental Beings*. We will see later that there are several classes of this type of creature.

But let's not get ahead of ourselves. What is important to remember, is that an action imprinted by a suggestion can wait a certain time before taking place, and can, when it occurs, arrest the person's will, if he isn't trained to break the impulse of the psychological organism.

These phenomena of hypnotism then, when carefully studied, lead to providing fresh proof of the action of the free, conscious mind (free will), rather than negating this action. But it should be noted that free will only exists in a man to the extent that he is in the habit of making use of it; and that a fine office employee or an excellent drunkard are both absolutely *determined* beings, yet very rarely beings who are truly free.

We shall speak in another part of the book about the phenomena of magnetism and second sight, as well as the discoveries of Colonel Rochas[40], who allowed us to link ancient magnetism to modern hypnotism, which is really a version of the former.

Before ending this section, let us note the interesting fact that each of the hypnotic phases recognized by the School of Paris[41] manifests the action of a specific impulsive center. Thus, lethargy manifests the physical center of instincts; catalepsy manifests the emotional center of passions; and somnambulism manifests the intellectual center. Since Mr. Charcot demonstrated the existence of the three souls of Plato, isn't this a little sad for Mr. Charcot?

---

[40] Eugène Auguste Albert de Rochas d'Aiglun (1837 – 1914) was a military engineer who also published historical translations (particularly of engineering projects in ancient societies), and was an officer in the Legion d'Honneur. However, his passion was the study of parapsychological phenomena, and he was particularly interested in hypnosis, as well as telekinesis, spirit photography, etc. He was particularly known for his study of 'externalization of sensibility' in which the hypnotist would prick himself and the subject would feel the result; and was a pioneer of past life regression.

[41] The Salpêtrière School, also known as the School of Paris, was run by a leading neurologist, Jean Martin Charcot, towards the end of the 19th Century, in what has been called the 'Golden Age of Hypnosis'. He was credited with a number of discoveries in the neurological world, including Lou Gehrig's Disease and Multiple Sclerosis. However, his studies of subjects under hypnosis led him to conclude, firstly, that hysteria was a genuine psychological condition and not simply an affectation of women seeking attention; and more importantly, that hysteria could be observed in men as well. His belief that these could also arise from physical injury paved the way for the diagnosis of PTSD. However, at that time, the idea that men could be hysterics led to considerable notoriety. Indeed, later on the diagnosis of hysteria was refuted, and in France at least, psychology was set back by decades. But the notoriety at that time might be what Papus was referring to at the end of the paragraph: after all, men don't have wombs, so how could they suffer from hysteria?

Insanity

All the phenomena that we have seen up till now – sleep, inebriation, hypnotic states – are all based on the natural evolution of a series of events derived from a single cause: the rupture of the equilibrium between the impulsive being and the conscious being. We are going to see that it's the same with insanity.

What is dangerous in organic activity is a brusque transition from one state to another, shocks to the system, be they physical or psychological.

Nervous energy, being identical for all the nervous centers, cannot move to one point without quitting another, and this passage must be progressive to be without danger.

It is for this reason that the obsessive thought of the drunkard, although dangerous for him and those around him at that moment, doesn't persist after the crisis is past: for the excessive movement imprinted on the intellectual center was progressive and not instantaneous.

But if a terrifying vision, unexpected news, or a moment of extreme joy or fear suddenly comes and has an overwhelming effect on the impulsive being, it could result in that effect taking on such great importance that all the nervous energy which links the organism to the mind is suddenly absorbed, and then the human being could die or go mad.

Insanity is a kind of permanent inebriation. In insanity, the impulsive being is definitively taken out from under the conscious being, and, if the latter remains vaguely connected to the organism, it no longer has any effect over the lower psychological centers. The consequence of the loss of the mind's influence over the impulsive centers is a loss of the balancing power, the destruction of commonsense, reason, wisdom, and the ultimate triumph of reflex over consciousness. The type of madness will depend on the impulsive center which prevails over the others. If the intellectual center dominates, obsessive and persistent delusions of grandeur will take hold. In this case, the madman will appear as a subject submitting to a permanent suggestion in such a manner that it annihilates all other impressions.

If the emotional center dominates, we will see ecstatic madness, with all that brings to bear, come to life.

Finally, if it's the instinctive center which gains the upper hand, hypochondria and melancholy will win over all other manifestations.

Note that absolute separation is very uncommon, and often the madman will pass from one state to another at random, following the motions imprinted on the impulsive being.

A madman is often half a being, if not in fact dead. Swedenborg[42] affirmed this consequence, and from it drew somber conclusions on the subject of vampirism, conclusions which we will return to in another book.

We could give many examples to support this theory of the impulsive being and his possible independence: we could speak about fainting fits, dreams and visions, go into greater detail on the subject of hallucinations, etc., etc., but we are neither writing a treatise on psychology nor a treatise on mental pathology. The attentive and impartial reader can certainly *perceive* the numerous consequences which can be drawn from this very Platonic theory; and only the future will show if Plato was wrong, Pythagoras was incorrect in his thinking, and Fabre d'Olivet misrepresented his opinions on the famous mathematician. Be that as it may, ancient Magic explains all these facts by means of the same cause. We will wait for future pioneers to replace this explanation with a better one[43].

Summary

Let us now try to summarize in a few lines the constitution of the human being according to all that we have said.

Plato conceived man as being a head to which the gods, ministers and servant of God had added members and a body to allow it to move around. This is also the notion we have of true man, if we consider the brain as being an instrument of reception and action.

But man, a stranger in the physical world because of his essence, cannot enter into communication with the material plane except by means of a series of intermediaries. From this we see the existence, inferior to true man, of a psychological center differentiated into three parts: that is impulsive man, charged with transmitting man's orders to the material world and transmitting

---

[42] Emanuel Swedenborg (1688 - 1772) was a Swedish mystic who believed he had been appointed by Jesus Christ to write books to reform Christianity. Devoting himself to scientific theory and discovery, it was not until he was 55 that he began having the strange dreams of visiting heaven and hell, that pushed him onto his new path. He also believed in a form of 'psychic vampirism', in that entities – and even other humans either consciously or subconsciously – could drain a being of its life force (sucking blood is really a romantic image of the true act of removing the vital force).

[43] Oddly, Papus uses the term *contemporains* or 'contemporaries' rather than 'future pioneers'. This is possible because he was impressed with the speed at which science was advancing at the end of the 19th Century. However, the substitution above hopefully makes the intent clearer.

impressions of this material world to man; and finally, as required, to replace man's action on Nature, when, controlled by habit, he acts automatically (reflexive acts). If the human being were constructed out of steel, like the machines we build, these two principles would suffice. But this isn't the case.

The material part of the human being is composed of cells which group together to form organs, which in their turn come together to form systems. Now, all this constitutes the machine part of the human organism, which has three principle objectives:

1. Since the organic systems acting in man are used all the time, it is necessary to repair and recreate the substance of the cells: this is the function of the albuminoid elements contained as dissolved particles in the liquid part of the blood which circulates around all parts of the organism.

2. But it is necessary, for the human machine to function well, not only that the constituent organs be renewed and that wastes be expelled, but also that the living organs be continually vitalized, that they receive a certain amount of energy, just as they received the substances necessary for their maintenance. The blood also contains special organs called red globules or red blood corpuscles which constantly carry oxygen, the origin of organic activity. Thus, the two primary functions of the human machine are accomplished by the blood whose only purpose is to maintain this machine itself.

3. But certain organs, called nervous, draw a new power from the blood: nervous energy which, spread in its turn throughout the body and condensed in the special ganglions, puts all the systems into action.

Besides, this power directly links the mind to the impulsive being and through this to the organism itself.

If we now set aside the purely personal functions of the human machine, and focus on those abilities which are useful to true man, we'll see that the overall purpose of this human machine is to create that nervous energy which links conscious man to the organism through feeling and will.

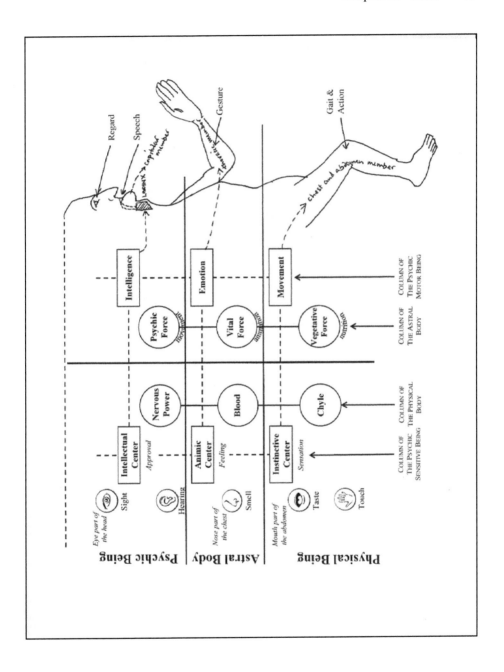

Bibliography

Works useful to consult for further information.

For occult science:

PAPUS...........................*Traité méthodique de Science occulte.*
                          (1st Part – Doctrine)
                          La Science des Mages (Chapter 1).

For psychology:

PAPUS.......................... *Essai de Physiologie synthétique.*
FABRE   D'OLIVET............*Histoire   philosophique   du   Genre   humain*
                          (Introduction).
                          Les Vers dorés de Pythagore (notes on will).
PLATO..........................Le Timée (Timaeus)
CHARDEL.......................*Psychologie physiologique.*

For scientific points :

MATHIAS DUVAL...............*Physiologie.*
                          Le Cerveau.
LUYS............................*Les Emotions dans l'Hypnotisme.*

CHAPTER III – NATURE

A SUMMARY OF ITS ANATOMICAL, PHYSIOLOGICAL AND PSYCHOLOGICAL CONSTITUTION

The preceding study of man is still quite incomplete, but it will suffice to show how the Magician must have a very specific understanding of the objects on which he should focus. Before returning to the human being, which always constitutes the point of departure and the point of arrival of any serious study of Magic, we must consider Nature.

Now, when I am sitting beneath a tree beside a road, while a stream flows a few steps away, bustling insects fly around in the grass, and above, the sun illuminates the whole scene with its rays, the word Nature summarizes for me all the impressions that I experience. This pebble before me, the tree under which I sit and the grass which surrounds me, the insects and birds I see, all this constitutes the manifestation of Nature across the three Kingdoms, Mineral, Vegetable and Animal.

But the earth on which everything relies, the water which makes the earth fertile and the air which I breathe, and which supports my life, as well as the warmth, light, electricity, modifications in many degrees of the subtle fire which constitutes the sun, all this is still Nature.

Finally, when night comes, all those fixed stars, all the wandering stars, and all their satellites which I can make out if I so wished, are still an aspect of what we call Nature.

In sum, Nature, such as we have just described it, is composed of everything which is visible around us, which is not us men. From this comes the term *not-me* which some philosophers have given to it.

But to think of Nature as the totality of the visible world and to study it as such is still like thinking about man only as his visible, external aspect: and that exposes us to confusing the habit with the monk. Nature is therefore more than this visible world which surrounds us, just as real man is more than this body which we are used to confusing with him. Let us consider this point more deeply.

The road by which I sat would certainly not exist in that state, if man hadn't applied himself to modifying the primordial work of Nature in this place. Even if the road wasn't regularly maintained, that is, if man didn't continually exercise his will over this road, we know that little by little Nature would take back its rights, and that weeds, trees and insects would soon destroy the works of man.

Human works only endure at the price of a constant battle against this power which directs the evolution of all that lives outside of us. If Nature, considered in its external aspect, appears to us as the ensemble of the visible world from the point of view of its progress, Nature shows itself under this new aspect as a specific force of prophetic character which presides over the progress of all these beings and all these worlds which we have just admired.

Compared to man, Nature represents the organic, mechanical part of the human being, and we know that a similar principle, widely modified, presides over the two great organic functions: nutrition one the one hand, and movement on the other.

This force acts on man outside of consciousness. From this comes the name *unconsciousness*[44] which the philosophers gave it, and the *astral body* which the Magicians gave it. We will soon see why.

In man, cells of very varied forms and functions exist, and yet it is a single principle, the activation by blood or life, which supports the animation of all of them, and which, when transformed into nervous energy, governs their movements.

A doctor who wants to act on a specific cell, wherever it may be, knows that by acting on the blood he will assuredly accomplish his objective. The only danger to fear in this case, is that this action on the total mass of blood won't affect many other cellular centers as well.

Now, in Nature all living beings, whatever their form and constitution, represent cellular masses equivalent to the organs in man, and are animated by the same principle which circulates through all Nature, as the blood circulates through all points of the human body.

Here we are touching on a most important point in the study of Nature in its magical context: and in order to focus closely on this, and avoid any possible obscurity on these matters, we must leave the visible and raise ourselves to the invisible, which is of particular interest to us.

If you asked your doctor to *show you the vital force*, he couldn't easily satisfy you. However, he could show you some blood and tell you that, if blood was prevented from reaching an organ, that organ would quickly die, which indicates that the blood contains the force which allows this organ to live, the vital force which you can learn to understand, but which you can no more *see* than you could see the 'springiness' of the spring whose use makes your watch work.

---

[44] Given the time this book was published, there is little doubt that Papus would have used the term 'subconscious', had it existed then! But to be fair to the times, we will continue to translate the word as 'unconscious' or 'unconsciousness'.

One can therefore understand the existence of these invisible forces by studying the material principles which serve to support them, just as the blood serves to support the vital force, or the watch's spring serves to support its tension.

Now, another remark of great importance, which we must say before proceeding is that, everything being analogous in Nature, the function of blood corpuscles regarding an organic cell is completely identical to the function of air in connection with the whole of man. In fact, the blood corpuscle carries what it needs to breathe, and it is this local respiration which results in the maintaining the life of the cell, just as our planet furnishes man with the air he needs to breathe; in other words, to maintain the man's life. So atmospheric air can be compared to the blood cell; and compared to the entire man atmospheric air is like blood, but the blood of the earth where man has been put.

The essential difference is that the cell is fixed in one point of the organism and the sanguine current comes and circulates around it; whereas man himself circulates in the atmosphere which bathes him on all sides.

But what we've said about man applies to all living beings on the earth, since a bird, insect orplant placed underneath a bell-glass from which air is removed to form a vacuum, will die more or less immediately.

Here, then, is why atmospheric air represents, for us, the material principle which supports terrestrial life. Just as one can only deduce the existence of the vital force by studying the action of blood, so one can only understand the action of life on terrestrial beings by studying the action of atmospheric air.

But you will then raise the following objection by saying to me: 'From the point of view of the cell in our organism, blood is certainly what air is to the whole man, I willingly admit. But that blood which comes and bathes the organic cell still has to renew its own powers by coming in contact with atmospheric air in the lungs.' Let us therefore set out the following point:

If I review what you have just told me, for man I find:

Cell = man
Blood = atmospheric air   compared to
Air = ?   the earth

I am missing one point: that is, what acts on the atmosphere concerning the earth, as air acts on the blood with regard to man?

To this I would reply by thanking you, for we are touching on the heart of this matter.

Indeed, organic cells are bathed by blood, as man is bathed by the atmosphere, and it should be sufficient to know what bathes the earth to discover the connection we are missing.

Now the earth, like all the planets of our system, bathes in *solar fluid*, which is the real origin of all the powers which are manifested in it as well as around it. Solar fluid is therefore the substance which maintains the mysterious force which presides over life in all of Nature, for, once again, all these visible things are simply the manifestation of invisible principles, and solar fluid is not in itself and materially speaking universal life, any more than blood is itself the vital force.

Thus, if we take this term blood as the basis for our definitions, we can say:

1. The blood of man is blood;
2. The blood of terrestrial life is atmospheric air;
3. The blood of planetary life is solar fluid, while remembering that all these elements: blood, air, and solar fluid are transformations of one another, and that the definitive origin of universal life, regarding its material basis, is solar fluid.

It's the reaction of each of the planets of our system to the solar fluid which results in the atmosphere of each of these planets, and it's the reaction of each of the beings on a planet to the local atmosphere from which the very life of each of these beings results.

Let us leave the other planets of our system for now, and just consider the earth, for it is that which interests the student of magic the most.

The earth, considered from the most external and clearest point of view, is composed of a mineral carcass, that is to say, formed by the Mineral Kingdom, which supports the liquid fluids (seas, rivers, springs, lakes, etc.) and gases (the atmosphere). Upon this base the vegetables and animals which form the two other Kingdoms evolve, and the whole is reacted on by various physio-chemical forces. Thus constituted, the earth is isolated in space, where it moves along a specific curve.

If we weren't to go any further in our study, we would stop at the elementary data of Astronomy and we would follow the paths of our contemporaries who only seek the obvious parts, the visible side of things, without considering the invisible side, the only side which is truly of use to us. The solely physical statements which we have just made only form the beginning of our research. Let's go on.

Each mineral, vegetable or animal being living on the earth is analogous to each cell in man; the atmospheric air which bathes all these beings is analogous to blood, and the solar and astral fluids which carry movement everywhere are analogous to the nervous fluid.

This already allows us to get a glimpse of a physiology of the earth, as we have rapidly described its anatomy, and to think that the earth may well be a living organism, just like each of us.

I know well enough that this idea will seem bizarre to contemporary people, but I repeat that he who unable to conceive the game of universal life in this already colossal organism which is a planet, will never be a Magician. He will be a preeminent physician, an observer of phenomena and an analyst of the first order; he will have a clear perception of the physical forces, but he will never be able to raise himself up to an understanding of life and the vital forces. Let's continue.

*

* *

The earth must be conceived by the Magician as an organism, in other words, as an animate machine.

This organism isn't static, and doesn't wait for the vital force to come and find it: it is, on the contrary, the organism which is in motion in the solar fluid, the origin and maintainer of the vital force which animates and moves the earth.

To avoid as far as we can any obscurity inherent in such things, let's go back to the human organism, which must be constituted like all other organisms in Nature. Let us go further and go back to one of the segments of the human organism (head, chest or stomach), for we know that the segments only differ between one another in their physiological or psychological function, but are identical with regard to the general law which goeverns their function and their constitution. So let's take the chest as an example.

The chest is composed of a crowd of cells of very different forms and functions, like the animate beings which populate the earth. The classification of these cells (general anatomy) will be similar to that of terrestrial beings. But this is a secondary point.

All these cells are bathed by a repairing fluid, and all movements, like the direction of nutrition across the entire system, are regulated by the nervous fluid. This nervous fluid, don't forget, is the instrument which the unconscious utilizes to act on the organism by firstly acting on the nervous cell. Now, in the human organism, the nervous fluid of a segment like the chest emanates from different sources:

1. There is a certain quantity in reserve in the sympathetic plexus;
2. But this very reserve is ceaselessly modified by the supply of new fluid coming from the anterior medulla.

In sum, if we admit that an intelligent principle, though not perceived by the conscious being, directs the exchanges and movements in the chest, we can localize its principle action in the medullary swelling, the true brain of the chest, and its secondary action in the sympathetic plexus.

In the chest itself, therefore, a specific center of activity is attached, the medullary center, which serves as an intermediary between the organic segment and the cerebral center. Now let's return to the earth.

In its specific spheres of action, the earth possesses an organ which is joined to it: the moon, its satellite. Let us seek this satellite's connections with the planet from a magical point of view.

Terrestrial beings correspond to the organic cells of man, and the terrestrial atmosphere corresponds to blood. With regard to the earth, what corresponds to the nervous fluid of man? The emanations coming from the stars which surround this earth.

In first place, then, we will put the solar fluid, the active emanation of the center of the system, strictly analogous to the cerebral center in man.

But, when the action of the sun and its fluid isn't preponderant on a point on the earth, when the phenomenon of night comes along, the emanation from the center of the system is replaced by that of the reflection of this center, and the lunar fluid comes into play.

The moon acts thus on the earth as the medullary and sympathetic reflexive center acts on the chest, and no longer like the cerebral center. This satellite is, to the planet, an organ of condensation charged with momentarily supplanting the function of the center of action. We also see the satellites augment this to the extent of how far away they are from the sun.

So, the luminous fluid which the earth receives is analogous to the nervous fluid in man and manifests the same action, that is to say, it rules over the progress and maintenance of terrestrial organisms.

The progress of life on earth, like that of many physical phenomena, is thus closely linked to the influx of the stars, or *astral influx*, and if the phenomenon of the tides demonstrates a purely physical action by these stars, a more serious observation will show us many other influences, not only physical but also psysiological and psychological.

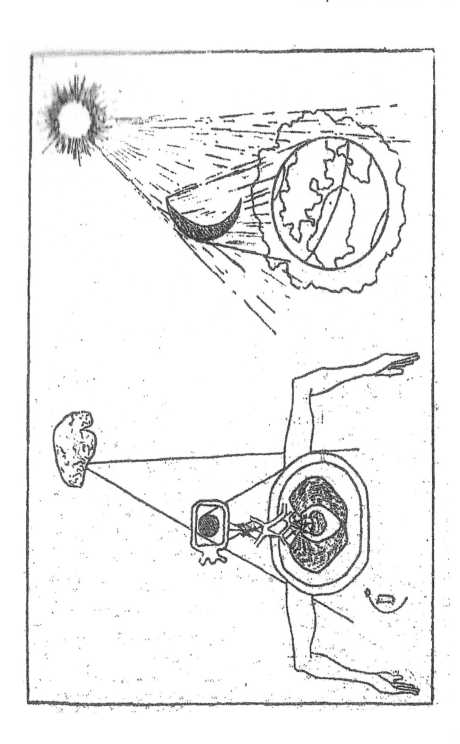

As the position of the earth in relation to the sun and that of the moon in relation to the earth varies at each instant, there are specific *phases* during which the astral influx makes modifications to a greater or lesser extent. Knowledge of these phases, called *morning, noon, evening, night* when they are connected to the movement of the earth; *first quarter, full moon, last quarter, new moon* when connected to the position of the moon in relation to the earth; and *Spring, Summer, Autumn, Winter* when connected to the position of the earth in relation to the sun, is of great importance to the Magician.

But if we go back a little, and remember that the earth and its satellite together only represents a segment of the human being, we would realize that we have talked extensively about the constitution of this segment and even the nervous action of the cerebral center on this segment, but that we've completely left the other segments of this human being to the side. We have done the same with Nature.

The chest and its medullary center, physiologically and psychologically, are the object of certain reactions to other segments of the organism: this is a point which we have already discussed in the preceding chapter. These reactions are less strong than those we have just talked about, but they exist none the less.

It's the same in Nature. The sun is certainly the center of our system, but to this center there are attached several segments or *planets* which not only submit to the action of this sun, but also act upon one another to some extent.

The earth doesn't escape this rule, and while studying the *astral influx* one must pay close attention to the action upon this influx by the various planets of our solar system. Also, a particular name has been given to each of the terrestrial revolutions – *day* – which takes place during a quarter of the moon, and each of these days has been dedicated to one of the seven planets of ancient Astrology. From this come the names of the days of the week[45].

*
* *

Here we are obliged to open a sidebar to talk about these seven planets and the choice of this number. The ancients, operating under principles and not phenomena, worried very little about the precise locations of these principles. It was enough for them to understand their action.

---

[45] This works better in French than in English: *lundi* (Monday) – Moon; *mardi* (Tuesday) – Mars; *mercredi* (Wednesday) – Mercury; *jeudi* (Thursday) – Jupiter; *vendredi* (Friday) – Venus; *samedi* (Saturday) – Saturn; *dimanche* (Sunday) – Sun. Although the last one isn't obvious, it comes from the Latin *dies solis*, a pagan festival.

Thus, the words Earth – Water – Air – Fire designated principles and not substances. From these we find the wonderful fabrications of our contemporaries who wish to see the substances themselves in these terms, and who, as a result, have understood nothing of the knowledge of the ancients. Today we divide our physics into: the study of solids, the study of liquids, the study of gases, and the study of forces. So, each corresponds exactly to a division of ancient physics in earth (solid), water (liquid), air (gases) and fire (forces). We haven't been able to come up with better divisions than those the Egyptians made, and with good reason. But that doesn't prevent our chemists, when they decompose water, from saying that the ancients were naïve and children to have considered water as a simple element. They made a fundamental error when they said that, since the ancients called everything that was liquid 'water'. *Eau régale* is chemically different to ordinary water (in French, *eau*), as is *eau fort* or *eau-de-vie*, yet all these substances were considered 'water' since they were liquids; just as magnesia was called *terre absorbante* (in French, earth is *terre*), pulverized iron phosphate was *terre bleu*, and acetate of mercury was *terre foliée mercurieile*[46]. Almost all these substances were solids.

A little good faith suffices to understand the naivety, not of the ancients, but rather of the moderns. It is exactly the same with the seven planets.

The earth makes seven revolutions which we call a quarter of the moon. Each of these new positions of the earth against the entire sky determines a particular state to which the name *influence* has been given, just as we have given this word to electrics in certain similar conditions. There are therefore seven specific influences acting successively upon the earth and which are themselves subject to a certain modification depending on the influence of the sun and the moon on the earth, since the influence of these two stars is preponderant, the first being the activating principle of the entire system, and the second being closer than any of the others. One may calculate for each day, and even every hour or every third of an hour of the day, the astral influences acting on the earth; and from this Astrology is derived, which is also decried by the moderns, as is alchemy; though, however, Mr. Selva has shown us that a well-educated Astronomer can draw very serious lessons from Astrology without leaving the purely scientific domain.

The ancients gave these seven influences we have just discussed the names of seven planets, and calculated these influences according to the position of these planets at a given moment. The heavens were divided into seven concentric

---

[46] In other words, elemental water included *eau régale* (hydrochloric acid), *eau fort* (nitric acid) and *eau-de-vie* (brandy); and elemental earth included the list of varying substances listed above.

spheres, and each of the seven parts of the heavens were considered to preside over a type of astral influence. Now, whether a planet or 36 planets moved in this sphere is of little importance. The influence always happens, and is calculated according to the star which is preponderant among the others, that is all. But even if there were 200 planets moving around the sun, the astral influence derived from the point in space in which the planets moved would not change. And if tomorrow someone proved that the system of Copernicus and Newton to be false, as Alcide Morin would hope (Thirteen Nights[47]), then what we took for other worlds under the name of fixed stars would now be simply the reflection in our atmosphere of the luminous emanations of the peaks of terrestrial mountains; and the sun is in fact an electric emanation from the earth and in itself very close, etc.; if all these ideas, absurd in appearance, came to be officially taught one day, all that wouldn't change one word of Astrology, based upon principles and not material localities, just like the four Elements we spoke about at the beginning of this already long sidebar.

Now, knowledge of the elements of Astronomy and later the elementary principles of Astrology is absolutely indispensable to know for the person who wishes to perform even a little Practical Magic. So, let us now move on to this question.

*
* *

We think that the reader is sufficiently well-versed in the teachings of occult knowledge to know that everything produced in the visible world is the result of the action of the invisible world upon matter[48].

In the human organism, when an accident or an illness has destroyed a certain number of cells but the sympathetic centers have remained intact, the unconscious repairs the organs, *and in their original forms*. The histological study of pneumonia *from the point of view of the modifications* of the pulmonary alveoli is typical as proof of this assertion. In the same manner, in the normal state it is again this unconscious which manages nutritional changes and respirations in every part of the organism.

---

[47] This appears to refer to the book by Morin, published in 1860, entitled: *Magic of the 19th Century, Darkness, Thirteen Nights, Followed by Half a Day Under Hypnosis*. This is available in print in French as a scanned book.

[48] "You can find the development of the themes outlined here in *Traité methodique de science occulte*." [PAPUS].

The school of Paracelsus gave this unconsciousness the name *astral body*. We'll soon see why. For now, let us simply remember that in man it's the astral body which directs all the manifestations of organic life, without which the will would have nothing to do.

The tool used by this astral body is nervous fluid.

Now, we saw that the fluid in Nature corresponding to the nervous fluid in man is the generally luminous astral fluid, but this astral fluid, unlike nervous fluid, is only the *tool* used by Nature in its actions.

Nevertheless, going forward we can establish the following conclusions. All evolution of terrestrial beings is made by means of the influence of the astral influx acting through its special fluid, and the speed or slowness of this evolution depends on the quantity of fluid available. Also, terrestrial life at the equator is a lot more active than at the poles.

So, there will be moments when a plant affected by a particular astral influence will be in a special state. Gathered at that moment, it will have properties different to those which it usually has, or at the very least they will be much stronger. From this comes all the knowledge of village witches, those seekers after "simples."

The evolution of all terrestrial beings is thus directed in the final instance by this special power which we have named Nature, or destiny. But this power acts on organisms through the light of the stars, or astral light, which is the universal intermediary (the horse) of creation. Each organism individualizes a portion of this astral light which, condensed in its nervous centers, becomes the astral body of this organism and evolves the material forms of this aforesaid organism. Now, the quality of this astral light will depend on many factors, among others on the position of the earth in space at the instant that the individualization of the astral light is produced to form the astral body.

Since the physical body is but the material translation for our senses of the action of the astral body, one may, by studying the *forms* of this material organism, determine the quality of the astral body which governed the evolution of these forms, and through this go back to the influence of the governing star at the moment of the individualization of this astral body. From this comes all the knowledge of divination by the inspection of forms. Each organism is considered by the Magician as being *signed* by one or two stars. And these sciences of divination have been given the name of *studies of the astral signatures*.

It follows from this that the astral body of any organism, being an adaptation of the astral light which circulates in our world, retains a permanent relationship with that astral light which supports its properties under the direction of Nature, just as the astral body itself supports the properties of the organism it governs.

The profane, when they want to act on an organism, always seek to modify the physical body, and have to fight constantly against the astral body, which following its inevitable path, forever seeks to re-establish the balance which has been destroyed; whereas the Magician, acting upon the astral body, modifies the *plane of action,* and as a result the physical body, without expending much effort at all. The whole difference between allopathy and homeopathy can be seen in that.

So Nature, or destiny, governs the progress of all the terrestrial organisms in the three Kingdoms, and, as a worthy result of such great attention, the human organism doesn't escape this Law, being an organism itself.

Indeed, the human organism represents the Mineral Kingdom with its skeleton, the Vegetable Kingdom with its vegetative life whose center is the abdomen, and the Animal Kingdom with its emotional life, whose center is in the chest.

We know that a similar power, modified in different ways, governs all these actions in man. Now, this power, in the final analysis, is simply the astral light fixed by the organic functions.

Now, if we have to represent the position of man in Nature, let's do it this way.

Only the head of man, the seat of the immortal soul, rules Nature.

The human organism, on the contrary, is completely beholden to the Laws and the influence of this Nature, which is itself the famous "unconsciousness" of our modern physiologists. Man, thus conceived, is truly the summary of Nature, the small world (Microcosm), containing within himself the three kingdoms, but also the divine spark which permits him to act as an equal with Nature.

What does he need to do in order to act on this Nature? If you have understood what preceded well enough, you will see that it is enough to act consciously upon one's own organism: for the powers in action in the human organism, being *exactly the same* as those which are acting in any terrestrial being, be it Mineral, Vegetable or Animal, as soon as will, by means of nervous fluid, rules the organism and commands it, it acts in the same way on the astral light and as a consequence on the forces of Nature. There lies the secret of magic in all its manifestations, from alchemy to theurgy.

But the man who hasn't subdued his passions, who is still susceptible to being moved, being affected, or being controlled by the reflexive influences of his organism, belongs completely to Nature and is a slave to his body: he doesn't have the right to expect to command himself and as a consequence, to command any other organism.

All the magic words in the world, all the talismans, all the ceremonies put to use by such a man will only produce zero or ridiculous effects, for a purebred horse is not used to being led by an inexperienced child.

The Indian fakir who *consciously* produces catalepsy in his own organism for a period of time, can change the form of an animal or make a plant grow rapidly, for he is acting on the very principles of forms in acting on his own astral body. This is the only lawful path of magical Operations: *training*.

In the second part, we will return to these questions. Let us now talk about the stars and the influences they can visit upon terrestrial organisms.

*

* *

If the stars weren't endowed with any particular movement, the astral influence wouldn't be very easy to determine. But this is not the case. From this arise certain facts which the student of magic, even the least advanced, must absolutely possess at the risk of failing in most of his works.

To begin, we must to get a clear idea of the important difference that separates the action of life in man from that action in our world. In man, the generating centers of movement, the sympathetic ganglions, like the other nervous centers, are immobile and fixed in their different places, each from one another. The character imprinted on the nervous fluid by these centers therefore depends uniquely on the position of these centers, and the cerebral cell gives this nervous fluid a movement different from that given to it by a nervous cell of a sympathetic ganglion governing over the circulation of blood, for example in the liver. In man, the centers of emission are fixed, and the material conductors join these centers of emission to the organ which is going to be imprinted. So it is that the arm is directly connected to the brain, and next to the grey medulla (thoracic swelling) which is itself connected to the other medullary centers. Nervous fluid emanating from these various centers flows into the arm, but these centers are immobile.

Suppose on the contrary, that at specific times the medullary swelling is put in motion and connected with the arm to act on it, and at other moments it's the brain which acts like this in turn, and you will have an idea of the physiology of our world.

Here, indeed, are those centers of activity, the stars, which circulate and come to be located, at certain times, in such a manner as to influence all that submits to their action at that time. As for us, we need to consider the action of these stars, true organs of the world, from the earth's viewpoint, so it is the action of these stars on the earth which we must study.

Now, a cell in the organism submits to the influence of the blood which is carried to it by specific channels from the stomach, and the influence of nervous fluid which is carried to it by the nerves from the head.

On the other hand, a terrestrial being, a plant for example, submits to the astral influence when the star which moves itself comes to be in an attractive alignment with this plant. In Nature, it is the centers which move, whereas in man it is only their emissions which do.

This may be a little obscure or difficult to grasp; nevertheless, it's an important point to remember if you want to understand something of the action of the stars upon the earth.

But it isn't sufficient to know that the stars move. It's also necessary to know the route these stars follow, observing their movements from a terrestrial point of view.

So, we'll to describe things as they *appear to take place* from our viewpoint on our planet, supposing that our reader knows enough about Astronomy to understand that, when we say that the sun moves, we imitate the teacher who describes this sensation before correcting this initial impression, which is furnished by the senses, through the use of reason.

If, then, you take the trouble to view the path the sun appears to follow in the sky sometime, this is quite close to what you will see, supposing you begin on December 21 and you know your cardinal points.

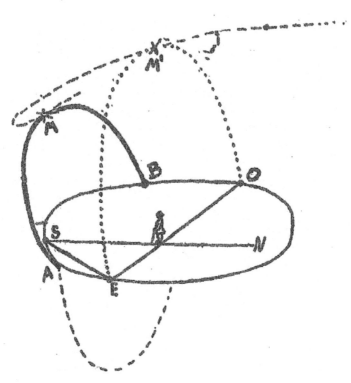

THE PATH OF THE SUN

The sun will rise in the East, at point A, and will climb into the sky from the morning until midday, where it will arrive at point M. From this moment the sun will descend, and in the evening, it will set in the West, at point B. The sun has thus described a semi-circle in the sky (A, M, B), and you know that when it sets it rises for the inhabitants on the other half of the world, which is to say that it completes the description of a circle of which we've only seen half.

But if you've noted that point M in the sky, where the sun was at midday on December 21, and then, a few months later, on March 20, recommence your observations, you'll establish that there are changes in the progress of the star which marks the day. It still rises in the direction of the East, but draws closer more than the first time to the exact astronomical point E. Finally, it arrives in the sky at midday at point M^1, which is higher than the point reached the first time. The half-circle E, M^1, O is larger than the preceding half-circle, that is to say the sun remains visible for a longer period, and, as a result, the day is longer during this period than the preceding period.

In noting, through many observations, the path of the sun in the sky, we will see that for six months, from December 21 to June 21, the sun rises more and more at midday in the sky, and after June 21 it returns on the contrary to its original path in becoming lower each day at noon. This diminishes the length of the day until December 21, at which it begins to mount again, and so forth.

The apparent path of the sun in the sky during the interval which separates its return to the same point has been divided into twelve parts. As the sun takes a year (365 days) to make this route, each of these divisions corresponds to a twelfth of a year, or a month. Each of these twelve divisions has been given a particular name, after the fixed stars which are seen there at the moment of this division. From this come the twelve Signs of the Zodiac.

To summarize, the sun appears to describe a circle around the earth in one year, like the end of the hour-hand of a watch describes a circle around the center of the watch over 12 hours. Each of these hours marked by the sun in the sky has 30 days, and here are the names of these 12 Houses crossed by the sun in a year:

Aries	March
Taurus	April
Gemini	May
Cancer	June
Leo	July
Virgo	August
Libra	September
Scorpio	October
Sagittarius	November

Capricorn	December
Aquarius	January
Pisces	February

You can give these names to the hours marked on your watch and give the name of the sun to the end of the hour hand, and you will then have an exact representation of the Zodiac and its Signs.

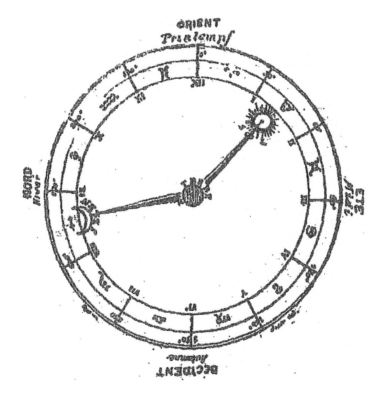

But I see you smile maliciously and tell me: 'I own a watch which has three hands, one for the hours, one for the minutes, and one for the seconds. Now, the hour-hand certainly counts twelve hours, from midday to midnight or midnight to midday, in making a tour of my dial, or as you put it, my Zodiac. But the minute-hand only takes a single hour to pass through the twelve signs of my watch. How do I relate that to the heavens?'

I would reply to this objection very easily, since if the sun, comparable to the hour-hand, takes one year to make a tour of the heavens, it is another star, the moon, which only takes a month to make this same tour. That is to say, it passes through all the Signs of the Zodiac. Thus, the moon can be closely compared to the minute-hand. You see that the sun and moon are the hands of this immense dial which is the heavens, if we hold to appearances. This is why men have divided time according to this celestial watch, and this is why the Magician must know to watch the hours in Nature if he wishes to become skilled in this art.

But the heavens, round like a dial, possesses not one, not two, but seven hands, which run at different speeds. We know two, the sun and the moon. Let us name the others, and moreover let us name them all, beginning at the earth:

Firstly, we have the Moon, our satellite.
Next, rapid Mercury.
Gracious Venus.
Majestic Apollo, the Sun.
Impetuous Mars.
Placid Jupiter.
Finally, somber Saturn, the most distant.

From the viewpoint in which we find ourselves, these stars appear to move around the earth, and pass through the Houses of the Zodiac, each in a determined period of time. These are the hands of our watch; but one, the closest, the Moon makes the tour of the dial in one month, whereas another, the most distant, Saturn takes 30 years to complete the same course. We have no intention to write a treatise on Astronomy, for good reason. Now let's summarize all that we have covered up to now.

*
* *

Having explained that the word Nature, like the word Man, indicates a particular group of beings and things under the direction of a unique principle, we have been led to establish certain categories while following our analysis.

So, we stated that the three Kingdoms which contain all terrestrial beings must obtain their support almost entirely from the atmospheric layer and from the physical forces which bathe all these terrestrial beings.

But a deeper analysis has led us to see, in this active environment which surrounds the earth, a simple effect of the reaction of this earth under the influences of which it is subjected by the other stars which comprise our solar system on the one hand, and by our satellite, the moon, on the other.

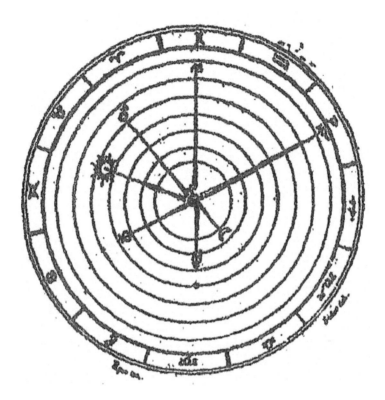

This led us to describe the constitution of our world, seen as a model for the constitution of all the other worlds, which together comprise the universe. We saw that, for an observer relying solely on his senses and neglecting for a moment the teachings of Astronomy, the stars of our world, together with their satellites, seem to form the organs of an immense organism, which is Nature or the Macrocosm. These organs are all in motion, and seem to move more or less quickly around the earth. It is during this course and according to the points in the heavens or "Celestial Houses" in which the stars are found, that the influence of these stars upon the earth and the beings which people it can be determined.

Since this analogy shows us that the other worlds must be constituted fairly similarly to ours, we can extend what we've said regarding our world to all of Nature. But for Magic, the study of the influences which control the earth alone are indispensable to know well.

This is the point we're at, if we're nevertheless careful to add that we have been led to see in this astral light an analogy to nervous fluid in man, and to consider each star as forming a cosmic machine. From this we've concluded (despite the fact that a more profound analysis would lead us to see the stars are considered to be organs, and not apparatuses of the Macrocosm) that the visible light is analogous to the blood in man, and this would be the attractive force which acts in this instance like nervous fluid. But once again, we can, without fear to making too great an error, hold fast to the considerations which preceded it. This should be ample for the rest of our studies.

We have just created what one could call the anatomy of a course of Nature: we also have spoken a little about its physiology. Does Nature have a physiology?

This is the big question, one which has always brought persecution or sarcasm (depending on the epoch) to both Magic and Magicians, from all the so-called 'right-thinking' souls.

When we described the stars and their emanations, it's as if we were talking about the nervous centers and their action. Now we know well that nervous energy is put in motion by a specific cell in the human body, the voluntary nervous cell or a special cell in a sensory organ. There is always a cell at the origination of any movement of nervous fluid, and as a result, the origination of any movements of the human being, be it organic or psychological. But for us, although this cell has its own particular individuality, it is still only a tool, a means of action of the power, whether that is the soul when it acts on the exterior world, or the external world when it acts on the soul. It's like the touch of a piano, which is certainly the origin of a sound, and a specific sound after a touch made it sound, yet which cannot put itself in motion by itself. "Every cell of the human body is represented in Nature by a being", Magic tells us: and we must now talk about these beings in action in all of Nature and acting according to the fatal impulse of destiny.

One can say that this particular vision of Nature has, from the beginning, separated seekers into two camps which have been utterly opposed and sometimes even hostile. Those who cling to the physical side, to the visible world, normally often won't admit to any reality other than that perceived by their senses. To them, it is the powers generated by matter which are the cause of everything, following to the Laws of Chance (?) and Probability (?). They also make themselves hoarse yelling at all those dreamers who come and speak of the existence of something other than the visible world. We have no doubt at all about the welcome reserved for such a strict study on Magic among this kind of critic! It is enough to read the biographies of all the Occultists across the ages, in the dictionaries created by these right-thinking types, to be enlightened on this point.

But those who have understood how, in man as in Nature, the form given to matter is the effect of the action of a local invisible principle, either in the nervous center or by means of astral fluid, know how to search with us for that intelligence which governs all these forms and all movement.

Only seeing the physical side in Nature is to remain at the first degree of study, the physical degree, and studying only those forces transforming matter is already to enter the physiological degree. Many stop there, already afraid, but one must have the courage to pursue the study to its conclusion, and remember that the psychological exists in Nature just as much as it does in man; but, at the same time, one must take care to separate the study of the psychological from that of the physiological or the physical, for otherwise one risks becoming mystical, which is an excess just as dangerous as the pure pantheism of seekers who stop at the second degree or the narrow materialism of those who stop at the first degree. Open an alchemical work of the 15th Century or a magical study of the 16th Century, and you will find taught there the existence of three connected planes of facts, laws, and principles called the Three Worlds.

Now, it's true that a star is a living organism. This organism, like all possible organisms, possesses:

1. A directing principle, the origin of general cohesion;
2. Emanations from this directing principle located in the principle centers of action.

One can object, by saying that a star isn't an organism and that advancing such an affirmation commits us to scientific heresy. As we are not writing a treatise to be used by candidates for a Baccalaureate at this time, we will permit ourselves to say what needs to be taught to students of Magic, and which we are convinced will surely be asked of Bachelors of Science in around thirty years' time, under the title of a history of theories of the 17th Century. These reservations established, let us proceed.

Nature conceived as living must also be conceived as intelligent: such is the teaching which results from all which precedes.

Thus, the evolution of any being on earth depends on the use of astral forces generating this being, by an intelligence.

Our contemporary studies, based on materialism, have so often habituated us to seeing the universe only as an immense cadaver moved by completely physical forces, and that the concept of a universe people by intelligences acting in accordance with the impulse of destiny seems bizarre, to say the least, as our prejudices tell us. Polite critics extricate themselves from this approach by saying that it is 'poetic'. For them it is a supreme injustice to address it by means of a philosophical system.

Now, the independent seeker mustn't flinch in the face of a mere word, and if Magic has always taught this theory of the universe – as living and intelligent, rasther than the theory of a 'cadaver' universe – then let's have the courage to preserve these intelligences in their entirety in Nature, if the practices we are studying here will shortly allow us to connect with these intelligences.

Some material masses – a stone, for example – can only be moved when acting on its periphery by applying physical force to the outside of this mass, which puts it in motion. The action in this case is an action from without to within.

A living being, on the other hand, since it is sufficiently evolved to be able to move, moves to act on its periphery with forces which it possesses within itself. In this instance, the motivated action is an action from within to without, and this work is of a completely different order.

Physicians have taught us only to see stars as enormous blocks of material, whose movement can only be conceived as a result of the application of physical forces to the star's outside.

Magicians teach, on the contrary, that the stars move under the influence of forces acting on the inside and outside, and that the action of the core of each star is no different to the action of the core of any organic cell. The future will show that this is true.

For now, let us content ourselves by noting this important difference, and continue.

Those who are up to date with the Occult Sciences know that every realization on the physical plane is the product of an action of the astral plane upon matter. We can verify these ideas in the human organism. Indeed, we know that a clean incision that destroys a piece of skin, or even one of those fine little whorls found on the end of the fingers, is repaired in a few days and in such a way that everything is recreated in its original form, including the lines and whorls. Physiology teaches us that it's the nearest nervous cells of the sympathetic ganglion which rule over this action. We also know that if the wound is deep enough to affect the nervous filaments or the ganglion itself, it's unable to reconstruct the original forms, and a lasting scar is produced. The memory of forms to reconstruct is therefore localized in some manner in the nervous cells of that ganglion, whose mission is to maintain and preserve these forms. Thus, each point of the human organism possesses small centers charged with watching over the preservation of a certain number of cells, and these centers enjoy a kind of autonomy in their action, since, when they are destroyed, the center-general is unable to replace their action.

What we see in man we can also find in Nature.

The form of terrestrial beings perpetuated through generation is also the result of the constant action of the present plane and the beings which populate it outside of matter. Subjects in a state of lucid vision in whom the material barriers have been lifted see this world of intelligences acting upon matter perfectly, a world which is also closed to our physical senses, so that the sight of a cell put in motion in man is impossible to him who adheres solely to teachings which provide him the aforesaid physical senses.

It is by acting on these intelligences that one can make forms *evolve rapidly*; but to modify the results normally produced by Nature, other actions are necessary which are almost impossible to produce by a human being. A fakir could indeed grow a plant in two hours; but it would be almost impossible for him to produce a pear on a vine, for that would be supernatural, and the supernatural cannot exist any more than miracles.

So, one can act on Nature in three ways.

1. *Physically*, by modifying the constitution of a being or some little part of Nature by the external application of physical forces used by the work of man. Agriculture in all its division, industry in all its transformation are examples of this kind of action.
2. *Physiologically or Astrally*, by modifying the constitution of a being through the application of certain principles and certain forces, not on the external constitution this time, but on the fluids which circulate in this being. Medicine in all its branches is part of the type of action, adding nevertheless that Magic claims that one can act on the astral fluids in action in Nature, just as one acts on those which drive the human being.
3. *Psychologically*, by acting directly, no longer on the fluids, but on the principles which put these fluids in motion.

Such is the magical theory concerning Nature. In the second part, we shall see its application.

Let us now endeavor to explain man's position in Nature.

True man, having his organs of action in the head, rules Nature and can act as its equal in certain circumstances.

Through his organism man is plunged into the very center of the forces of Nature, and it is in acting firstly on his organism that man can have any action on the natural forces.

Nature is double: physical and astral. But the astral is polarized into two modalities, physiological and psychological, which means that we should consider Nature as being triple in the final analysis.

Through walking and gesture (legs and arms) man acts mainly on physical Nature; and through word and regard on astral Nature. We will soon know the importance of these consideration in Magic.

Continue to remember that it's the forces of Nature themselves which circulate in the human organism and that, after all, this organism is simply a terrestrial being, an animal, placed by Nature in the service of the immortal spirit of true man. The key to all conscious magical activity is in this statement.

*
* *

I am sitting beneath a tree beside a road, while a stream flows a few steps away, bustling insects fly around in the grass, and above, the sun illuminates the whole scene with its rays.

All the impressions I experience at this moment come from physical Nature, from the world of manifested forms. But I've learned that these forms are only the clothing which covers each parcel of the conservatory power of the universe, and I know that in the pebble there before me, as in the trees under which I sit and in the grass which surrounds me, in the insects and birds I see, the same force circulates which maintains life everywhere under the impulse of the conservatory principle of the universe, of Nature. This power which circulates in me and which also governs the creation of the sap in this tree, is life; life, source of illusions here below whose secret province is love and which unites all created beings by the subtle chain of correspondence. While all the terrestrial beings seem strangers to one another by their forms, he who possesses the knowledge of correspondence, that is, the knowledge of love, always know how to find the vital link which unites all of creation into a whole.

But the earth on which all depends, the water which makes the earth fertile, and the air I breathe and which maintains my life, just as heat, light, and electricity are modifications to varying degrees of the subtle fire constituting the sun: all this comes to aid life in its manifestations. And we will say still more: all this constitutes the diverse sources thanks to which the life which circulate in terrestrial beings continuously purifies itself, transforms itself and renews itself.

When night comes, all the fixed stars, all the wandering stars and all their satellites which science permits me to see, will come to teach me how the earth is but one of the cells of this giant organism called the universe.

And it is then that I could understand how the diffusion of the animating force is regulated in the universe by the movement of the stars; it is then that I will see, from the earth where I am standing, the zodiacal dial appearing in the heavens, on which the sun, the moon and the planets of our world mark the hours of Nature in shafts of fire.

It is only then that I will understand the modifications brought to universal life by the different hours of the heavens, and at this moment, transported by prayer, my will puts the vital parcel which animates my organism into a communion of love with living Nature, the principle conservator of the forms here below.

I shall seize the first Unity in action in the infinite diversity, and, vibrant with enthusiasm, my liberated spirit will perceive, as if in a dream, the future reintegration of the divine spark which constitutes it in the brilliant majesty of eternal divinity.

"In the invisible order as in the visible nothing is lost, and the primary substance of any star preserves imprinted upon it, in its secret light, until the movement of a desire, until the radiation of a passion, the image of a thought."

(SAINT-YVES D'ALVÉYDRE – Lumière d'Orient)

Bibliography

For occult science:

PAPUS................................*Traité méthodique de Science occulte* (Doctrine).
        La Science des Mages (Chapter 2).
SAINT-YVES D'ALVÉYDRE.........*Mission des Juifs* (Chapter 4).

For Astrology:

OGER FÉRIER.......................*Jugements astronomiques sur les nativités.*
SELVA..............................*Traité d'astrologie.*

For the Elements:

POISSON............................*Théories et symbolisme des Alchimistes.*

For Astronomy:

CAMILLE FLAMMARION............*Qu'est-ce que le Ciel?*

PUB. DU BUREAU DES LONGITUDES...*La connaissance des Temps.* (An ephemeris)

CHAPTER IV – THE ARCHETYPE

Magic, viewed as a science of application, limits its actions almost solely to the correspondences which exist between Man and Nature.

The study of the relationships which exist between man and the superior plane, the divine plane in all its modalities, really belongs to the purview of Theurgy rather than Magic.

Since this present treatise is an elementary work on Magic and not a study of Theurgy, a study which would require considerable development, we will not weigh ourselves down by describing the intelligences of different orders acting in the divine world, intelligences formed to a large extent by the partial reintegration, in the form of an androgyne, of evolved human entities according to the Kabbalah. We will content ourselves here by reproducing a summary of what we said in "The Knowledge of the Mages" about the Archetype and Unity.

When we want to picture man, it's always the image of his physical body which first comes to mind.

However, a little reflection suffices for us to understand that this physical body is only the supporter and manifestor of the real man, the mind which governs him.

One can remove millions of cells from this physical body by cutting off an arm or a leg, but for all that the unity of consciousness suffers no harm. The intellectual man within us is independent of the organs, which are only the support and means of communication.

It is no less true however that, for us in our current state, these physical organs are most useful, even indispensable to allow us to rise up to the action of the mind and to comprehend it. Without this completely physical foundation, our deductions would take on the vague and mystical character of ideas which are exclusively metaphysical.

But a superficial analysis could, on its own, lead us to confuse intellectual man with organic man, or convey the idea that will is completely interdependent with the function of the organs.

Now, when we consider the question of God, most of the time we fall into one of the excesses which we have just indicated when talking about men.

The entirety of existing beings and things supports and manifests divinity, just as the physical body of man supports and manifests the mind.

Wishing to discuss God without relying on all these physical manifestations is to risk losing oneself in the mists of metaphysics; that is, to remain incomprehensible to the majority of minds. It is by considering the constitution of man on the one hand, and that of the universe on the other, that we can attempt to furnish ourselves with an idea of God.

In man, we see a physical – or rather organic – being, functioning in a machine-like manner both while awake and while asleep. Above this organic being we've identified another, an intellectual being, coming into action when waking up, and manifesting itself almost solely during the state of consciousness.

The organic part of the human being corresponds to the idea that we are made from Nature. This is the same inevitable and regular Law which directs the path of organic man like that of the universe, the latter being formed from cosmic organs instead of the being formed from human organs.

As a result, the intellectual being in man corresponds, but in a very elementary way, to the idea that we can make ourselves from God. The connections between physical man and intellectual man enlighten us on the connections between Nature and God, just as the connections between the physical being and man's mind can enlighten us analogically about the connections between man and God.

Through this we can now state in principle that, if the analogy is true, God, though manifested by Humanity and by Nature, though acting on these two great cosmic principles, has nevertheless His own, independent existence.

But the original unity thus conceived can no more intervene in the functioning of Nature's Laws, than the conscious mind of man under normal conditions, can intervene in the functioning of the heart or the liver.

Man is the sole creator and the sole judge of his destiny: he is free to act at will within the circle of his fatality, just as a passenger can, on a train or in a steamer, act as he wishes in his cabin or compartment. God can no more be accomplice to human faults than the train driver or the captain of the steamer are responsible of the fantasies of the passengers he is conveying in his vehicle.

We must therefore avoid an error on this point, recognizing that God, such as He appeared at the first instant, is the sum total of all that exists, just as man is the sum total of all the organs and faculties which appeared in the first place.

But true man, the mind, is distinct from the physical body, from the astral body, and from the psychological being, all of which he perceives and governs. Similarly, God-Unity is distinct from Nature and humanity which He perceived and governs. To use a somewhat gross phrase, Nature is the body of God, and humanity the life of God, but just as the material body is man's body and the astral body and the psychological being are the vital principles of man; so it is organic man and not spirit-man who, once again, only uses these principles as a means of manifestation[49].

It is no less true however that man's mind is, through the internal senses, connected to the least parcel of his organism, a parcel on which he cannot act directly, but which can manifest itself to the mind through suffrage. Similarly, God is present both mediating and immediately in the least parcel of creation. He is in each one of us, just as human consciousness is present because of the receptive or motor consciousness in each of our corporeal cells.

Thus, Nature and man act freely, surrounded on all sides by the circumferential divine action which draws the universe towards progress, without intervening despotically, either in the laws of Nature or in human activity. And so, the captain of a steamer who controls the helm of his ship sails towards the goal of the voyage without interfering in the details of the machinery which moves the vessel (an image of Nature) or in the occupations of the passengers. The captain circumferentially governs the overall system; he doesn't concern himself about the activities within the cabins.

In Kabbalah, the Father is called the divine principle which acts on the general movement of the universe (the action on the tiller), the *Son* the principle in humanity, and the *Holy Spirit* the principle in action in Nature[50]. The mystical terms indicate the several applications of the universal creative force.

UNITY

The universe, conceived as an animated entity, is composed of three principles which are: Nature, Man and God; or, to use the language of the Hermetists, the Macrocosm, the Microcosm and the Archetype[51].

---

[49] Firstly, God only exists as a potential in the ineffable unity: that is the first person of the Trinity, or God the Father. Then He reveals Himself and creates an entire intelligible world. He stands beside Himself as a thought, as universal reason: this is the second person of the Trinity, or God the Son. Finally, He acts and produces – His will is exercized and His thought appears outside of Him: this is the third person of the Trinity, or the Spirit. God, passing eternally through these three states, presents us with the image of a circle whose center is everywhere, and the circumference is nowhere. (*Philosoph. Mor.,* Sect. I, Book II, Ch. IV – R. Fludde, 16th Century). [PAPUS].

[50] One may assume that Papus is talking about the *Christianized* Kabbalah!

[51] There are three worlds, the archetypal world, the Macrocosm and the Microcosm, that is to say, God, Nature and Man. – R. Fludde (16th Century). [PAPUS].

Man is called the Microcosm, or little world, because he contains *analogically* within him the Laws which control the universe[52].

Nature forms the fulcrum and the center of general manifestation of the other principles.

Man acting upon Nature by action, on other men by word, and raising himself up towards God by prayer and ecstasy, constitutes the link which unites creation with its Creator.

God, enveloping within His providential action the domains in which the other principles act freely, rules the universe, in which He restores all the elements to a unity of direction and action.

God manifests Himself in the universe through the action of Providence, which comes to enlighten man on his journey, but which cannot actively oppose the effect of the two other primordial forces[53].

Man manifests himself in the universe through the action of will, which allows him to fight against Destiny and make it the servant of his thoughts. In applying his will to the exterior world, man has complete freedom to call upon the lights of Providence or to disregard its action.

Nature manifests itself in the universe through the action of Destiny, which, in an immutable manner and in a strictly determined order, perpetuates the fundamental types which constitute its basis of action.

Facts are from the domain of Nature, *Laws* from the domain of man, and *Principles* from the domain of God.

---

[52] Man, in himself alone, forms a complete world, called the *Microcosm* because he presents in summary all the parts of the universe. Thus, the head corresponds to the empyrean realm, the chest to the ethereal sky, and the abdomen to the elementary realm. – R. Fludde (16th Century). [PAPUS].

[53] It is nature which presides at our birth, which gives us a father, a mother, brothers, sisters, relatives, a position on the earth, a status in society. All this doesn't depend on us, all this for the common man is the work of chance; but for the Pythagorean philosopher, these are the consequences of an earlier order, severe, irresistible, called fortune or necessity.

Pythagoras opposed this constrained nature with a free nature which, acting on inevitable things as if on brute matter, modified it by drawing from it good or bad results as he wished. This second nature was called power or will: it is this which rules the life of man and which directs his behavior according to the elements that the first nature provided to him.

This explains necessity and will according to Pythagoras, the two opposing mobiles of the sublunary world where man is relegated; the two mobiles drawing their power from one higher cause which the ancients called *Nemesis*, the fundamental decree, and which we call Providence. (Fabre d'Olivet, *Golden Verses*, 5th examination, 1826). [PAPUS].

God never created anything except in its principle. Nature developed the principles thus created to constitute facts; and man, through the use made of his will over the faculties he possesses, establishing the relationships which unite facts to their principles, transform and perfect these facts by the creation of Laws.

But a fact, simple though it may be, is always but Nature's translation of a principle emanated from God, and man must ever re-establish the link which joins the visible fact to its invisible principle, and do this through the enunciation of a Law (which is the basis of the analogical method).

*

* *

A steamer is launched upon the immense ocean, and sails towards the goal assigned to be the destination of the voyage.

Everything the steamer contains is carried forwards.

However, each person is free to organize his room as he pleases. Each is free to climb the bridge to contemplate the infinite, or to descend to the bottom of the hold. Forward progress is effected each day upon the total mass, but each individual is free to act in his own way within the circle of activity in which he chooses to partake.

All the social classes are there, on this ship, from the poor emigrant who lies fully clothed in a sleeping bag, to the rich Yankee occupying a good cabin.

And the speed is the same for all. Rich, poor, large, small, all will end up at the destination at the same time.

An unconscious machine, functioning according to strict laws, moves the entire system.

A blind power (steam) channeled through tubes and metal organs and generated by a special machine (heat), animates the entire machine.

A will, ruling both the organic machine and all the passengers, governs them all: the captain.

Indifferent to the specific actions of each passenger, the captain, eyes fixed on the goal, hand at the helm, conducts the immense organism towards the end of the voyage, giving his orders to the army of intelligences who obey him.

The captain doesn't directly command the screw that moves the steamer; he only has an immediate action on the *helm*.

Thus, the universe can be compared to an immense steamer on which what we call God is at the helm; Nature is the combined machinery of the screw, which makes the whole system function blindly according to strict laws, and humans are the passengers.

General progress occurs for the entire system, but each human being is completely free within the circle of his fatality.

Such is the image which quite clearly paints the teachings of Occultism on this question.

PART TWO

PRACTICE

CHAPTER V – PRACTICAL APPLICATION

PRELIMINARIES – FEELING

In the first part, we summarized the constitution of Man and Nature, such as they should be understood by the Magician. Now we're going to see how we can practice and expand on the various elements we've just spoken about. Finally, in the third part, we'll show how we can use the outcome obtained in various kinds of Practical Magic.

Developing the various elements acting in the human being requires a very specific kind of study. Indeed, we know that prior to acting on Nature, man needs to have mastered himself sufficiently to resist the emotions of his impulsive being, and we also know that the key material used to achieve this is nervous energy. Now, the quality of this nervous energy depends on the quality of the blood; and the quality of the blood depends, on the one hand on the quality of the nutriments from which the chyle came from, and on the other hand on the quality of the air inspired and the respiratory rhythm. We'll therefore need to outline a series of training exercises applicable to these various elements: food and the air inspired, or the sensations man receives from Nature, over all of which he can exercise his will so long as they haven't yet entered his organism.

This is the grossest part of the preparations which he who wants to study this practice seriously and obtain some results, must make himself do.

With regard to man, we've seen how important the use of *meditation* is to the Magician; and we shall say a few more words on this subject.

We must then begin to educate the various organs of expression by means of which the human being acts on the external world. This includes learning how to look and the use of mirrors; educating speech as a prelminary to learning formulae; the study of gesture which, once learned, becomes the origin of pantacles; and finally, we will also focus our attention on learning about movement and the construction of the circle.

Man, educated according to the means we are going to summarize by returning to manuscripts on the Practical Kabbalah, will then become a conscious generator of *active* will, and can work firstly on those practices which need little training, then move progressively to more and more difficult endeavors. We will discuss these practices in the third part.

But, thanks to the earlier discussions about Nature, we can anticipate that he is not blind to the need to operate at specific times. This is the reason we'll need to return to a detailed study of the indispensable elements of Astrology for the Magician. At the same time, we'll publish tables provided by the Kabbalah on these subjects, as well as the characters and pantacles of the planets and the Zodiacal houses. This will form the study of activity in Nature, the corollary to the study of activity in the human will.

Thus, we will come to possess the two terms of all Magical Operations:

1.   The actions of the human being, and above all his will;
2.   The use of the powers of Nature over which he should operate this will.

Here our second part on preparations or practice will end, if we are careful to add that the magical concordances between Plants, Animals and Minerals and the stars will be explained as clearly as possible in our study of Nature.

We repeat once again that this current book is concerned with MAGIC, that is, with man's action on Nature, and is neither concerned with Theurgy (man's action on beings of the Divine Plane) nor with Psychurgy (man's action on the world of human souls). Nevertheless, we shall be compelled to say a few words about the latter.

We thought it useful to summarize the layout of our book first; and we will now begin with confidence.

NUTRIMENTS

Creation of the Instinctive Being

From what has been said earlier, the importance that the question of foods takes on for the Magician can be understood.

The ideal that magical training should strive for, is to make the greatest possible quantity of nervous energy available at a given time for the will to use. The symptom which lets us feel that the will has the energy it needs is called "freedom of spirit.[54]"

So, as a psychic feeling, the free spirit reflects the physiological state in which the will is able to freely wield a sufficiently large amount of nervous fluids.

---

[54] As a reminder, *esprit* can be translated as 'mind' or 'spirit'. However, in this instance the idea of 'spirit' doesn't have religious overtones. While the word 'mind' is used most of the time here, there are occasions when 'spirit' fits the flow of the narrative better, for example here, where spirit fits better with this sense of vertical movement. These words will be used interchangeably according to the circumstance.

Now, this state happens mostly in the morning, or while fasting; that is, at those times when the human is least occupied with the physiological work of the organism, and particularly digestion.

We'll also see that most magical practices lead to that state of progressive dematerialization of the Being and the separation of the organism and the psychic being, by means of fasting, and physical and even spiritual fatigue.

But we shouldn't forget that the psychic state of a man who is fasting, while it points to the goal to be achieved, is only a transitory state which can't be maintained by untrained people, since nervous fluid isn't being renewed in this case and the reserves are quickly exhausted.

To better visualize these concepts, let's represent the human being in a rough manner as a balloon which can reach various heights depending on the heaviness of the weight it must lift. The balloon represents the *spirit*, the weight the *organism*, and the hook the *nervous energy*. The different horizontal strata which the balloon can reach indicate the different states of the spirit.

Now, "freedom of spirit" can only occur by reducing the weight of the organism which pulls the balloon towards the earth. From this comes all the mysterious practices relating to the body, practices which are insane if one loses sight of the fact that they must be *occasional*, of *short duration* and never, absolutely never, continuous. I have seen wealthy American women, surrounded by extraordinary luxury, yet *literally dying of hunger* under the pretext of dematerializing themselves, by following a diet prescribed by one of the many mystical societies which abound in America. The founders of these societies, of which the famous *Theosophical Society* of charlatan memory is the classic example, by borrowing practices from Eastern religions or Western initiations which were only performed by priests or initiates at certain times, push their adherents into following these practices in a regular and continuous manner throughout their lives, paying no attention to the difference in climate or physical constitution of the candidate for initiation. This leads to those accidents and illnesses to which the poor, foolhardy person becomes a prime victim.

One can train oneself to release progressively greater quantities of nervous energy, and put it to the spirit's service. This is certainly true, but only when one remembers that renewing nervous energy is directly linked to the absorption of nutriments. And this leads us to our subject.

Psychic health is obtained by means of a harmonious balance between the mind and the organism. When, without any transition, the intellectual being gains the upper hand over the organism, there is a break in the balance *above*, with an attendant danger of fainting and madness. When, on the other hand, the organism suddenly gains control over the intellect, there is a break in the balance *below*, with a danger of somnolence and brutishness. Our will, ever seeking to restore the destroyed equilibrium, will use various means to this end which we must now study.

Imagine that, while on a fast, in that state of "liberty of the spirit" which we have just discussed, we introduce a lot of heavy food into our stomach. What will happen? We all know that as the stomach's instinctive sense of wellbeing has a proportional effect on sharpness, firstly ideas become dimmer, then confused, and finally they progressively diminish in terms of number and clarity. Physiologically speaking, a part of the nervous energy which was serving the mind has changed its location, and the active center of the human being which was in the intellectual sphere has now passed into the instinctive sphere: for a moment, the body has monopolized the mind's tool, nervous energy.

Instinctive man, for whom this state of satisfaction of the stomach constitutes one form of happiness, allows himself to fall into the joys of progressive brutalization which results in and facilitates the body's activity by having him fall asleep. Such a man is a total slave to his organism, and is unable to accomplish any magical action whatsoever.

The man in whom, on the contrary, intelligence is well developed, whom we call "an intellectual", is impeded in his action by this degenerate state, and does everything possible to come out of it as quickly as he can. This brings us to the use of *stimulants*.

Stimulating the organism diminishes the time during which the body has the upper hand over intellectual operations. Also, instead of letting it go to sleep, which increases the control of the material, the man of action can use various means, principally: 1. physical work; or 2. a substance taken from Nature and activated by physical means, normally called a *stimulant* (coffee, tea, alcohol, sugar, etc.).

The natural method is to take a rest from mindful work by doing something physical, while the artificial method of using coffee or alcohol is however more commonly used, although it is rather more dangerous.

Stimulants require special study, which we will do in a moment. For now, we'll simply note their existence and the goal being pursued by using them.

The student of Magic must therefore begin his practice with the conscious handling of his organic forces. Now, if he remembers that, in food and stimulants he has the two poles of action on his nervous powers, he will have already taken a great step forward. Indeed, food used on its own lowers enthusiasm and encourages avoidance, when he needs excitement to pursue mysticism. Stimulants in their turn, used on their own and while fasting are dangerous, but allow the mind to take magnificent flight in the world of ideas. Finally, combining the actions of foods and stimulants allows the accomplishment of those patient works for which Germany is currently considered the shining example. The design of this elementary treatise doesn't allow us to go into much detail on the classification of foods. Let's content ourselves with some indispensable facts about practice.

One should have seen that the human being is able to act through nervous energy depending on whether the stomach is at rest or working, and that the mind is more or less independent of the organism, according to the different states of the stomach, which is the anatomical center of the instinctive sphere.

But another choice can be made concerning the aliments themselves, depending on whether they come from the Vegetable or Animal Kingdom, without taking into considerationt the remaining parts, such as salt, provided by the Mineral Kingdom. Moreover, in our lands, the almost daily use of various stimulants (alcohol, tea or coffee, among others) also gives the will new opportunities to take control over the organic forces.

So, man is like the driver of a locomotive who has no direct control over the steel organs of the machine, but who can produce more or less heat in a given time depending on the fuel being used, and by means of that can call upon a greater or lesser quantity of steam at the desired moment, which gives him a variable pressure which then acts on the steel organs.

It's the same for the man who wants to practice the management of foods.

Let us summarize the effects produced in the most common cases.

With regard to *Vegetarianism*, we will see in the third part of this book that, during the time of magical training, a period which varies between 7 and 40 days, an exclusive diet of vegetables should be used. We can ask ourselves why.

If we remember that organic man is simply a creation of Nature and lent by Her to support the terrestrial existence of Spirit-Man, we will know that the human organism is immersed in two Kingdoms, the Animal Kingdom through the chest, and the Vegetable Kingdom through the abdomen[55].

So, aliments taken from the Vegetable Kingdom will, when taken regularly, act almost solely on the instinctive part, calming the organism. The will, acting on an organism which has been trained in this manner, will need to expend almost no power, since in this instance the rebellious nature of the impulsive being is almost completely in abeyance. Now, if you'd like to give yourself over to dreaming, and enjoy all of its charms without fear of anxiety, go into the country[56] and take up a Vegetarian diet, taking care to drink only milk or water, and soon your formerly troubled organism will experience profound peace.

---

[55] In this comment Papus is in fact referring to the vegetative – or involuntary – functions of the body, such as digestion, most of which take place in this region of the body, the abdomen (the other two being the head and chest).

[56] The way this is worded could suggest Papus means either physically live in the country, or to imagine this in the mind. However, a couple of paragraphs later he is most

But if you wish to go still further and awaken your dormant transcendent abilities, add tea several times a day to your Vegetarian diet, and meditate for an hour or an hour-and-a-half every morning and evening, and you'll become susceptible to having very clear experiences of telepathy or astral vision.

The Vegetarian diet, from which fish, meat and alcohol are omitted, can be used with success in the country, and perhaps in this environment it can be followed for many years without any danger – indeed, quite the contrary. This diet, which quickly makes any resistance the organism may have to the will disappear and makes a man passive, is essential for the student of Magic to practice. He should first follow this diet for periods of seven days, then for fifteen days: but on condition – and we cannot repeat this enough – that he is in the country, or in a similar environment which is safe from all material concerns.

Milk, eggs and cheese are normally used in Vegetarian diets lasting a long time; and eggs and cheese are omitted during periods of magical training. In this case the diet followed is the pure Pythagorean one.

But one consideration which should surpass any others is that concerning the time of year and the climate, after one has taken into account the environment, country or town.

In cold regions closer to the poles, the human organism cannot exist without the continual use of heavy fats and oils: the sauerkraut and beer of the Germans is an adaptation by the individual to the country's climate. But in India, Egypt and equatorial regions, the active nutrition provided by the solar influence is almost sufficient by itself, and a few grains of rice replaces the enormous plate of sauerkraut necessary to the Germans.

The diet, whether Vegetarian or another, must therefore vary according to portion size and the quantity of oil added depending on the climate, and you would be as ignorant as a Theosophist to impose the same alimentary diet on the English as the Hindus. It's the non-observance of these precepts drawn from climate and environment by the priests which has given birth to all the superstitions regarding fasting which are found in the majority of religions founded in the East. What is truly interesting is seeing how new superstitions have come to be implanted in the West under the influence of Vegetarianism.

---

explicit about living *à la campagne*, and we have to remember that, in the late 19th Century, far more people lived their lives in the country than in the cities, which were also far smaller, so the countryside was never far away.

Emotional Vegetarianism

Departing from the true fact that Vegetarian diets lead to organic calmness, various sects have outdone one another in the strictness of the diets they impose on their followers, caring no more about physiology than environment or climate.

It was then that arguments arising from emotion made their appearance. We mustn't kill in order to feed man, they said, forgetting that in Nature vegetable life only occurs as a result of the slow dissolution of minerals, and the animal life of herbivores which was cited as an example, is a result of the incessant sacrifice of vegetable beings.

But a vegetable is a living entity, another sect leader objected; and so was born a new school, which only took sustenance from grains and fruits. And from diminution to diminution the pure Vegetarians, becoming the repositories of strict emotionality, came to nourish themselves only from the earth....and so forth.

However, a little reflection will suffice to understand that we kill living beings every moment of the day, when we take a walk in the country, during those hecatombs[57] we call harvesting or haymaking, or again, most frequently by breathing in and drowning in the depths of our organism those millions of microscopic beings which flutter about in the air and which, unfortunately for us, are only too alive.

To avoid such a narrow sectarianism, one should understand that the human organism is an assemblage of living beings which makes use of other living beings from Nature to develop. Our intellectual being, the Spirit-Man, who is only nourished through sensations and can only act through nervous energy, can indeed play at emotionalism; but the organism which supplies nervous energy has no more right to be emotional than the *sundew*, that gentle plant which slowly sucks in the blood of insects, or the *spider* which throws itself on flies, or even the *ox*, that calm vegetarian, which pitilessly grinds up the most tender of sensitive plants.

And when we protest with all our strength against these practices, it's because we are bearing witness to facts which would revolt the good sense of the lowliest peasant.

---

[57] Large scale sacrifice. In ancient Greece or Italy these huge public spectacles involved the slaughter of 100 oxen or more.

In London, in the headquarters of a mystical society, we saw two members: Countess W...[58] and another, Mrs. M..., literally dying of hunger in order to avoid eating "living beings"; while the founders, feigning illness, sat at the dining table and devoured large slices of fish, followed by monumental plates of rice and assorted vegetables. Those ladies wished to have "visions." By following this approach, they were able to procure a jolly dose of cerebral anemia.

In France, we have followed the case of Madame L...with interest, the wife of a humble country doctor, who came to a point where she would only drink one glass of milk a day, in order to "spiritualize herself." She did this so well that she "spiritualized" herself completely after a year on this diet, and her death was due solely to starvation. But she could console herself by believing that, apart from the microbes in the milk and those she inhaled, that is, the hundreds of millions every day, no "living being" passed the threshold of her organism.

In these questions of practice, the great stumbling-block to avoid is mysticism. We can't repeat this enough. Mysticism, which has become the rule of spiritualist sects, leads the followers to sensual profligacy under the pretext of claiming that the soul sees nothing of the actions of the body, or to stupidity if not madness, under the pretext of "spiritualizing" the unclean organism.

The mind, which is master of directing the external actions of the human being, is completely responsible for *all* actions performed, just as one only truly "spiritualizes" oneself by acting patiently and continuously upon the organic functions which give rise to nervous energy.

So, before embarking on any magical practice which requires you to fast, you need to have a clear idea of the goal in mind and the abilities of the Operator. This is done by basing any calculation on two factors, the environment and the

---

[58] This is certainly Countess Constance Wachtmeister (1838 – 1910) who was Madame Blavatsky's companion for many years and a prominent member of the Theosophical Society. While there is no clear reference to the diet mentioned by Papus, he states that he saw this personally on a visit to London. In 1890 the Theosophical Society established its Esoteric School under Annie Besant, and housed in her home at 19 Avenue Road, London. Initially composed of twelve members (6 men and 6 women, including Countess Wachtmeister), the members lived there, and committed themselves to a strict regimen of study, service, meditation and lifestyle requirements. There is no mention of a "Mrs. M..." being among these initial 12 members, to which, interestingly, William Wynn Westcott (one of the founders of the Hermetic Order of the Golden Dawn) was added as a specially invited 'outsider'. Since this was established in 1890, and Papus' book was written in 1893, he must have visited this location in the preceding two years. Papus was initially a member of the French branch of the Society, but left due to its inclusion of Eastern practices, which he felt were unnecessary.

climate, to determine the number of days over which the preparatory diet should be followed.

One should only move from a regular diet to a Vegetarian diet progressively, firstly by cutting out stimulants like coffee and alcohol which are replaced with water; then cutting out meat from every other meal, and then from all meals. After this one could try cutting out fish, while continuing the use of butter and oil as long as possible.

One shouldn't forget that it's only in the final eight days preceding the most long and difficult of magical experiments, the conscious evocation of astral forms, that one should follow a rigorous diet of vegetables without salt, cooked by the Operator and boiled in water only. At any rate, these diets should be done in the country. In a city as feverish as Paris, where everything rotates around the sphere of passion and not around the instinctive sphere as in the country, any attempts to follow a Vegetarian diet will be disastrous. We can certify to having clear evidence of cerebral anemia in many people who have tried to follow this diet strictly, which nobody has been able to endure more than six months.

To summarize, a Vegetarian diet may be followed in our climate, but only for short periods, in the country, and while avoiding any practices due to sentimentalism.

An Animal Diet

Aliments taken from the Vegetable Kingdom mainly act on the instinctive center, as we've said. On the other hand, aliments taken from the Animal Kingdom act on the center of the passions and develop to a considerable extent the organism's resistance to impressions coming from the outside or from the will. An animal diet, therefore best suits men of action in everyday life or, in moderate proportions, to townspeople obliged to suffer the feverish life of the cities. This diet should not be followed during magical training; but it would be a good idea for anyone who wishes to better understand the effect of different food types on the organism to undertake some instructive experiments.

Following a period of around fifteen days following a vegetarian diet, performed during a waxing moon, the organism can be considered to have been brought to '0' in terms of impulsiveness. Then let the person try to ingest a significantly large amount of beef ($\frac{1}{2}$ to $\frac{3}{4}$ pound) and let them note down the effects. Then continue with the vegetarian diet for two more days, and then try lamb. Then, under the same conditions, repeat the experiment with pork. From this, especially if the temperature is sufficiently high, one will understand the considerable changes which various dietary systems can produce in the human organism.

The Use of Material Stimulants

Now we know how nutriments taken from the Vegetable Kingdom act on the instinctive center, and on the other hand the impulsiveness of the passionate center which arises from nutriments taken from the Animal Kingdom, let us focus on substances which act on the nervous reserves and, in consequence, on the intellectual center. We give these substances the name of *stimulants*.

As we said earlier, stimulants act physiologically on the nervous reserves. For example, you are tired, and are inclined to fall asleep, that is, your will no longer has sufficient nervous energy available. You want to resist this desire for a period, so you drink coffee, and soon work becomes easier until the next reaction. What is going on in this example?

We know that in the normal state a reserve of nervous energy exists in the neural plexus of the sympathetic nervous system. The first thing a stimulant does is act on these reserves and make the stored nervous energy available to the organism. The first consequence of this action is renewed activity in the intellectual center; but the mid-term consequence is profound fatigue in the organism which, if it is prolonged, can lead to serious problems.

Nothing has a higher cost to man than an excessive use of that precious deposit which is nervous energy, and although a problem with the digestive system can be repaired in a few hours, troubles with the nervous system require very fastidious – if not prolonged – treatment.

Balzac[59] wrote a marvelous "Treatise on Modern Stimulants" which we re-edited in the *Voile d'Isis*[60], and which we recommend to the attentive seeker. To

---

[59] Honoré de Balzac (1799 - 1850) was a French novelist and playwright who is considered to be one of the founders of realism in writing, and had a profound influence on many writers of the late 19th and 20th Centuries. His style reflected a depth of perception, and even his lesser characters were fully developed. He presented his stories, mainly focused around Parisian life, in a very unvarnished manner. He is believed to have been a Freemason, as was his father. His work ethic was strenuous, and probably led to his early death. He wrote for fourteen or fifteen hours a day, fueled by 30 to 40 cups of thick black Turkish coffee. Indeed, his book "Treatise on Modern Stimulants" included a graphic description of his addiction to, and withdrawal from, caffeine.

[60] The *Voile d'Isis* (or 'Veil of Isis') was Papus' companion periodical to *l'Initiation*, his predominantly Martinist magazine. Running from 1890 – 1935, though intermittently for periods, as a public organ of his esoteric education faculty, *le Faculté des Sciences*

keep ourselves within the bounds of our study, we will only consider the following stimulants: alcohol, coffee, tea, morphine and hashish. There are many other substances employed, which we can consider in a longer study than this one.

Alcohol

A product, like most stimulants, of the action of human will upon a product of Nature, alcohol is one of the most precious agents, and at the same time the most dangerous, that man makes use of.

The action of alcohol used in the form of brandy (Eau-de-vie) is very quick but not very profound, and therefore of short duration. Under the influence of alcohol, a very large quantity of nervous energy is released, and the mind seems to be illuminated by a richness and quantity of ideas which appear, and jostle for position in the intellectual center. At that moment, there is no need to think carefully in order to take a deduction or to solve a complex problem. All one needs to do is jot down the ideas which pass by as quickly as lightning, during the few minutes that the action of this stimulant lasts. A small glass of brandy taken half-an-hour before an intense intellectual exercise can allow the mind to perform extraordinary feats, but only fleetingly; in this respect, we can quote a personal fact. During the Congress of 1889, after taking half a glass of cognac, we succeeded in translating the addresses made by the Spanish delegation both accurately and instantaneously, with a delivery worthy of an orator, so that several stenographers there asked us for our "method", even neglecting to stenograph one of those speeches since they believed we had a new process for doing that. But this little intellectual exercise, which we repeated almost every day, required us to sleep two hours longer at the end of each day.

The action of alcohol only works for a very short time, and one can never go back to this stimulant two times in succession during the same exercise. And this is the danger of alcohol in all its forms; delighted by the results obtained and charmed to see the intellectual sphere set in motion so well without any effort of will, the weak man has a pernicious tendency to return to alcohol when the first effects are on the point of wearing off. Not getting the same result as before, the individual increases the dose, and soon he becomes drunk, and pays with long hours of degradation for the few minutes of stimulation at the outset. For the

---

Hermétiques, it initially covered reports of esoteric meetings held by Papus, but later broadened into coverage of general esoteric topics. Following Papus' death, René Guenon took over as editor.

mechanism behind this activity, see what we wrote about drunkenness in the first part of this book.

Alongside brandy in all its forms, modern industry has created a host of new stimulants by mixing alcohol with another stimulant: sugar. From these mixtures have come the liqueurs, some of which are truly compound medicines.

The action of liqueurs is slower than that of alcohol alone; but it develops the will more, while alcohol without sugar acts more on emotion. So, one should give preference to a liqueur over alcohol when it's more important to act than to give oneself over to meditation.

Coffee

Coffee is the most powerful stimulant, given the duration of its action, that one can always have available.

Coffee, made in the usual way, has two actions which are clear cut:

1.   During the hour following its ingestion, it acts locally on the nervous plexus of the abdomen, and assisted by heat, facilitates the work of the digestion and thus allows the mind to be provided with a great quantity of nervous energy.
2.   Two or three hours after its ingestion, the coffee begins to act on the intellectual sphere and this action lasts from one to two hours for one cup of coffee. Thus, if a coffee is drunk at 1 o'clock, the psychic action begins at 3 o'clock and lasts until 5 o'clock. After that time, the emptiness of the stomach itself acts as a stimulant, and intellectual work becomes easier and easier, so long as one is taking notes or making sketches or plans, and not writing or performing tasks. Taking coffee can be done in the morning, on an empty or nearly empty stomach, or in the evening, so long as one only has a light dinner.
3.   There is a third action produced by coffee on people of a nervous disposition, and this is an attack of melancholy which strikes the moment the stimulating effect on the intellectual center ceases, around five hours after drinking the coffee. The mechanism behind this phenomenon is sufficiently unusual to require explanation.

Indeed, like all stimulants, coffee acts by making part of the reserve of nervous energy in the ganglionic plexuses available to the mind. The energy, the tension which the coffee gives to the organism is therefore a trap, since this action is only produced at the cost of an erosion of the organic reserves. So, the use of coffee as a fortifier is only possible with energetic subjects, and certainly not with weak and anemic beings. Let's go on.

For a normal man, when coffee has produced its intellectual action, and this action has been ever so slightly magnified by the work of the individual, the sensation of emptiness in the condensing nervous centers manifests in the spirit in the form of an attack of melancholy and pessimism which lasts from ten minutes to an hour, and which can always be ameliorated by ingesting any kind of food.

To summarize, the psychic action of coffee appears to have an effect mainly on emotion. So, in the hands of the student of Magic, coffee constitutes a means to develop the artistic receptivity of the individual at will. Indeed, we can state that the ability to be affected by Art generally depends on the nervous state of the individual, and we know that on the other hand, coffee allows this nervous state to develop and even be magnified.

One can also drink Turkish coffee, a means of preparation where infusion is replaced by mashing, which considerably increases the power of the stimulant, since one absorbs a certain quantity of coffee in its raw form.

Finally, drinking coffee which has been finely ground, following the method described by Balzac, during a fast, gives the maximum effect which can be obtained from this precious stimulant.

Tea

If, after a period of stimulation, coffee gives a violent but passing crisis, tea acts much more insidiously.

The intellectual stimulation provided by tea is intermediate between that of alcohol and that of coffee; but this stimulation is very gentle and never offers the brusque periods of other stimulants. Tea makes the nervous centers progressively melancholic and anemic, but little by little. It is rare to see an attack of pessimism under the influence of tea; but on the other hand, we have often observed serious nervous anemia in Russian students who abuse the use of tea.[61]

The quality of this stimulant allows for sustained intellectual work. So, it is the only one which can be used during periods of magical practice.

---

[61] Surprisingly, even in a medical paper on drug abuse among Russian students dated 2013, Чифи́рь (chifir), or very strongly brewed tea, also prevalent in Russian prisons, was listed alongside amphetamine and ephedrine as an exceptionally strong stimulant.

But the main issue with tea is that it acts so profoundly on the nervous centers, that the period of recovery is longer than with any other substance. The nervous anemia which results appears as a complete absence of initiative and courage.

The individual who abuses tea allows time to pass him by in a state of melancholy. He complains quietly if he is unhappy, but he doesn't know how to address it, and he presents us the clearest kind of fatalism one can find in any sense of the term.

Hashish – Opium – Morphine

Many people imagine that hashish, which has gone back to being listed among the most dangerous class of drugs which can be governed from the mental point of view, immediately gives sublime visions and plunges the practitioner into ecstasy.[62] Now, this view of hashish bears little resemblance to reality. This substance, similar to opium but with far greater intensity, acts on the reserve centers of nervous energy, and empties these reserves in an instant, throwing the entirety into the intellectual sphere. Now the person's ideas are exaggerated, amplified, embellished to a prodigious extent; but it is still necessary for the oiginal idea and the original physical sensation to exist.

In this manner, a lamp seen under the influence of hashish becomes a magnificent palace lit by 10,000 lights and dripping with precious stones; on the other hand, when the ideas are vulgar, so are the impressions. A beginner taking

---

[62] The comment suggests that it hadn't been banned until shortly before the writing of this book. While it is difficult to determine its legal status in France in the 19th Century, in the late 1840s, there was a club in Paris called the *Club des Hashischins,* which counted Victor Hugo (*Les Misérables, The Hunchback of Notre-Dame*), Alexandre Dumas (*The Count of Monte Cristo, The Three Musketeers*), Charles Baudelaire (*The Flowers of Evil, Artificial Paradise* – about being under the influence of hashish) and Honoré de Balzac (*The Human Comedy*) among its members. This would lead one to presume that, if there was a law banning its use, it wasn't rigorously upheld prior to 1890. England, of course, was famous for its London Opium Dens, which featured extensively in the writings of Sir Arthur Conan Doyle and Oscar Wilde. Indeed, England only officially dismantled the opium trade with China as late as 1910, and let us not forget that opioids were freely available over the counter in England until the early 1900s; while Coca Cola contained cocaine until 1903, and the popular English over-the-counter remedy for diarrhea, Kaolin & Morphine, *is still available.*

hashish without any preconceived ideas and simply *waiting to see what happens*, will simply dream that he is a pipe and that he is smoking himself.[63]

Hashish is therefore an amplifier and not a creator. But this intoxicating action is followed by a terrifying reaction. The reserve centers, now empty of their contents, cause agony in the unfortunate taker, and the most horrible nightmares and the keenest suffering are the logical consequence of the enchanted dreams and astral sensations.

Opium, and morphine which is derived from it, have the same action, but with less intensity, and the unfortunate slave of these substances, wishing to escape the imminent reaction, progressively increases the dose of the poison until he reaches a state of complete exhaustion, soon followed by death.

From the magical point of view, the danger of these drugs is considerable, for the increase the control of the impulsive being over the will, and it takes a very strong will not to allow oneself to be ruled by these substances, the incarnation of the soul of the world in matter.

We don't wish to prolong this discussion too much, and we think that what we've just said is enough to understand the theory of these stimulants.

APPLICATION OR CREATION

How to Handle Stimulants

So, in these few substances which we have just reviewed, the practitioner has precious assistants, not only for Magic, but also for the regular management of his organic powers in everyday life.

If a strong intellectual effect needs to be produced, alcohol (unsweetened cognac, but a dose of only a small glass), taken half-an-hour before the event is a precious assistant. But one shouldn't forget that an hour's delay can destroy the effect, and take the individual by surprise in the midst of its effect.

If one needs to execute a plan whose outline has been broadly thought out, to develop an idea previously had, or to carry out some bibliographical or biographical research – in a word, work involving *application* – one should combine the action of alcohol, which can be taken following lunch, after coffee, with the action of a fatty and heavy food. For example, sauerkraut and sausages could be considered suitable as the basis for such a meal.

---

[63] This seems to predict Réné Magritte's famous painting *Ceci n'est pas une pipe* – but that wasn't painted until 1929.

If on the other hand, one needs to perform an act of *creation* rather than work, one should use very light foods in small quantity, and follow lunch either with a coffee on its own, or else with a sugary liqueur, such as yellow chartreuse. Then spend the first part of the afternoon re-reading previous notes, or in going for a walk around a favorite museum, and set to work around four o'clock if you ate at noon. After an hour, ideas will start to crowd in quickly; but one should only take notes and avoid doing any editing in this state of intellectual excitement. We'll shortly see how one can join respiratory rhythm, use of perfumes[64] and prayer to these several procedures.

We are convinced that the serious student who truly wishes to try these suggestions out will be able to verify the results, which we are only publishing after trying them out for many years both on ourselves and on many other individuals, for himself. This is the seed of an intellectual hygiene which really requires much explanation, but which is impossible to do in this small manual.

However, it is enough for now to remind oursleves once more the theory of the transmission of nervous energy from the plexus in the brain, or on the contrary the communication from the brain to the stomach. In the first instance, there is a production of ideas, but great difficulty in bringing them to fruition. In the second instance, there is a lack of creativity, but the ability to condense the nervous energy into a single point, as a result of acting deeply instead of acting superficially on the psychic centers. *Dissolve or coagulate*[65] the nervous influx by alternating stimulants and foods: this is the key to this first stage in the magical training of the physical being.

---

[64] Strictly speaking, the word *parfum* means 'perfume' and *encens* means 'incense'. However, Papus appear to use the two terms interchangeably, since most descriptions of Ritual Magic in this book discuss the use of a censer or cassoulet (earthenware bowl with a handle). However, a diffuser or even a spray could also be considered, for example, if the place of operation has fire detectors.

[65] It is interesting to note that Papus uses the French equivalent instead of the far more famous Latin motto of the alchemists: *solve et coagula*. Here he implies that the use of stimulants 'dissolves', and heavy foods 'coagulate'.

Inspired Air – Application of the Emotional[66] Being

We have quickly considered the modifiers of the physical body: nutriments and stimulants. We now come to the modifiers of the astral body: generally atmospheric air and perfumes, or volatile substances capable of being mixed with inspired air and acting directly on the lungs.

As a reminder, we will recall what we have been led to say about the theory of Nature, which concerns the relationship between atmospheric air and astral fluid, and its role as the general animator of terrestrial beings. For now, the important thing to remember is, that inspired air constitutes the most rapid modifier of blood one can have at one's disposition, and as a result, all actions produced on the organism by the pulmonary route need to be studied very seriously. Before entering the circulatory torrent, foods or stimulants have to pass through several organs, whereas all volatile substances which are inhaled act immediately on the blood, at the very instant that the corpuscle submits to the vitalizing action of the inspired atmospheric air.

We are now going to consider:

1.   The action of air on the blood, from the point of view of the nervous system;
2.   Respiratory rhythm, and the modifications which the human will can exercise over it;
3.   The action of stimulants, or *perfumes*, on the astral body, and volatile substances such as ether or chloroform.

Once he has learned to handle foods and stimulants, the student of Magic will then commence this study, the second phase of preparatory exercises.

After a run, or after ascending several stairs quickly you find yourself out of breath; that is, to compensate for the excessive use of the organic powers which you have just undergone, your respiration becomes more rapid, your heart beats more quickly, and a quantity of blood more considerable than when you are at rest flows through your nervous centers. As a consequence, nervous energy is produced in sufficiently large quantities to compensate for the losses endured. In this case, respiration acts as a rapid repairer. But the rhythm of the respiratory system is sufficiently connected to the rhythm of the heart, that any increase in

---

[66] *Animique*, is not a word one can find in contemporary French dictionaries. However, its root is the Latin word *animus*, meaning soul or spirit. However, in this translation the word 'emotional' has been used, as most closely following the intention of Papus. Here Papus is focusing on the chest region, which previously he associated with the emotions (the stomach being instinctive, and the head intellectual).

the rate of inspiration quickly translates into an increase in the frequency in cardiac movements.

This observation, which anyone can make thanks to the phenomenon of breathlessness, gives us a key to the conscious action of the will on the astral body through the intermediary of respiration.

Indeed, rapid inspiration will act as a stimulant on the nervous centers. Slow inspiration or better, prolonged and spaced out expiration will, on the contrary, calm the stimulation of the nervous centers. So, in the respiratory rhythm we find an analogy to the state of emptiness or fullness of the stomach with all its psychic consequences. This leads us to determine the respiratory rhythm.

Respiration or the circulation of air is performed in two steps, separated from one another by an interval.

The first period or inspiration is when atmospheric air is breathed into the lungs; then there is a short interval, and then the second period or expiration of the air charged with carbonic acid takes place. Finally, there is a longer interval which separates the expiration from the new inspiration, and the cycle begins again.

A little thought should be enough to note that the heart reproduces the same phases by analogy, but with a faster rhythm. So, during a minute one can count around twenty respiratory movements for sixty cardiac movements. But the pattern of the heart's movements is in every way similar to that of respiration, which we have reproduced diagrammatically below. Two silences, one short and one long, separate two equal beats.

The lungs and the heart can be considered as being two cog wheels connected to each other, which means that any increase in the respiratory rhythm is reproduced and multiplied in the cardiac rhythm and, as a result, in the entire circulatory system. Respiration is thus the great balancer of the organism, tasked with reestablishing equilibrium when this equilibrium is destroyed by some loss of energy.

When a material stimulant like alcohol has exhausted part of the reserve of nervous energy, it is through respiration that immediate repair is achieved, if it is possible to do this. Inspiration brings restorative energy, and expiration eliminates a part of the alcohol absorbed. But he must control his respiration to obtain this result, and above all keep it *very slow and very deep*. Rapid and shallow breathing will have the completely opposite effect, by adding a new stimulation to that already produced by the alcohol, and this will lead to a reaction which is as sudden as it is harsh. This explains the danger for drunkards who, leaving the table in a feverish state, breathe very rapidly and are, according to one of their expressions, "knocked out" by the outside world.

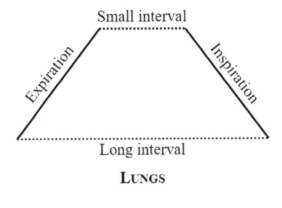

LUNGS

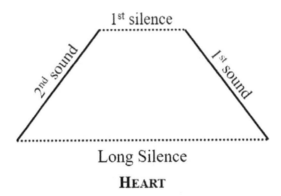

HEART

Practical exercises to train the respiration should be about increasing the interval which separates expiration from inspiration.

Books on the Yoga of the Hindus almost all discuss this point, whose result is to progressively lower the quantity of carbonic acid expired.

But the Magus should strive to take large inspirations regularly, and carefully observe the effect produced on his organism as well as the duration of that effect. Any important activity should always be preceded by three deep breaths, made while thinking strongly about the activity one is about to undertake.

The effect of respiration acting as an intellectual stimulant will be increased even more if one moves around while taking these deep breaths. That is why a walk after a meal can easily replace material stimulants.

Later on we'll see how the respiratory rhythm should be carefully managed during the day preceding an experiment in High Magic.

But, all in all, inspired air is only nourishment for the astral body, and we have seen that alongside foods there are other substances capable of acting not only on the instinctive center, but also on other centers of the human body: and these are the stimulants.

Regarding our study of material stimulants, we have studied the approximate action of each of these, and we know that overall their duration is quite long.

There also exist substances capable of stimulating the astral body, the soul, and these substances enter the organism mixed with the inspired air. These are the *perfumes*.

One should assemble a general list of perfumes divided into the classes on which they act the strongest: either on the center of instinctive behavior, the center relating to the soul or the center relating to intelligence. But we will reserve these details for a work which is more complete than this, to spare the reader from overly complicated explanations.

A typical perfume is musk, which comes from the Animal Kingdom, and acts very quickly and strongly on the center of the soul, to the extent that the presence of musk can sometimes replace beauty – a detail well known to all our flirts[67].

At the heart of the soul, musk reproduces the effects of alcohol, and when the two stimulants are combined, the impulsive being submits to such a drive that the will can barely resist it at that moment, particularly if there is also some music to support its effects, as we will see shortly.

The use of ether or above all of chloroform as substitutes for alcohol on the center of the soul can give us the key to the action of this type of stimulant. The individual who inhales the vapor of chloroform combines and manifests all the effects produced by the absorption of large amounts of alcohol. But these effects appear in barely a few minutes, whereas those of inebriation are only produced of a much longer period, one or two hours at least.

The means by which they act is the same for all stimulants. The weakening and the progressive anesthesia produced by chloroform are the result of a

---

[67] The word *coquette* is used, which refers to flirty women of the time, certainly the kind to be found in the *Folies Bergère*! The implication is that a little musk makes up for a lack of beauty, and remembering that in those days lighting in the evening was by candle or gaslight, so nobody had to endure that awful evening's end in a modern nightclub when, after Last Orders have been called, the electric lights come up, and...! Note we cannot include the *Moulin Rouge* in this category, since incidentally it was the first building in Paris to be illuminated by electric lights. Built in 1889, the electric lights were designed and installed by Adolphe Léon Willette, and each evening the streets of Pigalle would be lit up by its welcoming and innovative glow.

primitive hyper-stimulation of the nervous centers, similar to that clearly shown by that period called *stimulation* which precedes true sleep. This period is similar, but not identical, to that of hypnotic somnambulism, the mid-term result, as we have seen, of exaggerated stimulation of an organ of the senses or, to put it better, one of man's psychic centers.

The difference between the action of musk and that of chloroform clearly shows us the possibility of classifying perfumes. Several contemporary seekers, particularly Charles Henry, inventor of the *olfactometer*[68], have pursued this path. Generally, the Magister only retains the specific action of a perfume or volatile substances depending on its mineral, vegetable or animal origin.

But when one of the centers of the human being has been stimulated, it is rare for the other centers not to come into play as well, and this leads to the apparent difficulty in classifying it.

The Magister only needs to stock three principle perfumes, from the point of view of their action.

Incense and similar products, which act on the mind, and can be considered to be an intellectual stimulant.

Musk, which acts of the emotional being, but with very instinctive effects.

Smoking tobacco, whose principal action is instinctive, with a smooth intellectual stimulation at first.

Incense leads to prayer, musk to love, and smoking tobacco to sleep (the latter by means of the speed of its reaction).

Here, then, are three aids available to the Magician which are good to use. However, for those who claim that ether is difficult to manage, we would recommend smoking tobacco as also leading to calm and acting on the instinctive center, since its action is much slower, and it's easier to handle than ether.

Sensation: Training of the Psychic Being

---

[68] An instrument still in use in modified form to detect the presence of and measure the strength of scents. They are often used in laboratory experiments to detect a person's threshold of smelling a substance, particularly in the perfume industry. Charles Henry was an interesting character. A French librarian and editor, he was also the inventor of several unusual gadgets, and he was also a friend of artists, particularly the Symbolists and Neo-Impressionists.

The aim of magical training is the complete submission of man's impulsive being to the will. The Magister must not tolerate any impulse, any emotional reflex, without being able to resist it immediately and successfully.

We just discussed how the appropriate management of foods and the study of respiration helps this training. It now remains for us to consider sensation from this special viewpoint.

Every day we encounter people who say: "I can't touch velvet without my entire body being revolted." Others say: "I can't see a toad without fainting." Yet others say: "I can't bear the scent of lilies," etc., etc.

Now, all these aversions, all these purely reflexive impulses must be pitilessly dropped by the student of Magic, and this is a process which is both very easy and at the same time a very active training of the will.

The sensory organs, understood in philosophical terms, can be considered modifications in varying degrees of a single receptive organ. This is how the various sounds emitted by a harp are produced by a single material which comprises the strings, which only changes depending on the length and tension of each string.

Nevertheless, for ease of explanation we will preserve the generally established divisions, only noting that touch and taste belong to the physical body and to the instincts, smell to the astral body and the soul center, hearing to the psychic being and the intellectual center (which mainly concerns us here), and finally sight to the man of will.

We will only say a few words on each of these senses.

Touch – Whatever the sensation, viscous or otherwise, produced by the contact of an animal or some other body, you must train yourself to perceive it without the least emotion, above all if this sensation seems unpleasant. Moreover, constant and careful cleanliness is essential to maintain the organs of touch and the entire organism in a perfect state.

Also, we strongly recommend those who would like to do this, to take a cold bath every day on rising, followed by an oil rub, or better still a rub made with an infusion of verbena.

Be that as it may, this practice is essential during the eight days preceding a Magical Operation of any importance.

Taste – The practitioner must train himself to learn to like dishes which are generally available but which he doesn't much like. The same goes for popular drinks, such as milk and beer.

These practices, although apparently pointless, are in fact extremely important to overcome instinct, which, if it isn't controlled, will later impede all the Magister's endeavors. One mustn't forget that taste is, in fact, the only sense directly connected to the instinctive center.

You must also train yourself to vary the times of meals and to progressively diminish the size of meals, stop and then resume the habitual daily routine; for habit, marvelous as it is for educating the impulsive being, is also very dangerous when it's caused by the reflexes, and then it can often check the strongest efforts of will.

Smell – The gradual education of smell through perfumes should be pursued; for this will allow a correct understanding of the action of various perfumes on the soul center. It is also necessary to work to conquer the antipathy one may have for such and such scented flower; for this antipathy is only a reflex action.

And when we speak of conquering these antipathetic impulses of the senses, that's not to say that we hope that sympathy will replace the contrary impulse. We simply wish the will to be sufficiently developed to counter the impulsive manifestation of these antipathies. The reflex is still produced, almost certainly, but the will must completely prevent any external action arising from these reflexes. This is the *criterion* of a truly powerful will.

Hearing – The education of audition is most important to the Magister, since, along with sight, it is the key to the aesthetic sense. It is also important to train it to appreciate in general – if not in detail – the beauty of musical impressions. To accomplish this, frequenting symphonic concerts and the great musical productions, such as operas to some extent as well, is useful. The Magister will be strongly assisted in this task, which is of great importance for future work, by undertaking preparatory theoretical work preceding the auditory event, by taking a coffee each time a few hours before this event, and having conversations and discussions with true amateurs or even musical "snobs". Never be discouraged by the slow progress achieved: with work, regularity, and habit imposed by the will on the organism to hear and understand the impulses which music gives rise to in us, we will surely come to have that perception of rhythm which is so important to intellectual development.

Sight – Frequenting museums, and meditation in front of the works of the Masters, especially in the morning, will facilitate the aesthetic education of sight. In some cases, tea may be used to aid in this development.

But the issue on which the Magister must principally focus his attention is the complete domination of the will over the emotions, which can otherwise give rise to visions of strange or unexpected things. These emotions can certainly be produced, but they must be overcome the moment they appear by the energetic action of the will.

Most of the trials in the initiations of the ancients were concerned with this point. We are going to show why this training of sight is so useful.

The greatest danger which can assail the practitioner in a Magical Operation is loss of composure.

"To lose one's head" is to abandon control of the will to the impulsive being, and to submit the immortal being to all the terrors which cause every vision of the beyond.

Now, astral entities can only use fear against the practitioner who is isolated in his circle and magically armed. In addition, the individual who gives himself over to this kind of experience "for amusement" and "dabbling" must be above all very brave to avoid the most awful accidents, of which the most minor is falling into a prolonged faint. Courage in the face of such an occurrence will work better than knowledge.

In this regard, we will recall some characteristic anecdotes.

Two young Hindus, after very little study of Magic, decided to perform an evocation and, after a few days of preparation, did their experiment, somehow or other, at the edge of a wood. They stood in the circle and began their conjurations. Almost immediately they saw a furious bull coming from a long way off, horns lowered, and charging right towards them. One of the two practitioners lost his head and jumped outside the circle, where he fell in a dead faint. The other had the wisdom to remain still and determined that the vision of the furious bull was only a conscious hallucination.

The unconscious state of the unwise one took a long time to depart.

The story of this experiment was given in a Madras magazine: *The Theosophist*.

But here is another, similar story, and quite recent. This year (1892), one of our members, knowing the practice of Magic well enough from having read and studied it, had the opportunity to accompany a practitioner near Lyon. Once the circle had been drawn at the crossing of three roads, around midnight the evocation began, and soon our student perceived a carriage coming along one of the roads at a gallop. He could clearly make out the lit lanterns of the coach, the horses' hooves and the cracks of the whip. Thinking that the carriage was about to bear down on them, our young man wished to get out of the way, and filled with fear, was about to throw himself out of the circle, when the practitioner, who was used to such surprises, grabbed him forcibly and held on to him firmly. This, then, was another hallucination to which a young debutant had succumbed.

You can understand why training the sight, and the constant control of the will over the emotions, is so important for those who want to perform the challenging experiment of conscious evocation. But we should be quick to say that these experiments are unusual in Practical Magic, and there are many others which require neither detailed preparation nor rigorous training.

At any rate, it's good for the Magister to understand what he should take from the senses, which are the doors for Nature's direct entry into the human being.

Intellectual Stimulants: MUSIC

We've seen that alongside each order of substance which normally enters the organism, that is, food or air, there are also stimulants which allow a quick action on the organic centers. Is there a stimulant for emotion similar to those we have just discussed?

Absolutely! It's rhythm and meter applied to the senses, arising from musical sensations. Hearing is directly connected to the intellectual center and auditory impressions, whether they come from a human being or a completely different source, directly affect this intellectual center. Contemporary education of deaf mutes, where sight, the superior sense, replaces hearing, shows us that one can act *intermediately* on the psychic being; but the ear is the only *immediate* door to the intellectual center. We cannot repeat this enough.

Music moves the soul directly, and religious orders have always made use of this observation, as well as the ancient initiatory societies. But the psychic center only affects us to the extent that it is developed. There is also a great difference between the way in which a workman, a middle-class man and a man of the world perceive music, or rather between the various types of music capable of acting on these different classes of human beings.

So, just as the purely instinctive man will love above all popular Dance Hall music, while occasionally elevating himself to military music, the city workman and the blue-collar employee will find their ideal at the coffee-house concert, where smoking tobacco, the oompah of the brass band and the voices of local ladies create a physical simulation which is half instinctive and half emotional. But place a true artist in such an environment, and he will become very bored, and his entire intellectual being will be repelled by the brutalization which spreads over him. And so, what is stimulating to the man of instinct becomes a torment for the artist, and the opposite is so true that the lower middle classes, who are so partial to coffee-house concerts and comic operas, are famous for their incomprehension and boredom when faced with a symphony or a bel canto opera.

Music, as an intellectual stimulant, is therefore so varied that it can be adapted to the needs of all human beings, whatever their level of psychic development. Also, one can appreciate the power the Magister can draw from this stimulant which acts directly on the intellect.

We can establish a classification of music according to its magical effect, whether one studies it from the point of view of the triple action of the orchestra on the organic centers, when it is considered as a perfect tripartite being composed of instruments which are corporeal (Tympani and Woodwind), emotional (Brass) and intellectual (Strings), in which the Conductor is the mind; or on the contrary, where one focuses on rhythm and meter; or finally whether one classifies musical action according to the kinds of individual which it affects the most, and then we find along general lines instinctive music represented by comic songs, dancing-hall music and the coffee-house concert; music which appeals to the emotions represented by nationalistic music, from the military march and the national anthem, and such models, to comic opera; and finally intellectual music, which for the general public is romance and for the artist an opera by Wagner. Each of these types is itself capable of being divided into three.

Now, slow and solemn marches, accompanied by incense as a perfume, should be particularly studied by the Magister from the point of view of self-revelation of the soul in prayer.

Poetry, which is the music of words, should also be studied from this point of view of rhythm and its correspondences; but we will soon return to this subject. We have said enough for those who wish to work by themselves.

GENERAL SUMMARY

It is now time to summarize all we've just said about man's training by grouping together elements normally considered to be separate.

The will, which has power over the choice of substances in inspired air or sensations which enters the human being, can adjust the natural tendencies of the being, either by stimulating the power of the organic forces or, on the contrary, by diminishing this power. The use of stimulants allows one to quickly obtain those results – but only for a short time – which can only be obtained in a continuous manner through work and habit. But this use must be short term, for the habit of progressive work is excellent, but the habit of using stimulants is, on the contrary, very dangerous.

Possessing a good range of aliments and stimulants, the Magister stands before his organism like an artist before his piano: depending on which center he uses, that is, which octave, and depending on which note he presses down, a different sound is heard. It is good practice to have in mind the purpose of the desired result, then one can proceed with confidence.

Training for the Instinctive Being

Do you have difficulty in seeing your ideas to fruition, even though you have no problems conceiving them? Do you find it difficult to set to work, whereas the work of the imagination happens with no effort, so that the intellectual center always prevails over your instinctive center, yet it is really important that you act? Unless misfortune or urgent material needs force you to return to real life, you will never accomplish anything real, and little by little you will become one of those coffee-house or artistic brasserie dreamers who astonishes their audience with the originality and strength of their ideas, but who, powerless to create anything, give rise to that category of jealous "failures" who bog down the administrations by day and the bars by night. The work of physical creation is a suffering which one must become used to performing progressively to avoid intellectual death. Indeed, it is during the act of creation that the mind comes into play, and it will try everything in its power to prevent what is sees as a hardship. We know of only two means to overcome this suffering:

1. Cultivating the habit of always working at the same time every day;
2. Consciously brutalizing the mind's appearance by developing the instinctive being.

It is also a serious error to scorn the physical body and its needs. This is the source of intellectual weakness to begin with, which can lead to unproductive mysticism (which shouldn't be confused with ecstasy), and finally madness. Nature has given man three parts harnessed together to lead him through life, and it is not by killing the ox part of this team, claiming it is too slow, that he will accomplish anything; for then one loses the possibility of undertaking journeys which are slow, yet long and sustained.

He must therefore know how to materialize his mind as he knows how to animate it, and the Hermetic androgyne bears *coagula* on one of its arms, and *solve* on the other.

Now, we possess the ability to *coagulate* the nervous force, and this is how:

Foods	- Heavy foods and vegetables (e.g. sauerkraut).
Drinks	- (Stimulants) Milk or beer.
Respiration	- Slow and shallow.
Perfumes	- The smoking of tobacco.
Sensation	- Pleasure in taste.
Music	- (Facultative) slow, monotone and easy.

Time   - Afternoon or better, the evening.

Training for the Emotional Being

There are some men of pale complexion, with a piercing gaze, remarkable thinkers, often highly accomplished, but who, if they aren't protected from material adversity by firm friendship or sufficient good fortune, quickly succumb to the blows of implacable destiny, their wonderful talents doomed from the moment of their birth. They don't have sufficient organic resistance or material activity, and the source of this activity is the blood. How many artists or authors of genius fall into this category, and Villiers de l'Isle-Adam[69], to name only one, was an unfortunate example of this truth.

Now, control of the emotional part of the being isn't sufficiently developed in such men, and it was with good reason that the Egyptians, and then the Greeks, also required their philosophers to undertake physical exercise through the practice of gymnastics.

The mysticism inherent in the nature of such dreamers leads them to exaggerate this characteristic, and sentimental Vegetarianism will certainly exercise its ravages on such intellectual types. The only true approach for such individuals who are conscious of the need to control their organic powers is exercise. Magical training requires complete balance in the human being above all else, and the first duty of the Magister is to activate the dormant or weakened centers within him. The training of the character should also be the object of especial care on the part of the serious student[70].

The foundation of such training is as follows:

Foods   - Roast meats. Game.

---

[69] A symbolist writer which died in 1889, at the age of 51, from stomach cancer. Although he came from a distinguished aristocratic family, his father used up most of their money unsuccessfully searching for an alleged family fortune (his ancestor, was a Grand Master of the Knights Hospitaller). L'Isle-Adam appears to have lived most of his life in poverty, with success eluding him despite his genius, and he died shortly after marrying his childhood sweetheart on his deathbed.

[70] We should remember that this terminology is not referring to the 'soul' as modern-day people understand it. In this instance, the 'soul' is one of the three components of the human being, so that the 'animal' part is the unconscious activity of the human, the 'soul' represents taking care of the body through exercise, self-development and right eating habits, while the 'intellect' is the sentient and conscious control of the body. It can also refer to a person's character.

Drinks	- (Stimulants) Wine.
Respiration	- Rapid and deep.
Perfumes	- Musk.
Sensation	- Pleasure in smell.
Music	- Marches.
Favorable Time	- Immediately after a meal.

A few days of such training should already begin to produce results in those who claim their usefulness in training the Magician. On many occasions we have had an opportunity to apply these teachings, and through them have been able to confirm within a month or two the successful nature of such an approach, which has been applied so often in the past.

We would also comment that those are general rules, and that the result being sought is obtained by the addition of all the physiological effects which were described earlier, too. Someone who opened the book at this page without reading the preceding information concerning the action of food and perfumes, would no doubt be astonished to read that wine or musk could have an influence on thoughts. But we are writing down the results of our experiments for serious seekers, and we would refer anyone else to read the "Red Dragon" and the "Grand Grimoire"[71], certainly more entertaining than our lucubrations, which are no doubt far too physiological for those determined to conjure up Charlemagne between the fruit and cheese courses.

Training for the Intellectual Being

Do you have large hands and big fingers, with great strength for work, along with a real difficulty in assimilating facts quickly and understanding art? But do you have an intense *desire* to improve your intellectual being, and place your work and your appetite in the service of your brain? Work on your memory, which in you is excellent, if slow to begin with, and I promise you a better path in life, though it will take a long time to accomplish. However, you need to retain what you learn to conquer all those needs and appetites which currently continue to control your entire existence; and above all you will need to tame that anger which overtakes you at the slightest provocation, and you must follow precisely the intellectual gymnastics which we outlined concerning sensation and music.

---

[71] In fact, the *Red Dragon* is an alternative name for the *Grand Grimoire*, a book of black magic involving summoning and making pacts with demons.

Add to that the following diet as the basis for your development, and in six months I promise you, if you make these efforts, the first vibrations of your soul to the accents of the divine music.

Foods	- Fruit and dairy. Eggs. Little meat. Sugar.
Drinks	- (Stimulants) Coffee once a day.
Respiration	- Slow with delayed expiration.
Perfumes	- Incense with frequent psychic training (prayer).
Sensation	- Hearing should be developed as well as sight. The attentive study of and listening to music.
Music	- Sacred. Symphonic concerts. Opera. Modern German music (Wagner).
Time of Work	- Always before breakfast, from 7:00 – 11:00am. Afternoon, from 5:00 – 7:00pm. Work in the morning; invent in the afternoon.

Bibliography

BALZAC...............................*Traité des Excitants modernes,* reproduced in the journal Le Voile d'Isis, 1st year.

BAUDELAIRE..............................*Les Paradis artificiels.*

ELIPHAS LÉVI............................*Rituel de la Haute Magie.*

STANISLAS DE GUAITA..............*Le Serpent de la Genèse* (p. 360. Le Haschisch).

DR. NOBIN-CHUNDER PAUL............*La Philosophe yoga.*

LOUIS LUCAS............................*La Médecine nouvelle.*

CHAPTER VI – MEDITATION

THINKING

Have you thought about the many transformations a piece of food passes through before becoming an integral part of the organism? Now, the analogy to this is sensation, which is in fact simply the food of the psychic being, and which must also suffer major transformations prior to its complete assimilation.

The physical process can be considered as three overall steps:

1. Filtering of the sensations by the sensory and condensing organs in this process to produce ideas;
2. Fixing of these ideas;
3. Digestion of these ideas constituting the origin of thought.

The sensory organs are to sensation what the mouth, stomach and intestines are to food, being the organs of separation and preliminary transformation.

Once the ideas have been produced, analogous to chyle, they are concentrated in the memory as chyle is concentrated (to a large extent) in the liver. Chardel defined memory as the reaction of intelligence on sensations, and the phenomena of dual consciousness and hypnotism lend particular support to that definition.

But it is here that the work of impulsive or reflexive man ends, whose perfect example is the office worker, meticulous, routine and without initiative. Here, on the other hand, begins the work of the Magister, who considers memory, so dear to present day teachers, as a purely passive faculty.

When the chyle has been concentrated in the liver, it hasn't completed its evolution, for the circulation now takes it up and carries it to the lungs where, according to Louis Lucas, and corroborated by modern histologists, some of the white blood corpuscles are transformed into red corpuscles.

Now, in the psychic circulation, this preliminary and rudimentary process of the filtering and fixing of sensations is followed by another, far more complicated, process: that of digesting the ideas produced and stored. *Feeling* is now followed by the action of *thinking*, an action which is far more elevated, and which only some human beings can attain. "To have an idea", said Fabre d'Olivet, "is to feel. To have a thought, is to create."

Meditation is the exercise of thought: it is the origin of the development of man's latent abilities, *including prophecy and ecstasy*.

The special development of memory achieved through instruction, as currently practiced, isn't necessarily the only way of practicing meditation, and prophecy will develop much more quickly in the character of a shepherd who is contemplative by nature, than in an overqualified pedant with absurd prejudices.

Instruction is a tool, a means to an end, often a danger if it is incomplete, and never an objective, except for what Westerners call "practice".

Just as the various procedures which we have described up till now help to train *feeling* in us, the exercise of meditation develops *thinking* surely and rapidly, and this is one of the effects on which the Magister should particularly focus his attention.

But how should one approach the practice of meditation, you ask?

When Goethe wished to penetrate a secret of Nature, for example philosophical anatomy, he took the brain of some animal and, sitting down in solitude in his garden, he would spend a long period of time contemplating the object of his research. Little by little ideas would come, and connections which had previously been obscure would become evident, analogies would come together, and the existence of an intermediate bone between the jawbones, or the existence of cephalic vertebrae would become clear under the influence of meditation. Edgar Allen Poe, by showing in his story *Eureka* that meditation alone led the founder of contemporary Astronomy to the discovery of his laws, also teaches us the path to follow; for the truth always becomes clear by means of direct contemplation of Nature by a man who knows how to isolate himself enough to listen to the simple and eternal language of the creative power. Wasn't Socrates' *daimon* a better guide than all the moral codes then known?

FIRST PERIOD: LEARNING TO MEDITATE

If you still don't know how to give yourself over to meditation, permit me to try to explain this as best I can, by establishing some rules and some divisions, no doubt quite arbitrary, but which despite this may be of some use, in my opinion:

1. The first mental exercise which one should undertake is to replace all responses and ideas which are purely reflex and brought forth solely from memory, with responses which are measured and carefully thought out. There is no more terrible enemy of the effects of meditation than the floating mass of ideas "known by heart", responses which are all taken as given in educational books in response to those important questions we can be called on to

resolve each day. The individual who shows off the number of fixed ideas in his memory in order to give proof of his intellectual worth is like the man who recites old puns to demonstrate his wit. In addition, contradictory discussions and polemics should be assiduously avoided by the serious man. These are purely pointless exercises, since one almost inevitably wounds one's adversaries, and with the help of conceit, the half-convinced will be transformed into implacable enemies of the ideas put forward. Intellectual agreement is a completely personal result; so trust me, and leave impulsive people to discuss such subjects at leisure, and know how to keep silent every time an emotive discussion starts up in your presence. If needed, reread the "Gilded Verses" of Pythagoras: teach, state your thought as clearly as possible, but spare yourself from discussing anything, for, once again, this is a pointless use of your intellectual abilities.

To summarize, the first meditational exercise consists of having a clear understanding of every idea expressed, and always to prefer active thought over memory in mental endeavors.

2. Beyond that, you must become accustomed to paying close attention to, rather than just seeing, those things which come before us every day; and as far as possible seek to gain an understanding of the *invisible* idea disguised beneath the visible and material sensation.

Remember the teachings we gained from that rough experience of a Hansom cab passing by us in the road.

Just as you shouldn't impart an idea which hadn't been directed by intellectual process, so you shouldn't accept a sensation which hasn't been stripped of every reflex processes of the impulsive being, in order to allow the conscious process of the mind to work. This exercise, if carefully followed, will develop as much willpower as any of the longest and most complicated recommended practices.

3. When, through reflections brought about by the process of sensation, you begin to examine the invisible which separates itself from the visible, those ideas which separate from the form – the esoteric, as we say – which is hidden by the exoteric, you must go further still and seek the connections between those ideas.

This is where the use of analogy will play a considerable role. Some plant or some stone which has no significance to the profane, will manifest astral signatures to the Magister, who will then associate this plant or this stone with such-and-such animal or such-and-such planetary position. This, then, is the knowledge of the village "healers" or "witches", and, supported by their faith, these people can do more with their potions than the pedantic doctor who, while he thoughtlessly scoffs at them, can only make cadavers of the elements within his medicines, assembled without will and administered without faith! Magic is the knowledge of the connections between things, said Kircher, and this definition is wonderful, if limited.

Seeking natural analogies *on one's own and without the use of books* should be the third mental exercise of the Magister.

4. In addition to applying meditation to the works of Nature, we would also strongly recommend long periods spent before works of art. These periods should be made as much as possible outside the hours when many people are there, and at times when silence reigns. It is profitable to use many visits to meditate on one masterpiece alone, without devoting your visit to two or more different works.

    When reading a book, the same procedure should be followed. Devote many sittings to the attentive reading of the work in question, with pen in hand, and never read two different works at the same sitting. This procedure, formerly recommended by Montaigne, has lost none of its value. It is better not to undertake a reading session and pointlessly tire your intelligence, rather than to do it in haste and without meditating. However, we would add that this procedure should be applied to incontrovertible masterpieces, and that reading a popular newspaper[72], which only rouses the reflexes, requires no expenditure of the intellect – indeed, far from that.

---

[72] In the text Papus cites *Le Petit Journal*, in English 'The Little Daily', a highly successful daily newspaper which appeared from 1863 to 1944. By 1895, the time of this book, its circulation has reached 2 million copies, making it the world's biggest newspaper. However, it made the mistake of being partisan in the *Dreyfus Affair*, who the Editor was against, resulting in the newspaper losing a considerable number of its readers.

SECOND PERIOD: PSYCHOMETRY & TELEPATHY

We can now understand easily enough the very general lines of approach, which can vary considerably, concerning preliminary mental training. Now we come to some more difficult, but far more important, practices for the Magister. Those who have some difficulty in reaching a decision, or even those who want to extend their mental training, can make use of the following practice.

Every morning on waking, and as close as possible to daybreak, they should wrap themselves in a wool covering, one corner of which should be pulled down over the head, and sit in their bed, concentrating their thoughts on the work to be undertaken during the day, and examining their organism for impressions supplied by their inner senses. They should perform this exercise initially for 10, then 15, then 20 minutes each morning, six times a week. During this time, the respiration should be slow and deep. After a few days of this practice, according to François-Charles Barlet[73], a great sense of well-being should be experienced, and the being of will should gain more and more authority over the impulsive being. One can then experiment with Psychometry[74], and then Telepathy.

One should practice Psychometry as much as possible in the dark, and firstly with letters written by people who are known, letters which are mixed up prior to the Operation, and which are then held against the forehead, one at a time, allowing five minutes of meditation to each.

After a few days of this exercise, images will start to appear, and become clearer, and the vision or impression of the people who wrote them will manifest with greater intensity.

The letters should then be replaced with archeological objects, and visions of ancient civilizations will appear to the seer and in a conscious manner, if he is sufficiently developed.

One can find more complementary details concerning Psychometry in the work of the creator of the method[75], or in the magazine *Initiation*.

---

[73] Albert Faucheux (1838 – 1921), whose pen name was Barlet, was a contemporary of Papus, Peladan, de Guaita, Chamuel, Chaboseau and Sédir. He was an Occultist and Astrologer. He was a member, along with Papus of the *Ordre Kabbalistique de la Rose-Croix*, becoming its Grand Master in 1889 (Papus succeeded him), as well as being on the Supreme Council of the *Ordre Martiniste*, and later a member of the *Hermetic Brotherhood of Luxor*.

[74] *Psychometry*: the ability to discern information about a person by touching or being near an object connected to or which belonged to that person.

[75] An American physiology professor from Frankfort, Kentucky called Joseph Rhodes Buchanan, who experimented with his students in the 1840s and later. In 1893, he

When one has obtained some satisfying results from the use of Psychometry, one can try to communicate thoughts at a distance, which is called *Telepathy* by some contemporary observers.

Two participants start to meditate at the same time in two different locations. One of these thinks strongly about an object, while the other attempts to sense the thought of the first. The Arabs excel at this type of practice, thanks to their habit of meditating.

For complementary details, see in the *Annales des Sciences Psychiques* the very interesting experiments of two men of letters, Mr. Léon Desbeaux, current Director of the Odéon, and Mr. L. Henrique, author of *Amour*, a marvelous esoteric drama, and also our own experiments between Paris and Marseille, in our magazines *Voile d'Isis* and *Initiation*.

LOVE

Stimulant for the Man of Will

There are substances, perfumes and sensations capable of influencing each of our three organic centers; but is the total being, the man of will sheltered from similar actions? Absolutely not!

But it is not a substance or a perfume, or even a sensation, however elevated it might be, such as the most divine music which can affect the immortal soul in its hidden retreat. It is something better or worse, depending on the use the human being makes of it: it is *love*.

Love, from the mysterious affinity which pushes atom towards atom, from the insane impulse which brings man to the woman he loves despite every obstacle, to the mysterious impulse which casts down intelligence, bewitched by the unknown, at the feet of beauty or truth, love is the great motive of all created beings acting in the manner of immortality, and love has two paths to come to fruition: generation below, and ecstasy above; for the pivotal center of the immortal soul is the same as the center of the characterful center, only the ray is more extended.

This is why Magic, considered as a whole, is the science of love, the love of the stars for the sun or the love of the atom for power. This is why woman, the instinctual priestess of love on earth, whether she acts in a Lunar manner as

---

published a manual on his techniques, called *Manual of Psychometry: the Dawn of a New Civilization*.

mother to the family, or in the manner of Venus as lover, spouse or courtesan, is the Magician born of humanity; and thus the girl looking after swine last night is now enthroned in a luxurious hotel by the magical virtue of her regard, supported by the teachings of EVE, who enlightens all women who come into this world.

Now, he who tries to flee from love never know how to resist it, and a wonderful writer as well as a true connoisseur of the human character, Anatole France, powerfully exposed this magical law in his novel *Thaïs*, where the monk Paphnuce is completed prostrated by this power which he had so poorly understood.

And the foolhardy man who appeals to Magic in order to follow his amorous passion is ignorant or drunk, for he asks for arms to fight at the very moment he admits he is conquered. The Magister must not be mastered by love any more that he should ignore it; and complete chastity is only required of the practitioner during the 40 days preceding the magical working.

But if the Magister must be able to resist the anger and hate he finds within himself, he must control this formidable dynamic power that is love all the more, when he fimds himself encountering it on his path.

When a beautiful pair of marvelous horses are shown to you during your travels, and you can climb into the coach which they are pulling and therefore shorten your journey, what would you do? Waste your time which is already so precious, and fight against the impetuosity of those horses by barring their route; or jump into the coach, seize the reins with a steady hand and move ahead?

You must reach a conclusion, for in life this problem presents itself to you daily. You have two dangers to fear. Do you remain in the road, to be trampled underfoot by the coursers, or at least waste your time to no benefit? Or do you mount the coach when you don't have enough energy, and have the horses carry you away? Remember that courage is the first requisite quality of the Magister after knowledge, and learn to solve the Riddle of the Sphinx by yourself. We have already shown you the best path in our opinion: let the horses gallop, but hold the reins firmly.

Man cannot forget that he only forms one of the psychic poles of humanity, and that his idea can only become alive when it has been activated by a feminine brain. Can you show me the religious man who can succeed in his work without the aid of women? Plato, in the *Banquet*, gives us the key to the original separation of the human into two poles; all magical knowledge resides in the mental rather than the physiological use of the spark produced, and it is there, without any contradiction, that we find the most powerful force which can be given to the Magician to know and direct. The poets, those prophets of Nature, have always taught this across the ages. So never scorn the teachings of the poets if you wish to understand and practice the eternal science of the Mages.

But, just as the mental being takes wing, new and higher loves are revealed to man, and the Holy Kabbalah teaches us that the Sage who devotes his efforts and his vigils to the disinterested worship of Truth will be aided in his efforts by the increasingly perceptible presence of his *sister soul*, an astral entity which sacrifices her personal evolution to that of her beloved. This is one of the most profound arcana of the "Mysteries of Love", and those who study the Kabbalah will alone penetrate this secret in its entirety.

But alongside this ardent pursuit of Truth, how many base and vulgar appetites exist, squandered beneath this unfortunate title. Those who have sacrificed their entire lives to research the highest issues which have touched humanity are treated as mad and as dreamers by the rest. Ah, the rest...those for whom study is only a whimsy, and whose sole purpose is to lead to a fortune and to affluent recompense. These are the people who, indolently installed in a position which allow them to receive the protections and rents of their relatives, vigorously criticize the dreams of those good alchemists of the Middle Ages. Mr. X...[76] can't indignantly blast the conduct of Paracelsus enough, unworthy calumny from a turncoat former pupil.

And when we see the career of that wonderful genius who was Paracelsus, poor throughout his life and always sacrificing all his means to the worship of Truth, travelling across all of Europe and parts of Asia on foot, in order to obtain

---

[76] While it's not completely clear who the mysterious 'Mr. X' is, after talking with Dr. Christopher McIntosh and other experts of the period, there seems to be a general consensus that he is referring to Charles-Marie-Georges Huysmans (known as J.-K. Huysmans, 1848 – 1907). Firstly, he was thirty-year civil servant, and therefore earned a steady salary, as referred to by Papus. In 1889, he met Berthe Courrière, who instructed him in occult teachings. He also had a brief affair with Henriette Maillat, former lover of Sâr Péladan, among others. He copied her letters to him, which he used almost verbatim in his book *Là-Bas*, which was serialized in a Paris magazine in 1891, a scandalous but very popular series (later a book) concerning Satanism. His spats with Papus and De Guaita were legendary at the time, and La Guaita even challenged him to a duel after he had claimed in public writigns that the latter was a 'practitioner of sorcery' (see *Occult Paris* by Tobias Churton, pub. Inner Traditions 2016, p. 303 et seq.). Given all this bad blood between Papus and his colleagues and Huysmans, it is hardly surprising that he uses the occasion of a book to publicly attack his adversary; and it is most certain that anyone reading this book at the time would have known exactly to whom he was referring! While his book *Là-Bas* was not exactly negative in its treatment of Paracelsus, the fact that he included him in a book about Satanism was no doubt enough for Papus to suggest he had twisted his education from his two lady friends and thereby called Paracelsus' integrity into question.

secret teachings from those few centers of initiation which still existed, effecting miraculous cures by means of the genii he had enclosed in the pommel of his sword, and burning the official books of learning in front of his audience, finally dying as miserably as he did gloriously, and crucified ever since in every volume of so-called "historical" dictionary; when we see that, it is not before Mr. X…, despite his 12,000 Franc salary, that we would wish to kneel; for Mr. X… is a courtesan to Truth, selling his studies as a courtesan sells her caresses, to the highest bidder.

Now, if we can find true sages through the ages, such as Bichat or Claude Bernard[77], how many might be supposed to be like Mr. X…, acerbic critics and sworn enemies of all innovation and progress?

So, just as the great knowledge of the man of the world consists of distinguishing lovers from those who sell love, the first duty of the Magister consists of recognizing true love wherever it manifests itself, and unmasking without pity those sellers who dishonor the parvis of this, the most sacred Temple of all, for it has allowed the manifestation of two great figures in Christianity: the Magdalene, and St. Theresa.

OBSTACLES

Reaction of the Impulsive Being

However, one shouldn't believe that voluntary action in any sphere is as easy to accomplish as one might think at the outset.

In fact, each affirmation of the power of the will is preceded and above all followed by a contrary reaction of the impulsive being, a reaction sometimes so energetic that the individual who intends to act is overcome by such a sense of discouragement and lassitude that he puts off his action until the following day, to the great detriment of the power of his volition.

Indeed, intellectual work can only take place at the price of the complete submission by the impulsive man to the intellectual man for a few moments. But very focused training is needed for this, without which we would be powerless to accomplish it.

---

[77] Marie François Xavier Bichat (1771 – 1802), despite his short life, is considered to be the father of Histology: while Claude Bernard (1813 – 1878) established the use of scientific method in medicine, and created the 'double blind' methodology for experimentation. In both cases medical boundaries were expanded through the creative thoughts of these men.

These things might appear naïve or paradoxical to individuals who are not used to taking personal action, and above all to completing projects; but there is no artist or author who hasn't felt the phenomena we have just mentioned taking place within him.[78]

Let's suppose that, after successive procrastinations and crises of laziness and pessimism, you are finally harnessed to your work of intellectual accomplishment. You imagine that the effort of will you have expended to get there is all that is required, and that, now, everything will proceed without further difficulty.

But hardly have you come to the point of writing or drawing, when an overpowering need to get up and go for a walk seizes your being. It seems to you that outside, the idea which is currently vague will come into focus. This need soon takes on such an importance that, if you are not instinctively inured to it, you get up, leave your work and go out. You have succumbed to the snare erected by the impulsive being, which physical stillness would have overcome, and you can be sure that your idea is no clearer than before; quite the opposite, in fact. In this instance it's the instinctive center, for whom walking is the characteristic means of action, which has fooled your vigilance.

Let us suppose, however, that you recognize this pitfall, and instead of giving in to it, your will on the contrary focuses on accomplishing the task. Then the action of the impulsive being manifests in another way.

The need for physical movement disappears as if by magic, and now a thirst, equally strong, makes its presence increasingly felt in proportion to the intensity of the cerebral task. This is another snare of the instinctive center, for each draught of liquid absorbed then uses up a part of the nervous energy in the brain and reduces the projected accomplishment of the task a little.

But once again you overcome this sensation, and finally the pen starts to write on the paper. It's then that the other impulsive centers come into play. The physical needs are silent; but emotional needs come to replace them. Images of past fights, former lovers, tomorrow's ambitions make themselves felt little by little, and an apparently invincible power pushes you to drop your pen, and you go backwards, allowing your mind to dwell on the tender melancholy or the impetuous ardor of the dreams which now describe themselves. How many young writers who have not become inured to this give themselves over to such

---

[78] "Here, faced with the blank sheet to which you come with your indecisive, vague, floating idea, and now you need to cover this paper sheet with black scrawl to give a precise, exact, logical and rigorous solidification to the fog in your brain, the first hours are truly difficult, truly sorrowful." (De Goncourt, *Mémoires*, Echo de Paris, 5 December 1891). [PAPUS]

temptation, and how many times has their work remained once more unrealized! And we are not talking about action arising from the need for action combined with feelings which often add themselves to these two isolated impulses. Those are reactions which every author believes is personal, and which are only overcome by an instinctive habit of enforcing strict regularity in the work ethic or in the timing of the work; for these reactions against instinct are engendered by the sphere of the soul.

It remains for us to describe the most dangerous snares to avoid, which can affect almost all of those who have managed to resist the previous effects.

When the author has resisted the need to move, for foods and stimulants, anger, nerves and emotions, and obstinately begins to follow his path, he immediately stops, enlightened by a marvelous idea, unperceived until then, and which is going to open grandiose horizons which have not yet been explored. After this idea another one follows, then a series, and all this is so unexpected, so ravishing, that he quickly throws them down on the paper or canvas, and feverishly takes notes...progressively distanced from his original subject. When he returns to himself, the brain, now fatigued by the effort he has just accomplished, no longer has the strength to continue. He carefully scours the precious notes he has just made, and this is how he fills his draws with these notes every day, and how he never gets to finish writing his work. This is the result of the action of the intellectual sphere which, not wishing to submit to the despotism of the will which constrains it for a moment into immobility, tempts the author's mind with the beauty of its ideas, and very quickly shakes off the yoke of power which had just held it in check.

An understanding of these reactions by the impulsive being is very useful, for it provides the means to avoid them. Indeed, patience and obstinacy in standing up to this impulsive being will allow a quick and sure accomplishment of the goal on which the author is focused, and he mustn't lose sight of this goal for an instant. Remember the legend of the sirens in the old myths.

Bibliography

For the artistic side:

ANATOLE FRANCE...................*Thaïs,* I Vol. in – 18.
EMILE MICHELET....................*L'Ésoterisme dans l'art,* in – 18, 1890.
                                 Conférences ésotériques.
DE GONCOURT...........…............*Mémoires.*

For Occult Knowledge:

PAPUS...............................*Traité méthodique de science occulte,*
                                  p 21.
WILLIAM DENTON....................*The Soul of Things.*
LOUIS DEINHART.....................*Psychométrie,* Brunschwig, 1891.
YVON LE LOUP....................*La Psychométrie* (Initiation No. 6,
                                5th Year, March 1892).
GURNEY ET MYERS................*Les Hallucinations télépathique,* Alcan
                                1892, in-vol. in – 8th.

CHAPTER VII – THE PRACTICE OF THE WILL

Classical philosophy has the singular merit of having chosen, as a basis for its affirmations about the human character, a ternary which corresponds on every point to occult teaching: that which feels, or sensibility; that which thinks, or intelligence; and that which wishes, or will.

We have seen how special training allows man to develop what feels and what thinks. It remains for us to consider the last part of our study. The development of the will begins with those various physiological or mental exercises which we have just discussed, in order to train the organs of expression in man, which number four: sight, speech, gesture and movement or general activity. Now Magic, when considered to be above all the external signs of occult connections to things, attributes to each of these organs of expression various symbolic implements whose knowledge is indispensable to the student. Thus, magic mirrors serve primarily to educate the sight, the magnetized wand and sword to educate gesture, as well as pantacular figures, commonly called talismans. Finally, circles and movements lead to the education of the last of the organs of expression in man. We must now concern ourselves with the various orders of development.

THE EDUCATION OF SIGHT[79]

Magic Mirrors – Magnetism

Magic mirrors are essentially vehicles for the condensation of astral light; charcoal, crystal, glass and metals can also be employed in their construction depending on the use one wishes to make of it.

Without concerning ourselves here with the Operations which contribute to the consecration of a magic mirror, we are going to focus mainly on the material construction and the effects produced by this type of object.

The simplest magic mirror is a crystal glass filled with pure water. The glass is placed on a white cloth and a light put behind this glass.

---

[79] The French word used is *regard*, which is closer to 'looking' since this implies an active state, whereas 'sight' really implies a passive act. However, 'sight' will be used in this case, and the reader is asked to remember that this is an active process or studying the object in view, rather than simply holding it in one's gaze..

We've been able to obtain very interesting results with this rudimentary equipment. This is how, to convince a skeptic, we had one of his children, a young girl, stare at the center of a glass of water, while we placed our right hand upon the child's head. The young seer immediately described a scene taking place at a distance from this place, and once verification had been made, everything turned out to be correct.

We've even tried out this process, made famous by Cagliostro, with women who are completely immune to hypnosis, and were able to obtain immediate results, which were as convincing as they were interesting. In this case it was necessary to quickly consecrate a mirror and make an appeal to ANAËL following the ritual described in the third part of this book. The results worked well both in speed and intensity.

But there is another category of mirror used by Arabic Magicians and very easy to make. Al that is needed is to blacken the thumbnail of a sufficiently excitable child with boot polish, while making the evocation prescribed above and burning perfumes appropriate to the hour or day of the Operation, to obtain satisfactory results.

One can also blacken a square of coarse paper (paper for sketching) more or less completely with carbon, or better still with drawing charcoal to obtain an excellent mirror, capable of affecting even only slightly susceptible subjects.

Travelers have described many kinds of magic mirrors used in the East.[80]

We have personally experimented with a magic mirror brought back from India, and which is formed from a crystal ball which reflects the light. Beneath this crystal is a little compartment to hold the object which the seer wishes to use in the consultation. Experiments made with ordinary hypnotized subjects have produced very interesting results.

In summary, all these mirrors have the singular effect of concentrating a particle of astral light into a point and puts the individualized life in each of us in direct connection with the universal life, the conservator of forms.

Don't think for a moment that it's enough simply to look into a magic mirror to distract yourself a little before dinner, and then you will immediately see the forms you wish to evoke appear. Magical Operations, even the most futile ones, require a great spiritual tension, absolute calm and above all a deep sense of the difficulty of the task being undertaken. Thus, it is only by progressive training that you can become accustomed to seeing visions in the mirror, and here certain counsels are necessary for the Operator.

---

[80] See *Coup d'oeil sur la Magie* ("A Quick Glance at Magic") by Un Badaud, pub. Dentu, 1892 [PAPUS]. Note: *badaud* is a pseudonym, and means 'Idler', 'Stargazer', or 'Ninny'!

Assuming the experiment is done with the necessary calm and meditation, these are the obstacles you will need to overcome. When you've looked fixedly for a few moments at the center of the mirror, you'll feel a characteristic pricking in the eyes, and one is often forced to close the eyelids for a moment, which destroys all the efforts made up to that point. Blinking the eyelids is due to the impulsive being and is purely reflex; so, it's necessary to fight it using one's will, but this normally only takes a few days, by holding a session lasting a maximum of twenty minutes each day. The moment you feel the characteristic pricking of the eyes, you must strain your will to prevent the eyelids from closing, and this begins to take place soon enough, and we've said.

Once this initial result has been achieved, firstly you'll see the mirror take on a different hue from that it habitually displays; red emanations, then blueish, similar to what electrical emanations exhibit, and it is only then that forms will appear. In the third part of the book are all the details concerning the use of perfumes and the consecration. Studious seekers can also read with benefit the chapter in Cahagnet's book *Magie magnétique*[81], about magic mirrors and their creation.

What we said about the education of sight in the sense of fixing the focus to obtain results, is closely related to the magnetic process of *fascination*. In the latter case, the eye of the one being fascinated acts as a mirror and receives the fluidic impulses emanated from the eye of the fascinator. True magnetism needs another practice added to that of the emission of fluid: this is *condensation*, the accumulation around the magnetizer. This is the sole secret behind the healings obtained by the use of *love* of humanity, remembering that one can wish in two ways: on the one hand, by emitting a large quantity of fluid by wrinkling the forehead and adopting a sullen attitude, which is the process of *repulsion*, particularly used to defend oneself against an attack by psychic beings; on the other hand, by *intensely desiring* the result one wants. Then, there is an attraction of fluid to the magnetizer, who only has to send it out having activated it. In Spanish, *querer* means both to love and to want, and this is the key to the magnetism called curative. We must magnetize with the heart rather than with the head, perhaps a rather coarse image, but which correlates precisely with factual reality. We will no doubt discuss *desire* again, and its power which is so much stronger than brute volitional impulse.

---

[81] *Magie magnétique, ou, Traité historique et pratique de fascinations, miroirs cabalistiques, apports, suspensions, pactes, talismans* ("Magnetic Magic, or Historical and Practical Treatise on Fascination, Kabbalistic Mirrors, Spiritual Manifestations, Suspensions, Pacts, Talismans") by Louis Alphonse Cahagnet (1858) is readily available in PDF on the internet, in French.

Speech

We know the position the study of vibration holds in present-day science; but this study has almost exclusively focused on the domain of physical facts, and it is hardly as if the captivating concepts of Camille Flammarion[82] have attracted attention in the mental results obtained from these studies. Now, Occult Science teaches us that every vibration on the physical plane results in specific changes of states in the astral and psychic planes. It is by understanding this affirmation and its results that we can conceive the enormous influence that human speech can exert over all the planes of Nature.

The emission of speech effectively includes three simultaneous effects:

1.   The emission of a sound activating the psychic plane of Nature.
2.   The emission of a certain quantity of vital fluid activating the astral plane.
3.   The liberation and creation of a psychic entity which is the *idea*, to which sound gives a body and articulation gives life.

Each idea so realized and manifested in the material world acts like a real being for a certain time, then fades and is progressively extinguished, at least in the physical plane. The duration of the action of this idea depends on the cerebral tension with which it has been given out, that is, the quantity of vitality with which it has been invested. In certain cases, the entire man sacrifices his own life in the interest of the idea he is defending, and then creates currents of considerable power in the astral and especially in the divine world. It is there that we can seek the true influence of the persecutions of martyrs on the future of philosophical or religious doctrines.

Speech is the generative instrument of the spirit, and this truth, proclaimed by Malfatti de Montereggio in 1839, has been reinstated and even clarified further thanks to the contemporary work of Mr. Vurgey on philosophical

---

[82] Nicolas Camille Flammarion (1842 – 1925) was an Astronomer and author. As well as popularizing Astronomy, he wrote a large number of books, including science fiction. His main claim to fame was his belief in the transmigration of souls. His first book, the *Plurality of Inhabited Worlds*, published in 18632 at the age of 20, coincided with his being fired by the Paris Observatory. He believed man was a 'citizen of the sky', passing through successive reincarnations on different planets. This combination of science, science fiction and esotericism attracted many people and later authors, including Edgar Rice Burroughs and Sir Arthur Conan Doyle.

anatomy. An old Christian legend teaches that the devil is incapable of taking hold of thoughts, so long as they aren't materialized in speech.[83]

There is a knowledge of speech composed in a few names and carefully preserved in two initiations: in the East, with its *mantras* in the Sanskrit language; and the West with its *kabbalistic* formulas in the Hebrew language. The second, more in conformity with our spirit, alone interests us for now.

Even students who are not very advanced know the Kabbalah well enough, a subject we have studied in particular, so there is no point going over the same ground here.

Let it suffice to recall that Kabbalists, who are generally very expert in Magic, assign a specific influence to Hebrew words in Astral Operations. It is from this that all those words come which we so often see horribly mangled in the Grimoires, and which we find scattered through the conjurations and prayers.

We are simply going to summarize the most important names to know according to established rituals. These names, simple garments for sublime ideas, are the most often found in the compound formulas reminding the astral beings of man's knowledge. Also, the Operator activates his formulas with all the faith he can muster to ensure the success of the experiments previously attempted either by the Masters or himself. This explains the considerable outpouring of fluidic projection particularly in the case of village witches, who have an unshakeable confidence in the formulas they only weakly understand. Now, these witches, who concoct vulgar recipes or recite some banal Hebraic phrases often obtain remarkable results, not because of the Hebrew words, which are simply the body for this emanation, but rather because of the vital intensity with which their imaginations clothe the words uttered by them.

Learning to develop speech is therefore of the highest interest to the Magician, and the rules of this training are implicitly contained in the ritual of prayer, which we explain in the third part of this book.

Let it suffice for now to remember that the only difficulty one may encounter in practice is to have one's speech interrupted by a violent emotion; so, the Magister must be a sufficient master of his impulsive being to avoid this accident, which could have dire consequences. Personal development is therefore most important in this matter.

---

[83] This is close to the similar view that, if you know the true name of something, you can control it. This is especially used in exorcisms, where the priest or Operator attempts to force or trick the entity into revealing its true name. The idea probably comes from Genesis, 1:26 and 2:19-20, in which God gives Adam dominion over all the animals, and has him name them as a further exercise of his authority over them.

Gesture

Sight and speech, considered to be organs of expression, have the great problem of not being permanent. This is the main reason for the importance of gesture, considered as the organ that makes ideas permanent. In fact, it is fact through the more or less great transformations effected by gesture which has given birth to drawing, writing, painting, sculpture and all the arts which leave a permanent imprint of their creation for future generations. Writing is simply the materialization of ideas, as is drawing. Now, those who have studied the Occult Sciences to some extent know that forms exist in essence in the astral, before being manifested on the physical plane; which is a way of saying that everything which populates the astral plane is only stimulated by the shapes of physical beings, the future origin of those beings themselves. That is why the man-made image of a physical power, the outline of this power which corresponds directly to the astral plane, will have a very marked influence on the beings which populate that plane.

For example, a human being whose will is sufficiently developed, will not affect an astral intelligence in the same way he would affect a physical man. Man, such as he is on earth, is perceived by other men through the eyes, which are physical organs. We see his habits, the color of his hair, his bearing; but, other than through habit or inference, we will have no perception of his moral being. In the astral state, on the contrary, we only perceive his moral being, and then man appears as a more or less luminous being, depending upon his psychic level of development, formed from fluidic[84] lines of various colors, whose whole representing to a large extent the figure of a *magical pentagram*.

Therefore, when a pentagram is shown to an astral power, thanks to the vital earthly fluids, the astral power receives an impression which is as strong as if it had standing before it a man of strong will, for the perception is identical, since it can only perceive general outlines on that plane.[85]

---

[84] There is no real equivalent to the French word *fluidique*. Perhaps the nearest is 'auric' or pertaining to the aura. It's seen as a mysterious force which emanates from beings, things and the stars. One way of visualizing it is as the force which comes out of the hands of a person charging a talisman.

[85] This is very important to understand. Papus is saying that, since the astral plane deals with what are considered archetypes or prototypes of ideas and things manifested in the physical world, so inhabitants of this astral plane would not see things in the same way that we do, but rather in symbolic or outline form. He makes the point that, instead of seeing a man in terms of height, weight, hair color, etc., an astral being would see man in terms of his metaphysical worth, which would be perceived in terms of the color and intensity of his astral form or aura. However, he develops this theme further by

This is the origin of the bizarre symbols called *planetary* or *angelic signatures*, and which we see drawn on most talismans, and which are composite summaries of moral laws of the greatest importance. This is no doubt seem paradoxical, even strange, to most readers who are not familiar with occultism, but experiments we have performed over the past three years on hypnotic subjects and results obtained from other sources have confirmed us in our statements. In another fifty years, we will better understand these astral forces whose influence we recognize today, and then we will see well enough if the secret teachings of the Kabbalah are ridiculous lies or, on the contrary, an expression of truths incomprehensible to the profane.

But in order to act in the astral, a gesture does not need to be fixed in a physical substance[86] and the sign of the cross, made by a simple gesture of the hand as taught to Christians, is a talisman of singular power when it is executed with great intention and faith; for it is the summary of the union between man and God to fight against the impulses of substantiality.

Magic also gives the Disciple a series of implements created to support his gestures, and we will give some technical details on the fabrication and consecration of these instruments in the third part.

The Magic Wand

To indicate and focus the projection of his will, the Magister possesses an implement formed out of wood and magnetized iron, called the *staff* or *magical wand*.

This wand has the sole function of condensing a large quantity of fluid emanated from the Operator or from substances arranged by him to this effect, and to focus the projection of this fluid upon a particular point. It supports the astral force condensed by the Operator around it, and this implement greatly facilitates experimentation.

But it contains no mysterious power within itself, and it only submits to the reactions of physical forces; and people who think it is enough to own a magical wand to conjure up magical phenomena are no different from those ignorant

---

suggesting that man would appear in the astral not so much as a glowing outline of a man, but rather as a glowing symbolic form of man. Thus, since the symbol of Man as Microcosm is the Pentagram (indeed, we will see a figure of this in part three of this book), the astral being would perceive a man as a pentagram formed from glowing lines emanating from man's fluidic form. We will see how he continues this analogy to explain the importance of sigils used in talismans, magical implements and circles as the only truly effective means of communicating with entities on the higher planes.

[86] That is, in a painting or a book, or a talisman.

types who believe they only have to purchase a nice flute in order to play it... It is far more important to know how to make use of the musical instrument, and a good musician knows how to delight you with a two-cent flute. Similarly, an expert Operator could use any kind of wand made from an insulating substance as a fluidic condenser: and therein lies its secret.

The Sword

The wand therefore serves to act on the astral, and it can be formed from rings and metallic bodies with no point. The same cannot be said of the sword. The purpose of the magical sword is to defend the Operator, and its point gives it this quality. This is why Paracelsus replaced the sword with a trident; and this is why an old nail driven into a piece of wood can absolutely hold its own with the best and the most expensive of magical swords, as the story of the sorcerer of Cideville shows us.[87]

The fluid accumulations formed by the union of astral powers acting like a soul, with the ambient vital fluids acting like a body, have a very strong analogy to electrical accumulation. The astral can only act in the physical by means of the fluids of physical life, or we can say vital energy. And when the Operator supposes that the astral power which appears wishes to misuse its power by acting against the goal being pursued, the Operator has no other decision to take than to place the point of his sword in the fluidic being which appears. The metallic point immediately draws off the astro-electric fluids which had formed

---

[87] This story could refer to one or two events, both of which occurred in Cideville! The more obscure one is that of Pierre-Robert Le Cornelier de Cideville, who counted Voltaire among his good friends. He recounts a story from the mid-1700s, when Voltaire had cured a farmer of fever, who repaid the kindness by promptly accusing Voltaire of being a sorcerer! However, the story referred to here is the famous one about the Poltergeist of Cideville, which took place in 1850-1851. In this interesting episode, reminiscent of the Salem Witch trials, a shepherd, called Thorel, had a Mr. Tinel summoned to court, accusing him of spreading calumnies about his by accusing him of being a sorcerer. Mr. Tinel ran a presbytery, where he taught a number of schoolboys. The boys reported extensive activity which we would now recognize as being poltergeist in nature. After a protracted trial, while the judge announced that not all the phenomena could be explained, confessions from some of the boys to the fact that they had faked at least some of the events led Mr. Tinel to apologize for spreading rumors about Thorel, though the judge dismissed the claims by Thorel for damages, and ordered him to pay all costs. It is interesting to compare the attitudes in 1750 to 1850: if the case had been brought and it had been determined in 1750 that Mr. Tinel was right to accuse Thorel, the fate of Thorel at the hands of the Inquisition would have been unthinkable. As it was, we shall see towards the end of this book that Thorel did not come out of it unscathed.

the body of the being endowed with evil intent, and this being is suddenly deprived of its means to act on the physical plane. It goes without saying that the lead grains violently expelled by a gun, like a revolver's bullet, act almost exactly in the same manner, which can be seen in many articles, among which is the one published by the Count of Larmandie (*Eureka*, p. 135), or the following taken from *Initiation* (April 1893).

Dissolving a larva on a steel point – Repercussion on the physical body of the witch.

"The following facts have seemed worthy of attention, since they allowed me to seek an explanation for the phenomenon of the luminous apparition cited in Issue No. 5 (February).

"I should say in advance that in drawing conclusions, I can only propose a hypothesis.

"As I said earlier, the population of P. is comprised of twenty-six people living in six houses. I hadn't mentioned a seventh house, which is situated in the middle of the village and which, together with the farm, had become my parents' property. This house was uninhabited. At its side was a little house, or rather a kind of cabin, inhabited by a woman who lived on her own. This woman, Mrs. B., was widely reputed to be a witch! The peasants attributed all kinds of occult powers to her, beginning with knowing how to make callouses disappear almost immediately, up to the blackest of evil magic, such as casting spells on people, inciting illnesses in animals, making cows abort, etc.

"I had an opportunity to see this woman for the first time a few months after my parents had moved into P. for the summer holidays.

"Mrs. B. came to the farm regularly every Saturday to purchase eggs, butter and cheeses, which she sold in local markets.

"She was a person aged forty to forty-five years old, small, stocky, a little chubby, with a face which was unpleasant without being ugly. She had a large mouth, with thick lips, slightly drooping to the right side, a short and big nose, with nostrils widely flared, a very low forehead, and dark chestnut hair beginning to turn gray. Her eyes were particularly remarkable: and weren't of the same color. Small, piercingly alive, the right eye was gray, while the left eye was a very clear blue, almost green at the top, while the lower part was dark brown.

"I was familiar with the stories circulating about this person, and, without paying the least attention to them, I had nevertheless noted them with some curiosity.

"I should now interject a detail whose importance will become clear later.

"When my parents had acquired the farm, it belonged to an Austrian gentleman and administered by a kind of steward, an uneducated peasant, who was notorious in the region for being under the domination of Mrs. B. Their exploitation of the farm resulted in no benefit accruing to its owner, and this is why it had been sold. All the animals, including a dog, had been included in the sale. This was a large sheepdog with reddish-brown hair, which was completely inoffensive during the day. However, the dog was scarcely familiar with anyone outside the members of the family, but he had a remarkable affection for me.

"This dog had peculiar eyes: the right eye was gray, while the left one was a very clear blue, almost green at the top, while the lower part was dark brown. In a word, the dog had eyes identical to those of Mrs. B. Moreover, the animal, which normally wasn't at all badly behaved, had an extraordinary animosity towards that person. On the days that Mrs. B. came to the farm we had to take care to put the dog on a chain. He barked furiously, he yelped, and didn't stop until B. had left. The dog ended up knowing the day that Mrs. B. came to make her purchases, and from the morning on he was in bad humor, and sought to free himself from this chain.

"The causes of this animosity were unknown. One day, I asked Mrs. B. if she had perhaps done something bad to the dog in the past, but she denied it and only replied that he was a bad animal, which would do something really bad one day if he wasn't taken care of. It was noticeable that the dog, when outside the house, was afraid of Mrs. B. If he saw her on the road, he would run off.

"At the farm, we were used to his caprices and didn't pay him any attention, save to put him on his chain each Saturday morning.

"In the August of 1876, a few days following the appearance of the *lantern*[88], on the night before my departure to rejoin my regiment, I was going for a walk with N…, mentioned earlier. The dog followed us as usual. We made our way towards the inhabited house, which I wanted to go into to examine some bits and pieces in the loft.

"As I mentioned earlier, Mrs. B. lived next door.

"Mrs. B. must have seen us enter. When we came out half an hour later, Mrs. B. was at her door, leaning against the wall. The dog followed behind us. Hardly had he come around the corner than he cried out, just like a dog which had unexpectedly been hit hard, and took off in the direction of the farm. N. and I watched the dog run off in surprise for a few moments, when Mrs. B., who was still at her door beside us without our paying any attention to her, began to laugh.

---

[88] This is a reference to the previous story, which recounts the *lantern* or luminescent figure appearing in the village and surrounding fields in more detail, and which is given later.

"I turned back towards her, feeling very vexed, without knowing why. No knowing what to say, I half turned, intending to look for the dog. But he had stopped a hundred meters or so away, and looked at us. We both stood where we were, and I called him over with a whistle. The dog obeyed my repeated calls. He began by approach slowly, stopped at each step and crouching on the ground. As he came closer at the sound of my voice (I chatted to him all the time), he became visibly bolder. The dog was now around twelve meters from me. He crouched on the ground and started to growl quietly. I called insistently to him. He didn't move, but his anger appeared to grow.

"I had a feeling that something was about to happen (N. told me later that he felt almost sick). Instinctively, I glanced at Mrs. B. and was taken aback by the hard and hate-filled look on her face, whose expression had completely changed. I've never forgotten the strangely evil expression on that face, as well as the intense and uncontrollable anger which overtook me at that moment.

"I called to the dog in a short, sharp tone; feeling sure he would approach. The dog pricked up his ears, eyes sparkling. Then, barking furiously, he bounded forward towards the door of the cabin. The instant the dog launched himself forward, Mrs. B. stepped back precipitously and threw the door shut behind her with a crash.

"The dog, upright against the door, barked and scratched furiously against it, as if he wanted to force his way in. It took a great effort to make him leave the place: we both had to take him by the collar and drag him back to the house.

"N. and I were not disposed to go to bed, and we discussed the bizarre attitudes of the woman and the dog far into the night, losing ourselves in conjecture.

"The following day I left for my garrison.

"At the end of December, I obtained a new leave for the New Year, and returned to our home at P.

"Since space at the house was limited and all the bedrooms occupied (relatives had come to visit us), I had a bed put in the empty house in the village.

"I went there around 11 o'clock in the evening, accompanied by the housekeeper, who carried water, towels, etc. Our shepherd dog followed me. After the housekeeper had made the bed, she left, taking the dog with her.

"The room I was sleeping in was on the first floor, accessible by a corridor which led to the door of a first room. This room was empty and completely stripped of furniture. By means of a second door facing the first, it communicated with my bedroom. My bed was set up in the corner, next to the communicating door between the two rooms, so that this door, which opened inwards into my room, touched the foot of the bed when it was opened.

"After the housekeeper had left, I locked the front door of the house and went upstairs. I closed the door of the first room behind me, without locking it, and went into my bedroom leaving the door partly open, touching the corner of my bed.

"I undressed (for I was in uniform), placing my cavalry saber against a chair which I was using as a night table. I went to bed and blew out my candle.

"When I had extinguished the light, I heard a very loud scratching at the door of the first room. It was an identical noise to the one produced by a dog wishing to enter or leave a room. But the scratching I had heard was very intense, as if the dog wanted to force the door open.

"Once the first moment of surprise had passed, I thought our dog was perhaps staying in the house. However, the scratching seemed to me to have been produced against the *inside* of the door of the first room and not against the corridor side. I called the dog several times by his name, "Sokol." Each time the noise increased in response.

"As I said earlier, I had left the communicating door between the two rooms open. Since this door was resting against the foot of the bed, I was able to reach it with my feet. With a brisk movement, I violently pushed the door with my right foot, which shut with a loud noise. At the same instant, the scratching increased in a very violent manner against this door on the other side.

"I must admit that, after calling the name of the dog to no avail, and the strange noise had grown louder, I was frightened for a moment, and it was this which had made me kick the door shut. But at the moment I heard the noise of this door closing right next to me, the feeling of fear immediately disappeared. I prepared to light my candle, and once light had returned the scratching stopped.

"I got out of bed, put on my pants and went into the first room.

"I still had the idea of the dog in my mind, despite the material impossibility of his presence. There was nothing in the room.

"I went out of the room, descended the stairs and looked around the ground floor. I called the dog. Still nothing.

"There was nothing more I could do but go back up to my room, and, not understanding any of this I went back to bed and blew out the candle.

"Hardly had I laid down when the racket started up again with even greater intensity outside the communicating door, which this time I had closed behind me.

"Then I experienced a feeling of annoyance and anger. I was aroused and, without taking time to light the candle, I jumped out of bed, seized my saber which I drew from its scabbard and ran into the first room. When I opened the door I felt a resistance, and in the darkness, I thought I saw a glow, a luminous shadow, if I can call it that, vaguely appearing against the door leading into the first room.

"Without thinking, I jumped forwards and struck a powerful blow with the saber in the direction of the door.

"A shower of sparks flew out from the door as if I had hit a nail stuck in the panel. The point of the saber had gone into the wood and it took an effort to withdraw the weapon. I hurried back to my room to light the candle, and, saber in hand, I then returned to look at the door.

"The panel was sliced from top to bottom. I searched for the nail which I thought I'd hit, but could find nothing. The sharp side of the saber no longer seemed to have encountered anything made of iron.

"I went downstairs again and looked everywhere, but found nothing out of the ordinary.

"I went back to my room. It was now eleven forty-five.

"I thought about the things that had just taken place. No explanation came to me, but I experienced a real feeling of peace after being overly excited, and I remember very well that I stroked the blade of my sword almost involuntarily as I went back to bed, and I put the weapon next to me in the bed, beneath the covers.

"I slept without further incident, and I only awoke around eight o'clock in the morning.

"In the cold light of day, the incidents of the previous night and the broken door appeared even more strange.

"Eventually I left the place and returned to the farm, where everyone had come together to have breakfast, and were waiting for me. Naturally I recounted my adventures, which seemed unbelievable to the youngsters visiting. As for my parents, as well as N., they were very concerned.

"Once breakfast was ended – it was now around ten o'clock – everyone wanted to see the broken door, and my parents, the young visitors, N. and I made our way to the house in the village.

"On the way, a woman from the village can to meet us and said she had wanted to come to our home to ask N. to come and see Mrs. B. who was ill. Another woman, who had gone to find Mrs. B. for some reason a few minutes earlier had found her on her bed unconscious and covered in blood.

"We walked more quickly. As for me, I was particularly moved by the woman's words.

"The delirious woman, lying on her bed, had a face almost completely covered with coagulated blood, her eyes closed and stuck together by blood, which was still pouring out of a mortal wound on her forehead. He wound, made by a sharp implement, began around two centimeters above the hairline and continued in a straight line to the bridge of the nose, extending seven and a half centimeters. The brain was literally split open, and the cerebral mass poured out through the crack.

"N. and I ran through the house, N. to find the necessaries to make a dressing, and me to have our groomsman go and find the doctor in a small neighboring village.

"Once the carriage had departed, I returned to Mrs. B., who had been temporarily dressed by N. The cabin was filled with all the village inhabitants, including the hostess of the inn. Nobody had any idea what could have happened to Mrs. B. The wounded woman, who had always been feared by the population, now only seemed to inspire the curiosity of the people present, with the exception of the hostess of the inn, who appeared not only to have been attracted by curiosity, but also seemed visible happy, and wasn't afraid to say out loud: "At last, Mrs. B. has got what she deserved."

"I must say that, from the moment I had laid eyes on Mrs. B. on coming into the house, laid out on her bed with her brain exposed, I had the feeling that something hidden was suddenly beginning to make sense in my head. At that moment, I realized that it had been Mrs. B., the "witch", who had been touched by the point of my weapon when, the previous night, I had given the blow with my saber which had broken wide the door of the room.

"Once the wounded woman was dressed and cleaned up, I left with N. We went up to the first floor of the empty house, towards the broken door. N. looked at it without saying anything: he was visibly affected. As for me, I was no less so. Eventually I broke the silence, and shared my ideas with N.

"I should mention that, at that time, I had no knowledge of occult matters or powers; nor did N. The connections I had made between what had passed in the night and the state in which we had found Mrs. B. were only intuitive.

"N. only replied to my explanations, if one could call it such, with: "I don't understand anything, but some terrible things have taken place." I didn't understand either, and we fell into an agreement not to speak any further about the events of the night, or what had happened to Mrs. B.

"She was in a comatose state, and the delirium had given way to a deep prostration from which she would never recover.

"After recommending that the ladies present continue to replace the cold compresses until the doctor arrived, we all returned to the farm. The family members had completely lost sight of the original purpose for our walk, which was the broken door; and both N. and I refrained from returning there. All the thoughts and conversations revolved around Mrs. B.'s accident, and when one of the younger people reminded me that we had forgotten to visit the door, I replied that it wasn't worth the effort to make another journey, and that I believed I had allowed myself to be overly affected by a dream.

"At one o'clock that afternoon, the doctor arrived. N. and I accompanied him to the home of Mrs. B.

"The doctor could only emphasize the gravity of the wound, and warned us that Mrs. B. only had a few hours to live. When he asked about the possible causes for the wound, we held our tongues, as we had agreed beforehand, and gave no suggestions.

"In expectation of a fatal outcome happening soon, the doctor stayed with us in P. He put together a report on the matter, and I immediately had a man leave to deliver this report to the nearest police station, which would have to come to make an inquiry about the cause of the accident.

"A brigadier arrived at 7 o'clock in the evening. He held an inquiry on the event in the same room as Mrs. B., where the doctor was, along with N., myself, the woman who had first discovered Mrs. B., and yet other inhabitants of the village.

"The policeman's inquiry continued until 7:30 o'clock, when Mrs. B. suddenly sat up in her bed, supporting herself on her elbows. She opened her eyes very wide, remained like this for a few moments, then fell back with her eyes still open. She was dead. The doctor closed her eyelids.

"Since nobody could give any indication at all on how Mrs. B. was wounded, the brigadier ended his inquiry and left. A magistrate arrived the following morning, on January 1st, to complete the customary reports with the doctor who had stayed overnight at our house, and in the evening Mrs. B. was buried in the nearest cemetery in the village.

"An inquiry, ordered solely for form and justice, reached no result and was abandoned after a few days. An accidental fall was concluded.

"I have nothing to add to the facts as stated, but I should mention a coincidence: and this is, that following the death of Mrs. B., all talk of seeing the *lantern* in P. and the neighboring areas ceased.

"Since that time, for the following seventeen years, I have had the opportunity to observe a great number of events with a supernatural aspect, or at least inexplicable by ordinary explanations. But I have never had an occasion to see any spontaneous phenomenon produced which is at all similar to the *lantern*. I have always found that the most miraculous phenomena have their basic origins in human powers (which is not to say that I would deny the existence of other kinds of powers out of hand) and I believe myself able to conclude:

"1st: That Mrs. B. had been a very powerful 'medium of physical effects', but one who could act consciously;

"2nd: That, consequently, Mrs. B. had been either well endowed with extraordinary abilities to send out her astral body, or that she had been initiated into certain practices to that end;

"3rd: That the nocturnal noise in my room had been produced by Mrs. B., that is, by her astral body, with the intention of scaring me in revenge for my having taught our dog to resist the occult power which she had exercised over him outside our house. This is why she had decided to imitate the noise that the dog had made at her own door when he had thrown himself at her;

"4th: That, by thrusting the saber against the door, or against the luminous shade, the steel had touched the astral body, and that a molecular severance of this body, due to the contact of the steel point crossing it with considerable force, had resulted in the wounding of Mrs. B.;

"5th: Finally, that the apparition of the *lantern* had only been an astral emanation of Mrs. B., who enjoyed affecting the local people and making them afraid.

"Regarding this last point, I was led to believe that if I had been able to fire my pistol at the phenomenon when the *lantern* has appeared, which had been my intention, I would probably have killed Mrs. B. on the spot."

"Gustave Bojanoo."

The wand and the sword are the two implements which are truly indispensable for the Magister to own. All the others, the lamp, the cup, etc., are luxury items which are only used in exceptional circumstances. In current practice, you can even combine the two implements into a single one, and this is how. You should obtain a sword-stick whose top ends with a ball of magnetic iron which has been strongly magnetized, and on which a magic sign and the required characters has been embossed in gold. The lower part of the cane should end in a lead tip encased in a sheath of silvered copper. A ring made from an alloy of tin and mercury should be added to the upper part of the cane which should form a reasonably large guard. The external part of the implement is now a magical wand which will go unnoticed by the profane.

The sword contained in the inside of this wand should also be as long as a regular small sword, triangular and covered with the necessary signs. Moreover, the guard of this sword is formed from a length of the cane long enough for the hand holding it only to be in contact with the varnished wood, and as a result completely isolated from the metallic blade. We own an implement of this kind which has served us very well in our practical studies; for you should always have it with you, and learn how to use it against all psychic manifestations.

Such are the precious assistants to gesture in magical Operations.

Talismans

We mentioned the theory of talismans earlier, in the context of precise figures of creative astral forms.

The knowledge and management of pantacles are, if we may be permitted this comparison, the proof of diplomas which the Operator can present to the astral powers. They are in a way the Baccalaureate of Magic. And the ignorant man who carries a talisman on him whose purpose and action he doesn't understand, whether it be a negro with his gris-gris or a Christian with the image of Our Lady of La Salette (a figure of Isis, between parentheses), is like the savage to whom one gives a copy of the works of Homer…in written format. Pantacles therefore have a value in Ceremonial Magic, like the Urim and Thummim of the Jews, and no less than the Christian host, all of which are talismans of a similar kind, since worship is most often but a magical ceremony, as misunderstood by the assistants as it is by the the Operator, or priest. The Grimoires and Clavicles contain a host of talismans. Without going into all these complications, we are going to going to look at one of the most esteemed figures, very instructive in its symbolic teachings, Agrippa's Great Talisman.

The talisman constitutes a second magical application of gesture. It remains to us to speak about the indispensable consecration in every Operation, however small it may be.

Reading the *Thousand And One Nights*, these Arabic stories so filled with magical rites (from which the French translator Galland has carefully excised the erotic details), we often come across stories of a Magician who, wishing to act on some being, soaks his fingers in a glass of water while pronouncing some mysterious words, then throws some drops of this water on the face of the person who is the object of this action, and the unfortunate being is suddenly changed into a beast, unless the opposite takes place.

"The Fairy ordered a gold chafing-dish to be set with a fire in it under the porch of her palace, with a box of the same metal, which was a present to her, out of which taking a perfume, and throwing it into the fire, there arose a thick cloud of smoke."

The Story of Prince Ahmed and the Fairy Paribanou

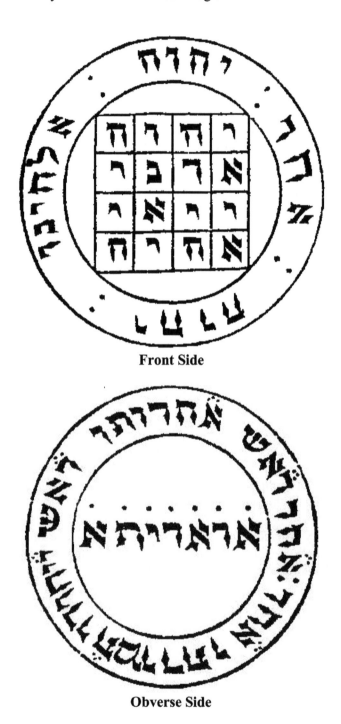

Front Side

Obverse Side

"Then this girl took a vase filled with water, and said words over it which I didn't understand, and then addressed the calf: 'O Calf, she said, if the Almighty and Sovereign Creator of the World made you like this, so that you appear at this moment living in this form, or if He is angry with you, don't change; but if you are man and were changed into a calf by enchantment, take back your natural form by permission of the Sovereign Creator.'

"After saying these words, *she threw water on him*, and immediately he took on his original form."

A Thousand & One Nights (5th Night)

"The Calif sent to fetch the two dogs from Zobeide, and when they had been brought a cup full of water was presented to the fairy, who had asked for it. She said works over it which nobody understood and threw it over Amine and the two dogs. They were changed into two ladies of surprising beauty and the scars disappeared from Amine."

(69th Night)

"The Magician took a cup of water and said words over it which made it boil as if it had been on the fire. Then she went to the room where the young Prince, her husband was, and threw this water over him, saying: 'If the Creator of All Things formed you as you presently are or if he is angry with you, don't change; but if you are only in this state by virtue of enchantment, return to your natural form, and become once more what you were before.'

"Hardly had she said these words when the Prince arose on his own."

(26th Night)

Now, this brings us to a magical reality: Consecration.

A Magister should never use an implement, burn incense, or use fire and water which hasn't been blessed.

Consecration is a kind of magnetization of objects through action combined with word and gesture. The use of an aspergillum in the Catholic religion is intimately linked to this part of Practical Magic, and recalls the use of water activated by sorcerers in *The Thousand & One Nights*. A very interesting experiment by Mr. de Rochas[89], one which we have personally verified often,

---

[89] Albert de Rochas (1837 – 1914) was a French parapsychologist, writer, translator, historian and military engineer. He is mainly known for his work in trying to find a scientific basis for paranormal events. His books covered parapsychology, hypnotism, telekinesis, reincarnation, spirit photography, etc.

shows us the theory behind this magical action (see the third part of this book, in the chapter on Spells).

From all which has preceded, we can see the considerable importance of gesture in the studies which concern us. And that is natural, for gesture which depends on the action of the thoracic members, the animal being's organs of expression, should comprise the coming together of dependent actions, both of the impulsive being and the man of will.

We could continue to talk about gesture in choreography or the symbolism of gesture in the theater; but these ideas take us completely out of the current scope of our work. Therefore, we will set these aside for now.

Movement

Sight, speech and gesture have just been examined. It remains for us to talk about movement, by means of which the human being transports the totality of his actions to different places.

The displacement of the physical body in the material plane is accompanied by the by the displacement of the fluidic shell in the astral plane. At each step man attracts or repels fluids which endlessly cross in the place of formation in Nature. The majority of men, true playthings of the fatal powers, have no anxiety or awareness of this action, and dark forebodings, mysterious voices from infinity, mostly only affect poets and women given over to the despotism of Eros. Now, he who, having learned to control his will, describes a specific work, and leaves a fluidic and dynamic trace of his passage on the path he follows. So, the Magister who draws a circle and who continues to affirm his will by returning twice along the same path, raises up a visible enclosure in the space contained by his walk to seers which is insurmountable to astral beings.

Remember the triple circuit executed by the witches around their cauldron in *Macbeth*, and you will see once again how these traditions were familiar to Shakespeare.

Before harvesting a plant, before arriving in a feared place where one intends to enclose the evil powers, the Magister will formulate his will by means of the triple fluidic enclosure containing the place of Operation.

Movement, therefore, including action on the astral, is the equivalent of gesture, following a material design or plan.

But the training recommended by Eliphas Lévi, and which is of considerable importance, consists of conquering tiredness resulting from a prolonged walk to use one's will upon some material object. Thus, if you come back home quite late in the evening after a tiring walk, and if your whole being is looking forward to a well-deserved rest, make an effort of will and go out again to a place half an hour from your home and pick up the first stone or some other object you find there, and then return home. This object, the symbol of the voluntary effort you have accomplished, is a personal talisman which is more effective than all the amulets and all the chaplets you could buy outside famous churches. The whole secret behind the psychic action of pilgrimages is in the practice of this training through walking.

A small stone which we found one night around two o'clock in the morning at the top of Butte-Montmartre, after we had returned, exhausted from a long walk, to our home, allowed us to perform magnetic activities of great interest.

THE COMPLETE TRAINING OF THE HUMAN BEING

Love and Chastity

In parallel to the study of stimulants on the various parts of man, we laid down procedures for training the various organs of expression. But we also discovered a stimulant for the whole being: *love*. This stimulant corresponds to a center of expression which is equally composite: *generation*.

Generation can be psychological, physiological or physical, and the union of two brains to a common end creates living ideas, just as the union of two hearts towards a common ideal creates emotions which survive physical death, and the physical union of two complementary beings creates children. The knowledge of the Magister consists of progressively replacing the pleasures which physical love procures with the more delicate pleasures of enduring emotions; and finally, with the still less deceptive enthusiasms of intellectual creations. And the discouragement and apathy which takes hold of an aging *bon viveur* for whom physical love had been everything, are unknown not only to the Mage but even to the Sage trained to some extent in works of the intellect.

But this training must be long and progressive, and it would take all the ignorance of the theologian or theosophist to impose, from one day to the next, complete chastity on young people who are, in practical terms, barely educated and ignorant of life. On the contrary, the greatest among the founders of Religious Orders were usually former military men or former *bon viveurs*, and it was only at an advanced age that a human being could truly make a serious determination in this regard.

It is clear that the being who aims for exceptional powers must be able to resist feminine suggestions: but the most rigorous rituals impose fifty days of abstinence prior to the Magical Operation, even to the most advanced practitioners.

A Magician is not forbidden to love, but he is absolutely forbidden to be ruled by love to such an extent that his will might be annihilated by desire for s female. The impulses of love must be treated like reflexes over which the man of will should maintain absolute control at every instant. Nevertheless, Fabre d'Olivet wonderfully elucidated the motives which make man and woman act. Man wants to enjoy himself before possessing. Woman wants to be sure she possesses the loved one completely before she feels satisfied. This results in the more or less silent battle in which Eve almost always engages in with Adam.

And woman never allows any sharing, and the love that the intellectual devotes to truth or to Magic will be like constant suffering for the lover, since she will sense a rival in this study which is far more dangerous than her charms, and which grows over time while feminine beauty fades like everything which is on the physical plane. Now, the untrained person will give in little by little to the desires of his beloved, and progressively lose the control he should have gained over the impulsive center.

The Magister's training should be concerned with the possibility of giving himself over to or resisting love when and how he wants. A man whose higher sphere is developed should be capable of being able to stop at an instant a love about to be born, for in that case he acts out of passion, that is, from the ability of the passive being to gain the ascendancy over the being who alone should be master. This is why the development of the intellectual ability requires more or less long periods of continence; but a physiologist should never lose sight of the very grave psychological issues resulting from a omplete sexual continence imposed on a large peasant dressed in a black robe, whose intellectual training consists of reading a book written in bad Latin and letting his larynx act under the reflex impulse of a series of incomprehensible words, called prayers. The person clothed in a sacerdotal function must be chaste and abstain from meat during the fifteen days which precede and the fifteen days which follow the accomplishment of his sacerdotal function, for this accomplishment is an act of High Magic. But to make a salaried career of worship instead of making it an occupation, to make priests functionaries vowed to abstinence instead of making initiates of free men, this merits death ten times over for a religion organized so pathetically.[90]

---

[90] While it is clear that Papus is not a fan of organized religion, and holds the Church (and Theosophy) in similar contempt for imposing what to him are unsupportable

And we can't repeat to the Magister enough that the illusions of physical generation are purely in the physical domain, yet he mustn't lose sight of the fact that in our earthly state we have a material body, which requires us to give account of the scorn we show towards it.

All the organizations which have made themselves more or less wealthy from selling the idea of "pure love" or "enforced continence" of human beings are the product of hypocrisy or ignorance. Let's leave the old ladies who are eager for sentimentality to assemble there; but let us have the good sense ever to remember that, if the intestines are not very poetic, at least we all have them, and that we aren't put on earth to have contempt for the body, which is the indispensable instrument for the evolution of purely spiritual principles.

To rule any suggestion of love with all the power of a strong and steely will, but never to ignore it; to learn to endure more or less long periods of complete abstinence, periods filled with study and work, and alternated with other periods filled with the regular occupations of daily life; these should be the two overriding rules in the Magister's conduct regarding the gracious representatives of universal life; or Eve to the profane.

Besides, the act of generation hides a very profound mystery, which we consider pointless to go into in such an elementary study.

Summary

The section of our elementary study concerning the main achievements of which the human being is capable is now completed.

We were able to see how *that which feels* in us was capable of being developed under the influence of foods, inspired air and sensations, helped by material stimulants, by perfumes and music.

We have also sensed how *feelings* in us are also capable of great development under the influence of meditation, and this despite the scorn which affects modern education, made to develop the memory in connection with the true superior abilities of man.

---

demands for continual celibacy, and the degredation of what should be a vocation into a career, the comment about abstaining from meat for 15 days prior and 15 days following the celebration of Mass may seem odd. Doinel's Gnostic Church instead saw the priesthood as being a collective of celebrants, each of whom might celebrate the Mass but once a year. In this manner a different priest would celebrate each month, or week, and this explains the rigorous period of following a Vegetarian diet for 15 days prior to celebrating Mass. Why this was extended for 15 days following this 'Magical Operation' is not so clear. He revisits this theme in detail in Chapter XIII.

Finally, we quickly embarked on the beginnings of educating *will*, speaking about sight, speaking, gesture, movement and generation, the result of the arcana of love.

Perhaps one finds these details too difficult or too diffuse; one may be tempted to reject Magic itself due to imperfections and errors which are solely due to our own fault. These details are necessary, in our opinion, to show those who believe that Magic is the art of seducing women quickly, or "posing" in front of one's comrades, is on the contrary about long and difficult study and, moreover, is very dangerous for the weak. They would be better off consulting somnambulists to find out the future, going to spiritualist circles to have emotions at a discounted rate, and to study so-called esoteric Buddhism to amuse social gatherings. All of this carries little danger, and will certainly be of more value to them than the practice of meditation and the development of the will.

But the training of the human being is not sufficient for Magical Operation; one must also take account of the potential education to be had from *Nature*, that precious auxiliary to man. It is that which will be the subject of the following study.

Bibliography

Works useful to consult for theoretical development:

A. – MODERN

PAPUS.................................*Methodical Treatise on Occult Science*
(3rd Part).
The Knowledge of the Mages (Ch. 1).
MARC HAVEN........................*A Plate by Khunrath* (Initiation,
December 1892).
U. N. BADAUD.......................*Magic in the XIXth Century,* in-8°,
Dentu.

B. – CLASSICAL

ELIPHAS LÉVI........................*Ritual of High Magic.*
FABRE D'OLIVET....................*Golden Verses of Pythagoras.*
LOUIS LUCAS........................*New Medicine.*
CHARDEL.............................*Physiological Psychology.*
AGRIPPA.............................*Occult Philosophy.*
AGRIPPA.............................*The Book of Love.*

C. – ADAPTORS

SHAKESPEARE.......................*Macbeth – Hamlet.*
GALLAND.............................*Translation of A Thousand And One
Nights.*
PLATO................................*The Banquet.*

For Philosophy:

AD. FRANCK.........................*Philosophical Dictionary* (article on
Love).

CHAPTER VIII – THE PRACTICE OF NATURE

Let's imagine that the human being is suitably developed and capable of great power of will whenever he wants. Is that enough?

We know that it isn't, for if Magic is the action of the dynamic human will to effect a rapid evolution of the forces of Nature, then we only possess the solution to the first part of the problem. It remains for us to study how active Nature functions.

Man endowed with sufficient initiative to act freely is surrounded by such a network of fatal forces that all his efforts will be in vain if he is ignorant of the most propitious moment to put his will into action. On the other hand, the least schooled village sorcerer always seems to act in the appropriate manner, thanks to a simple understanding of lunar movements, and will produce specific results without much expenditure of will.

We've already learned in the first part of this treatise about the forces acting in Nature and their origin: the stars and their positions. We won't repeat this topic, but will content ourselves here, in the following few pages, to lay out some elementary but practical principles about Astrology which are necessary for practicing Magic. For the technical part of Astrology, we will turn to the remarkable work of Mr. Selva, Director of such studies at the *Independent Group for Esoteric Studies*. We will then consider the intelligences acting in the sublunary world. Although this question is more in the realm of Psychurgy than Magic, we will look at this for a moment. Then the Magister will be in full possession of the *knowledge* necessary for all undertakings, and will be able to adapt the knowledgee which forms the subject of the third part of this book to his benefit.

ELEMENTS OF ASTRONOMICAL ASTROLOGY

The astral fluid which circulates in terrestrial beings and things passes through states of condensation or successive dilatation, and according to Esotericism, those states depend upon the position of the celestial bodies at that instant.

For better clarity, the path followed in appearance by each of the stars is divided into twelve sections or *Houses*, each one corresponding to one of the twelve Signs of the Zodiac.

Here we would recall our comparison with the dial of a watch, where each hour represents a Sign of the Zodiac. Just as, on a watch, the second, minute and hour hands go around the dial at differing speeds, so the stars make their tour around the heavens at greater or lesser speeds. In order to avoid the complicated calculations which are needed, we recommend the practitioner to purchase an annual *Astronomical Almanac*[91], in which all the necessary information can be found, as we will see later. To return to our example, remember that the moon, which represents in the heavens the minute hand on our dial, makes a complete tour of the Zodiac in a (lunar) month, whereas the sun, which represents the hour hand, only advances by a single division each month, just as the hour hand only advances one division each hour.[92]

An understanding of the Signs of the Zodiac and their action, and a knowledge of the planets and their properties and correspondences are indispensable to the Magister to avoid all his works grinding to a complete halt. Nevertheless, we have restricted the account of the principles needed to what is strictly required, and we have excluded all conventional teachings which don't correspond to natural reality.

We will now focus on the Signs of the Zodiac or the heavenly hours.

The Signs of the Zodiac

The Signs of the Zodiac are twelve in number. Their numeration begins with Aries, which corresponds to the month of March, and each of them occupies 30 degrees on the celestial sphere. Since one can find the position of the stars in the *Astronomical Almanac* indicated in *degrees*, it is very important to know the Signs of the Zodiac in connection with the celestial spheres. The positions are as follows:

Month	Sign	Degrees	Hieroglyph
March	Aries	0 to 30°	♈
April	Taurus	30° to 60°	♉
May	Gemini	60° to 90°	♊
June	Cancer	90° to 120°	♋
July	Leo	120° to 150°	♌

---

[91] This is the American and English source. Another term is *Ephemeris*.
[92] We feel we should remember that the 12 lunar months do not strictly correspond to the solar year. These are elementary principles of Astronomy, with negligible effects for now, but which all readers should certainly possess. [PAPUS]

August	Virgo	150° to 180°	♍
September	Libra	180° to 210°	♎
October	Scorpio	210° to 240°	♏
November	Sagittarius	240° to 270°	♐
December	Capricorn	270° to 300°	♑
January	Aquarius	300° to 330°	♒
February	Pisces	330° to 360°	♓

Take your watch and compare it with the following figure, remembering that each hour represents a month or 30 degrees.

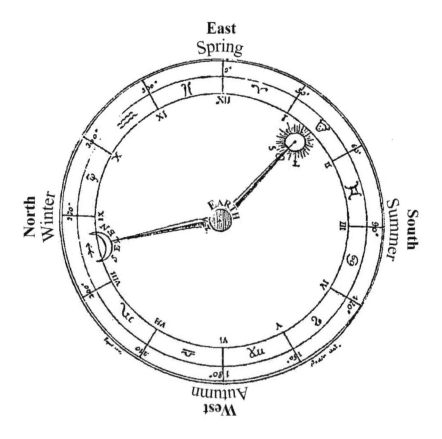

You have in front of you the field of activity in which the seven stars operate which Magic considers to be the only relevant ones, taking no account of the rest.

These stars are, in order:

Saturn	♄
Jupiter	♃
Mars	♂
The Sun	☉
Venus	♀
Mercury	☿
The Moon	☾

We know that this classification is based on their appearance, taking earth as the center. Astronomically, the order of the stars is, as our readers know, as follows: (Neptune – Uranus), Saturn – Jupiter – Mars – Earth & Moon – Venus – Mercury – Sun, taking as the starting point the true center of the System: the Sun.

The seven stars turning the heavens like the extremities of the hands of a watch turning around the dial. But the celestial watch, in the teachings of the Hermetists, has seven hands endowed with faster or slower movements.

As the stars are for the majority intelligent centers of emission of astral powers, it is very important to obtain as clear an idea as possible about them; and we should only move progressively towards more technical details to avoid as much as possible the obscurity hidden in these kinds of questions. So firstly, let us review each of the stars individually, without looking at their connections with one another or the Celestial Houses, beginning with our satellite.

THE MOON – The Moon especially rules what we call the physical world on Earth, which in Hermetic terms is called the 'sublunary' world. This satellite, which is only of a negligible size if one considers it in context of our solar system, nevertheless acquires an exceptional importance for the inhabitants of the Earth, an importance such that in Practical Magic the Moon always moves in lockstep with the Sun, and in a strict sense *one only needs to be guided by these two stars to almost certainly succeed in all Operations one undertakes.*

The Moon is the astral matrix of all terrestrial activities in which the Sun is the living father. We have already talked about the activity of the satellites viewed as the nervous ganglions of the planet to which they are attached. Everything which comes to the Earth, fluids and souls, passes by the Moon, and everything leaving the Earth passes by it, too.

In its phases, the Moon analogically reproduces the universal law of involution and evolution in four periods. During the first half of its course (New Moon to Full Moon) the Moon grows, in terms of its appearance. This is the *only* time the Magician should use for Operations of Light: it's also the time that the lunar influences are truly active.

On this matter, I will open a sidebar. A wealthy manufacturer who enjoys life and laughs at "prejudice" as he calls it, had previously owned a tree-felling company in the Jura. Seeing that his competitors were careful not to cut down trees during the period of the waning Moon (Full Moon to New Moon), he laughed heartily at their superstition, and profited from the cheapness of the labor during that time to exploit his property. Two years later our manufacturer had become more superstitious than the others; for it wasn't long before every tree cut down during that lunar period had become rotten... 'We don't know why this happened', he told us, because it was indeed him who told us this story. So, the growth phase of the Moon has a very great importance according to the teachings of Magic. We will soon return to this star in more detail when we consider the Lunar Houses.

The color corresponding to the Moon is white.

MERCURY – The fastest of the planets and closest to the sun, Mercury represents childhood with its outburst of vitality and movement. It completes its cycle in 88 days, which allows it to use its influence from a magical point of view at least four times a year. The color corresponding to Mercury is that of the prism in its totality, that is, the juxtaposition in its of different colors, which clearly indicates the inclination to change which affects everything which comes from Mercury. In the ancient Grimoires, the name of this planet was written in a different color for each letter composing its name.

VENUS, the Morning Star – Feminine youthfulness with all its flirtatiousness, seductions and dangers, the goddess of love in all her forms, who reigns over the lover just as the chaste Diana, the Moon, reigns over the mother. Venus' cycle is completed in 224 days and 16 hours, which makes Operations made under its influence very important, since a missed date means a wait of almost a year before the favorable moment returns.

Venus corresponds to the color green.

THE SUN, fiery Apollo – Youth in his generosity, noble ambitions and pride, and also his temerity and inexperience in practical matters; art with its divine intuition, its horror and its disdain for the vulgar.

The Sun is the father, the universal generator in our world; also, its influence in Magic is considerable.

This influence is calculated according to the position occupied by the star relative to the Zodiacal Signs.

The Christian festivals of Christmas, Easter, Saint John are solar festivals, as we shall see shortly.

The color corresponding to the Sun is golden yellow.

MARS – The nearest planet to the earth. Ruddy and violent, it is the image of the man of war. Mars possesses his courage, energy, anger and violence. The influences of Mars are used in Magic for action. But the cycle of this planet being 687 days, almost double that of earth's orbit, the direct influence of Mars isn't always used for the creation of pantacles. Either the days and hours dedicated to Mars, or the analogical connections of the Moon in its signs are used instead.

The red of fire corresponds as the color of Mars.

JUPITER – The man of reason and will in whom youth's violence and fits of passion have abated, and who is truly master of himself: such is the aspect under which Jupiter reveals itself to us. Calm and methodical, Jupiter is 12 times slower than the earth, taking exactly 11 years 10 months and 17 days to complete its cycle. It is true that the vivifying influence of the Sun disappears more quickly than on our planet, since its day lasts half the time it does on earth.

In Magic, the influence of Jupiter, which bestows honors and glory can only be used in exceptional cases. In 1893, Jupiter will leave Aries on February 10 and enter Taurus where it will remain until the end of the year.

The color of Jupiter is metallic blue.

SATURN, the Old Man, the Sad Man, but with great experience. Taking nearly 30 years (29 years and 187 days) to complete its cycle, it gives long but somber life to all those who unite beneath its influence. Saturn is the beloved star of Black Magicians, as is the waning Moon.

The color of Saturn is that of lead: metallic black.

Such is the first concept one can have of the living stars of our system. As we can see, Mercury, the Sun, Mars, Jupiter and Saturn represent different stages of human life from childhood to old age, and they also indicate the moral and intellectual character of each of these periods which traverse human life. It is the Saturnians who are already old at 16, and the Mercurians who still show gaiety and enthusiasm at 70 years old. The Moon and Venus correspond to the feminine in her two great modalities: maternity and love, and have the color of sea-green and the white of purity as their respective symbols.

Remember, too, that each day of the week corresponds to one of the seven planetary influences: Sunday to the Sun, Monday to the Moon, Tuesday to Mars, Wednesday to Mercury, Thursday to Jupiter, Friday to Venus, and Saturday to

Samedi[93], and you will add to the first ideas you should have concerning the stars from the magical point of view.

ALLIANCES AND HOSTILITIES

When you are received into a society you are not familiar with, one of the first elementary rules of politeness requires you to become acquainted with the alliances and hostilities of your hosts, to avoid committing a blunder.

Admitted to a knowledge of the superiors of our planetary world, take great care not to offend any of them when calling to them, when one of its enemies holds the keys to the heavens. This is why the table below will be of great use.[94]

In general, be wary of Saturn and Mars, the two most wicked planets in the system. On the other hand, make as much use as possible of Jupiter, the Sun and Venus.

PLANET	FRIEND OF	ENEMY OF
SATURN	MARS	All the others
JUPITER	All the others	MARS
MARS	VENUS	All the others
THE SUN	JUPITER & VENUS	SATURN, MARS
VENUS	SUN, MARS, MERCURY, MOON	SATURN
MERCURY	Good with the Good	Bad with the Bad
THE MOON	Neutral	Neutral

---

[93] Remember, the French days of the week correspond far more closely to the planetary names: Monday – *lundi* (Moon); Tuesday – *mardi* (Mars); Wednesday – *mercredi* (Mercury); Thursday – *jeudi* (Jupiter); Friday – *vendredi* (Venus); Saturday – *samedi* (Saturn); Sunday – *dimanche* (Sun).

[94] While the advice is sound, the actual Friends and Enemies listed bear little resemblance to modern lists. The reader wishing to make use of this aspect is strongly advised to consult more modern books in this particular instance.

RESPECTIVE POSITIONS OF THE PLANETS

Aspects

We now come to another important question, also within the domain of Astrology, but which seems to us to be useful to explain to our readers: that of the Oppositions and Conjunctions of the planets. Since these planets all pass along the same path with different speeds, and since this path is circular, so there will be times when they cross one another, and other times when, on the contrary, they become increasingly distant from one another.

To better understand these states called Aspects, and the names given to them once and for all, take your watch and imagine that the ends of each of the two hands (hours and minutes) represent different planets and the hour signs on the dial, the various points in the heavens.

Conjunction

At 3:15 or 4:20, the two hands on your watch are superposed upon one another in the same perpendicular plane, and the two stars have the same longitude in the heavens.

Quadrature

At 3:00 or at 9:00 exactly, the two hands form a right angle, as the two stars have longitudes which differ by 90°.

Opposition

At 6:00 exactly, the two hands form a straight line. These two stars show longitudes which differ by 180°.

Given the narrow compass of this treatise, we cannot go into all the considerations which follow from the various aspects between these stars. Let us simply remember that the Moon has her maximum influence when she is in conjunction with the Sun, and as this phenomenon takes place each month (as the hands of a watch superpose one another every hour), the Magister must be familiar with this fact, which will suffice for most of his Operations.

THE RELATIONS WHICH EXIST BETWEEN THE PLANETS
AND THE SIGNS OF THE ZODIAC

Planetary Houses

Now that we have seen the character of the planets in isolation and the influence of the planets on each other, let us consider the most useful influence of the planets' positions to the Magician for his Operations.

Firstly, one must know that each of the Signs of the Zodiac is considered in terms of its preferred abode, a planet's *House*. Then, we need to understand that a planet is happy to return to its House after its journey, and how the specific influences of this planet, good or bad, is then intensified.

These are the planets' Houses:

SATURN	– in Capricorn and Aquarius.
JUPITER	– in Sagittarius and Pisces.
MARS	– in Aries and Scorpio.
SUN	– in Leo.
VENUS	– in Taurus and Libra.
MERCURY	– in Gemini and Virgo.
MOON	– in Cancer.

Also look at the astronomical figures of the Tarot in my work on the Tarot[95], which points out all these connections. However, there are adjustments to make concerning the *diurnal or nocturnal* domiciles of the planets which are often the inverse of one another.

---

[95] Papus is referring to 'Tarot of the Bohemians', which was originally published in 1892, the year prior to this book. This book is widely available in English, the usual translation being that of A.P. Morton..

The Moon in the Twelve Signs

We now come to the study of the connections between the Moon and the Signs of the Zodiac. This study is extremely important for the Magister.

We know that each Sign contains 30 degrees. To describe it in summary form we have divided the some of the following Signs into three parts: head, middle and tail, for each 10°. We have drawn the following traditions from one of our manuscript "Clavicles."

ARIES (*Head*, 1° to 30°) – At this time, the Moon spreads a very positive influence for the prosperity of travelers and negotiations. Characters and talismans which are created under this influence protect against the dangers and perils of voyages and negotiations. (*Middle*, 10° to 20°) – The Moon influences wealth and the discovery of treasure. This time is favorable to make talismans and characters to be lucky in games of chance, principally if the Moon has a benign aspect with Jupiter (conjunction).

TAURUS (*Head*, 30° to 60°) – The influence of characters and talismans leads to the ruin of edifices, wells and fountains, to the rupture of friendships, marriages and other similar things. (*End*, 60°). Twenty-five minutes after departing from Taurus, the Moon influences a healthy happiness, a great disposition to learning the sciences and to procure the goodwill of people of distinction, and if, during this time, it is in conjunction with Venus, the talismans and other figures made under this constellation will be infallible for obtaining the love of the fair sex.

GEMINI (60° to 90°) – Good hunts, successful military campaigns. The influence of the Moon at this moment makes those who carry talismans, mysterious figures or characters formed under the auspices of this constellation insurmountable.

CANCER (90° to 120°) – Malign influences, success in acts of treason, conspiracies and other outrages. However, if the Moon is in a fortunate aspect with Jupiter, Venus and Mercury, the talismans will be favorable to love, games of chance and the discovery of treasure.

LEO (120° to 150°) – In aspect with Saturn influences all deadly enterprises from the beginning of its entry into the sign. But the moment it leaves this sign (the 10 last degrees), this constellation is liberal in all kinds of prosperity.

VIRGO (150° to 180°) – Good influence, at least in an aspect with Saturn. Talismans and characters constructed under this constellation are very advantageous to gamblers, travelers, as well as those who aspire to great honors.

LIBRA (180° to 210°) – Favors enterprises concerning treasures, the discovery of riches, mines of metal and fertile sources of fountains.

SCORPIO (210° to 240°) – Extremely harmful to travelers, to those who marry or who begin an association.

SAGITTARIUS (240° to 270°) – Good influence over honors and long life.

CAPRICORN (270° to 300°) – Favored by a benevolent connection with Venus or Jupiter, it influences health, also love of the fair sex, so that talismans and characters constructed under this constellation infallibly solves puzzles and prevent the evils which harm marriage, and supports friendship and good understanding between married couples.

AQUARIUS (300° to 330°) – Bad influence over health and travels.

PISCES (330° to 360°) – There is only one aspect of Saturn to fear for those who wish to construct talismans and characters under this constellation: for, so long as she has a friendly aspect with Jupiter, Mercury or Venus, she infallibly influences games of chance.

*

* *

We see from these brief notes how a knowledge of the Moon's influences can, in a strict sense, be enough for the current practice of Magic. Practitioners of folk magic have no other knowledge in any case.

Here is a composite summary of the lunar influence, which can be consulted quickly.

If it is not possible to observe the hours, one can at least take account of the Signs.

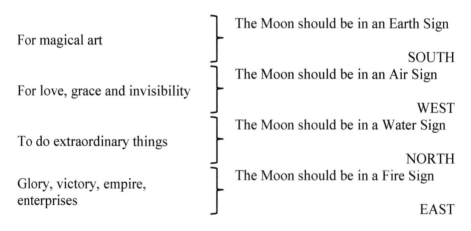

For magical art

    The Moon should be in an Earth Sign

        SOUTH

For love, grace and invisibility

    The Moon should be in an Air Sign

        WEST

To do extraordinary things

    The Moon should be in a Water Sign

        NORTH

Glory, victory, empire, enterprises

    The Moon should be in a Fire Sign

        EAST

Moon ascending = Good Operations
Moon descending = Evil Operations

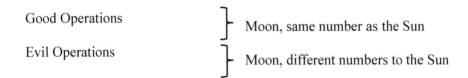

Good Operations — Moon, same number as the Sun

Evil Operations — Moon, different numbers to the Sun

These divisions, moreover, have been taken much further, and even elementary Astrology studies the influences of the Moon each day of its revolution, which in round figures gives 28 *Lunar Houses*, the true origin of the favorable and unfavorable days of the month. We cannot enter into all these details, and we will simply give the following table from memory (*see next page*):

Certain very interesting traditions exist on this subject. Here is a summary of how they are formulated:

1.   For the first child
The mother should refer to the position of the Moon at the time she will give birth (which can be done easily with an Almanac dated the year of this birth). If the Moon is new within the nine days following that date, the future child will be a girl. In the opposite case, if there is no New Moon within the nine days in question, it will be a boy.

2.   For the other children.
The birth date of the latest child born is noted. If the moon is new in the nine days following that birth, there is a change in the sex of the child which will be born. In the opposite case, there will be no change in the sex.

The Other Planets

We cannot go into the details concerning the other planets, details which are more properly associated with Astrology than Magic. However, we will look at the following dates connected with the Sun which are particularly favorable to the success of important Operations. The dates are fixed according to the type of influence.

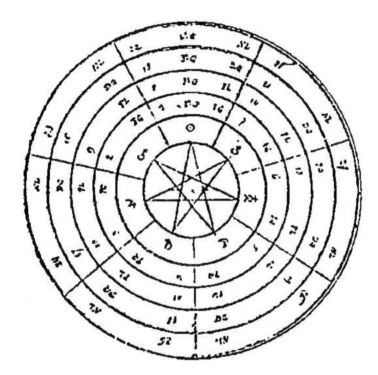

INFLUENCE OF THE MOON ON THE SEX OF INFANTS
(Unfortunately, the image is illegible in the original, possibly suggesting Papus took it from another book and reproduced it himself)

Sun: Magical Agenda

For the commencement of Operations, *March* and all passages of the Sun in Aries. It is at this moment that one should harvest verbena.

For love, *April*, particularly the 26th, as well as *May* 1st (in fact the Eve of Easter is the most favorable day of the year).

In *June* virgin parchment should be prepared. Talismans for journeys are also made in this month.

June 20th is a very propitious day for all Operations. On the Eve of St. John, the magic wand should be prepared. One should also harvest herbs during this period.

July – excellent influence for wealth and searching for treasure (above all, on Sunday). After July 24th, prepare the skin of a toad for the month of December (see that month).

This is when one should harvest magical herbs, and particularly heliotrope, the lily and the nettle.

August – good influence for evocations and the conscious appearance of spirits.

The 15th is a particularly favorable day for making talismans of love.

The 21st (and the Wednesday closest to this date) is good for making talismans for gaming.

September – the 12th should be used for making the following talisman of love:

For Love

Around September 12th, during the day, in the hour of Venus, you will create a medal of red copper on which you will engrave these characters on one side, and on the other side the words JEOVA DE NONA[96], and then hang it round your neck with a cord, along with a piece of woolen stocking from the person you desire, every morning before the sun rises. Throughout the month of October, you will go to the door and loudly say the following: Amapoylfac, repeating it twelve times; and the first day of the following month, that person cannot stop themselves from coming to you to ask you what you desire, and to do what you want.

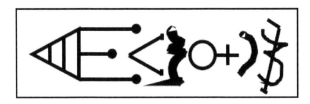

October – On a day and hour of Mars, make the talisman of war:

---

[96] An alternative given on some internet sites is "Jeora De Nona."

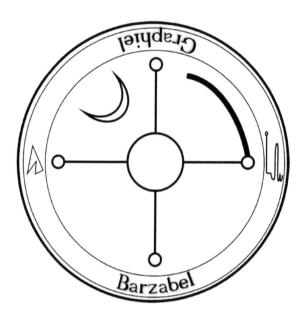

On October 22nd make the second of these talismans:

November – Favorable for evocations of spirits of Jupiter.

November 23rd is also very favorable for the evocation of bellicose spirits of Mars and Sagittarius:

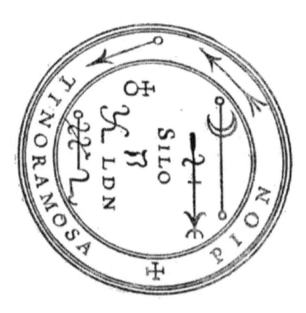

December – At the moment of the new Moon, on the day and hour of Saturn, in this month you can make a very interesting pantacle most favorable to the raising and purchase of animals. It is one of the great secrets of folk magic:

January – Very favorable for evocations of spirits of Saturn.

Here is another part of a very curious secret and which we don't hesitate to transcribe in detail. It is drawn from an exemplar in the *Clavicles* in the Bibliothèque Nationale:

To Make Yourself Invisible

Make a small image of yellow wax, in the form of a man, in the month of January and on the day and hour of Saturn, and at that time write with a needle above the crown of its head and upon its skull which you will have skillfully raised, the following character:

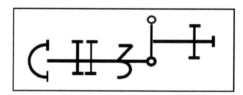

After which you will replace the skull in proper position. You will then write upon a small strip of the skin of a toad or frog which you had killed, with the blood from the same toad, the following words and characters: HELS, HEL, HELS, and

You will then go and suspend the said figure by one of your hairs from the vault of a cavern at the hour of midnight, and perfuming it with the proper incense you will say:

METATRON, MELEKH, BEROTH, NOTH, VENIBBETH, MACH, and *vos omnes, conjuro te figura cerea per Deum vivam, ut per vitutem horum caracterum et verborum me invisibilem reddas ubique te portavero mecum. Amen.* [97]

---

[97] "All ye, I conjure thee, O Figure of wax, by the Living God, that by the virtue of these Characters and words, thou render me invisible, wherever I may bear thee with me. Amen."

And after censing it again, you will bury it in the same place in a small deal box, and every time you want to pass or enter into any place without being seen, you will say these words, carrying the aforesaid figure in your left pocket:

Veni ad me et numquam, me derelinquas ubicumque ivere.[98]

Afterwards you will take it carefully back to the afore-mentioned place and cover it with earth until you have need of it again.

February – Good influences for the evocation of spirits of Jupiter. You can make the following talisman against apoplexy during this month. This talisman should be made of steel on the day and hour of Mars:

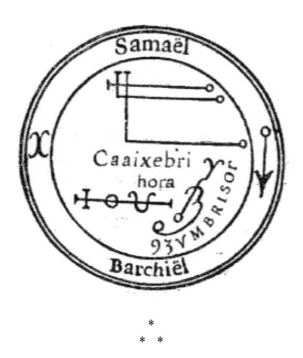

*
* *

For everything concerning the other planets, which is, in reality, beyond an elementary treatise, we would recommend technical astrological works, in particular the very scientific work of Mr. Selva.

---

[98] "Come to me and, never leave me wheresoever I may go."

The Hours Attributed to the Planets

The divisions we have studied up till now roughly correspond to natural phenomena, and are drawn from the effective position of stars in the heavens. Now, we think that we should, so far as possible, stick to these simple divisions.

Nevertheless, magical tradition attributes considerable influence to the theoretical connections established between the planets and the hours.

To obtain the exact magical hours we divide the time which separates sunrise from sunset by twelve and as a result one has 'hours' which, in winter, are much less, and in summer more than 60 minutes, as one can see. For the hours in the night, divide the time which separates sunset and sunrise by twelve.

We have created a *magical clock* which immediately provides the planet which rules any hour determined from one of the days of the week, as well as the name of the genius and several other complementary indications. Here is that clock[99]: (*see overleaf*)

To use this figure, detach the central section within the double line, and turn the name of the day on which one wishes to operate next to the 1st hour (Yayn). You then have the correspondences for all the hours of that day.

The hours of h, σ^{7}, φ and ☾ are excellent for performing Magical Operations and to speak with spirits. The 1st hour of the appearance of the sun on the days of these planets is the best.

The hours of ☉ and ♀ and their days are very good for love.

The hours of h and σ^{7} are excellent for actions of hostility.

The hours of ☿ are for the most interesting and difficult things.

Finally, the hours of ♃ and ♀ for love and extraordinary experiences.

---

[99] To use this magical clock, it should be copied onto a white sheet and then the central part (separate by a double line) should be detached from the rest. This central part is then fixed in its place by a nail or some kind of point so that it can rotate. When one wishes to know which influence corresponds to a particular hour of a day of the week, one takes the following actions: (1) Move the day of the week in question in front of the first hour by turning the central part. (2) then look for the selected hour and read the name of the planet found there. The Arab figures indicate the daytime hours and the Roman figures the nighttime hours.

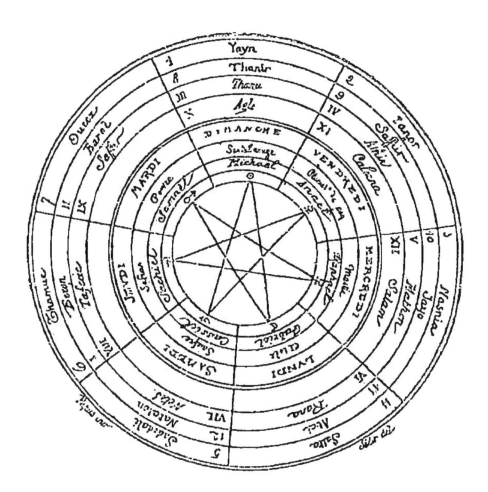

THE MAGICAL CLOCK

———

Bibliography

CAMILLE FLAMMARION............*The Heavens.*
RAGON..............................*Hermetic Initiation.*
OGER FÉRIER.....................*Astronomical Judgements – Keys of Solomon* (Ms in the Bibliothèque Nationale).

CHAPTER IX – PLANETARY INFLUENCES
IN THE THREE KINGDOMS OF SUBLUNARY NATURE

Natural Astrology

We have more or less completed our study of the action of the planets in the heavens; but this action isn't the only one which takes place, and for us, inhabitants of earth, the influence exercised by the astral fluid on the three Kingdoms of sublunary Nature takes on a particularly special importance.

Given the magical theory which accepts that every natural creation is produced by an action on the astral plane, we understand that every terrestrial being results from a predetermined astral influence. We say that this being is *signed* by the star which most rules him, and men are ruled like the rest of creation by signatures of the invisible world.

Our aim above all is to be as clear as possible in this study. Let us now leave behind all the details of those planetary correspondences with our world, to focus solely on those general things which are essential to know.

In all Operations, the Magister can group together in his circle all the influences of a planet in the three Kingdoms; and we will give such a list which is a simple as possible and reduced as often as we can to only one representative for each Kingdom. You will find more complete details in the little Dictionary of Practical Magic at the end of our treatise, under the name of each of the planets.

We warn our readers in advance that, since each planet rules over a large number of planets or precious stones, we will stick to the most practical classification. One can find further correspondences in the Grimoires and specialized books.

THE MINERAL KINGDOM

Various Metals

The Mineral Kingdom provides the Magister with metals and magical stones. Metals have a host of uses and are most used as conductors of astral fluid.

The seven metals corresponding to the planets are as follows:

Lead	corresponding to	Saturn.
Tin	corresponding to	Jupiter.
Iron	corresponding to	Mars.
Gold	corresponding to	The Sun.
Copper corresponding to	Venus.	
Quicksilver	corresponding to	Mercury.
Silver	corresponding to	The Moon.

Metals are used to make medals, pantacles, talismans, rings, implements, etc.

Stones

There are a large number of more or less precious stones which are used to decorate magical rings and spirits.[100] You can find a very odd treatise on stones, taken from a book on the numbers of *Evax and Aaron* (?) in the Grand Albert; but the materials contained in this treatise are not classified according to planetary correspondences and we have had to make a particularly careful study of this subject.

We eventually adopted the following correspondences after compiling the different tables available, including the "Clavicles", as well as the particular treatises of Agrippa and Kircher.

Stones Attributed to the Planets

SATURN..............................*lodestone, chalcedony*
JUPITER..............................*sapphire, beryl*
MARS..................................*amethyst, diamond, jasper*
THE SUN..............................*carbuncle, chrysolite, blood-stone*
VENUS................................*lapis lazuli*
MERCURY............................*emerald, agate*
THE MOON...........................*crystal, pearl, white coral*

---

[100] This is an odd phrase. In French "*qui servent à orner les anneaux et les esprits magiques.*" Yet saying that precious stones decorate magical rings and *spirits* is strange – yet there is no other possible translation. Either Papus is quoting a Grimoire, or he is referring to the genii which sometimes inhabit rings?

As far as possible we have eliminated from this list all generally fantastical stones found in birds' nests, animals' stomachs, or certain unknown trees, such as the famous stone from the hoopoe's[101] nest (read, as Lévi suggested, this as *trickery*[102]), which makes one invisible.

Nevertheless, we will outline, *for the sake of pure curiosity*, the marvelous properties attributed to stones corresponding with the seven planets according to the Grimoires, which comprise the catechism of our country sorcerers.

CURIOUS TRADITIONS CONCERNING THE VIRTUE OF CERTAIN STONES

Saturn

Lodestone – Very useful to the Magister, since it enters into the creation of the wand. This lodestone, which is a natural product, should not be

confused with magnetic iron obtained industrially.

If a man wants to know if his wife is chaste and wise, he should take the stone called *lode* and put it under his wife's head. If she is chaste and honest, she will embrace her husband, and if not, she will immediately jump out of bed.

Moreover, if one puts this stone after reducing it to powder, on burning charcoal in the four corners of the house, all those who are asleep there will run out and abandon everything, and then the robbers can do what they like without fear (sic) (*Grand Albert*).

---

[101] The hoopoe is indigenous to much of Europe, Asia and Africa. It is a colorful bird with a very distinctive crest. Perhaps its regular appearance in folk magic is due to three particular legends or old wives' tales, as well as the fact that it was sacred to the Egyptians, appearing in many temple frescoes; and named the King of the Birds in Aristophanes' comedy *The Birds*. Firstly, hoopoes were associated with thieves, like the magpie, and this would explain the reference here. Secondly, it was associated with death, and some rituals required the death of a hoopoe to summon evil forces. We will see this toward the end of the book where a hoopoe features in summoning the devil. Finally, and most importantly for us, in the Koran (and similarly known in the West), there was a legend that the hoopoe brought messages from the Queen of Sheba to King Solomon (as in verbally spoke them, as opposed to carrying a message tied to its leg), and given Solomon's prominence in magical Grimoires, this connection with the hoopoe bird is quite appropriate.

[102] Eliphas Lévi was famous for his hostility towards the unscrupulous.

Chalcedony – To get rid of illusions and all kinds of vain imaginings, take the stone *chalcedony*, which is pale and dark. If you pierce it in the middle and hang it around your neck with another stone called *serenibus* (?), you will no longer have to fear fantastic illusions. By means of its virtue you can prevail against all your enemies, and it keeps the body in strength and vigor.

Jupiter

Sapphire – To bring peace to someone take a *sapphire* stone, the yellow one which isn't so bright is best. This stone, carried on you, brings peace and concord, makes you devout and pious, inspires good, and tempers inner fire and passion.

Beryl – He who wishes to mock his enemies and end his lawsuits and quarrels should take a *beryl* which has a pale and transparent color like water. If you carry it on yourself, you will not fear your enemies; and you will win lawsuits, if there are any. It also has an admirable virtue for children, for it makes them able to advance in education.

Mars

Amethyst – To have a good spirit and to never get drunk one should take a piece of *amethyst* colored purple; the best is found in the Indies. It is marvelous for drunks and makes the mind ready for knowledge.

Diamond – Those who wish to overcome their enemies will take the stone called *diamond*, which has a brilliant color and so hard that it cannot be broken except with the blood of a *he-goat*. If you place it on the left side it is wonderful against enemies, preserves judgement, puts wild and venomous beasts to flight, and confounds the evil plans of those who wish to assassinate you or do something similar, and ends differences and legal suits. Moreover, the diamond is strong against poisons and wanton spirits.

Sun

Carbuncle (we haven't been able to find anything about this stone in any tradition except its ability to shine in the dark).

Chrysolite – If you wish to become wise and never be mad, you have only to take a stone called *chrysolite*, which has a color which is green and brilliant. It should be set in gold and carried on yourself. It chases away phantoms and delivers you from madness and is admirable for fear.

Blood-stone – To make the sun appear to be the color of blood, take the stone called *heliotrope*, which is green and resembles the emerald, and is varied in color with what look like drops of blood. All Necromancers commonly call it the precious stone of Babylon; and if you rub this stone with the juice of the herb of the same name, it makes you see the sun red like blood, as during an eclipse.

It is this stone, as I've learned, that was formerly used by the temple priests to divine and interpret oracles and the responses of idols.

This stone comes from Ethiopia, Cyprus and the Indies.

Venus

Lapis Lazuli – If you wish to heal someone of melancholy and malaria, you should obtain the stone *lapis lazuli*, which is the color of the sky, with little golden flecks within. This aid is infallible and recently proven. Carry this stone on yourself for the ills listed above.

Mercury

Emerald – He who wishes to become wise, amass riches and know the future, will take the stone which we normally call *emerald*, which is strong, clear and brilliant. Yellow is the best type.

If a man carries it on him, it gives him a clear mind and memory, helps him to amass riches, and if he puts if under his tongue, it communicates the gift of prophecy.

Agate – If someone wishes to avoid all kinds of dangers and never fear anything in the world, or wishes to be generous, he will carry an *agate* which is black with white veins. The agate is very good against adversity.

Moon

Crystal (quartz) – To light a fire, take a crystal, expose it to the sun, and put something which is easy to burn opposite it. As soon as the sun shines, the fire will take. If it is drunk with honey, it will give milk to wet nurses.

Coral – If you wish to calm tempests and storms and pass over rivers, carry coral. There are red and white forms. It is tried and tested to staunch blood immediately; and he who carries it on him will always be right and prudent. Many prominent people and worthy of trust have proved this recently. Coral is admirable against tempests and the perils one can face when on water.

MAGICAL HERBS
(THE VEGETABLE KINGDOM)

The knowledge, search for and preparation of "simples" hold a very important place in Practical Magic, and in the following pages we have devoted a particularly close study of plants corresponding to the planets.

For other so-called magical herbs, the reader is referred to the word *herb* in the Magical Dictionary at the end of this book, and from there to each of the herbs listed in that entry. In the third part of this treatise we will revisit them and the manner of harvesting the plants.

Firstly, here are the usual planetary correspondences with the different parts of a plant.

Vegetable Correspondences

FRUIT	♃	Jupiter
FLOWERS	♀	Venus
SEEDS AND BARK	☿	Mercury
ROOT	♄	Saturn
WOOD	♂	Mars
LEAVES	☾	The Moon

Saturn

The herbs of Saturn are classed under this influence according to the connections they have with the planet:

1. Firstly, poisons which numb and make dizzy like most of the Nightshades;
2. Plants which don't seem to produce fruits;
3. Those which produce black roots, leaves or branches, and fruits (black fig, pine, cypress trees).
4. Those who have a bitter taste, with a strong odor, a black umbra or which are deadly, like wild celery dedicated to Pluto (*Apium graveolens*, umbelliferous).

The following are herbs characteristic of Saturn:

HELLEBORE (*Helleborus Niger*), family of ranunculus, grown in gardens under the name *Christmas Rose*. *Helleborus fetidus* or Griffin's Foot can replace the former if required.

The first belongs to Saturn and is called Offodilus[103]. Its sap is good for alleviating and curing pains in the kidneys and soreness of the legs. It is also given to those who have problems with the bladder. If one lightly boils the root, those who are possessed or suffer from melancholy who carry it on them in a piece of white linen will be set free. Finally, this same root makes evil spirits flee from homes.

Jupiter

Jupiter's herbs are characterized by their pleasant and aromatic odor, and their fruits (almost always oil-producing) by their pleasant taste (walnuts, almonds, hazelnuts, etc.). The trees are those which are particularly majestic, such as the oak, or considered to be fortunate, for example: hazel, popular and white fig, and especially the olive tree.

For characteristic herbs of Jupiter, we would particularly include, as well as mint, bugloss (*Anchusa officinalis*, boraginaceae) which one should always use in preference in magic.

HENBANE (*Hyosciamus niger*, solanaceous), whose action is characterized by the Grand Albert thus:

The sixth is of Jupiter and commonly named *Octharan*, and by some *Henbane*. Its root being taken for ulcers, removed them and prevents any inflammation from coming to those places where the ulcers were. If one carries it on oneself prior to getting an ulcer or boil, it will prevent them forming. Its root is extremely good for gout if, after crushing it, one places it in the place one feels pain, especially at the time of the astral signs which rule the feet. When its sap is drunk with honey, it is marvelous for problems with the liver, since *Jupiter* rules over it. It contributes much to love and is used for coition. Those who want to obtain the love of women only have to carry this herb on themselves, since those who carry it are very joyous and pleasant.

---

[103] The list of plants and descriptions have been taken directly from Book Two of the *Grand Albert Grimoire*, although Papus appears to have introduced some spelling errors at least from the version consulted here. It was not possible to find English transcriptions of all the plants in either French of Latin dictionaries, so it is possible the others are fictitious plants. The order of planets is also taken from the *Grand Albert*, but again is given no explanation for this unusual order: 1. Saturn, 2. Sun, 3. Moon, 4. Mars, 5. Mercury, 6. Jupiter, 7. Venus.

Mars

The herbs of Mars are classed according to the following properties:

1. Those which are venomous due to an excess of heat (e.g. euphorbius, garlic);
2. Those which have spines or which prick and who cause itching or inflame the skin through touch (e.g. nettles);
3. Those which cause crying when peeling and particularly when eating (e.g. onions, shallots, mustard, etc.).

We give the following examples of herbs characteristic of Mars:

EUPHORBIA (wart-weed, umbellifer, snake milk, tithymaloides, little cypress, poor man's rhubarb), of which there exist around 700 species.

Under the name of ARNOGLOSE (language of the birds), the Grand Albert describes a herb whose virtues seem connected to those of Euphorbia.

The fourth is of Mars, and called *Arnoglose*; its root is good for headaches, for it is generally believed that it is Aries which rules the head of all men, which is the reason for *Mars*[104]. It is used for ailments of the testicles and for rotting ulcers, when *Mars* is in *Scorpio*, which is a sign which retains semen. Its sap is admirable for dysentery and hemorrhoids, and for the stomach when imbibed.

Sun

The herbs of the Sun are generally aromatic.

These herbs are also classed according to their movements towards the sun such as the sunflower (Helianthus[105]) or those which reverse or close their leaves when the sun is distanced or setting and which open them little by little and extends them when the sun rises, like the laurel, peony, celandine, etc.

We give the following examples of herbs characteristic of the Sun:

1. HELIANTHUS (sunflower, wart grass, flower of Saint-Fiacre), from the borage family, to which the Grand Albert attributes the following magnificent properties:

---

[104] This is probably a play on the fact that 'Aries' sounds the same as 'Ares', the Greek God called Mars in Latin.

[105] Interestingly, Papus writes 'Heliotrope' here, yet that is a completely different plant. The Latin for Sunflower is *Helianthus*.

It possesses an admirable property if one cooks it in the month of August, when the Sun is in the Sign of Leo. For if, being wrapped in a laurel leaf, with a wolf's tooth, and carries upon oneself, none will be able to say anything bad about or harm with lies he who carries it. Moreover, he who places it under his head during the night will see and know those who could come to burgle him. Also, if one places this herb in a church where there are women, those who have violated the fidelity they have promised to their husbands will be unable to leave, if the herb is not removed from the church. This secret is assured, for it has often been tried out.

2.   POLYGONUM (knot-grass, pig grass) (*Polygonum aviculare*), of which the Grand Albert also gives the following description:

The second is the Sun and is called Poligoine, Corrigiale or Rensuée. It draws its name from the Sun because it is powerfully fertile; some have also called it the House of the Sun. This herb heals ailments of the heart and the stomach. He who touches this herb receives a virtue which comes to him from the influences of the planet which ruled over his birth.

If one drinks it, it will strongly incite love, and give him the powers for coition; and also, if one carries it in root form, it will heal ills of the eyes. It calms frenzied people who place it on their stomach. It is good for consumptives and gives them good breath and free respiration. It also works on the flux of blood in melancholia.

Venus

Venus' herbs are remarkable for their perfume, their aroma, like verbena, valerian, Venus hair (*Capillus Veneris*), and the fruits dedicated to this planet are very sweet, like pears, figs, oranges. Roses are also particularly devoted to Venus, above all in Operations performed in the morning.

We will list characteristic herbs such as:

VERBENA (the Sacred Herb). One of the most powerful and mysterious magical plants that exists. You will find some details on this subject in our magical dictionary. This is what the Grand Albert says:

The seventh is *Venus*, and is called *Pisterion*, some call it *Colombaria* or *Vervaine*. Its root placed under the neck heals scrofula, mumps, ulcers, and the loss of urine if one makes an ointment of it and applies it to the place which is bad. It is sovereign for deep grazes and hemorrhoids.

If its sap is drunk with honey in warm water, it gives one good breath and free respiration.

It makes one amorous because its sap creates a lot of sperm. Moreover, if someone carries it on oneself, he will be strong and vigorous in coition, seeing that it's the best herb for this.

If it's put in a house, in the earth or a vineyard, a great income will be made.

Also, its root is good for those who wish to plant vines and trees; and children who carry it will be well-raised and will love knowledge; they will be intelligent and of good humor. It is also useful for purges, and chases away evil spirits and demons.

Mercury

Mercury's herbs are comprised of several natures and different colors.

As well as hazel, coltsfoot, annual mercury (*Mercurialis annua*, euphorbiaceae) called dead nettle, these can be considered as characteristic:

CINQUEFOIL (*Potentilla reptans*), from the family of Rosaceae and whose properties are described by the Grand Albert thus:

The fifth is of *Mercury* and is called *Pedactilius* or *Pentafilon*, in French *Quintefeuille*. The root of this herb cures sores and scurfy if it is made into an ointment, and it quickly relieves scrofula if its sap is drunk in water. Its sap also cures aches of the stomach and chest. Put in the mouth, it relieves toothache and any other oral problems one may have. If it is carried, it will be of great assistance. Moreover, if one wants to ask something of a king or a prince, one has only to carry it on oneself, and then it makes one wise and able to obtain what one wants.

Moon

To the Moon are dedicated water plants or those which are particularly subject to the influence of the lunar phases, such as the palm which, it is said, grows a branch each hour of the Moon; the herb *Chinostares* which grows and wanes like the Moon both in substance and the number of leaves.

This herb, called such by Agrippa, called on the contrary *Chrynostates* by the Grand Albert, is very difficult to determine and seems to be particularly connected to the *White Lily* (το κρινου) as much by its name as by its medical properties, principally with regard to the eyes. Among lunar herbs we include the following:

1. NENUPHAR (*Nymphea alba*, the white nenuphar, water lily, etc.);
2. WHITE LILY (*Lilium candidum*) whose description from the Grand Albert we gave.

The third is of the *Moon* and it called *Chrynostates*. Its sap purges acidity from the stomach. The flower of this herb flushes the kidneys or heals them; it grows and diminishes like the Moon. It is very good for problems with the eyes, and makes the sight good. If its crushed root is put in the eye, it is marvelous for increasing and clarifying the sight, since the eyes have a close correspondence with the Moon and strongly depends on its influence. It helps those who drink it in the digestion of meats in the stomach, or those who have scrofula.

THE ANIMAL KINGDOM

Animals are used in Magic for releasing the astral fluid necessary for certain Operations. All of witchcraft is based on the principle of animating consecrated objects, animation obtained through the astral body of a toad which is fixed in the objects in question (the toad is Saturnian). In case of necessity, one of the Disciples in the invocation can be replaced by a dog whose magnetic *aura* is sufficiently powerful. Feathers from birds connected with the planets are used as a sprinkler for water activated by the magnetic influx. We will now list three correspondences for each planet: a bird, a quadruped (except for some) and a fish. As with the previous correspondences we will follow this list of "secrets" attributed to them with folk magic for some of these animals.[106]

Saturn	Lapwing	Mole (Toad)	Cuttlefish
Jupiter	Eagle	Deer	Dolphin
Mars	Vulture	Wolf	Pike
The Sun	Swan	Lion	Thimallus
Venus	Dove	Goat	Seacalf
Mercury	Stork	Monkey	Trout
The Moon	Owl	Cat (Frog)	Seal

---

[106] The list of birds, animals and fish appears to vary depending on the translation. However, since it is unlikely anyone determined to sacrifice one of these poor creatures in the interest of Magic would be using this book, but would rather be referring to the original Grimoires, this list is the best available. No accurate translation for 'Thimallus' was found.

TRADITIONS OF FOLK MAGIC
ON THE SUBJECT OF PLANETARY ANIMALS

Saturn

HOOPOE – He who carries its eyes will become large, and if they are carried in front of the stomach, he will be reconciled with all his enemies, and to avoid the fear of being duped by a tradesman its head should be carried in a purse.

MOLE – It has admirable properties and virtues. If one of its feet is wrapped in a laurel leaf, and placed in the mouth of a horse, it will immediately flee and be afraid; or if one puts it in a bird's nest, the eggs will become useless and will not develop. If one wants to chase moles away from a place, one needs to take one and put in in this spot with natural sulfur which is then burned: very soon all the other moles will no longer assemble there. If one rubs a black horse with water in which one has boiled a mole, it will become white.

A mole enclosed in a earthenware pot with lit sulfur powder will call others to help it with a piteous voice and cry.

If one wants to catch a mole, one must put a leek or an onion in front of its hole: for they will come out immediately, as if giddy.

Jupiter

EAGLE – If one reduces its brain to a powder and then mixes this with the sap of hemlock, those who eat it will tear out their hair and won't stop until they have removed all of it. The reason is because its brain is so hot and passionate, it creates fantastic illusions.

Mars

WOLF – If one buries a wolf's tail in a village, it will prevent other wolves from entering.

If one puts a wolf's tail in the manger of cows or small cattle, no wolf will come near until it is removed.

Sun

LION – If one makes a belt out of its skin, he who wears it will never fear his enemies.

If someone has a fever and eats its meat, or drinks its urine for three days, he will be cured.

If he carries this animal's eyes in his armpit, all animals will flee before him who has them, with their heads lowered.

Venus

TURTLE-DOVE – If one carries the heart of this bird in a wolf skin, he will extinguish all the fires of concupiscence and amorous desire. If this heart is burned and then put on the eggs of some other bird, which then tries to incubate them, they will produce nothing. If one places its feet under a tree, it won't bear any fruit. If one rubs its blood, mixed with water in which one has boiled a mole, somewhere with fur, or even a horse, any black hair will fall out.

HE-GOAT – If one puts its blood and boiled vinegar in a glass, the glass will become soft like paste and won't break when thrown against a wall.

If this composition is put in a vase and then rubs one's face with it, one will see horrible and terrifying things. Or if one throws it in a fire, and if there is someone present who is in decrepit old age, by giving him a *magnetized* stone he will fall to the ground as if dead; but if he is made to drink water and the blood of an eel, he will immediately be cured.

SEAL – If one takes its blood with a little of its heart and puts it in water, it is a sure thing that all the fish around will assemble there. And if one carries it under one's armpit one will surpass everyone in judgement and in spirit, and the criminal who has surrendered will be judged gently and favorably.

Moon

The frog and the owl make man talkative and principally frees the tongue and the heart. In this manner, a frog's tongue put under the head will make a man speak while asleep, and an owl's heart put upon a woman's left breast who is asleep in this condition will be caused to tell him all her secrets.

(Agrippa)

ACTION OF THE PLANETS ON MAN

The ancients observed and determined the different stages crossed by the universal power by its action on matter. They noticed that every generation passes through identical phases in every plane of Nature, and to engrave these teachings in the spirit of its Disciples, they gave these phases the name of 7 planets, not because these 7 stars individually have a natural influence in this action, but because these stars are themselves the expression to a great extent of this universal law of creation constituting a kind of common measurement applicable to all of Nature. Such is the key of these planetary applications which seem bizarre or absurd to those who haven't understood the true teachings of esotericism on this subject.

This is why the study of the embryology of how a bird or a rabbit develops serves as a model to understand the development of the human fetus, but without there being any possible confusion between the two planes of generation.

The Hindus, with their seven universal principles, are simply expressing the same ideas a lot less clearly. But we prefer to read *jiva, linga sharira, manas*[107], etc., etc., rather than the *Moon, Mars, Jupiter*, since Sanskrit terms aren't used to have many different meanings.

We are convinced that the serious student who truly wishes to pursue this question in the manner we have suggested will draw very important conclusions by doing so. That said, we are going to expose all the stages of the universal power applied to man, stages given the generic names of the planets which serve as a basis for all septenary[108] correspondences.

To avoid any confusion, we will firstly provide a table of the planetary influences over the organs and functions of man; then, we will follow this table with an explaination why these correspondences have been established, an explanation very well laid out by the Albert the Great in one of the rare works genuinely published in the Grimoires which bear his name.

We will end this explanation with a general table laying out the traditional Hermetic correspondences as they were known in the 16th Century. In this table, everything which is connected to the "astral signatures" is contained.

---

[107] That is, universal life, the astral body, and the astral soul, as described by Mme. Blavatsky. It is interesting to note that Papus, while not being a fan of Eastern theosophy, at least recognizes the fact that Sanskrit terms tend to have only one meaning, whereas many Western terms, in this case planetary names, can have multiple interpretations.

[108] It is interesting to see that Papus uses a word which doesn't exist in normal French. This word *septenaire* comes from the writings of Martines de Pasqually and Louis-Claude de Saint-Martin.

THE INFLUENCE OF THE PLANETS ON THE MICROCOSM

A. The Intellect

The *primum mobile* which, in its daily rotation contains all the lesser spheres, communicates the virtues of existence and movement by means of its influence over matter. This globe of fixed stars not only gives the fetus the power to distinguish itself through its different features and accidents, but also communicates to it the power to differentiate itself in accordance with the various influences of this globe. The sphere of *Saturn* is immediately after the firmament, and the soul receives discernment and reason from this planet. Then *Jupiter* gives it generosity and many other passions. *Mars* communicates hate, anger and many similar traits. The *Sun* gives it an influx of knowledge and memory. *Venus* provides the stirrings of sexual desire, *Mercury* of joy and pleasure. Finally, the *Moon*, which is the source of all the natural virtues, strengthens it. Although all things come from the soul, and although it received them from various parts of the celestial bodies, one still attributes them to the character and to the whole body, since a simple accident of fate isn't enough to explain everything.

*

* *

B. The Physical Body

Now, regarding the body which is created and formed from the *embryo* through the efforts and operations of the stars which are called planets, we should note in the first place that the matter from which man is generated, being taken and held by the coldness and dryness of *Saturn*, receives from this planet a strengthening and vegetative virtue, with a natural movement, since there are two powers in Saturn: one to prepare matter in general, and the other to give it a certain specific form.

During the first month *Saturn* rules over the conception of the embryo. *Jupiter* takes its place in the second month, and by virtue of a special favor and a singular virtue it disposes the matter to take and to receive the members it needs to have. Moreover, by means of a marvelous warmth it strengthens the fetal matter, and moistens all the parts which had been dried by Saturn during the first month.

PLANET	INTELLECTUAL INFLUENCE	CORRESPONDING ORGAN	PHYSIOLOGICAL INFLUENCE	SOCIAL INFLUENCE
SATURN	Meditative Spirit	Spleen	Has power over melancholy and parties which give rise to this humor.	Allocates treasures and reveals secrets.
JUPITER	Dominating Spirit	Liver	Controls the mass of blood and the vessels which enclose it both perfecting the elements and converting them into blood.	Allocates dignities, honors, respect and delectation.
MARS	Strong Spirit	Stomach	Controls the bile.	Give victory.
SOL	Spirit of Purity	Heart	Presides over vital warmth and over the heart which is the principle of life and the animal's movement.	Gives the friendship of Kings, Princes and the Great.
VENUS	Susceptible Spirit	Kidneys	Prepares the seed and exercises its power over the vessels necessary to generation.	Gives the love of women, peace and harmony.
MERCURY	Turbulent Spirit	Lungs	Work of the animal spirits. As its mission is to constantly circulate the sun, it vivifies the brain by stimulating its functions.	Give knowledge, commercial success and success in gaming.
MOON	Spirit of Light	Brain	Governs the natural powers and all the parts which depend on this ability.	Facilitates voyages and turns away misfortune.

During the third month, *Mars* with its heat creates the head, then distinguishes all the members from each other. For example, it separates the neck from the arms, the arms from the ribs, and so forth.

The *Sun*, ruling the fourth month, imprints the different forms of the fetus, creates the heart and gives movement to the sensitive character, if we believe the doctors and certain Astronomers; but Aristotle has another idea and says that the heart is created before all the other parts, and that it is from the heart that they are all derived. Others, wanting to go higher, say that it's the Sun which is the source and origin of life.

In the fifth month *Venus*, by means of its influence, completes the exterior members and forms others, such as the ears, the nose, the bones, the shaft and prepuce in males and the vulva in females. It also separates and distinguishes the hands, feet and digits.

During the sixth month, under the rulership and influence of *Mercury*, the organs of the voice are formed, as well as the eyelids and eyes; and under the same planet the hair grows, as do the nails of the fetus.

In the seventh month, the *Moon* completes what was begun by the other planets, since it fills all the gaps found in the flesh through its moistness. *Venus* and *Mercury* moisten the whole body, giving it the nourishment it needs.

The eighth month is attributed to *Saturn*, who through its influence greatly cools and dries the fetus once again, and thereby tightens it up. But *Jupiter*, who reigns over the ninth month, delights the fetus with its warmth and its humidity.

It is appropriate now to consider the influence of the planets which the ancients called the Gods of Nature, which rules over man's body as well as his character.

Saturn, which is higher, darker, heavier and slower than all the other planets, gives the man born under its influence a body which is dark in color, with black, greasy hair, a large and bearded head, and a small stomach, and he also has clefts in his heels. Regarding the older person, he is bad, perfidious, traitorous, angry, melancholic and leads a bad life. He loves filth and delights in having bad habits. He is not a slave to luxury or bawdiness; on the contrary, he hates them. In sum, one might say, using the words of my Master who is experienced in these matters, that all men who come into the world under the planet of *Saturn* possess all the evil qualities of body and soul.

Jupiter, which is a gentle, brilliant, temperate and happy planet, gives the man born under its influence a handsome face, clear eyes and a round beard, and moreover the upper two front teeth of this man are large and equally long. He also has a complexion which is white mixed with red, and long hair. Anyone who looks at his character, sees that he is good, honest and modest; and will have a long life. He loves honor, nice clothes and trimmings, and enjoys pleasant tastes and scents. He is merciful, beneficent, agreeable, virtuous and sincere in word and sober in deed, often casting his eyes downwards.

The man born under the planet *Mars* is immoderate in his hotheadedness and abruptness, and his complexion is ruddy, like someone who is sunburned. He has short hair, small eyes, and a rounded and gross body. He is inconstant, deceitful, dishonest, subject to anger, a traitor, haughty, capable of sowing discord and dispute.

The *Sun*, which is ordinarily called the eye of light of the world, gives to him who comes into the world under the influence of this planet a fleshy body, a pleasant face, large eyes, a fulsome beard with long hair. Some write that the man ruled by the Sun is a hypocrite and only appears to be nice; while others say that he loves knowledge and becomes very wise. Some believe that he is normal, pious, devoted, wise, wealthy, loves good and avoids and hates evil people.

He who is born under *Venus*, which is a beneficent planet, is handsome, and has fleshy, elevated eyes and eyelids, and is of a medium height. With regard to his character, he is frank, pleasant, knowledgeable, and loves music, pleasure, diversions and dancing. He likes to cultivate good habits and his gait is pleasant.

Mercury, which the Astronomers say is always close to the sun, from which it draws its light, sees that the man born under its rulership has a well-proportioned body, a height which is neither too tall nor too short, and a nice beard. Regarding his character, he is wise, subtle, loves philosophy and study, speaks truly, makes friends, and never has a lot of money; yet however he gives good counsel, is sincere, keeps his word, is incapable of infidelity or treason, and never asks anyone to do something wrong, and never finds himself in bad and evil company.

The *Moon*, which is far more troubled than the other planets, makes men who wander and are fickle, indecisive in speech and good-for-nothing, agreeable and of mediocre height. He has unequal eyes, and one is always bigger than the other.

One should know that all the planets and the other parts of the celestial sphere influence and communicated through divine virtue and must always necessarily act. Therefore, we can confirm, without fear of being wrong, and as a result of all which has gone before, that all terrestrial things are governed by superior, celestial ones, and that the sacrifices and holocausts offered in the world are useless and cannot prevent the influences of the celestial bodies which give life or death.

The Influence of the Signs of the Zodiac and Their Connections

But it must also be noted that all the parts of the body are dependent upon the 12 Signs of the Zodiac. *Aries* is the first of all the celestial Signs which, when it contains the Sun with moderation, communicates warmth and humidity and stimulates generation. It is for this reason that the movement of the Sun in Aries is called the source and principle of life. Thus, it's attributed to the head of man with all its parts, for just as the head is the most noble part of the body, Aries in the heavens is the most noble of all the Signs, and with good reason, since joined with the Sun it moves and excites the warmth and humidity of Nature, in the same way that man's head is the principle of the vital spirits.

Taurus rules the neck; *Gemini* the shoulders; *Cancer* the hands and arms; *Leo* the chest, heart and diaphragm; *Virgo* the stomach, intestines, ribs and muscles. All these Signs which divide up the heavens only rule over and govern half the body. *Libra* in the second half watches over the waist and is the origin and principle of the other members; *Scorpio* rules the parts proper to reproduction, both for men and women; *Sagittarius* the thighs; *Capricorn* the knees and what is beneath; *Aquarius* the legs; and *Pisces*, which is last of all, sheds its influence on the feet.

Here in a few words are the twelve Signs of the Zodiac with regard to the different parts of the body. However, one should not imagine that these things are simply sham and imaginary, since we have been able to confirm this through experiments in several places.

Therefore, know that it is dangerous to offend any member when the *Moon* is in the Sign which rules it.

———————

SIGN	ORGANS & ACTS	HERBS	TREES	ANIMALS	BIRDS	STONES
ARIES	Head, sight and blindness.	Sage	Olive	She-goat	Owl	Sardonyx
TAURUS	Neck, hearing and deafness.	Male Verbena	Myrtle	He-goat	Dove	Carnelian
GEMINI	Shoulders, smell and its absence.	Female Verbena	Baytree (*Laurier*)	Bull	Cockerel	Topaz
CANCER	Hands and arms; speech and mutism.	Primula	Common Laurel? (*Lorille*)	Dog	Black Stork	Chalcedony
LEO	Chest, heart, swallowing and hunger.	Cyclamen	Oak	Stag	Eagle	Jasper
VIRGO	Stomach, intestines and castration.	Calamint	Appletree	Sow	Sparrow	Emerald
LIBRA	Kidneys, activity and impotence.	Sunflower	Box	Ass	Goose	Beryl
SCORPIO	Genitals, gait and limping.	Wormwood	Service-tree	Wolf	Green Woodpecker	Amethyst
SAGITTARIUS	Thighs, anger and removal of liver.	Mace	Palm	Hind	Crow	Hyacinth
CAPRICORN	Knees, laughter and removal of spleen.	Yellow dock	Pine	Lion	Heron	Chrysoprase
AQUARIUS	Legs, thought and removal of heart.	Snakeroot	Buckthorn? (*Raminus* – assumed to be 'Rhamnus')	Ewe	Peacock	Crystal
PISCES	Feet, sleep and languor.	Buckwheat	Elm? (*Ulme*)	Horse	Swan	Sapphire

Bibliography

STANLISLAS DE GUAITA.................*The Witches' Arsenal* (in the Serpent
of Genesis).

P. SÉDIR...................................*Urim and Thummim.* Study on the hieratic
gemstones of the High Priests
(Initiation, Feb. 1893).

PAPUS.............................*Methodological Treatise on Occult
Knowledge* (Nature) - *The Tarot of the
Bohemians* (Astronomical Tarot).

Ancient authors:

GRAND & LITTLE ALBERT – AGRIPPA – KIRCHER, ŒDIPUS EGYPTICUS – PIERRE
D'ABAN – KEYS OF SOLOMON

*(The following two pages contain the 'General Table of
Planetary Correspondences drawn from the Works of
Ogen Férier, giving the tradition of the 16th Century.)*

PLANET	CARD. PT.	ELEMENT	TEMPERAMENT	ORGANS	SIGNATURES (MEN)	TRADES	AILMENTS
SATURN (♄)	North East	Earth & Water	Melancholy, and sometimes gross phlegm.	Ears, spleen, vessels, stomach, nerves and bone.	Pale or black people, thin, thoughtful, fearful, serious, contemplative.	Laborers, masons, buyers, usurers, messengers, fishermen, sellers of oil, tiles, stones, alum, etc.	Difficulty in breathing, leprosy, chancers, eruptions,
JUPITER (♃)	West	Air	Blood and vital spirits.	Lungs, sides, liver and arteries.	People of good stature, full-faced, white with a pleasant redness mixed in, quite large eyes, quite short nostrils, main teeth also large.	Honest men, gracious, benign, monks, abbots, bishops, prelates, officers, pages.	Gallstones, pleurisy, convulsions, apoplexy, phlegm, other blood ailments.
MARS (♂)	South	Fire	Choleric humors.	Kidneys, liver, nostrils, gall, genitals.	People red from employment, red hair, round face, yellow eyes, horrible stare, furious, cruel, hazardous and seditious people.	Mercenaries, captains, forgers, bakers, alchemists, armorers, butchers, surgeons, barbers.	Lasting fevers, plagues, migraines, boils, pustules, jaundice.
SUN (☉)	East & South	Fire	Pure blood and vital spirits.	Eyes, brain, heart.	Wise people, prudent, discrete, hungry for glory and honors, mediocre and small stature, brown color, large beard, yellow eyes, marked face, loud voice and quite unpleasant.	Honorable men, officers, magistrates, lords, princes and kings, governors, big game hunters.	Colds, cardiac problems, palpitations, headaches, high blood pressure.
VENUS (♀)	Far East	Air & Water	Phlegm, blood, spirit and generating seed.	Kidneys, abdomen, liver, back and parts serving generation.	White and brown people with redness mixed in, attractive face, pleasant look, aquiline nose, full hair, joyful, laughing, liberal.	Dancers, keepers of women, actors, perfumers, musicians, messengers of love.	Fistulas imbecility, stomach issues, kidney issues, syphilis.
MERCURY (☿)	North	Water & Earth	Animal spirits and confusions in the humors.	Hands, feet, arms, nerves, tongue, mouth, teeth.	People neither white nor black, thin and small stature, long-fingered, tall forehead, small hateful eyes, ingenious, inconstant.	Poets, rhymers, attorneys, orators, philosophers, diviners, sellers, mathematicians.	Vertigo, mad fancies, paralysis of the tongue, leg and foot ulcers.
MOON (☾)	West (right part)	Water	Phlegm, sweat, menstruation.	Stomach, abdomen, brain, lungs, breasts, eyes.	People of good stature, white, round spotty face, eyes a little black and eminent, long beard, eyebrows joined, friendly, pacific, modest people.	Travelers, huntsmen, ambassadors, assessors, town governors (police).	Gout, sciatica, hydrops, apoplexy, paralysis.

PLANET	AGE	SEASON	COLOR	TASTE	DAY	REGIONS	PLACES
SATURN (♄)	Old age	Autumn	Black, livid, lead, tawny tones.	Sour and astringent, sharp with austerity.	Saturday	Bavaria, Saxony, French Switzerland, Constance 1st Region.	Caverns, lakes, ponds, cesspools, ruins, cemeteries, places which are sad, hidden, deserted and stinking.
JUPITER (♃)	Mature age	Spring	Clear like satin, verdant citron drawing a little on red.	Soft and pleasant.	Thursday	Babylon, Persia, Hungary, Spain 2nd Region.	Churches, palaces, privileged places, honest and religious places.
MARS (♂)	Flower of youth	Summer	Bright red, bloody and drawing on iron.	Bitter and pungent.	Tuesday	Sarmatia, Gitulia (?), Lombardy, 3rd Region.	Blacksmith's homes, butcher's, furnaces, all places connected to iron, fire or blood.
SUN (☉)	Youth	Beginning of Summer	Yellow, clear red, color of gold.	Sharp with an agreeable sweetness intermingled.	Sunday	Italy, Sicily, Bohemia, 4th Region.	Princes' houses, great palaces, theaters, other ample, magnificent and light places.
VENUS (♀)	Adolescence	Beginning of Spring	White, green, red and a little yellow.	Soft, delectable, delicious.	Friday	Arabia, Austria, Switzerland, 5th Region.	Places, gardens, fountains, rooms, beds and places dedicated to luxury.
MERCURY (☿)	Childhood 7 to 14	Autumn	Strange, diverse, mixed.	Strange, and with a bad taste.	Wednesday	Egypt, Greece, England, Flanders, Paris, 6th Region.	Shops, fairs, markets, schools, law courts.
MOON (☾)	Young Childhood	Winter	White, blond, yellow, verdant.	Salted, insipid or unpleasant.	Monday	Flanders, Africa, 7th Region.	Foundations (springs), fields, mountains, rivers, beaches, woods, roads, deserted places.

CHAPTER X – SUMMARY OF KABBALISTIC ASTROLOGY

Up till now we have only studied the planets from the Astronomical point of view. These elements are not sufficient for the Magician.

These should be supplemented with the manufacturing or study of talismans, as well as divinatory applications, using the Kabbalistic part of Astrology.

The Kabbalah attributes specific characteristics or *signatures*, numbers, talismans, angels and daimons, etc., etc. to each planet. All the details can be found in the Grimoires and "Keys", as well as in the works of Agrippa, Pierre d'Aban, Kircher and Eliphas Lévi. We are going to give our readers a summary which is succinct and clear as possible concerning all those things, referring them to our work on the *Kabbalah* for the theoretical part.

Firstly, we will establish the Kabbalistic correspondences between the seven planets, considered both in totality, and in isolation, focusing on the talismans of each of these planets.

We will then consider the Kabbalistic connections between the Signs of the Zodiac, and end this short summary by speaking about the elements.

Despite the brevity of this volume, it is one of the most useful and complete published up till now, which moreover our readers can judge for themselves.[109]

---

[109] That said, it is sufficiently inaccurate to carry a warning that the reader is strongly encouraged to refer to more modern sources if intending to make use of anything in this section. In particular, the Seals appear to diverge from those listed in Agrippa's books, and it is unclear which book Papus was clearly copying and pasting from (manually in those days). Therefore, the Seals sections have simply been taken directly from Papus' book. Note that *Sceaux* = Seals; *Caractères* = Characters; and *Lettres* = Letters. That said, this book is an impressive framework for Solomonic Magic which has not, to the translator's knowledge, been equalled.

Saturn

1. MAGIC SQUARE

Table of Saturn in numbers   **in Hebrew characters**

4	9	2
3	5	7
8	1	6

ד	ט	ב
ג	ה	ז
ח	א	ו

Signs or Characters of Saturn

Seal or Character
of Saturn

Sigil of the Intelligence
of Saturn

Sigil of the Spirit
of Saturn

"It is said that this Table engraved upon a lead plate representing lucky Saturn helps childbirth, makes a man sure and powerful, and brings success to his requests in the courts of princes and powerful men; but if this table is dedicated to unlucky Saturn, it works against buildings, plantations and such things; it sees men stripped of their honors and dignities, brings about quarrels and discord, and disperses armies."

2. REVERSE OF TALISMAN

PLANETS	HIGHEST PLANETARY ANGELS	PLANETARY SPIRITS[110]	LOWEST PLANETARY ANGELS
SATURN	TZAPHKIEL	ARATRON	CASSIEL
JUPITER	TZADKIEL	BETHOR	SACHIEL
MARS	SAMAËL	PHALEG	SAMAËL
THE SUN	MICHAËL	OCH	MICHAËL
VENUS	HANIEL	HAGITH	HANAËL
MERCURY	RAPHAËL	OPHIEL	RAPHAËL
THE MOON	GABRIEL	PHUL	GABRIEL

---

[110] Taken from the Grimoire known as the *Arbatel*, and lists the Olympian spirits associated with the planets.

Mystical names connected to the numbers of Saturn:

3 – AB
9 – HOD
15 – YAH
45 – AGIEL
45 – ZAZEL

3. LETTERS & SEALS

Sceaux de Saturne.

Caractères de Saturne.

Lettre de Saturne.

4. SYNTHETIC FIGURE

SATURDAY

Angel: CASSIEL

Seal:

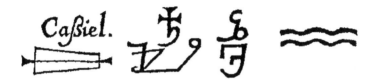

Angels of Saturday:	CASSIEL – MACHATAN – URIEL.
Angel of the Air:	MAYMON, KING.
His Ministers:	ABUMALITH – ASSEIBI – BALIDET.
Wind:	South-West (African wind).
Perfume:	Sulfur.

Jupiter

1. MAGIC SQUARE

Table of Jupiter in numbers

4	14	15	1
9	7	6	12
5	11	10	8
16	2	3	13

in Hebrew characters

ד	יד	יט	א
ט	ז	ו	יב
ה	יא	י	ח
יו	ב	ג	יג

Signs or Characters of Jupiter

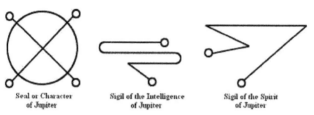

Seal or Character of Jupiter   Sigil of the Intelligence of Jupiter   Sigil of the Spirit of Jupiter

"If this table is engraved on a silver plate representing powerful and dominant Jupiter, it gives riches, favor, love, peace and concord with men, reconciled enemies, assures honors, dignities and counsels; if it is engraved on coral, it prevents misfortune."

2. REVERSE OF TALISMAN

Mystical names connected to the numbers of Jupiter:

4 – ABBA	16 – TAIE
16 – EHIE	34 – ELAB
136 – IOHPHIEL	136 - HISMAEL

3. LETTERS & SEAL[111]

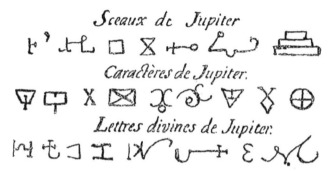

4. SYNTHETIC FIGURE

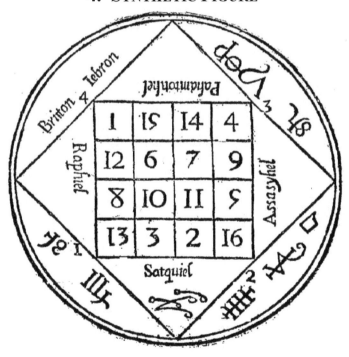

---

[111] As a general comment, there are a number of apparent typographical errors in this chapter. Also, it is very apparent that Papus has literally taken a pair of scissors to other books and pasted them into the original manuscript, since there are several page numbers (from an unknown book or books) next to many of the images.

THURSDAY

Angel: SACHIEL

Seal:

Angels of Thursday:	SACHIEL – CASTIEL – ASACHIEL.
Angel of the Air:	GUTH, KING.
His Ministers:	MAGUTH – GUTRIZ.
Wind:	South.
Perfume:	Saffron.

Mars

1. MAGIC SQUARE

Table of Mars in numbers

11	24	7	20	3
4	12	25	8	16
17	5	13	21	9
10	18	1	14	22
23	6	19	2	15

in Hebrew characters

יא	כד	ז	כ	ג
ד	יב	כה	ח	יו
יז	ה	יג	כא	ט
י	יח	א	יד	כב
כג	ו	יט	ב	יה

Signs or Characters of Mars

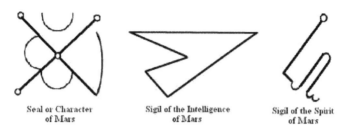

Seal or Character of Mars — Sigil of the Intelligence of Mars — Sigil of the Spirit of Mars

"This table, engraved on an iron plate or on a sword representing favorable Mars, makes man powerful in war, wise in judgements, happy in his requests, terrible to his adversaries, and gives victory against his enemies; engraved on a coral stone, it staunches blood and the monthly course of women."

2. REVERSE OF TALISMAN

Mystical names connected to the numbers of Mars:

5 – HEH (letter of the Holy Name)
25 – ZEI
65 – ADONAÏ
325 – GRAPHIEL
325 - BARTZABEL

3. LETTERS & SEAL

Sceaux de Mars.

Caractères de Mars.

Lettres divines de Mars.

4. SYNTHETIC FIGURE

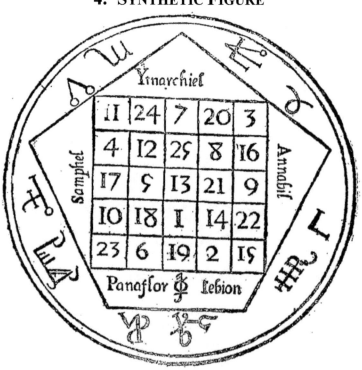

TUESDAY

Angel: SAMAEL

Seal:

Angels of Tuesday:	SAMAEL – SATAEL – AMABIEL.
Angel of the Air:	SAMAX, KING.
His Ministers:	CARMAX – ISMOLI – PAFFRAN.
Wind:	South-East.
Angels of the 5th Heaven,	*East:* FRIAGNE – GUAEL – DAMAEL – CALZAR – ARAGON.
for whom it is necessary to	*West:* LAMA – ASTAGNA – LOBQUIN – SONCAS – JAXEL – ISAEL – IREL.
call the 4 parts of the world:	*North:* RAHUMEL – HYNIEL – RAYEL – SERAPHIEL – MATHIEL – FRALIEL.
	South : SACRIEL – JANIEL – GALDEL – OSAEL – VIANUEL – ZALIEL.
Perfume:	Pepper.

Sun

1. MAGIC SQUARE

Table of the Sun in numbers

6	32	3	34	35	1
7	11	27	28	8	30
19	14	16	15	23	24
18	20	22	21	17	13
25	29	10	9	26	12
36	5	33	4	2	31

in Hebrew characters

ו	לב	ג	לד	לה	א
ז	יא	כז	כח	ח	ל
יט	יד	יו	יה	כג	כד
יח	כ	כב	כא	יז	יג
כה	כט	י	ט	כו	יב
לו	ה	לג	ד	ב	לא

Signs or Characters of the Sun

 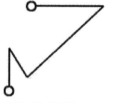 

Seal or Character of the Sun   Sigil of the Intelligence of the Sun   Sigil of the Spirit of the Sun

"This table engraved upon a gold plate representing the fortunate Sun, makes him who carries it on himself glorious, pleasant, gracious, powerful in all his works, and makes him like kings and princes by raising him up to the height of his fortune, and allowing him to obtain all that he wishes."

2. REVERSE OF TALISMAN

Mystical names connected to the numbers of the Sun:

6 – VAV (Letter of the Holy Name)
6 – HEH (Final) (ditto)
6 – ELOAH
212 – NAKHIEL
666 - SORATH

3. LETTERS & SEAL

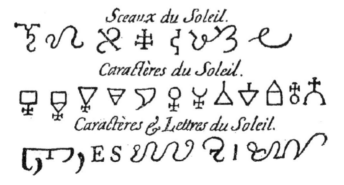

4. SYNTHETIC FIGURE

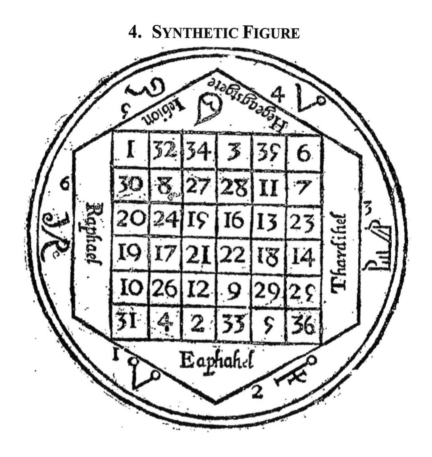

SUNDAY

Angel: MICHAEL

Seal:

Angels of Sunday:	MICHAEL – DARDIEL - HURATAPEL.
Angel of the Air:	VARCAN, KING.
His Ministers:	THUS – ANDAS – CYNABAL.
Wind:	North (Boreas).
Angels of the 4th Heaven,	*East:* SAMAEL – BACHIEL – ATEL – GABRIEL – VIONATRABA.
for whom it is necessary to	*West:* ANAEL – PABEL – USTAEL – BURCHAT – SUCCRATOS – CAPABILI.
call the 4 parts of the world:	*North:* AIEL – ANIEL – VEL – AQUIEL – MAGABRIEL – SAPIEL - MATUYEL.
	South : HAPUDIEL – MASCASIEL – CHARFIEL – URIEL – NATOMIEL.
Perfume:	Red Sandalwood.

Venus

1. MAGIC SQUARE

Table of Venus in numbers

22	47	16	41	10	35	4
5	23	48	17	42	11	29
30	6	24	49	18	36	12
13	31	7	25	43	19	37
38	14	32	1	26	44	20
21	39	8	33	2	27	45
46	15	40	9	34	3	28

in Hebrew characters

כב	מז	יו	מא	י	לה	ד
ה	כג	מח	יז	מב	יא	כט
ל	ו	כד	מט	יח	לו	יב
יג	לא	ז	כה	מג	יט	לז
לח	יד	לב	א	כו	מד	כ
כא	לט	ח	לג	ב	כז	מה
מו	יה	מ	ט	לד	ג	כח

Signs or Characters of Venus

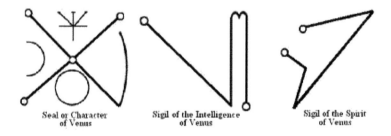

Seal or Character of Venus   Sigil of the Intelligence of Venus   Sigil of the Spirit of Venus

"This table engraved on a silver plate representing fortunate Venus procures concord, destroys dissent, and gives one the benevolence of women. It contributes to conception, prevents sterility and makes one powerful in copulation. It delivers from misfortune, brings peace between men and women, and produces an abundance of all sorts of animals. Placed in a columbarium it multiplies pigeons. It is good against melancholic illnesses and gives strength. Carried on one's person, it makes travelers happy."

2. REVERSE OF TALISMAN

Mystical names connected to the numbers of Venus:

7 – EHEIEH
49 – HAGIEL
157 – KEDEMEL
1252 – BENI SERAPHIM

3. LETTERS & SEAL

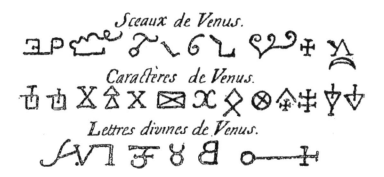

4.   SYNTHETIC FIGURE

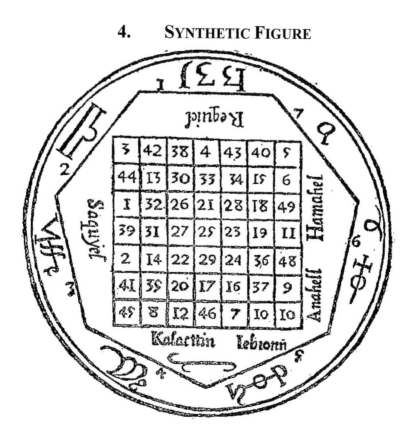

FRIDAY

Angel: ANAEL

Seal:

Angels of Friday:	ANAEL – RACHIEL – SACHIEL.
Angel of the Air:	SARABOTES, KING.
His Ministers:	AMABIEL – ABA – BABALIDOT - FLAFF.
Wind:	*The Zephyr.*
Angels of the 3^{rdh} Heaven:	*East:* SERCHIEL – CHEDUSITANIEL – CORAT – TAMAEL – TENACIEL.
	West: TURIEL – CONIEL – BABIEL – KADIEL – MALTIEL – HUSATIEL.
	North: PENIEL – PENAEL – PENAT – RAPHAEL – RANIEL – DORMIEL.
	South : PORNA – SACHIEL – CHERMIEL – SAMAEL – FAMIEL.
Perfume:	Coq (?)

Mercury

1. MAGIC SQUARE

Table of Mercury in numbers

8	58	59	5	4	62	63	1
49	15	14	52	53	11	10	56
41	23	22	44	45	19	18	48
32	34	35	29	28	38	39	25
40	26	27	37	36	30	31	33
17	47	46	20	21	43	42	24
9	55	54	12	13	51	50	16
64	2	3	61	60	6	7	57

in Hebrew characters

ח	נח	נט	ה	ד	סב	סג	א
מט	יה	יד	נב	נג	יא	י	נו
מא	כג	כב	מד	מה	ימ	יח	מח
לב	לד	לה	כט	כח	לח	לט	כה
מ	כו	כז	לז	לו	ל	לא	לג
יז	מז	מו	כ	כא	מג	מב	כד
ט	נה	נד	יב	יג	נא	נ	יו
סד	ב	ג	סא	ס	ו	ז	נז

Signs or Characters of Mercury

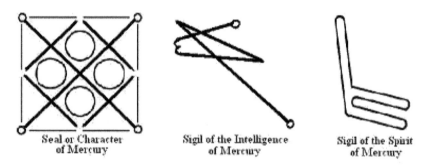

Seal or Character of Mercury

Sigil of the Intelligence of Mercury

Sigil of the Spirit of Mercury

"Engraved on a silver, tin or yellow copper, or if it is written on virgin parchment with Mercury fortunate, this table makes him who carries it gracious and happy in obtaining what he desires. It makes one win and prevents poverty; and it gives a good memory, an understanding of the gift of divination and makes hidden things known in dreams."

2. REVERSE OF TALISMAN

Mystical names connected to the numbers of Saturn:

8 – ASBOGA
64 – DIN
64 – DONI
260 – TIRIEL
280 - TAPHTHARTHARATH

3.   LETTERS & SEAL

4.   SYNTHETIC FIGURE

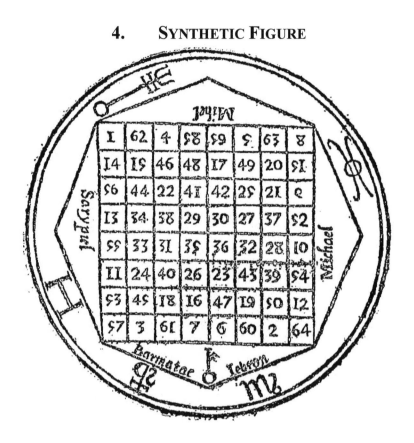

WEDNESDAY

Angel: RAPHAEL

Seal:

Angels of Wednesday: RAPHAEL – MIEL – SERAPHIEL.
Angel of the Air: MADIAT *VEL* MODIAT, KING.
His Ministers: SUQUINOS – SALLALES.
Wind: West.
Angels of the 2ⁿᵈHeaven, *East:* MATHLAI – TARMIEL – BARABORAT

for whom it is necessary to *West:* IERESCUE – MITATRON.
call the 4 parts of the world: *North:* THIEL – RAEL – IARAHEL – VENAHEL – VELEL – ABUIORI – UCIRNUEL.
South: MILLIEL – NELAPA – BABEL – CALUEL – VEL – LAQUEL.
Perfume: Mastic.

Moon

1. MAGIC SQUARE

Table of the Moon in numbers

37	78	29	70	21	62	13	54	5
6	38	79	30	71	22	63	14	46
47	7	39	80	31	72	23	55	15
16	48	8	40	81	32	64	24	56
57	17	49	9	41	73	33	65	25
26	58	18	50	1	42	74	34	66
67	27	59	10	51	2	43	75	35
36	68	19	60	11	52	3	44	76
77	28	69	20	61	12	53	4	45

in Hebrew characters

לז	עח	כט	ע	כא	סב	יג	נד	ה
ו	לח	עט	ל	עא	כב	סג	יד	טו
טז	ז	לט	פ	לא	עב	כג	נה	יה
יו	טח	ח	מ	פא	לב	סד	כד	נו
נז	יז	טט	ט	מא	עג	לג	סה	כה
כו	נח	יח	ג	א	מב	עד	לד	סו
סז	כז	נמ	י	נא	ב	מג	עה	לה
לו	סח	יט	ס	יא	נב	ג	מד	עו
עז	כח	סט	כ	סא	יב	נג	ד	מה

Signs or Characters of the Moon

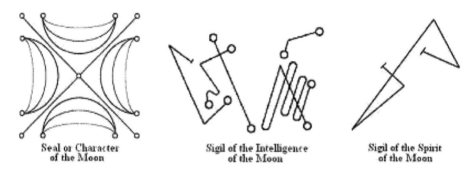

Seal or Character
of the Moon

Sigil of the Intelligence
of the Moon

Sigil of the Spirit
of the Moon

"This table engraved on silver with a fortunate Moon makes him who carries it gracious, amiable, gentle, gay, honored and prevents all malice and ill will. It gives certainty in travel, advancement in wealth and bodily health; it chases away enemies and all other harmful things from any place you desire."

2. REVERSE OF TALISMAN

Mystical names connected to the numbers of Saturn:

9 – HOD
81 – ELIM
369 – CHASMODAI
3321 – SCHAD BARSCHEMOTH HA-SCHARTATHAM
2321 – MALKAH BE TARSHISIM VE-AD RUACHOTH SCHECHALIM

3. LETTERS & SEAL

Sceaux de la Lune.

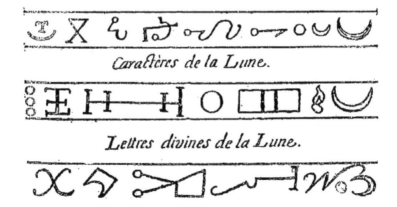

Caractères de la Lune.

Lettres divines de la Lune.

4. SYNTHETIC FIGURE

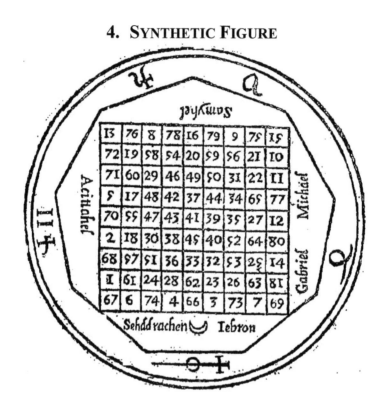

MONDAY

Angel: GABRIEL

Seal:

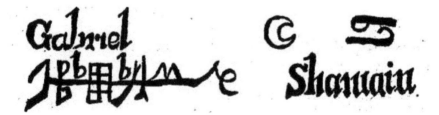

Angels of Monday:	GABRIEL – MICHAEL – SAMAEL.
Angel of the Air:	ARCHAN, KING.
His Ministers:	BILET – MISTABU – ABUZAHA.
Wind:	The Zephyr.
Angels of the 1ˢᵗ Heaven,	*East:* GABRIEL – MADIEL – DRAMIEL – JANAEL.
For whom it is necessary to	*West:* SACHIEL – ZANIEL – HABAIEL – BACHANAEL – CORABIEL.
call the 4 parts of the world:	*North:* MAEL – VIRAEL – VALMUM – BALIEL – BALAY – HUSMASTRAU.
	South : CURANIEL – DABRIEL – DARQUIEL – HANUM – ANAEL – VITUEL.
Perfume:	Aloe.

Season of the Year[112]

Spring................. Talvi
Summer............... Gasmaran
Autumn............... Ardareal
Winter................. Fallas

SPRING	*Angels*...........................	CARACASA – CORE – AMATIEL COMMISSOROS
	Head of the Sign.................	SPUGLIGUEL
	Name of the Earth in Spring.....	AMADAI
	Name of the ☉...................	ABRAYM
	Name of the ☽...................	AGUSITA

SUMMER	*Angels*...........................	GARGATEL – TARIEL – GAVIEL
	Head of the Sign.................	TUBIEL
	Name of the Earth in Summer....	FESTATIVI
	☉ ATHEMAI	☽ ARMATUS

AUTUMN	*Angels*...........................	TARQUAM – GUABAREL
	Head of the Sign.................	TORQUARET
	Name of the Earth in Autumn.....	RABIANARA
	☉ ABRAGINI	☽ MATASIGNAIS

WINTER	*Angels*...........................	AMABAEL – CTARARI
	Head of the Sign.................	ALTARIB
	Name of the Earth in Winter.....	GEREMIA
	☉ COMMUTAF	☽ AFFATERIM

---

[112] This information is taken from the first pages of the Heptameron, by Peter de Abano.

SIGNS OF THE ZODIAC	KABBALAH (SPIRITS)	THEOLOGY (ORDERS OF ANGELS)[113]
ARIES	MALCHIDIEL	SERAPHIM
TAURUS	ASMODEL	CHERUBIM
GEMINI	AMBRIEL	THRONES
CANCER	MURIEL	DOMINIONS
LEO	VERCHEL	POWERS
VIRGO	HAMALIEL	VIRTUES
LIBRA	ZURIEL	PRINCIPALITIES
SCORPIO	BARBIEL	ARCHANGELS
SAGITTARIUS	ANNACHIEL	ANGELS
CAPRICORN	HANAEL	INNOCENTS
AQUARIUS	GABRIEL	MARTYRS
PISCES	BARCHIEL	CONFESSORS

[113] Virtues and Powers are sometimes reversed, as are Principalities and Archangels.

*
* *

Summary

The Magister now possesses the two elements necessary to resolve the problems which interest him.

Human creation or *realization* teaches him how to activate the will in an expedient manner, which is the origin of all serious action; *Natural creation* or *realization*, through the knowledge of the stars and their courses, as well as their correspondences in the three Kingdoms, allows him to await or to determine the moment where the cycle of evolution is most appropriate to receive the volitional influence.

It now remains for us to enter upon the technique which is properly called *Adaptation*. This is the third and last part of our work. It is also the most difficult and one which requires the most attention on the part of the reader.

Bibliography

PIERRE D'ALBAN.........................*Heptameron.*
AGRIPPA.................................*Occult Philosophy.*
KIRCHER..................................*Œdipus egyptiacus.*
ALBERT LE GRAND.......................*[Memoires attributed to him].*
SALOMON................................*[Manuscripts on practical Kabbalah attributed to him].*

THE SEALS OF THE SPIRITS OF THE PLANETS[114]		
Part of the world where it presides	*Names of the Spirits*	*Seals of the Spirits*
SOUTH	ARATRON ($\hbar$)	
EAST	BETHOR ($\qopname$)	
WEST	PHALEG (σ)	
WEST	OCH ($\odot$)	
EAST	HAGITH ($\female$)	
NORTH	OPHIEL (ϱ)	
SOUTH	PHUL ($\mathcal{D}$)	

---

[114] The sigils appear to have been copied wholesale (even including the page numbers) from an early French version of Rabbi Abognazar's text of the Veritable Clavicles of Solomon. A correspondence with Joseph H. Peterson, an acclaimed expert in this field, suggested that Papus would have had access to a version in the French National Library, particularly the version by F.F. Fyot, who he believes introduced the black on white seals. Indeed, BNF manuscript 25,314 appears to be the one Papus used, and the Seals and Characters have been reproduced here.

THE SEALS OF THE SPIRITS OF THE PLANETS

Part of the world where it presides	Names of the Angels[115]	Seals of the Angels
SOUTH	CASSIEL	
EAST	SACHIEL	
WEST	SAMAËL	
WEST	MICHAËL	
EAST	HANAËL	
WEST	RAPHAËL	
NORTH	GABRIEL	

---

[115] These have been corrected to the usually accepted correspondences. As noted above, these originally came from F.F. Fyot's interpretation of Rabbi Abognazar's version of the various books attributed to Solomon. There, the angelic names were listed, in order, as follows: Cassiel, Sachiel, Samaël, Anaël, Raphaël, Michaël, Samaël (repeated). Therefore, these seals may not accord perfectly with the angelic names. However, the very fact that the two times Samaél is used there are different seals, would suggest the original list is not overly accurate, either!

CHARACTERS OF THE ANGELS & THEIR SIGNS		
Zodiacal Sign	*Names of the Angels*	*Seals of the Angels*
ARIES	MALCHIDIEL	
TAURUS	ASMODEL	
GEMINI	AMBRIEL	
CANCER	MURIEL	
LEO	VERCHIEL	
VIRGO	HAMALIEL	
LIBRA	ZURIEL	
SCORPIO	BARBIEL	
SAGITTARIUS	ANNACHIEL	
CAPRICORN	HANAEL	
AQUARIUS	GABRIEL	
PISCES	BARCHIEL	

PART THREE

ADAPTATION

CHAPTER XI – ATTRACTION

ADAPTATION - PRELIMINARIES

All the practices we have been talking about up till now are preparatory and can therefore be executed separately. It now remains to us to study magical *adaptation*, that is, bringing together man's training and the various influences of Nature into a number of rituals. Each of the Operations we are now going to describe is such a synthesis, and requires us to work on most of the actions we have described, and have a serious understanding of theory. But those impatient people who would find the previous studies pointless, yet wish to start on the following practical work are warned that they can only expect mediocre results if they try.

And so, the activated human unites with the astral influences to bring about the rapid evolution of forces normally borrowed from a living creature in each Operation whose description is going to be covered. That is to say, we can no longer maintain our distinction between actions which are purely human and influences which are purely Natural, since all come together for the goal we wish to attain. This is why we will divide this part of our work into four chapters, corresponding to the prevailing actions: ATTRACTION – CONCENTRATION – RADIATION – AGGREGATION, which form the Genesis of all magical work.

Moreover, we will carefully seek how to accomplish the *application* of the practices mentioned in the old Grimoires to our environment and our times. The progress made in the material world allows the Magister to use tools more powerful and more perfect than those described in the "Clavicles." It is here that a deep understanding of *theory* is so important; for it is important for us to resolve the true problems of Ceremonial Magic at every instant. We must not forget the Century in which we now live, under pain of committing the greatest errors and sacrificing everything pointlessly to unnecessary archaism. That is why the good American visionaries who claim to incarnate Christ "mimic" the person described in the Gospel, and through this only come to show their true role: that of a bad actor. Now, the well-instructed Magister *adapts*, but does not copy. Every age determined by destiny has its own needs and its own Laws. Now, one would no more take humanity backwards through the course of the ages than one would make water in a river return up the path it had followed. The initiate evolves, frees, but never goes backwards and never wastes time complaining or protesting about the acts of destiny. To create a book made of verses created by committees and written in one of our Western idioms, in the pretext of continuing the method of the Bible, is to make a ridiculous copy of another poor copy which is the fantastical translation adopted by the Holy Ignorance: The Roman Church. One might be able to write in this manner in hieroglyphic Hebrew, if one had been a seer of genius, having long studied the Hermetic Mysteries of Osiris in Egypt, being named Moses, and living a few thousand years before our time. But to attempt to recreate a Bible in the same mold in French is as naïve as to want to live nowadays as an "elegant" Phoenician. You would be considered to be a charlatan, or at least as an actor whom poverty had reduced to wearing stage costumes, and with good reason. To be an actor is to "copy." Now, once again, *adaptation* differs as much from a copy as a literary work differs from a dictionary. The terms in the dictionary are adapted depending on the phrase being used in the book. Orpheus, taught at the same time and in the same place as Moses and, as the possessor of the same principles, *adapted* his teachings to the corsairs and poets who later populated Greece, just as Moses *adapted* the same teachings for the brigands and practical men whom he had chosen as the instruments of its application.

We hope that you now understand what is meant here by the term *adaptation*.

Personal Practices

Fly away, ye profane and ye profaners![116] Whoever you are, you who wish to pursue theory into practice, reflect well, and if you fear prejudice, sarcasm or madness, throw these blackened pages into the fire.

Remember that, as Master of your impulses and knowing the mysteries of the stars, you should never allow the feminine whirlwind to control your being. If you come to Magic in the hope of destroying your rivals you are a slave, and only Masters have the right to penetrate into the Mystic Temple. If you come to Magic hoping to satisfy your appetites and instincts through the possession of riches, you are a servant to Destiny who rules over material illusions, and you will never attain that peace which proceeds from disdain for what is below.

Slave or servant, return to your lovers or your gilded chains; but do not work to revive the knowledge of another age, for it will remain forever hidden from your base cupidity. Shrug your shoulders or laugh out loud, call the Disciples of Hermes charlatans or lunatics. But do not seek to practice these

---

[116] Members of the Hermetic Order of the Golden Dawn will recognize these words, and the Paris Temple was running by the time the book was written. However, the words come from the Greek Mystery Schools, normally rendered as "Hekas! Hekas! Este bebeloi!"

bizarre rituals any longer: They are deadly for those of weak constitution and, like subtle poisons, only heal those who understand them and how to handle them.

Prayer

The aim of prayer is the momentary fusion of the self[117] and the superior unconscious, the higher self, through the action of idealized feeling on the magically developed will.

*
* *

Thus, prayer is a magical ceremony of the first order, and it is with this that the student must being all his work.

But prayer is a voluntary and cerebral act, and doesn't only consist of moving the lips to pronounce predetermined and always identical words, which, as a result, becomes a simple reflexive act.

Speech should only be the vestment in which the initiate clothes his idealizations; and we counsel the Magister always to create new words to use each time, or at least to rephrase the traditional words in different terms.

The elevation of the animal being to intellectuality, the effect which prayer has, is an act of too great importance to become mere habit, and the ardent supplications of a mother over her sick child moves the invisible far more than the movements of a priest's lips, a salaried functionary of the State and servant of a cult whose teachings he barely comprehends. The few exceptions to this case only serve to prove the rule. How many priests are there, indeed, who feel their soul liberated following a prayer which they have *sold*...usually for thirty pieces of silver.

Among all the rituals of magical prayer, here is the one which we like the best:

---

[117] Although Freudian psychoanalysis did not really come into existence until the early 20th Century, in a way this begins to anticipate it, and notwithstanding Papus' slightly cynical comment about the hypnotherapy work being performed by Charcot in the School of Paris (see footnote 41). Freud studied with this doctor for a time in Paris, and the experience affected him enough to specialize in neurology, which eventually led to his theories on psychoanalysis.

The supplicant should not have ingested any food for at least three hours. He begins with a meditation lasting around five minutes, preceded by three slow, deep breaths. Then he turns successively towards the four Cardinal points, beginning with the East, invoking each of the geniuses and angels of these points, preceding this invocation by pronouncing the corresponding letter of the Sacred Name. We also recommend that, if he can, he should stand on woolen fabric (rug or blanket).[118] Once the cycle of these preliminary invocations has been done, the Magister should give himself over to a new meditation for three minutes. Then, turning once more to the East, he begins his prayer, hands extended with palms turned outwards.

We have said that the words of the prayer should be personal to the Operator. Also, if he cannot accompany himself on a musical instrument, it is essential that he chant these words to a slow and solemn tune: and one should choose from among preferred tunes (the *Noël d'Adam*[119] would work, for example).

Firstly, invoke the Invisible Masters who constitute the magical chain, and then the psychic beings which preside over the evolution of humanity, and one will raise oneself progressively up towards the higher center of all existence and all hierarchy. The prayer is usually made while standing, with the eyes fixed upon the magic mirror over the altar; but neither the time nor the place nor the implements are essential for this essentially spiritual act. Use of the expressive faculties is enough, and the ritual we have just described makes use of movement, gesture, speech and sight.

Later, when the magical laboratory has been constructed, incense may be added to the preceding ritual, together with the sword, the wand and the cup, as implements which one turns towards the four cardinal points.

Such should be this magical prayer which one can develop further by studying the teachings given by Eliphas Lévi in his *Ritual* (p. 888 et seq.) on the

---

[118] This is a common practice in invocation, and represents a layer of insulation between the Operator and Malkuth, or the earthly plane. Thus, at least symbolically, he is operating in Yetzirah, or the plane of the angelic forces.

[119] This once ubiquitous and well-beloved French hymn ("Adam's Noel") sung at many Christmas Eve Midnight Mass in France, has a rather odd provenance. The lyrics were written in 1847 by Placide Cappeau, a 'free-thinker' (i.e. atheist) in those times when an atheist could still be moved by Christmas carols and be inspired to write something along those themes. The meter was quite unusual, and eventually Adolphe-Charles Adam, a minor composer and Israelite, put music to the words in a single day. So, every Christmas all over France, devout Christians sang a beloved carol written by an Atheist and set to music by a Jew! Note also that the 'Adam' in the title refers to the composer, and not the first man of Genesis!

esoteric verses of the *Our Father*. Nevertheless, we have given all the essential elements for this esoteric ritual.

The effects produced by magical prayer are considerable. In the astral plane, the elementary forms are attracted by the action of human speech. For the Operator himself, the effects on the animal center are assured. It seems that the soul finds itself in its true element; a hitherto unknown sensation of well-being and calm invades the Magister, and often visions appear after the first attempts. Note that one should reserve the use of magical prayer for important circumstances, and assiduously avoid making too regular a habit of this elevated practice at the same hour each day. In this instance meditation and mental evocation will suffice. Under normal conditions the complete ritual should be executed once every seven days at a maximum.

The Magical Chain

When the ritual of prayer is well known and has been sufficiently practiced, the Operator can complete it by forming the *magical chain*.

Isolation is a guarantee of failure for the Operator; for the fluidic currents which are put into action will produce terrible reactions if they do not encounter a center of condensation and drainage which is just as powerful. Put a small horseshoe-shaped magnet in front of a strong electro-magnetic field and you already know what will happen. The action of the first will be instantaneously destroyed and absorbed by the force of the second.

Now, in Magic, one must create a fluidic field of attraction around oneself which is as powerful as possible, both in the visible world as well as in the invisible one, but commencing in the latter. This field of attraction, once constituted in the three planes, forms the magical chain which will frustrate all the efforts of jealous or hateful individualities. Prayer, simple or collective, has the purpose of always maintaining the magical chain at the same tension, that is, to continually re-magnetize the center of action.

As we said, one should begin with the invisible world. To this end, one should select from among the passed Masters, ancient or modern, a preferred guide, whose doctrines or works are held by you to be particularly dear. The name of this Master, activated by desire and the disciple's admiration, will serve as the primordial nucleus of the magical chain.

At the commencement of each ceremony or each prayer, firstly one will call upon the beloved Master, symbol of the will of the Magister in the invisible. Then one invokes the psychic influences in action in the astral and which come either from the visible or the invisible world. To end, one addresses the planetary genius which especially dominates your temperament by pronouncing its name, loudly, three times.

Once this is done, after a prayer, you state the spiritual assistance you desire, whether it be for study, for the accomplishment of a vocation, or even for defense against astral attacks. In the case of danger, or at the moment of completing an important action, it is enough to call the Master's name three times in a low voice to feel his psychic influence manifest itself almost immediately.

We have been able to appreciate the efficacious influence of the magical chain, both personally and around us. Although destiny sowed dangers and challenges around us every day, whose strength was increased by our then social situation (in the army), we were alerted every time a danger was about to appear, and were able to avoid all of them. But don't forget that silence on personal Operations is the first condition imposed on the Magister. As another example of a different order, we have seen a young seeker who has a great desire to study the Kabbalah, and in the most modest conditions, suddenly find all the precious books he needed over time, and, to accomplish this, he had simply created his magical chain in the invisible. Finally, the serious practitioner will see their effects on his own clearly enough, so it is pointless for us to stress them.

Once the chain operating in the invisible world has been created, one must endeavor to realize it as far as possible in the visible world. For this, an intellectual association with a serious and discreet friend is very helpful, and this is the reason for the existence of most initiatory societies. If you are able to join a society formed by people presenting guarantees of education and the necessary discretion, you can do this; and never forget that, working in isolation, sooner or latter you will become the victim of the two great dangers faced at the beginning of such studies: egotism and pride.

We will see later that the magic circle is nothing more than the material configuration of the chain which protects you, and which guards you in the invisible; but let us remember that, in any case, it is one of the greatest secrets of practical Kabbalah.

THE MAGIC LABORATORY

PREPARATION AND CONSECRATION OF THE OBJECTS NEEDED[120]

Every intention which is not translated into action is a pointless exercise, and the words which express it are futile. Action is proof of life, and action also proves and attests to the will.[121]

This is the theoretical origin of all the accessory implements used in Magic. We are going to describe the various preparations to which each of the elements comprising the laboratory should be subjected in as much detail as possible, and the assiduous reader will find those extra details we don't feel worth repeating here in other parts of this short treatise.

Depending on one's means, one can devote either an entire room (which is essential for Great Operations) or just a part of a room to these studies. Firstly, we will quickly consider the first possibility, and then we will pay particular attention to the second, which corresponds better with the elementary character of this little treatise.

Let us first remember that any furniture, implement or object used must be new and that all be blessed, each one separately, according to the following rituals:

1.   Purchase or preparation in accordance with the correct planetary correspondence.
2.   Aspersion with holy water.
3.   Fumigation with blessed incense.
4.   Anointing with holy oil.
5.   Figuration with a sacred name.
6.   Blessing with a prayer.
7.   Setting apart.

---

[120] The majority of the following Operations appear to be a mixture of the "Key of Solomon" and Eliphas Lévi's book "Transcendental Magic". It seems highly unlikely the version of the "Key of Solomon" was that of McGregor Mathers published in 1888, since he omitted a considerable amount included in this book. More on this topic will follow in later footnotes.

[121] *Eliphas Lévi*, Ritual, p. 31. [PAPUS]

The Room[122]

If one has a whole room at one's disposal, one will make the following installations:

1. The walls should be covered with a white fabric which can be stretched over wooden frames, so that they can be put up easily and always stay clean;
2. The positions of the four Cardinal Points should be carefully determined with the aid of a compass, and a cardboard star covered with gilded paper should be attached to the wall to permanently indicate East;
3. The *laboratorium* (Hermetic Laboratory) should be set up in the West of the room, formed by a long, wide table purchased, consecrated and signed under the auspices of Mercury, and covered with thick sheet of glass or a waterproof white cloth. A pipe and opening are placed over the table to allow for the expulsion of noxious gases to the outside. It is also good to install gas burners in this laboratory. But we won't insist on these details which relate to Alchemy, which is not the subject we are considering in this present work.

In the East are placed three pieces of furniture comprising the *oratorium*:

1. The altar (approx. 1 – 1.4 meters in height) permanently covered with a fine white cloth, which we will discuss shortly;
2. To the left of the altar a small wardrobe covered inside with white cloth, closed to all profane eyes, and containing the magical implements;
3. To the right of the altar, there is another wardrobe completely covered inside with gold paper and which contains the symbols of the principle forms of worship practiced on earth.

---

[122] "Circa autem ea quæ accedunt as hunc invocandi ritum primum est ut eligatur locus mundus, castus, occlusus, quietus, remotusque ab omni strepitu, nullis alienis aspectibus subjectus. Hic primo exorcisandus est, atque consecrandus" (Agrippa, Practical Magic, book IV of Occult Philosophy) [PAPUS]. *English translation:* "Now concerning those things which appertain to this Rite of Invocation, the first is, that a place be chosen, clean, pure, closed, quiet, free from all manner of noise, and not subject to the view of any strangers. This place must first be exorcised and blessed..."

All these pieces of furniture should be purchased, consecrated and signed under the auspices of the Sun.

4. A curtain which can be drawn at will should separate the Laboratorium and the Oratorium, and two light fittings, one placed in the East and the other in the West, will illuminate the room as needed;

5. A circular area two meters in diameter is set aside for the circle in the center of the room.

These are the principle measures to be taken in the Magister's experimentation chamber; but in the case where such a laboratory cannot be set up, one needs to know how to adapt one's works to the parts which are strictly necessary, which we shall now consider.

*
* *

In an urgent case and for preliminary Operations, a piece of furniture which can serve both as an altar and a wardrobe for the blessed objects will suffice. A small bookcase 1.4 meters tall is excellent for this purpose. The top part serves as the altar, and the body for storage.

One can also use a simple table made of white wood as the altar, and a large chest lined with white material for storage. This is the setup usually shown in the manuscript Clavicles.

Whichever setup is chosen, one will obtain the objects which follow, which will decorate the altar, that indispensable base for all Operations, as we shall see.

The Altar

The altar will be covered, as we have said, with a fine, white cloth. It should represent a Pantacle of the Universe with its three planes, human, natural and divine, and to accomplish this, we recommend the following arrangement which has given us very good results.

A Pentagram is placed in the center of the altar. The one by Eliphas Lévi is compound, while that of Agrippa is purely microcosmic. The latter is preferred when one can procure the required metals, while the first is better in all other cases.

This Pentagram is drawn on a virgin animal skin (a newly-deceased calf, for example) or on virgin parchment, or better still, on paper made from commercial paper pulp by the Magister himself, firstly consecrated under solar influences.

The Magic Chamber

Seven small metallic cubes of each of the planetary metals are placed about the Pentagram (the cube of Mercury is enclosed in a small cube of crystal). These metals are laid out in the order of the seven-pointed Egyptian star.

At the four corners of the altar are placed the following objects: 1 – at the top right-hand corner (*Yod*) the light; 2 – at the upper left-hand corner (*Heh*) the perfume vaporizer or censer, depending on the situation; 3 – at the lower left-hand corner (*Vav*) the magical salt; at the bottom right-hand corner (*Heh final*) the holy water.

Magic Mirror – Above the altar and attached to the wall one may, if one is able to do so, place a concave magic mirror with a black back.

Let's now discuss the preparation of the water, the salt and the incense, as well as the creation of the lamp and mirror.

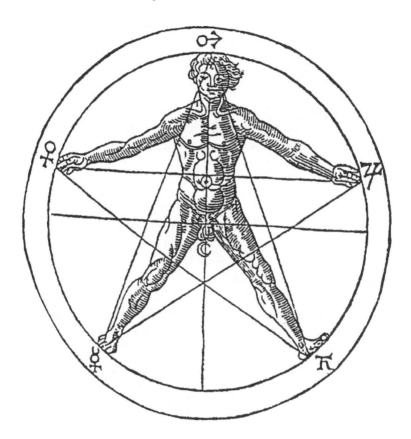

The Water

Following a preparatory prayer made in accordance with the ritual, on the day and under the influences of the Moon, the water is blessed (which should be as pure as possible, but not distilled) in a crystal vase.

Firstly, the hands are imposed on the water, and one blows three times on this water, each time pronouncing the Divine Name of the Tetragrammaton, and stating the intention for which the consecration is being performed (when this is done with a specific purpose in mind). The water is then censed with lunar incense, and the Prayer of the Undines is recited.

Prayer of the Undines

"Dread King of the Sea; Thou who holdest the Keys of the floodgates of Heaven and who enclosest the subterranean Waters in the cavernous hollows of the Earth; King of the Deluge and of the Rains of Spring; Thou who openest the sources of Rivers and of Fountains; Thou who commandest moisture, which is like the blood of the earth, to become the sap of plants: We adore thee and we invoke thee! Speak thou unto us Thy inconstant and changeful creatures in the great Tempests of the Sea, and we shall tremble before Thee. Speak unto us also in the murmur of limpid waters, and we shall desire thy love. O Vastness wherein all the Rivers of Being seek to lose themselves, which renew themselves ever in thee. O Ocean of infinite perfections! O Height which reflectest Thyself in the Depth! O Depth which exhalest thyself into the Height! Lead us into Immortality through sacrifice, that we may be found worthy one day to offer unto Thee the Water, the Blood, and the Tears, for the remission of Sins! Amen.

This is the usual blessing of water which is currently used.
For Great Ceremonies and to leave water permanently upon the altar, one should operate in the following manner:

Following the imposition of hands and the triple breath, a small quantity of blessed salt is mixed with the water, as well as a little of the ash of the similarly blessed incense.[123] During this mixing the following is said:

In sale sapientia æterna et in aqua regenerationis et in cinere germinante terram novam, omnia fiant per ELOHIM GABRIEL, RAPHAEL et URIEL in sæcula et æones. Amen.[124]

In the salt of eternal wisdom, and in the water of regeneration, and in the ashes whence the new earth springs, let all things be accomplished by the Elohim Gabriel, Raphael and Uriel, unto the ages and aeons. Amen.

---

[123] Note the admixture is essentially of the four elements, since it contains water, salt, the product of fire, and breath – air – was introduced. Also note that Papus has listed these in the incorrect order. The serious student should first bless the water, then the salt, then the ashes, and finally mix them together with this blessing.

[124] Papus took these Latin blessings, and the Prayers of the Elementals, from Eliphas Lévi's book *The Doctrine and Ritual of High Magic* (Pub. 1854), Part Two: The Ritual of High Magic, chapter IV.

The Altar

Then the exorcism of water is recited (see below) and, after three minutes of meditation, the Prayer of the Undines is said. Once the water has been blessed it is placed permanently on the altar, in a crystal goblet covered with a lid of the same material.

Exorcism of Water

Fiat firmamentum in medio aquarum et separet aquas ab aquis, quæ superius sicut quæ inferius et quæ inferius sicut quæ superius, ad perpetranda miracula rei unius. Sol ejus pater est, luna mater et ventus hanc gestavit in utero suo, ascendit a terra ad cœlum et rursus a cœlo in teram descendit. Exorciso te, creatura aquæ, ut sis mihi speculum Dei vivi in operibus ejus, et fons vitæ, et ablutio peccatorum. Amen.

Let there be a firmament in the midst of the waters and let it separate waters from waters, so that which is above may be as that which is below, and that which is below as that which is above, to perform the miracles of the One Thing. The Sun is its father, the Moon its mother, and the wind has carried it in its belly. It ascends from the Earth to Heaven and descends again from Heaven to the Earth. I exorcise thee, Creature of Water, that you may be for me a mirror of the living God in His works, and a fount of life, and an ablution for sins. Amen.

The Salt and the Ashes

The salt, which should preferably be sea salt, is blessed by breath, in the same way as for the water, and then the following exorcism is said:

Exorcism of Salt

In isto sale sit sapientia et ab omni corruptione servet mentes nostras et corpora nostra, per Hochmaël, et in virtute Ruach-Hochmaël, recedant ab isto fantasmata hylæ ut sit sal cœlestis, sal terræ et terra salis, ut nutrietor bos triturans et addat spei nostræ cornua tauri volantis. Amen.

Let wisdom abide in this salt, and may it preserve our minds and bodies from all corruption, by Chokmaël, and in the power of Ruach-Chokmaël, let the phantoms of matter depart from it that it may become a heavenly salt, salt of earth and earth of salt, that it may nourish the threshing ox and strengthen our hope with the horns of the Winged Bull. Amen.

*

* *

Once blessed, the salt is place in a crystal vase upon the altar and will be kept free of impurities.

The Ashes

The remains of the incense should also be carefully collected and blessed using the following words:

Exorcism of the Ashes

Revertatur cinis ad fontem aquarum viventium et fiat terra fructificans et germinit arborem vita per tria nomina quæ sunt NETZACH, HOD et YESOD in principio et in fine, per Alpha et Omega qui sunt in spiritu AZOTH. Amen.

Let these ashes return to the font of living water and become a fertile earth, and bring forth the Tree of Life by the three names, which are Netzach, Hod and Yesod, in the beginning and in the end, by Alpha and Omega, which are in the spirit of Azoth. Amen.

*I *
*

This ash is then preserved in a phial with wide neck, carefully kept in the wardrobe set aside for the magical objects.

The Prayer of the Gnomes is used in the consecration of the salt and the ash.

Prayer of the Gnomes

O Invisible King Who, taking the Earth for Foundation, didst hollow its depths to fill them with Thy Almighty Power. Thou Whose Name shaketh the Arches of the World! Thou who causest the Seven Metals to flow through the veins of the rocks! King of the Seven Lights! Rewarder of the subterranean Workers! Lead us into the desirable Air and into the Realm of Splendor. We watch and we labor unceasingly, we seek and we hope, by the twelve stones of the Holy City, by the buried Talismans, by the Axis of the Lodestone which passes through the center of the Earth. O Lord, O Lord, O Lord! Have pity upon those who suffer. Expand our hearts, detach and upraise our minds, enlarge our natures. O Stability and Motion! O Darkness veiled in Brilliance! O Day clothed in Night! O Master who never dost withhold the wages of Thy Workmen! O Silver Whiteness! O Golden Splendor! O Crown of Living and Melodious

Diamond! Thou who wearest the Heavens on Thy Finger like a ring of Sapphire! Thou who hidest beneath the Earth in the Kingdom of Gems, the marvelous Seed of the Stars! Live, reign, and be Thou the Eternal Dispenser of the Treasures whereof Thou hast made us the Warders! Amen.

The Incense and the Censer

The incense and perfumes used in magic are great in number, and classed according to the planetary correspondences. Because of this we find a host of differing lists, so we will provide the simplest and most practical one. Another may be found attached to our magical clock.

It should suffice to recall that *incense* should always be used in all white Operations; since it is a kind of synthesis of good influences.

Incense or perfume may be thrown on glowing coals in a magic censer; or one may put them in a perfume vaporizer, in the latter case to be used in ordinary circumstances[125].

It should always be remembered that the smoke produced should be thick enough and that, during evocations, it should be upon this smoke that the colored ray from the magic lamp should be directed.

Incense and perfumes are purchased, then blessed with aspersion and prayer under the influence of the corresponding planets. They are then kept in glass vials bearing the seal of the planet.

In the consecration of incense, the Prayer of the Sylphs is said.

Prayer of the Sylphs

O Spirit of Life, O Spirit of Wisdom, whose breath giveth forth and withdraweth the form of all living things; Thou, before whom the Life of Beings is but a shadow which changeth, and a vapor which passeth; Thou who mountest upon the clouds, and who walketh upon the wings of the wind; Thou who breathest forth, and endless Space is peopled; Thou who drawest in Thy breath and all that cometh from Thee returneth unto Thee; ceaseless Movement in

---

[125] Strictly-speaking, a perfume vaporizer is a regular perfume sprayer, which suggests that one may either throw incense on coals in a censer for special Operations; or use an atomizer containing the essential oil of the scent required in regular practice. It is assumed the following paragraph is referring to major Operations, given all the previous instructions about the power of smell, which may be obtained without using a censer or thurible.

Eternal Stability, Be Thou eternally blessed! We praise Thee and we bless Thee in the changing Empire of created Light, of Shades, of reflections, and of Images and we aspire without cessation unto Thy immutable and imperishable brilliance. Let the Ray of Thine Intelligence and the warmth of Thy Love penetrate even unto us; then that which is volatile shall be fixed, the shadow shall be a body, the Spirit of Air shall be a soul, the dream shall be a thought. And no longer shall we be swept away by the Tempest, but we shall hold the bridles of the Winged Steeds of Dawn, and we shall direct the course of the Evening Breeze to fly before Thee. O Spirit of Spirits, O Eternal Soul of Souls, O imperishable breath of Life, O Creative Sigh, O mouth which breathest forth and withdrawest the Life of all Beings in the Flux and Reflux ebb and flow of thine Eternal Word which is the Divine Ocean of Movement and of Truth. Amen.

THE PERFUME OF EACH PLANET:

♄ Sulfur
♃ Aloe Wood
♂ Styrax
☉ Laurel
♀ Musk
☿ Juniper
☽ Magnetite/Lodestone[126]

SYNTHETIC PERFUME: Incense

Prayers for Incense

Hagios, Athanatos, Beron, Ciel Dedotois,
O Eternal One, Being of beings, Sanctifier of the Universe,
Bless and hallow this incense which is burned for Thee,
And deign to hear my prayers. Amen.

---

[126] Literal translation of *aimant*. No reference to an actual perfume called *aimant* can be found.

Et æterne ens entium, sanctificator universi, benedic et consecra hoc incensum, et sicut fumus incensi ad te ascendit sic exaudire digneris preces meas. Amen. [127]

Exorcism of Fire

Throw salt, incense, white resin, camphor and sulfur into the fire, and say the three names of the Geniuses of Fire three times:

MICHAEL, King of the Sun and the Furnace; SAMAEL, King of Volcanoes HANAEL, Prince of Salamanders.

The Magic Censer

Purchase an earthenware pot under the auspices of Mars and bless it following the ordinary ritual.

Here is an interesting extract from the *Keys* on this subject.

Exorcism of Censer, Fire and Incense

It is also necessary to have a censer suitable to hold fire for censing. This should be made from a new glazed black earthenware pot, and the fire from new charcoal, when one should have a small taper with matches and tinder, or a wick and a candle, and the charcoal, once lit with new fire, should be exorcised by saying:

God of Moses, God of Aaron, God of Abraham, bless and purify this creature of fire, so that it may be acceptable, and purify all the places where it may be lit. Amen.

Deus Moyses, Deus Aaron, Deus Abraham, benedic et purifica hanc creaturam ignis tuo honori preparatum, ut digna sit complacere et purificare omnia loca in quibus accensa erit. Amen.

Once this is done, throw incense specific to the Operation which is exorcised, saying: "Hagios, Athanatos, Beron, Ciel Dedotois…" as before.

---

[127] Papus only quotes the French version of the blessing, so the original Latin from the Rabbi Abognazar version is included here: similarly, for the exorcism of the censer.

The Magic Lamp

The lamp used in the Operations should be constructed so as to bring together the planetary influences. In his Ritual, Eliphas Lévi established this synthesis based upon the correspondences of metals, which is wonderful, but which is also most inconvenient in requiring so costly an object which only the most powerful of initiatory societies could own. Also, we prefer the color correspondences of the planets to those of the metals, which allows for a more practical object for the student Magister.

Therefore, you should procure seven panes of glass, colored according to the color or each planet, and also a varnished wooden base will allow the panes to be fixed upright, which should be purchased on separate days according to the day of the planet, and then consecrated according to the ordinary ritual before being put into service. One can also place one of the metal cubes from the altar, or a metal ring, on the wooden base. The glass pane dedicated to Mercury should be created by joining together parallel pieces of glass panes from all the other planets. The glass panes can also be replaced by colored bulbs – which is far more practical.[128]

The light is provided by one, three or seven candles of virgin wax, according to the importance of the Operation. A strong lens can condense the light coming from these candles towards the magic mirror or the smoke from the incense. The appropriately-colored pane of glass is placed between the lens, and the mirror or the smoke. At any rate, a carefully designed casing can prevent the luminous rays from shining in any other direction than the one we have just described.

*
* *

This is what one may call the lamp, so created, which the Magister will use.

---

[128]The first electric street light was installed in Paris in 1878, near the Arc de Triomphe, and by the Paris International Exposition of Electricity in 1881, they were installed on the major streets. However, this would suggest it was unlikely that the average consumer would have access either to lightbulbs nor the circuity to connect them in 1893. However, we see here that that Papus was talking about colored glass to go around oil or candle lamps, which were still very common at the time, as we see in the next sentence. Of course, the numbers one, three and seven speak for themselves.

If you wish to build a permanent lamp, the most practical means consists of obtaining a commercial magic lantern[129], which is lit using blessed oil (using the same ritual as for water), and in which the colored glass panes correspond to the planets replacing the figures. We will simply add that you can purchase anywhere for a low price a base to allow it to be rotated easily. A contraption made out of cardboard (found in commercial use) is always preferable to one make of metal.

The lamp should be blessed before it is used by the usual ritual (aspersion, and fumigation by incense), then successively under the auspices of each planet when inserting the colored panes. The complete consecration of the lamp will therefore take seven days.

Prayer of the Salamanders

Immortal, Eternal, Ineffable and Uncreated Father of All, borne upon the Chariot of Worlds, which ever roll in ceaseless motion; Ruler over the Ethereal Vastness, where the Throne of Thy Power is upraised, from the summit of which Thine eyes behold all, and Thy pure and Holy ears hear all, hear Thou Thy children, whom thou hast loved since before the Ages began. Thy Majesty Golden, Vast and Eternal, shineth above the Heaven of Stars! Above them art Thou exalted, O Thou Flashing Fire! There Thou illuminateth all things with Thine insupportable Glory, whence flow the ceaseless streams of splendor which nourish Thine Infinite Spirit. This Infinite Spirit nourisheth all, and maketh that inexhaustable treasure of generation whichever encompasseth Thee, replete with the numberless forms wherewith Thou hast filled it from the beginning. From this Spirit arise those most Holy Kings, who surround thy Throne and who compose Thy court. O Universal Father! One and Alone! Father alike of Immortals and of Mortals! Thou hast created Powers marvellously like unto Thy thought Eternal and unto Thy venerable Essence. Thou hast established them above the Angels who announce Thy Will to the World. Lastly, thou hast created us third in rank within our Elemental Empire! There our continual exercise is to praise and to adore Thy desires! There we ceaselessly burn with Eternal Aspiration unto Thee! O Father! O Mother of Mothers, O Archetype Eternal of Maternity and of Love! O Son, the flower of all Sons! O form of all forms, Soul, Spirit, Harmony and Numeral of all Things! Amen.

---

[129] The magic lantern is really just an exoteric recreation of the Operational lamp made by an intiate. [PAPUS].

*
  * *

Once the Magister has made all these preliminary preparations, he will be in possession of all the objects necessary for the decoration of the altar.

Before passing on to other Operations, it only remains for us to talk about the construction of the magic mirror which should be placed above the altar.

This mirror should be either made of clear, concave plate glass, or a silvered mirror which is also concave, or a mirror made of metal.

Although we want to restrict ourselves to use only those extracts and citations which are necessary, we are obliged to take the following extract concerning the detailed preparation of the magic mirror from the "Clavicles."

The Magic Mirror

Take a shiny and well-polished plate of fine steel, slightly concave, and write upon it these names with the blood of a male white pigeon in the four corners:

Jehovah   -   *Elohim*   -   *Metatron*   -   *Adonai*

And place the steel plate in a new, clean, white linen cloth. When you perceive the new Moon at the first hour after sunset, go to a window, look at the sky with devotion and say:

"O Eternal One! O Eternal King! Ineffable God, who created all things for the love of me, and by an occult judgement for the health of mankind, look on me, N…, your most unworthy servant and on my pure intention. Deign to send me your angel ANAËL into this mirror, who mandates, orders, and commands his companions, your subjects, whom you made, O Almighty One, Who was, and is, and shall be eternally, that in Thy Name they may judge and act with integrity, instructing me and showing me whatever I may ask of them."

Then throw some appropriate incense on the glowing charcoal, which is oriental saffron[130], and say while adding it:

---

[130] This detail is only included much later in the *Grimoirum Verum*, edited and translated by Joseph H. Peterson (pub. CreateSpace, 2007, ISBN 978-1434811165), which is a very

"In this, for this, with this offer I pour before Thy Face, O my God, Who art Three in One, great and most sublimely exalted, who watches over the Cherubim and Seraphim, and who will come to judge the Ages by Fire, hear my prayer."

Then cense the mirror by placing it over a new black earthenware pot, so that it becomes impregnated with the fumes of the incense, holding it in the right hand and saying the preceding prayer three times.

After saying this, blow on the mirror three times and say:

"Come, ANAËL, come, and let it be your good pleasure to come to me by your will, in the name of Almighty God ✠, in the name of the Most Wise Son ✠, in the name of the Most Kind Holy Spirit ✠; come, ANAËL, in the name of the terrible Jehovah, come, ANAËL, by the arms of the all-powerful Metatron, come to me, N… (say your name over the mirror), and command Thy subjects that, with love, joy and peace, they may reveal to my eyes those things which are hidden from me. So mote it be.[131] *Amen.*"

Once this has been done, raise your eyes to heaven and say:

"Almighty Lord, Who causeth everything to move according to Thy will, hear my prayer, and let my wish be agreeable to Thee. If it pleaseth Thee, O Lord, look upon this mirror and bless it, so that ANAËL, one of Thy subjects, may remain with it with his companions to satisfy N…, Thy poor and unworthy servant, O blessed and highly exalted God of all the celestial spirits, who liveth and regineth in everlasting good. Amen."

When you have completed these things, make the sign of the cross upon you and on the mirror, one the first day and on the following forty-five days, at the end of which, ANAËL will appear in the form of a fair child. He will greet you and command his companions to obey you.

Note that it doesn't necessarily need forty-five days to perfect the mirror: the spirit often appears on the fourteenth day. This depends on the intent, devotion and fervor of the Operator. When he appears to you, ask him what you

---

good reference work for this material. Indeed, this entire section is taken by Papus from that *Grimoire.*

[131] In French: *ainsi soit-il*, which is often used as *Amen* in prayers. The 'Masonic' Amen has been substituted here. 'So be it' can also be used.

desire, and pray him to appear at any time you will call him to grant your requests.

Then, when you want to look in the mirror and obtain what you desire, it is not necessary to recite all the afore-mentioned prayers; but having censed the mirror, say: "Come, ANAËL, come, and let it be your good pleasure...." Etc. up to *Amen*.

When the Operation is ended, send the spirit on his way, saying:

"I thank thee, ANAËL, for coming and satisfying my request. Go in peace and come when I shall call thee."

The incense of ANAËL is saffron.

There are those who perform the Operation by means of a crystal globe filled with the seven waters of the seven maps of the world[132]

The following writing was presented and unfolded in the globe by the angel ANAËL to a seer. It was read by her and written under her dictation on December 28, 1797:

"Charged by the Almighty One to watch over the prosperity and tranquility of humans, I fulfill my mission by submitting to the desire of the truly faithful who ask me questions concerning what happy and unhappy events will take place; but, as the prosperity which God prepares for His elect does not consist of vain riches, I avoid any question which concerns obtaining them, or if I consent to satisfying them, I only do this in a way which leaves the choice of means to them, in conformity with the liberty which God gives to all His creatures. Nothing is more pleasant to me than being able to communicate good news true believers, since they aren't in the category of those to whom I am not permitted to explain myself as clearly as they might wish. However, I can answer the questions which some ask me, provided that they are asked in a very precise manner, and their main object is not to know all the precise odds of success."

---

[132] The term used by Papus (or his source) is *mappemondes*, from the Latin *mappa mundi*. These were images of the world predominantly in Medieval times. These maps were not intended for navigation, but rather illustrate a particular Christian or esoteric point. Most divided the world into three parts normally with Jerusalem in the center (Europe, Asia and Africa) or four (reflecting the four elements). However, there appears to be no reference to seven maps, and indeed most *mappæ mundi* show the continents surrounded by a 'universal sea'.

SIMPLIFIED PROCESS OF DIVINATION BY THE MAGIC MIRROR

Make a cross on a crystal phial with olive oil, and write *St. Helena* beneath the cross.

Then give the phial to a virgin child from a legitimate marriage to hold, and kneel behind them and say the following prayer three times:

"Deprecor, Domina S. Helena, mater regis Constantini, etc., etc."[133]

When the child sees the angel, they will be able to make whatever request the Operator wishes.

Talismans

We have spoken at length about talismans in the second part of this book (performing the gesture). It now remains for us to consider a few practical details on this subject.

The creation of each talisman is truly a small magical ceremony in itself; and the student cannot practice this subject enough.

The necessary implements are as follows:

1. The material on which the talisman is engraved, which may be metal, virgin animal skin, parchment derived from this skin, or paper hand-made by the Operator himself under favorable influences;
2. The objects needed for this Operation: pencils, compass, ruler and penknife for the skin, parchments and paper; engraver, virgin wax and acid for metals;
3. Silk envelopes of various colors in which the talismans, once made, will be preserved.

---

[133] According to the book *Les Miroirs Magiques* by Ernest Bosc, published in 1912, this is the sum total of the prayer, which translates as: "I beseech Lady St. Helena, Mother of King Constantine." It is certainly an odd prayer, as it doesn't contain a request. It is possibly an extract from a longer prayer, and St. Anselm is indicated. However, detailed research is outside the scope of this work. Incidentally, the book by E. Bosc closely matches this section by Papus, but expands on it, and is well worth seeking out by the curious student.

Concerning the Talisman's Material

A. Metals

Obtain the planetary metals corresponding to the talismans. We will repeat the list of these correspondences: for Saturn, *lead*; for Jupiter, *tin*; for Mars, *iron*; for the Sun, *gold*; for Venus, *copper*; for Mercury, *mercury* (in this case this will be an amalgam with silver and gold); and for the Moon, *silver*.

For planetary talismans you will engrave the image of the planet on one side; and its magic square, as previously described, on the other. This engraving is made directly with an engraver on softer metals, or using wax and acid as we have just described.

B. Skin, Parchment and Paper

Skin – On a day ruled by the Sun (the Eve of St. John) purchase a freshly-deceased lamb or calf skin, and after consecrating it according to the usual ritual, keep it carefully wrapped in a white cloth.[134]

Parchment – For present-day use, commercially-made virgin parchment is perfectly fine, but skin made as described above is certainly preferable for talismans.

Paper (for talismans and one's personal book of magic) – The paper required for Operations can be made oneself by purchasing from commercial vendors of paper paste (see le Bottin[135]) the finest paper paste you can find which can be easily stretched in water, then laid on metal plates and finally pressed on an ordinary copier which is sufficient for this purpose. One can even make a watermark of the planet, under whose influence the paper is being made, with an iron thread.

For detailed instructions one can study *making paper in a vat*, either in the manuals of Roret (Manuals made by Le Normand, National Library, Vol.

---

[134] In the country it is easy to prepare a lambskin on the day desired, and it was in this manner that they were made by the ancient Egyptian initiatory colleges. In Paris one may substitute this preparation by purchasing it on the specific day, and after many hours of research, at 65 rue de Gravilliers we have been able to find a tanner called Anthony who specializes in freshly-deceased calfskins. Thus, our readers will avoid much searching. [PAPUS]

[135] Published by the publisher Didot Bottin, this directory was a reference manual to locate service providers. By now it has expanded to cover just about any kind of list of services or professionals.

27.338, 27.339 and 27.340), or also in the *Encyclopedia*, which provides useful plates on this topic.

Engraving Characters on Metals

The most practical means consists of firstly covering the metal medallion with a thin layer of virgin wax melted at a gentle temperature and which has been asperged and censed under the auspices of the planet to which the Operation is dedicated. Then one uses the engraver to engrave the magic characters on the obverse side and the figure of the planet on the reverse of the medallion by simply removing the wax from the required places.

Then it is enough to plunge this medallion into a suitable acid, appropriately diluted with water at the hour and day of the planetary correspondences.

An appropriate consecration of the talisman is made while it is in the acid.

Once the talisman is retrieved, it is washed in slightly alkaline water and wrapped in a piece of silk in the appropriate color.

ENGRAVING TOOL (BURIN)

For the consecration of the engraver one can simply follow the traditional teachings in the "Clavicles."

Exorcism of the Engraving tool

The burin is a very useful implement in all Operations, and since one can do nothing without it, it should be the first implement one makes, in the following manner:

On a Tuesday (Mars) or a Friday (Venus) make a small steel point like the one shown in the table of implements, on which you will engrave the following words and characters on the same day and hour of Mars or Venus.

Then you will create a small Boxwood sleeve for it, similar to that which is shown, and after washing and censing it with a little Juniper, say the following prayer:

"O Eternal God, my Father, bless this implement prepared in Thine honor, so that is will only serve for good and healthy purposes for Thy glory. Amen.

Asophiel, Asophiel, Asophiel, Pentragrammaton, Athanatos, Eye, Eye, Eye, Kellon, Kelloi, Kelli."

After censing it once more, you will set it aside until needed.

Design of Talismans on Parchments or Skin

PENCILS

Firstly, one should obtain seven pencils colored according to the seven planets. Each of these pencils should be consecrated separately on the appropriate day. They will then be prepared for use by cutting the point with a little knife or the special penknife.

Exorcism of the pens

According to the Operations, one will obtain different pens and all are purified in the same manner, that is: that, after being censed, take the blood of a ewe, and you will moisten the ends of the feathers up to around two fingers of the quill, saying this prayer:

"Hamiel, Hel, Miel, Ciel, Joviel, Nasnia, Magde Tetragrammaton. Great and Powerful God, hear my prayers and deign to grant to these feathers the fruit of Thy benediction. Amen."

You can then use them as required.[136]

PENKNIFE

Under the influence of Mars, purchase a new penknife with a white sleeve and several blades, one long and strong which will serve to cut herbs or branches on the desired day, and one or two small ones for the pencils and to cut the

---

[136] This consecration is something of a hybrid between blessing the ink bottle, ink and blessing the quill pen outlined in the *Clavicles*, which make no mention of pencils or crayons.

parchment, skin or paper. In this manner one will replace several implements indicated in ordinary rituals with one only. Here, now, is the traditional teaching on this subject:

Exorcism of the Penknife

One must have a penknife made which will serve no other purpose than that of cutting the quills you need for the Operations, and whose blade is made of pure and thin steel. With regard to the sleeve, it is not important what it is made of, so long as it is new, and having been thoroughly washed and wiped dry, you should place it on a table covered with a white cloth, and after asperging and censing it, say the following prayer with close attention:

"Agiel, Asiel, Sadon, Paliel, Alma, Mammiel, Dilaton, Kaday, Catilua, Utanzaral, Zalphi, Carsali, Faffua, Hictimi, On, Agla, Agios, Hamon, Yoth, Luphat, Miel, Ciel, Miel, Ciel, Miel, Deus Moyses, Deus Israel."[137]

After which you engrave the following characters on it, on one side the Holy Names and on the other the seal:

Having censed and blessed them say the prayer once more: "Agiel, Asiel, Sadon" etc. After which, wrap the aforesaid penknife in a piece of taffeta of different colors, and keep it on its own to be used as needed.

"Agiel, Asiel, Sadon, Paliel, Alma, Mammiel, Dilaton, Kaday, Catilua, Utanzaral, Zalphi, Carsali, Faffua, Hictimi, On, Agla, Agios, Hamon, Yoth, Luphat, Miel, Ciel, Miel, Ciel, Miel.

God of Moses, God of Israel. Great God, do not forget Thy servant N..., but condescend to bless this implement prepared for Thine honor, by Thy great power which Thou revealed to my Father, and by all the angels whose names Thou hast revealed to Him, and by Thy Name which is mighty, Tetragrammaton."

---

[137] It is not clear why the first section was only partially copied by Papus. It is recommended that the latter, longer prayer is said both time in full.

COMPASS AND RULER

A compass purchased on the day of the Sun and a graduated ruler purchased under the lunar influences are most useful for designing talismans. These objects are consecrated and wrapped, the one in yellow silk, the other in white silk, and are set aside only for this use.

Design of Talisman – Under the favorable influences one will cut out the section required for the creation of the talisman with the penknife. Then one traces the circles with the compass and the requisite colored pencil. Finally, one will draw the figures with the pencil

That done, the talisman is blessed according to the ritual for all consecrations, adding the triple breath. Also, it is good to say the prayer of the day of the week corresponding to the Operation at the end of the consecration.

Consecration of Talismans – When the talisman has been created, either etched on metal or drawn on another material, it should be wrapped in a piece of silk in the color corresponding to its action and carefully set aside in a small casket which will be kept in the magic cupboard.

REMARKS ON THE SUBJECT OF TALISMANS AND THEIR CONSECRATION

From the theoretical point of view, a talisman is in fact the material sign of the joining of the will of the Magister with an astral influence, and in accordance with the primary[138] characters of the astral. And a talisman simply purchased and not blessed by the Operator is no more than a symbolic object without any particularly special influence. When the Magister finds himself in a position to purchase a more or less ancient talisman, he should first attend to discovering its meaning, which will be easy for any well-instructed occult student, thanks to the images we gave in the second part of this book. When the influence under which this talisman works is known, one must bless it again, but in a great ceremony, using the wand, the cup, the sword and the pentagram.

One should also recall that one must consecrate an object in accordance with the correspondences of the Moon and the Planets, which only requires a delay of 24 hours at most. This consecration performed in accordance with the place the earth occupies with regard to the celestial Houses only has power for a month. If one consecrates an object according to the correspondences of the days of the week (the quarter of the Moon), the influence lasts a little longer, but only

---

[138] *Principiateur* in the book. There is no such word.

a little. If on the contrary, one consecrates it according to the location of the Moon in the Signs of the Zodiac (considered to be Planetary Houses), the influence will endure for a year or more. Finally, a consecration made at the moment the Sun indicates a correspondence is the most efficacious, and should be preferred over all the others for the magical wand or sword.

Establishing the Horoscope for the Operation

In all Operations of any importance it will be most useful to establish the position of the stars in the heavens on the day chosen for this Operation.

To this end it will be indispensable to produce the following items in advance:

1. LA CONNAISSANCE DES TEMPS published by the *Bureau des Longitudes* for each year (five years of this publication are generally published in advance). Price: 4 Francs, rue Chamuel, 29, rue de Tréviste.

2. UN PLANISPHÈRE CÉLESTE, above all the excellent card of Camille Flammarion edited in Paris (rue Serpente, 25, Bertaux editor) and whose price is 8 Francs.[139]

These are the two most useful tools for every Magister.

This is what one should do if, for example, establishing a horoscope for Sunday, April 23, 1893:

*

* *

Firstly, trace a circle on a sheet of paper. Then divide the circle into 12 parts like the face of a watch, and write around it the degrees from 1° to 360° (every 30° if one wishes to write quickly). Then write the name of each of the Signs of the Zodiac in its place as indicated in the following figures.

Once this is done, one takes the Ephemeris and seek successively the longitude of the various stars, beginning with our satellite, the *Moon*.

For the MOON, open the annual at the Table of Longitudes and Latitudes, for the month of April (23 page 52). There you will find several hours listed. Take 12 o'clock, for example. At this moment the Moon occupies 169°22′56″. For the magical horoscope this is sufficient for very rudimentary observations: now we return to our figure and place the Moon in the Sign of Virgo a little after

---

[139] The first book is an Astronomical Ephemeris, and the second a Celestial Star Chart. The equivalent should be purchased.

the center. If our sphere was divided exactly into 360°, we would place it on the exact degree.

The SUN (page 30) – Longitude of the Sun at midday, April 23, 33°31′56″, which gives us the Sign of Taurus (30° to 60°).

MERCURY (page 236) – Longitude at midday, April 23, 258°45″, which gives us Mercury in Sagittarius (240° to 270°), a little before the middle of the Sign.

VENUS (page 260) – Longitude, 27°56″, which places it in Aries nearly at the end of the Sign.

MARS (page 284) – Longitude on April 23, 102°12″, which places it in Cancer, a little before the middle.

JUPITER (page 297) – 37°30″, which places it in Taurus almost next to the Sun.

SATURN (page 312) – 190°15″, which places it in Libra, a little before the middle.

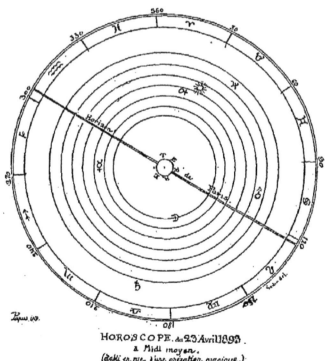

HOROSCOPE. du 23 Avril 1893.
à Midi moyen.
(établi en vue d'une opération magique.)

*

* *

You now have the state of the heavens on this day and can quickly understand the connections between the planets. But there is one more indication required: that is setting out the Signs of the Zodiac below the horizon at that moment, and those which are above it, also known as the demarcation of the two parts of the heavens, visible and invisible.

It is here that you must use the *Mobile Celestial Planisphere* of Camille Flammarion.

Set it to noon or XII hours on April 23, which is placed at the top of the Table and see which Signs of the Zodiac are at the East and West of the horizon.

On the West you will see Aquarius which is close to setting. One then draws a first thick horizontal line between the end of Aquarius and the beginning of Capricorn.

On the East the line passes between Cancer which is rising, and Leo which is still invisible.

The Signs above the horizon are Cancer, Gemini, Taurus, Aries, Pisces and Aquarius, and the planets which rule at this moment are: Venus, the Sun, Jupiter and Mars, as may be learned by studying the figure above.

This example will work for any Operation. This is why we have gone into such technical detail.

Summary

The instructions we have just given are in summary, but they should definitely enough to understand the attraction of the astral through will, thanks to prayer on the one hand (the origin of the Magical Chain), and the preparation of the required objects for the Magic Laboratory on the other hand. The minute details which may seem puerile to some are of great importance, since, indeed, it will be enough for us to note the dangers which lurk among the many works and the Grimoires which are so easy to obtain. Our intention is to create a *practical* and *elementary* treatise, and we will expend all our efforts to accomplish this goal without going beyond that.

Bibliography

PIERRE D'ALBAN………..…………….*Heptameron.*
AGRIPPA……..……………………….*Occult Philosophy.*
KIRCHER……………….....................*Œdipus egyptiacus.*
ALBERT LE GRAND...…………………*[Memoires attributed to him].*
SALOMON...……………....................*[Manuscripts on practical Kabbalah attributed to him].*

CHAPTER XII – CONCENTRATION

ADAPTATION – 2ⁿᵈ PHASE

The Magister's Week – The Seven Mysterious Prayers

The attraction of psychic forces should be performed in silence. It is only through perseverance, calm and above all through the exclusive search for truth for its own sake and not for a material and vile purpose, that one will come little by little to an understanding of the astral and possession of the practical. "Seriousness" of character is therefore indispensable in this preparatory period, and the unfortunate whom vanity drives to want to boast that they are "Mages" or "Grand Initiates" are more to be pitied than blamed, for pride and affectation are the most perfidious perils which destiny presents to the beginners' imagination. Pythagoras, if the tradition is to be believed, firstly imposed a long period of silence on his disciples, a very practical procedure to develop meditation and concentration in those ardent natures in the midst of which the Master most often taught his wisdom. A bugler advancing into enemy territory holds back from playing the bugle if he doesn't wish to be discovered and murdered. Therefore, he who wants to give himself over to the practice of Magic should use the greatest discretion and disguise his true occupations under various pretexts, as the marvelous Eliphas Lévi taught. A sure friend pursing the same studies can sometimes be the sole confidant chosen. But, once again, the most important rule for everyone to observe is the fourth teaching of the Sphinx: *to be silent.*

And, whatever the jesting or sarcasm with which sceptics of rank prejudice greet these studies of talismans and magical wands made at the end of the 19ᵗʰ Century, whatever the epithets with which they please to weaken our research, we will pursue our work with calm and perseverance, while never be discouraged by these procedures which appear in every age and have ever been just as powerless to destroy what should be made manifest. We are convinced of the reality of the facts which we set forth and are convinced by it, for we have the proof; but we are also convinced that only those who *are able to understand* will follow us in our studies, and that the rest will only see in them the fruit of an ingenious dilettantism, or the ramblings of someone alienated from the current age. When a teacher writes a fairly complicated algebraic formula on a blackboard, only certain advanced students understand it, and without doubt if some rustic or ignorant student sees all these figures, no doubt he will consider them to be "useless scribbles." Isn't that the most ironic of punishments? Also, those of you who understand, and who worry that we have said too much, rest assured that these subjects can be discussed in the light of day without fear. Occult knowledge has nothing to fear from the light: it is its element, and if you still don't believe me, look directly at the sun for two minutes, and you will then understand the esotericism of the preliminary warning in our book concerning psychic concentration.

The practice of concentration is intimately linked to the development of meditation and to the exercise of prayer and, as a result, is connected above all with *Psychurgy*. We won't dwell on this point, and will content ourselves by showing how we understand this practice along general lines, leaving each person to adapt this teaching to his nature, his environment and his occupation.

What we are going to say is therefore rather another suggested example to adopt than a line of conduct to be strictly adhered to: this is what should be understood above all. Each Magister should apply his own intelligence and not his memory to the study of the following counsel.

DURING THE DAY

The day is divided up into four parts corresponding to the four seasons of the year and to the four weeks of the lunar month: Morning or Spring of the day, the period of intellectual advent; Midday or Summer, the period of flowering; the Afternoon or Fall, the period of fructification; and finally the Evening or Winter, the period of repose and meditation.

The Magister's day should be dedicated to prayer in its three forms: speech, work and meditation.

On rising, after purifying yourself physically as completely as possible with water, say the prayer of the day before the altar (for this we give the seven mystical prayers from *The Enchiridion*[140] later). Then perform that work which is most useful and efficacious to prayer ('*He who works, prays*' says the Gospel). Work associated with *a profession or trade* which one pursues in order to live should be carefully distinguished from work linked to *an occupation* which one has chosen. All men worthy of that title should have a profession, a trade to assure his physical well-being, and an occupation to develop his intellectual life. It is in confusing these two elements that the majority of present day social

---

[140] This refers to the Enchiridion of Pope Leo III, which, according to legend, was presented by Pope Leo III to Charlemagne on the occasion of his coronation. However, no copies prior to the 16th Century have been located. The book is more a Sacramentary than a Grimoire, though later parts of the book certainly contain what would be called spells.

inequalities arise. Therefore, one should devote a greater or lesser part of the day to one's profession, and it's when these professional duties are accomplished that one will give oneself over to meditation, practice, reading magical or other works, educating the senses through the influence of esthetic manifestations (theater or music), and finally to such occupations one may desire.

Finally, in the evening, before going to sleep, devote a few moments to meditation on the observations and teachings one has been able to acquire during the day which has just passed. A moral examination, such as is recommended in the *Golden Verses of Pythagoras*, will conveniently end the day.

It goes without saying that during periods of training with regard to Magical Operations, attention should be given to the various procedures for accomplishing these outlined in the second part of this book.

THE SEVEN MYSTERIOUS PRAYERS

SUNDAY

Our Father, Who art in Heaven, Hallowed be Thy Name. Thy Kingdom come, Thy Will be done on Earth as it is in Heaven. Give us this day our daily bread, and forgive us our trespasses, as we forgive those who trespass against us. And lead us nor into temptation, but deliver us from evil. For Thine is the Kingdom, the Power, and the Glory, forever and ever. Amen.

Deliver me I pray Thee, O Lord, who art Thy creature, N... from all evil past, present and to come, both of soul and body. In Thy goodness give me peace and good health, and by propitious unto me, for I am your creature, by the intercession of the benevolent Virgin Mary, and by your Apostles St. Peter, St. Paul, St. Andrew, and by all the Saints. Grant peace to Thy creature, and health throughout my life, that, being aided by Thy mercy, I shall be neither the slave of sin, nor fear any trouble, by the same Jesus Christ Thy Son, Our Lord Who, being God, sits and reigns in the unity of the Holy Spirit, forever and ever. Amen. May the peace of the Lord be always with me. Amen.

O Lord, may that Heavenly Peace, which Thou hast given your Disciples, remain forever constant in my heart, and always stand between me and my enemies, both visible and invisible. Amen. May the peace of the Lord, His face, His body, His blood, help me, comfort me and protect me, who art Thy creature, N..., as well as my soul and body. Amen.

O Lamb of God, Who deigned to be born of the Virgin Mary, and Who, being on the cross, cleansed the world of its sins, have pity upon my soul and my body. O Christ, Lamb of God, sacrificed for the world's salvation, haver pity upon my soul and my body. O Lamb of God, through Whom all the faithful ones are saved, give me Thy peace, which must endure forever, in this life and the next. Amen.

MONDAY

O Great God, by Whom all things are delivered, deliver me also from all evil. O Great God, who grants consolation to all beings, grant consolation unto me also. O Great God, who has aided and assisted all things, help me also. In my needs, my miseries, my enterprises, my dangers: deliver me from all opposition and the obstacles of my enemies, both visible and invisible. In the Name of the Father, Who hath created the whole world ✠. In the Name of the Son, Who redeems it ✠. In the Name of the Holy Spirit, Which hath accomplished the Law in all its perfection. I throw my whole being into Thine arms, and place myself completely under Thy holy protection. Amen.

May the blessing of Almighty God, the Father, the Son, and the Holy Spirit, be always with me. Amen ✠. May the blessing of God the Father, who has made all things by His Word alone, be always with me ✠. Amen. May the blessing of Our Lord Jesus Christ, Son of the Great Living God, be always with me ✠. Amen. May the blessing of the Holy Spirit with Its Seven Gifts, be always with me ✠. Amen. May the blessing of the Virgin Mary, with her Son, be always with me. Amen.

TUESDAY

May the blessing and consecration of the bread and the wine, that Our Lord Jesus Christ performed when He gave them to His Disciples, saying unto them: "Take and eat all of this: For this is my body which shall be given for you. Do this in remembrance of me, and for the remission of all sins," be always with me ✠. May the blessing of the Holy Angels, Archangels, Virtues, Powers, Thrones, Dominations, Cherubim and Seraphim be always with me ✠. Amen.

May the blessing of the Patriarchs and Prophets, Apostles, Martyrs, Confessors, Virgins, and all the Saints of God be always with me ✠. Amen. May the blessing of all God's Heaven be always with me ✠. Amen. May the Majesty of Almighty God support and protect me; may His eternal goodness lead me; may His limitless charity inflame me; may His supreme divinity lead me; may the Power of the Father preserve me; may the Wisdom of the Son vivify me; may the Virtue of the Holy Spirit always be between me and my enemies, both visible and invisible. Amen. Power of the Father, strengthen me. Wisdom of the

Son, enlighten me. Consolation of the Holy Spirit, comfort me. The Father is Peace. The Son is Life. The Holy Spirit is the Remedy of consolation and safety. Amen. May the Divinity of God bless me. Amen. May His Piety warm me. Amen. May His Love preserve me. Amen. O Jesus Christ, Son of the Great Living God, have pity upon me, a poor sinner.

WEDNESDAY

O Emmanuel, defend me against the mischievous enemy and against all mine enemies, both visible and invisible, and deliver me from all evil. King Jesus Christ has come in peace, made man by God, and has suffered patiently for us. May Jesus Christ, the compliant King, be always between me and mine enemies, and defend me. Amen.

Jesus Christ triumphs. Jesus Christ reigns. Jesus Christ commands. Jesus Christ delivers me continually from all evil. Amen. May Jesus Christ deign to give me the grace to triumph over all my adversaries. Amen. Here is the Cross of Our Lord, Jesus Christ. Then flee at this sight, mine enemies, for the Lion of Judah has triumphed. Line of David. Alleluia. Alleluia. Alleluia.

Savior of the world, save me and aid me. Thou, who hast redeemed me by Thy Cross, and by Thy most precious Blood, I beseech Thee, O my God, O Hagios, O Theos, Hagios Ischyros, Hagios Athanatos Eleison Imas: Holy God, Mighty God, Merciful and Immortal God, have pity me, Thy creature, N... Be my support, O Lord: do not abandon me, do not reject my prayers. O God of my salvation, be always mine aid, O God of my salvation.

THURSDAY

Enlighten mine eyes with True Light, so they are not closed in eternal sleep, lest mine enemy should say I had prevailed over him. So long as my Lord is with me I shall not fear the malice of my enemies. O most sweet Jesus, preserve me, aid me, save me; that by saying only the Name of Jesus every knee shall bend, be it heavenly, earthly or infernal, and that every tongue shall confess that Our Savior, Jesus Christ, enjoys the Glory of His Father. Amen. I know beyond doubt, that as soon as I invoke the Lord, at any hour or any day, I shall be saved. O most sweet Lord, Jesus Christ, Son of the Great Living God, who performed such great miracles through the power of Thy Most Precious Name alone, and enriched the poor so abundantly, since by its power all demons flee, blind men see, deaf men hear, the lame walk aright, the dumb speak, the lepers are brought back to life, the inform are healed, the dead brought back to life: for once the most sweet Name of Jesus Christ is spoken, the ear is charmed and the mouth filled with what is most agreeable. And only by pronouncing it, it demons take flight, all knees bend, all temptations cease, and even the most evil are uprooted, all infirmities are healed, all disputes and combats between the world, the flesh and the devil dissipate, and one is filled with Heavenly joy; because, whoever invokes or shall invoke the Holy Name of God was, and shall be, safe. This Holy Name, which was spoken by the Angel before He was conceived in the womb of the Blessed Virgin.

FRIDAY

O gentle Name, Name which strengthens the heart of man, Name of life, salvation, joy; that precious, radiant, glorious and pleasant Name; that Name which fortifies the sinner, that Name which saves, leads, preserves and governs all; may Thou be pleased, most precious Jesus, by the power of that most precious Name, keep far from me the demon. Enlighten me, O Lord, for I am blind. Remove my deafness; rectify my lameness; give me speech, for I am dumb; heal my leprosy, restore health to me once more who art sick; resurrect me, for I am dead; give me life again, and surround me in every part, within as well as without, that being provided for and strengthened by this Holy Name, I may abide forever in Thee, praising Thee and honoring Thee, because all that is due to Thee, because, Thou alone art worthy of glory, the Lord and Eternal Son of God through Whom all things rejoice and are governed. Let praise, honor and glory be forever rendered unto Thee forever and ever. Amen. May Jesus be forever in my heart, and in my affections. Amen.

May Our Savior, Jesus Christ be ever within me, may He restore me, may He surround me, may He preserve me, may He be before me, may He lead me, may He be behind me, that He might preserve me; may He be above me, that He might bless me; may He be in me, that He might vivify me; may He be close to me, that He might govern me; may He be beneath me, that He might fortify me; may He be forever with me, that He might deliver me from the pain of eternal death; He Who liveth and reigneth forever and ever. Amen.

SATURDAY

Jesus, Son of Mary, salvation of the world, may the Lord be favorable unto me, gentle and propitious. May He grant me a holy and willing spirit to render the honor and respect which is due to Him who is the Liberator of the world.

Nobody can lay their hand upon Him, because His hour is not yet come, He Who is, Who was, and Who shall ever be, Who has been God and man, the Beginning and the End. May this prayer I make unto Him forever protect me against mine enemies. Amen. Jesus of Nazareth, King of the Jews, honorable title, Son of the Virgin Mary, have pity on me, a poor sinner, and according to Thy mercy, lead me in the path of eternal salvation. Amen.

Now, Jesus, knowing the things must come to pass concerning Him, came forward and said unto them: "Whom do ye seek?" They answered him, "Jesus of Nazareth." And Jesus said unto them, "I am he." Now Judas, who was to deliver him, stood with them. As soon as He had said unto them, I am He, they fell backwards upon the earth. Then Jesus asked them again, "Whom do ye seek?" They said again: "Jesus of Nazareth." Jesus replied, "I have already told you, I am he. If it is me that ye seek, let these men go their way (speaking of His Disciples).

The lance, the nails, the cross ✠, the thorns, the death which I have suffered, prove that I have erased and expiated the crimes of the unfortunate. Preserve me, O Lord Jesus Christ, from all afflictions of poverty and the snares of mine enemies. May the five wounds of our Lord be unto me a continual remedy. Jesus is the Way ✠. Jesus is the Life ✠. Jesus is the Truth ✠. Jesus has suffered ✠. Jesus has been crucified ✠. Jesus, Son of the Living God, have pity upon me ✠. Now, Jesus, passing went through the midst of them, and no-one could place his murderous hand upon Him, because His hour was not yet come.

THE SEVENTH DAY

The day of the Sun should be, so far as possible, dedicated solely to *occupation* and not to profession. We will recall that the only true rest from an intellectual point of view is the exercise of this preferred occupation; for the complete cessation of all physical or intellectual work may constitute the ideal situation for the brutish man, but not for a man who is sufficiently developed.

The prayer said on this day shall therefore be given in as complete and solemn manner as possible, either in the Magic Chamber, or preferably in a church, which is a wonderful Magic Laboratory, open to all, rich or poor. In winter and during bad weather, the first part of Sunday morning is therefore dedicated to this ceremony. In good weather, it is profitable to replace the temple, that work of men, with the direct manifestation of Nature, and prayer in the heart of the forest or the country is particularly recommended.

Sunday afternoon will be given over to either the preparation of magical objects provided by Nature and then adapted by the natural sciences, or to the esthetic education of the senses in museums or symphonic concerts, or to the performance of minor Operations of Ceremonial Magic, depending upon the time, place and arrangements taken. Finally, the evening will be dedicated to review and classify the results obtained during the week regarding one's occupations, whether in reading or in copying formulas and preferred works, or even at the theater, still depending upon the time and arrangements.

Returning to his laboratory, the Operator will end this day with a long meditation followed by a prayer before the altar or in the Magic ircle. It is at this moment that the use of insulators such as glass and wool should be especially studied.

Besides, adapting meditation to the environment and the individual cannot be explained in detail in such an elementary treatise: we hope that the examples given above will serve as a guide for the student, and that exercise and practice will easily activate the work begun by his desire and his efforts.

It is through this progressive exercise of meditation that one will come, little by little, to develop superior psychic abilities, from which flow the three most important orders of phenomena, classed by ancient authors under the names of *rapture*, *ecstasy* and *prophetic visions*.

RAPTURE

Rapture is a consequence of meditation on spiritual things, combined with a special respiratory rhythm in which expiration is progressively delayed. In this state the body is in catalepsy and the astral body is illuminated by its sudden elevation to the spiritual plane. An intense faith, a powerful and enduring *desire* for truth or justice are the primordial motives for the development of this psychic stasis. All the visions of Joan of Arc belong to this state. The various rituals of religious mysticism, and the fasts and prayers required are excellent guides for the Magister who wishes to develop these abilities, which we no longer insist upon, for this practice is dangerous and requires very specific teachings.

ECSTASY

Ecstasy manifests itself externally by the same phenomena (catalepsy or a fixed regard, particular respiratory rhythm, etc.); but in this state, there is an exteriorization of the astral body and vision at a distance. Certain deep states of hypnosis recently described by Colonel de Rochas come close to ecstasy, but in a passive mode. We will have an opportunity to discuss this state further in our last chapter. We will also find most interesting historical details in Volume II, chapter 50 of Agrippa (*Occult Philosophy*).

PROPHETIC VISIONS

One mustn't confuse visions with dreams.[141] A dream is often produced by the sudden afflux of nervous forces in the intellectual center, and the images born from these depending upon the last ideas which had disturbed this center. It is in fact on this observation that the majority of materialistic philosophers have based their theories.

On the other hand, a prophetic vision, which is generally very rare, is produced through an sudden illumination of the soul by the astral plane. The impressions which the vision so perceived leaves in the memory are profound and lively, and have a character such that those who experience them are never misled as to their value. Moreover, the spirit, truly freed from the shackles of matter, is susceptible to consciously experience the influence of the divine plane.

We have personally been able to judge the truth of these revelations from visions in many circumstances. But we think that meditation and above all prayer are the principle elements of training, and, for the rest, we advise you to take note of the following instructions:

"He who now wishes to receive divine visions should be disposed in his whole body, and to not have the brain subject to vapors nor the spirit to passions, and for him never to eat on that day nor drink anything which might cause inebriation. His room should be tidy and very clean of all dirt, also exorcized and blessed, and fumigated with incense. Once he had anointed his temples, his fingers wearing rings of dreams, a celestial image placed on his head and a consecrated card, having invoked divinity with holy prayers, the Operator shall lie down on his bed, having his thoughts focused on what he wishes to know; for it is thus that he will have visions most true and very certain, with a true illumination of understanding." (*Agrippa*).[142]

---

[141] In this translation the word *songe* has been translated as 'vision' and *rêve* as 'dream'. However, 'vision' is both a French and an English word and means the same in both language. *Songe* really refers to lucid dreaming, while *rêve* refers to general dreaming. For clarity we will use the word 'vision' for *songe* in this section.

[142] This is from Book III, chapter 51 of *Occult Philosophy*. *Three Books of Occult Philosophy* edited and annotated by Donald Tyson (pub. Llewellyn, 2014, ISBN 978-0-87542-832-1) is particularly recommended.

CHAPTER **XIII** – **RADIATING**

ADAPTATION – 3rd PHASE

The Magister and Society

Up till now we've taught the simplest practices which will provide the Magister with a progressive education of his will, while working on becoming more and more aware of psychic beings. We're implying, therefore, that the practitioner has succeeded in creating an atmosphere of sympathy both in the invisible and visible worlds around him, and we're going to ask him to use his work and his knowledge for the benefit of the profane and the ignorant: those who, far from understanding him, will respond to each kindness with peevish attacks, to each revelation with sarcastic remarks. This is the plainest outcome of this apostleship, and only those who have been in this situation know how much energy and doggedness is required to remain "good-natured" and smile before all those curious and feckless people of today who will become the adversaries and enemies of tomorrow, with only rare and noble exceptions. For it is but rarely that, from time to time, a generous heart reveals itself to be prepared for all the intellectual sacrifice and devotion necessary to endure the scrutiny of the common people; and this is the story of all the Adepts of Occultism from Pythagoras to Raymond Lully, and from Paracelsus to Martinez de Pasqually and Louis-Claude de Saint-Martin.

But those obstacles should never stop the seeker, and it is now that he should describe to us what the conduct of the Magister in society should be: what his intellectual influence in these hostile environments should be, and how, as a Knight of the Idea, he should rush into the fray without counting the number of his allies any more than he should count the number of his adversaries.

Oh, how many times do we counsel the independent disciple never to go beyond the studies of attraction and concentration! Surrounded by a few close friends, guided by the counsels of his seniors in group study, where silent work is the first rule observed, he can thus avoid the battles and vexations that apostleship prepares for him in the profane world. Out of reach of the temptations of triumph following the battle, may he remain a living vessel of the High Sciences, unknown to his enemies and also the curious. It is thanks to such men that the Hermetic Tradition has not been lost, and the wise Alchemist of the 15th Century, quietly pursuing his work in the depths of a cave instead of publicly triumphing over clerical ignorance, has bequeathed to posterity treasures which are more real than the Philosopher's Stone and the Elixir of Life.

Never forget, you who would forge ahead and model humanity as you have learned to model your own substance, never forget that, if you have a single moment of weakness, the matter which you have united within yourself will revolt against your actions, and you will become the first victim of the powers which you were unable to master. And now, if you are still ready, let us study together the possibilities of psychic radiation in the environment you are going to confront. [143]

Reading the Signs

Master of your passions and instructed in the mysteries of Nature, cast your eyes around you. [144] You are in the 19th Century, counting time from the revelation of the Essene Jesus. Gnosticism, finally vanquishing clerical oppression, manifests itself on all the planes through an unbelievable explosion of liberty. Ideas, finally freed from the time-honored constraints of tradition and

---

[143] This entire passage appears to reveal some of Papus' very personal thoughts and ideas. It is clear from the first part, as we have read earlier, that he took some of the betrayals by people he held as friends very personally, as he warns the budding occultist to beware of those who will support you for a time, before turning against you, either because of disbelief or to go along with the crowd. Yet his solution is by no means clear. On the one hand, he counsels the student to remain silent and hidden, so as neither to attract attacks nor to participate in the easy hubris of winning a fight, and in this he is close to the Martinist concept of remaining 'unknown', or drawing the mantle closely about him and hiding from the gaze of the profane, or in Saint-Martin's words, not wishing to make any noise; yet on the other hand he tells the reader that hardships and difficulties should not prevent him from going out to 'radiate' or transmit and share his ideas with the profane world, which he describes as a 'confrontation'. And, of course, this is exactly what Papus himself is doing!

[144] This first section is as poetic a description of the *fin de siècle* feeling as one may read anywhere, which is all the more remarkable when we remember that Papus was only 27 when he wrote this book! We can sense the exquisite tension between hope and despair, the possibilities and also the challenges of a society undergoing enormous change due to the relaxation of the iron grip that the Church and the State had previously held, over a people who are now free to pursue any avenue of study or thought. In a way, we are beginning to experience a similar feeling in the second decade of the 21st Century, where the initial promise of the internet, with its promise of instant connection and communication and the unlimited sharing of information and history, is beginning to manifest a darker side, with persecution, the promulgation of false news, the influencing of elections in other countries, and a general hardening of attitudes towards the weaker and more vulnerable members of society.

dogma, manifest their power through unbelievable affirmations and disconcerting negations. The existence of Homer is questioned, and the literary existence of Shakespeare is denied. Orpheus is seen to be only a wonderful myth. Pythagoras is a revealer of Chinese teachings; and the Buddha contends for the scepter of spiritual royalty with our Jesus. Faltering faith collapses beneath the bold revelations of science, the five thousand years of the Bible amuse many orientalist commentators on the chronology of the Brahmans, and the geologists are joining this chorus. Finally, Jacobus Burgundus Molay, Grand Master of the Temple, plants the banner of his Order on the black papal citadel, the last vestige of the Roman she-wolf.[145] An old world is perishing, and a new world is being born, and like Alexandria in the first Centuries of our era, the modern barque of Isis, Paris, sees a thousand rival school rising up, espousing a thousand contradictory philosophies; while over there in the East, dark rumblings make themselves heard, a clear indication of invasion by the barbarous Germani and Tartars. [146] Remember that you are called to do battle in such a moment. Remember the device inscribed on Isis' barque, the symbol of our science: FLUCTAT NEC MERGITUR [147] . Leave despair to the faint-hearted and the

---

[145] For those unaware of the myth of the founding of Rome, two twins abandoned at birth, Romulus and Remus, were nursed by a she-wolf. On reaching adulthood they decided to establish a city, but argued over it, with Romulus killing Remus and establishing the city in his name: Rome. Thus, Rome began with a fratricide, as did many Roman myths. One should note that Papus is conflating Roman mythology with the Vatican, Rome being founded, according to its Romulan mythology, in 753 B.C.E., and therefore all dates in the Roman Empire were counted from that date, or *Ab Urbe Conditur* (A.U.C., from the founding of the city).

[146] Papus is careful to use the old version for Germans, *germains*, rather than the contemporary term: *allemands*. To preserve this nuance, the Latin word for the germaine tribes, 'germani' has been used here.

[147] A Latin motto, meaning "She is tossed by the waves, but never sunk." It has been the motto of Paris since at least 1358, and appears on the coat of arms of the city as a ship sailing on rough seas. Now, given that Papus was at least aware at this time of the basic details of the lives of Jean-Baptiste Willermoz, Louis-Claude de Saint-Martin and Martinez de Pasqually, it seems unlikely that he would be unaware of the Scottish Rectified Rite which, following the Convent of Wilhelmsbad in 1782, modified the rituals of Baron von Hund's Rite of Strict Observance, initially practiced in Germany but which had spread at least to the Eastern part of France. In the 1770s. Two images used in the Grades which were retained in the French rewrite were that of a ship with a broken mast in stormy seas, with the motto: *In Silentio Et Spes Fortitudo Mea* (adapted from Isaiah 30:15, meaning 'In silence and hope is my strength'), and a broken column with the base intact, with the motto: *Adhuc Stat* ('It still stands' or 'It still endures'). Given Papus' earlier reference to Jacques DeMolay, with his implication that his

unlearned. Leave them to foretell the decline and fall of the Latin peoples. Remember that the Celtic strain persists, that the country of the druids and the fairies endures. Today you are born in the heat of battle, intellectual today, moral tomorrow, and perhaps physical at any moment. Learn, therefore, to conquer yourself and know how to die at your station, for that will be your supreme honor. Let the infirm and the unfit crowd around the rear-guard, and discharge jibes in the form of bullets. What does it matter to you! The society in which you come to live is created like this: accept the conditions which our epoch imposes upon you, and, as a true Magister – that is to say, as Master over external impulses and contingencies – calmly examine what remains to be done to make known the power of the apostleship of the Idea in such an age and in the bosom of such a civilization. You are surrounded by human beings: it is from them that you should expect salvation or doom, and it is on them that you will have to act. So, what is a human being, then?

According to circumstance, he is an ox or a pig guided by instinct and the grossest appetites; a tiger or a wild boar impelled by passions and governed by egotism and hate; a vulture or a parrot obsessed by selfishness, paltry things or prejudice; or sometimes even a man fantasizing about often false beliefs and always despotic and blinded by pride.[148]

Now, each of these beings bears the signature of the animal impulses which drive and dominate him written on his face. You, possessor of the secrets of Hermes, can first learn to tear away the mask on the human face which hides all the latent bestialities at the foundation of all beings, and as a person who has conquered their impulses, you should know how to conquer all the manifestations of impulses in Adam-Eve.

---

successors had finally toppled Rome, it is interesting to wonder whether he saw the close connection between these images, if he was aware of them, and the coat of arms of Paris.
[148] If these creatures appear vaguely familiar, they are indeed based on the four animals of the Merkabah, and the Sphinx is a theme to which Papus returns frequently. In his *Elementary Treatise of Occultism*, he included three tantalizing plates depicting "The Four Elements constituting the Sphinx", being the Eagle, Man, the Lion and the Bull or Ox. Later, he shows two more images described respectively as "The Evolved Sphinx" and "The Involuted Sphinx." Frustratingly he makes no reference to these images in the text, but so far as can be made out, the "Evolved Sphinx" has evolved the Eagle into a Dove, Man into an Angel, the Lion into a domesticated Dog, and the Ox into a Horse. Conversely, the "Involuted Sphinx" show the Eagle degenerated into a Vulture, Man into an Ape, the Lion into a Wild Boar, and the Ox into a Pig. From his description of the somatic types of man, it is clear that he sees these symbolic forms as manifesting physically in man, too.

This, then is how you may recognize the Adversary of Will, both in your own being and in those of men, your brothers.

The face, complexion, gait, writings, gesture which is the *origin* of handwriting, and the voice can all serve to quickly establish a diagnostic of the moral being. Since all human beings are a more or less balanced synthesis of the three impulsive centers which are governed by will, there is little point, at least in the early stages, to look for anything more than the two dominant elements of activity, and this is certainly sufficient for the present needs of the Magister. The four temperaments of the ancients (phlegmatic – sanguine – nervous – melancholic and bilious), the four forms of the Sphinx, and the four letters of the Tetragrammaton correspond to those gifts, whose origin may be discovered in man's constitution provided by Plato (Timaeus).

It would take a small volume to provide even a summarized study of all human characteristics, and although we have undertaken this task in a treatise which will appear at the same time as this one, we are going to attempt to summarize the indispensable points to know, in order be able to diagnose the characteristics of individuals which the Magister may encounter, in just a few pages.

The impulsive being is manifested in us through three modifications: the instinctive, the emotional and the intellectual, and the being of will combines all three. This is truly a point which will have been clearly grasped by anyone who had studied the theoretical side (in the first part of this treatise).

Now, all individuals in whom the instinct rules will be tranquil and slow, but also have the endurance of the ox, his sign, and will reveal himself to the observer's eye through the *whiteness* of his complexion, the moistness of his skin, and the slow manner of his gestures and his voice, as well as his gait. We will see the details shortly.

He who manifests the emotional being will be an active person, hurried, violent depending on the situation, demonstrating the image of his sign, the lion, which he bears in his being. He may be recognized at first glance by his *red* complexion, the firmness of his skin, the briskness of his walk and gestures, and the speed of his speech.

These are the first striking features of individuals in which matter predominates in a being's impulses.

But has the intellectual being gained the ascendancy? Then we will find the characteristics of the bird, so developed in women, with their mixture of excessive impressionability and a fast ability for assimilation. Here, *yellow* is the basis for the complexion, and the gestures are rapid and abrupt, like the speech.

Finally, the beings in whom the will, and therefore ambition, dominates are characterized by the somber color of their complexion and by their profound regard, the broadness of their gait and their gestures.

A quick and practical way to get a sense of these broad divisions is as follows: take a white point of reference, such as a piece of paper or, for the face, the collar of a shirt, and using this as reference, determine the color of the complexion of the individual you need to judge. By placing the closed fists of three different people on a piece of white paper, it is rare not to see at least two of the characteristic colors where just spoke about, in recalling that:

1. A white or clear yellow complexion (almost white) indicates an essentially phlegmatic and tranquil character, a person dominated by instinct;
2. A red complexion indicates an emotional character, active and passionate;
3. A yellow complexion indicates a melancholic or pessimistic character, and intellectual;
4. A black complexion or at least very dark, on the contrary, indicates will.

It is useful to perform these initial studies often and preferably with the hands, for, on the face, as we are going to see, one can find two complexions superposed: at the base a real and fundamental hue (as one sees in the hand), and on the surface an additional hue, which will determine the secondary element of the individual temperament. It is even through this secondary hue that one may further refine the diagnosis.

*
* *

Man isn't simply formed from an instinctive, emotional, intellectual or willful element; nor is he formed from the juxtaposition of two or several of these elements, but rather by their intimate union. It's similar to a chemical salt which one must first determine by decomposing its acid and alkali elements, and then further decomposing the acid in order to discover its constituent elements.

So, the preliminary analysis which the practice described above permits is sufficient to give a general indication of the problem we need to solve. A tranquil person can in fact appear at first glance as sensual, or meditative, or simply calm, depending on the elements which intimately come together in his fundament, which is the calm of the body. Thus, a phlegmatic who gives himself over to impulses is at his base no longer like the hieroglyph of the ox, but rather the pig;

but if he acts in the contrary sense and modifies his natural indolence, his hieroglyph will similarly change and become the horse instead of the ox. It is the same with the other divisions (active, intellectual and willful).

Unfortunately, the limited size of this treatise doesn't allow us to talk in as much depth as we would like about this subject, since as we have said before, an entire volume would be necessary. Nevertheless, we'll summarize the various practical processes to diagnose the characteristics in a series of tables

This diagnosis will be founded in the following manner:

1. From a distance one can make a preliminary determination based upon the *gait*, whether rapid or slow, and the length of the steps, whether long or short (refer to the tables);
2. Then examine the *complexion* following the procedures we have already outlined;
3. Next, one can make a specific study of the profile and above all of the nose, where concave traits indicate instinctive and emotional people, while convex suggests intellectuals and those driven by the will;
4. This initial examination will be concluded with the mouth, chin and eyes, to correct any errors made in the diagnostics already performed, as needed;
5. If possible, it is then permissible to examine the *hand*, which is studied from the point of view of its firmness, color and its lines;
6. Then one can verify all these elements by examining the handwriting, if one can procure a few lines written by the individual whom one wishes to know better.
7. A moderate study of the table below will allow the student to stay within the bounds of this preliminary classification.

Each of these general divisions is subdivided in practice into three groups corresponding to real Nature, and which one should know well. For the quickest and most practical way to do this, in our opinion, we recommend studying the face (above all the shape of the nose seen in profile) and studying the handwriting, when one can obtain it.

If the basic complexion appears to be white, when comparing the hand with a reference point (in this case a sheet of blueish-white paper), look closely at the face and see if the cheekbones are rosy. If, on the contrary, the face appears to be slightly yellow like old ivory on a white base, or if there is an extraordinary energy in the regard together with a dark complexion, this indicates the particular influence of will.

	GENERAL CHARACTERISTICS OF SIMPLE ELEMENTS	INSTINCTIVE OR TRANQUIL	ANIMAL OR ACTIVE	INTELLECTUAL OR PESSIMISTIC	ACTING THROUGH WILL
TRAITS	GAIT	Small, slow steps (Like a priest's walk)	Large, quick steps (The soldier)	Small, quick steps (The hopping of a bird)	Large, slow steps (Processional walk)
	HUE	WHITE	RED	YELLOW	DARK OR BLACK
	LIPS	Thick, white and weak	Thick, red and firm	Thin, tight and governed by the lower one	Thin, tight and straight (knife-like)
	CHIN	Large	Square	Receding and pointed	Projecting
HAND	HANDSHAKE	Weak and damp	Firm and warm	Bony and dry	Hard and cold
	FINGERS	Large and short, knotty	Thin and short, knotty	Thin and long (smooth)	Large and long (smooth or lightly knotty)
	FINGERTIPS	Spatulate or square	Square	Angular	Square or angular (the two thumbs often of a different type)
	LINES ON THE HANDS	Large, white and not very numerous	Deep and red, and not very numerous	Fine, thin and very numerous	Fine, deep and numerous
HANDWRITING	GENERAL CHARACTER	Round and luxurious (Calligraphy)	Hesitant and zigzag	Angular and sloped	Straight, firm and equal
	THE O'S AND A'S (in general)	Rounded and firm	Rounded and open	Angular and open	Angular and closed
	THE T'S	Cross bar omitted or hesitant	Ascending cross bar	Cross bar fixed, long and often descending	Short, straight cross bar, in the middle and very firm
	THE N'S	Rounded and well-formed	Round and poorly formed	Angular and elongated	Angular and compact
	HIEROGLYPH	OX	LION	EAGLE	MAN

The four following tables, covering the four basic divisions (instinctive, emotional, intellectual and willful), are sufficient, with a little work, for the Magister to obtain a preliminary sense of the beings on whom he wishes to act. Thus, the first part of the social part of the work, *diagnosis*, will have been accomplished.

To be absolutely complete, these tables should also include the influence of two other elements which modify certain details by their presence; for the human being always contains not just two, but *four* constituent principles. These divisions would lengthen our discussion and we do not include them here: these Tables, such as they are, will suffice amply for our current practice.

Once the diagnosis has been made, it is easy of act on them; for the will now possesses a firm foundation. Of all the actions which one could be called on to initiate, there are two kinds: defensive and offensive; that is, one can act in turn like an acid and an alkali towards the external environment. Now, the character of each of these actions will depend upon the diagnosis which was previously established.

The means to manage all types of men depends upon the following statement: *by exaggerating the dominant center of his impulsive being, man is always rendered passive, that is to say, disarmed*, since control of his reason, his good sense and his wisdom is erased in the face of passionate impetuousness, and because, through *attenuating the dominant center of his impulsive being* man is on the contrary active, on the defensive, and enlightened by good sense if he is instinctive, by reason if he is emotional in nature, and by wisdom if he is intellectual.

So, what is the main outcome of amplifying the active center in the four general human types we have studied?

Amplifying the instinctive center produces laziness, gluttony and inertia.

Amplifying the emotional center produces a flush of anger, lust or vanity.

Amplifying the intellectual center produces cold anger and envy.

Amplifying the will produces despotism, ambition and pride.

If you therefore wish to gain control over an instinctive person, seek to satisfy his gluttony, his laziness and his tranquility in the environment in which he moves. In this manner, you'll create around this being an atmosphere of absorbing habits which he will find hard to give up, without a strident appeal to his will.

To master the emotional person, seek to make use of his energy, contrive to always find new enterprises to begin, new obstacles to conquer, know how to make him angry from time to time, and don't forget that flattery is the surest weapon you possess in this instance.

INSTINCTIVE OR TRANQUIL

INSTINCTIVE OR TRANQUIL – GENERAL CHARACTERISTICS	TRANQUIL ANIMAL SENSUAL (taste)	TRANQUIL PESSIMIST CONTEMPLATIVE	TRANQUIL WILLFUL CALM
HUE: WHITE PROFILE AND NOSE (*Concave with a round end*)	Red on a white base Large head and short neck; large, wide and often colored nose; no bump on the nose which is completely concave	Yellow on a white base Large head, but skull gently projecting backwards and upwards; neck well detached from the shoulders, but not very long; a small bump on the *upper* part of the nose which is concave and larger at the base	Dark on a white base Large head, square at the top; short and slender neck. Calm but imperious gaze; a little bump on the *middle* part of the nose, which is also concave and large at the base
HAND (*Weak and damp*) LINES	Weak and hot Large Heart Line; Fate Line broken in several fragments, but cleanly; Mount of Venus grooved and well-developed	Weak and dry Fate Line well-developed and clean; Mount of Apollo bears some vertical lines	Weak and cold Big Head Line, long large and straight. Very few minor lines. Mount of Jupiter predominant as well as that of the Moon
HANDWRITING (*Round and luxurious*) T	Full downstrokes throughout, almost no upstrokes. Childish writing of a peasant Cross bar at the base, a gently rising bar but shaky and clumsy when present	Very clear but exaggerated writing in its roundness. Each letter is written carefully Missing or very thin cross bar, and very poorly drawn	Calligraphic full of well-drawn upstrokes Thin cross bar, quite long and ending in a club
O AND A HIEROGLYPH	Very heavy and an open A PIG	Closed and heavy OX	Closed but all well-drawn HORSE

ANIMAL OR ACTIVE

ANIMAL OR ACTIVE – GENERAL CHARACTERISTICS	ACTIVE INSTINCTIVE GAY	ACTIVE PESSIMIST PASSIONATE	ACTIVE WILLFUL OPTIMISTIC
HUE: RED PROFILE AND NOSE (*Concave with a pointed end*)	White on a red base Skull square on top; nose completely concave but pointed at its end; quite large nostrils	Yellow on a red base Skull inclined at the front and behind; a little bump on the *upper* part of the nose immediately after its root	Dark and black on a red base Skull inclined at the front and at the top, which gives a little pointed head with an arched forehead; a small bump on the *middle* part of the nose
HAND (*Firm and warm*) LINES	Firm and moist Red and large but not deep, except for the Saturn Line which is straight and deep; Mount of the Moon and Mars well-developed	Firm and dry Red and thin; Mounts of Venus and Mercury well-developed; Ring of Venus broken; Good Heart Line; grate pattern on the Mount of Venus	Firm (muscled) and warm Red and deep; Head Line well marked; Saturn Line double and broken; Mounts of Jupiter and Mercury predominant
HANDWRITING (*Hesitant and zigzag*)	Infantile stress, hesitant but quite readable; not sloping much	Thin, aristocratic, hasty, very sloped, not very readable; flourishes	Hasty, the letters lack the ends of words which is only *indicated*; writing small and often illegible although lacking flourishes
T	Big ascending cross bar, placed at the bottom of the letter	Thin and long cross bar, quite often a flourish	Short and straight cross bar, but thin
O AND A (*Round and open*)	Very round, well formed	Long and thin	Poorly formed but thick
HIEROGLYPH	WILD BOAR	DOG	LION

INTELLECTUAL OR PESSIMIST

INTELLECTUAL OR PESSIMISTIC – GENERAL CHARACTERISTICS	TRANQUIL PESSIMIST MELANCHOLIC	ACTIVE PESSIMIST INTUITIVE	PESSIMISTIC WILLFUL PERSON A PESSIMIST (properly called)
HUE: YELLOW PROFILE AND NOSE (*Convex with a pointed end*)	White on a yellow base Large head, projecting at back and on top; flat forehead; a little concavity on the *upper* part of the nose which ends in a convexity which is often round	Red on a yellow base Pointed head, projecting at back and top; forehead retreating; a small concavity in the *middle* part of the nose, ending in a parrot's beak with nostrils which are often red	Dark and black on yellow base Elongated head projecting at back and on top; forehead arched; nose completely convex with a thin bridge, ending in the beak of an eagle
HAND (*Bony and dry*) LINES	Bony and moist; fingers short and smooth Many pale lines; Mounts of the Moon and Saturn well-developed; Fate Line well indicated although often broken	Bony and hot; fingers long and smooth Many fine, red lines; Mount of Apollo and Venus well-developed; good Heart Line; ring of Venus of hepatic color and quite long	Bony and cold; fingers long and knotty Many fine and deep lines thought dark-colored; Mounts of Saturn and Jupiter very well-developed; Mount of Venus flat; Mount of Apollo grooved, fine hepatic lines and strong; good Head Line
HANDWRITING (*Angular and sloped*) T	Clear, relatively round, well formed; full and loops shown; large flourishes at the end of words; quite high and sloping Long cross bar, thin and hesitant	Small, jerky, pointed; often very sloping, neither full nor with well-drawn loops; many flourishes even in the middle of words; heavy writing Cross bar accompanied or ending with a flourish (often missing, or placed beneath the letter). No club at the end	Fine writing, very pointed, tall letters, spidery and light; some flourishes at ends of words, writing often original in its details, and aristocratic Cross bar ending in a club but long and fine
HIEROGLYPH	DOVE	PARROT	EAGLE

WILLFUL

WILLFUL – GENERAL CHARACTERISTICS	WILLFUL CALM AMBITIOUS	WILLFUL ACTIVE ENTREPRENEURIAL	WILLFUL PESSIMIST PRIDEFUL
HUE: DARK AND BLACK **PROFILE AND NOSE** (*Convex with a round end*)	White on a dark base Gross head, large and square; forehead large, white and arched at the base, for the head is projected up and out; aquiline nose with a concavity at the upper part, round and often large at its end; large, round and advancing chin	Red on a black base Head mainly small and pointed; forehead large and colored, arched at the top and bottom, with head projected up and a little outward; aquiline nose with concavity in middle, round end, narrow at the base; chin pointed and advancing	Yellow on a black base Long head with forehead projecting up, high and arched without concavity; nose completely convex with a thin bridge, with a round end
HAND (*Hard and cold*) **LINES**	Hard, thick and moist, short fingers and knotty but white Head Line large and pale, predominating; Mount of Jupiter and the Moon predominant	Hard, thick and warm, short fingers, knotty and colored Heart Line long and colored; Head Line deep: Mounts of Jupiter and Mercury predominant; Plain of Mars filled with lines	Hard and cold. Long and knotty fingers. Well-developed Apollo Line; Head Line dark and thin, but straight; Mounts of Jupiter and Apollo predominant
HANDWRITING (*Straight, closed and equal*)	Small, round, well-formed letters; closed As; no loops, straight and well-spaced lines; clear overall; writing not sloped and almost straight	Great elliptical letters formed in haste; open As; straight lines but unequally spaced; writing sloped and thick	Great elliptical and original letters; closed As; with straight lines, but very unequally spaced. The writing indicates vanity and pretention, elongated writing but a little pinched, with many flourishes
T (*Characteristic of different groups*)	Straight cross bars, firm and uniformly applied	Rising cross bars, beginning with a loop and ending with a club	Straight cross bars descending or at least ending in a point, often loops, always with original touches
HIEROGLYPH	MATURE MAN	CHILD / APE	OLD MAN / SATURN

For the intellectual, on the contrary use admiration, and contrive to replace the physical activity he really needs. Satisfy his little whims, which you have taken the time to get to know, and don't forget that jealousy or envy, stirred up from time to time against some person or other, will make him its slave whenever you have need. For the intellectual's weakeness is that he is prepared to do things out of spite!

But concerning the fiercely willful, he who seems so frightening at first, quickly learn about his hidden ambitions, and strike him directly by fanning his colossal pride. Accept his despotism and direct his vanity, and you will create a child who believes that he governs you, when in fact he's the instrument of your plans.

So, this is how you attack. And it is truly an outline of this knowledge which women possess instinctively, without any need to understand the rules. The woman profits from her apparent passivity to penetrate the intimate nature of the man on whom she wishes to work. She analyses his whims, ambitions and passions, and many months are devoted to this preparatory work, made all the easier by man's abandonment of his intelligence with regard to the one he loves. By the time this study is concluded, the woman knows her companion better than he knows himself. She slowly shrouds him from his actions, and progressively replaces his desires and resolutions with habit, with cherished ideas which she regularly invokes, and within a few years the being is imprisoned in a circle of reflexes more difficult to break out of than chains of steel. Then love can disappear, for habit has taken its place, and the sorceress has, once again, accomplished her Great Work.

Woman, the Guardian born from the mysteries of Eros, instinctively knows well those magical secrets, which normally demands long work and constant study to be penetrated by means of deductive reasoning.

So as not to drag out our discussion, we are going to summarize, symbolically, the rules to be followed by the Magician in the current political environment.

Do you want to act upon an ox? Be like *grass* if you need to keep and disarm him; and be like a *spur* if you need to evolve him.

Do you need to have authority over the lion? See how he makes himself endearing and gentle to *the one who bring his fodder* to the cage; but if you need to govern him completely, be the *tamer*.

Now, do you need to attract the fickle bird? Quickly spin the *mirror* with a thousand faces, and the fascinated lark will let you hold him in your hand. In the other instance be the *fowler*, and firmly close the cage in which you have enclosed the imaginative intellectual, so flighty in his nature.

Man presents himself through pride, male vanity and his despotism as a strong being; yet remember that *woman*, though frail and delicate, causes this wild man to fall to his knees. Know, too, that the scintillating *Idea* carries lovers of the divine along in its wake.

Such then, symbolically described, are the rules of opposition that one should observe in all intellectual battles. Disciples of the Occult Sciences are well acquiainted with these symbols, so it's pointless to stress them any further. The rest of mankind wouldn't understand these several simple points any better even if they were given extensive explanations. Now, let's end this topic here.

*
* *

The Magister now knows the individual or collective environment in which his actions are going to radiate. How, then can he use these actions?

Just as the tiny piece of yeast which acts and works on the large mass of inert dough, the Initiate must be ready to awaken the forces and ideas latent in all humanity. Nothing is contemptible in Nature, neither a gain of dust nor a man, and each being who possesses reason contains hidden treasures within him which the Magister must discover and use. For this, adaptation is indispensable.

As an intellectual, if you despise the company of instinctive people, if you flee their circle for fear of its pervasive moral impurity, avoid the crowd for concern for its vulgarities, and shun the patriots in the cafés for terror of their silliness, you are both a moral and physical coward, and you have no concept of dying for a moment for the ideal so that you may be reborn more alive to truth. Remember the company in which the divine personality of the Essene Jesus evolved, and ask his disciples if he fled from the common people or the uneducated? Now, these impure collectives are the dough which the magical yeast must make rise, and the first condition for this action is to plunge yourself as deeply as possible into that inert mass, so full of unrealized potential.

So, for a moment, adjust your personality to the social environment: your training will protect you from every stain, and like a pure diamond, you will come out of the mire without a speck of mud penetrating the outer skin of your moral being.

Go into the circle, and throw out countless divine ideas as food for those who are ignorant of good; manifest your wisdom on the level of commonsense for the crowd, and may your hearty laugh correct morals and help the torpor of the ignorant; abase your universality to the level of the sectarianism of the false patriots so that, by suddenly opening them up, their repressed divine power might evolve in these narrow brains. Finally, always be courageous, and remember that the social activity of the Magister can be summarized by these three verbs:

TO HEAL
TO SOW
TO CONSOLE

You must know how to cure people of ignorance as well as pride, of false knowledge as well as false belief, and moral illness as much as physical illness.

You must sow now and leave the harvest to the future; you must sow without counting the seeds, without anticipating the value of the terrain, and without waiting for the rains of heaven to come and fertilize the unthankful earth.

And finally, his knowledge of the mysteries of death and those of birth should make the Magister a fleeting incarnation of the source of all good, when destiny has ravaged a soul, a family or a people.

Then the voice of *knowledge* should he raised, and the calm of the infinite should be evoked while the revelations of the Absolute are recalled. Rhythmic and slow, the magical prayer is begun, and the invisible forces of the chain come to enchant the souls of the living and to preside over the evolution of the dead. Such should be the threefold mission of the true Adept of the Science of the Mages.

The Magister and Religion

Few problems are as troubling for the sincere Magister as religious ones. Faced with the revolting ignorance of a fanatical clergy for whom wealth has become the sole representation of Divinity upon earth, and faced with the obtuseness and depth of the mysterious books delivered as fodder to the jibes of skeptics, what direction should he take?

The Magister is the living guardian of a lofty truth of which religions are but pale emanations. But in the West no religion better manifests the esoteric teaching than Catholicism, and no religion is more given over than this to the sectarianism of its priests, against which Jesus' judgement concerning the Pharisees would be ignored nowadays.

Prayer is no longer understood or practiced. The Mass, that purely Magical Ceremony, is sold to the living for the dead, and to atheists for the naïve, and in the absence of the triple meaning of the Hebrew hieroglyphs drawn by Moses, superstition and pride have invaded the very temples where we should be seeing the Divine Word adapted to human nature. But the end of clericalism is near, and the Gnosis will be made known and be revealed before long in all its splendor.

The priesthood should be exercised FREELY, during the periods of psychic rapture which will not last longer than a lunar month, and whose post will be consecutively filled by well-instructed men, in a faith which is entire and reflective and in the spirit of total self-sacrifice. This would be the sacred occupation of those who practice a trade during the other eleven months of the year.[149]

The Magister should also remain independent in the midst of all religions, all of which deserve equal respect. Each continent has generated its own flora and fauna and human nation. Each nation, each great people has crystallized its psychic aspirations into a religion; and each religion is alive due to its possession of a particle of the one, sole Truth. The Magister should know how to pray as easily in a church as in a temple, in a synagogue as in a mosque, for the Divine Word reveals itself equally in all, only beneath a different veil. Leave it to the guardians of these veils to quarrel over the different colors, and let us instead commune in unity with the Adepts of the Sanctuary.

We said that the Catholic Mass was a Magical Ceremony. It now remains for us to end this study by expanding on our comment in a few lines.

The Mass is divided into three principle parts: *The Preparation*, which extends from the Introit up to the Consecration of the Bread and Wine; *The Consecration*; and finally, *The Conclusion*, which lasts from the Communion of the Priest until the end.[150]

In esoteric terms, this is the meaning of this division.

------

[149] This was the year when Papus was admitted into the newly-formed *Gnostic Church* of Jules Doinel, or Tau Valentin II, which was based on his spiritual initiation into the Cathar Church through a series of visions or dream in the latter part of the 1880s. This particular paragraph reflects the enthusiasm of this 27 year-old for a new Church devoid of money and cynicism, and probably also reflects the manner in which Doinel originally intended his new church to function. Although we are now used to the concept of Independent Catholic and Gnostic priests and bishops holding down a job and following their sacerdotal occupation in their space time for no salary, often in a chapel at home, this was certainly a radical concept when first envisaged towards the end of the 19th Century.

[150] Remember that in the Roman Catholic faith, it used to be only the priest who took communion, though this tradition changed following the introduction of Vatican II in 1962. Before then, from 1570 to 1962, the Tridentine Mass was said entirely in Latin, and the congregation did little more than watch the priest perform all the actions of the Mass on their behalf. Now the people hear the Mass in their native language and receive the bread, though the wine is still often reserved to the priest alone.

During the first part, the Priest, symbolic image of the Microcosm, after making confession of his faults, offers himself as an expiatory victim in the name of all the faithful present. In this manner he raises up the soul of these faithful as a sacrifice to God, and he concludes by offering in a visible sign of sacrifice that which Nature has most perfectly produced: bread and wine.

That is the *evolution* of the mortal and natural inferior towards the Divine, an evolution which can be drawn as a triangle pointing upwards, the symbol of fire.

It is then that the Priest magically consecrates all these symbolic objects. The Great Mystery is almost accomplished.

Indeed, once the consecration has begun, the fluidic current changes direction. It is no longer the inferior which rises up towards the superior. Now the Divine Word rushes forth from the highest heavens to be united with the matter offered as sacrifice. The Bread becomes the symbolic flesh of the Son, and the Wine becomes the miraculous Blood involuted from heaven to earth. The incarnation of the Universal Spirit in the Celestial Virgin is once more accomplished.

It is then that the Priest communicates with the Divine power and incarnates this power into himself. The union of God and Man is accomplished.

Turning towards the faithful, the Priest extends his hands, and his benediction unites the congregation with the symbolic receptacle of Divinity.

Solomon's star perfectly expresses this double action of evolution and involution, of which the Mass is just a translation for our eyes.

Every religion possesses a similar esotericism, yet the priests of all the religions of the West only have one point in common: their ignorance and their inveterate bigotry.

And so, we should leave each country to practice its preferred religion, and focus all its efforts on transforming the clergy through education. That is still the best service one can provide. And in the meantime, if you are Catholic, go to church, hear the Mass, and learn its lessons on Magic. Also meditate on the first two Pythagorean verses:

- Worship the immortal gods.
- Then keep your Faith.

The Magister and his Country

Destiny weighs so heavily on current societies, that at any moment the Magister can find himself seized by pitiless teeth which would grind him up if he ignores his duty. Whether it be in the battle to provide for his material existence through exercising his trade, or whether it be through contact with the crowd and ambitions of every shade, or in connection with the State, all around him blind and deadly powers oppress the will.

He whose initiation is imperfect, he who loses his courage and audacity at the least attack by Nahash [151] will flee the battle, and pay his duty to the collectivity with cowardice and insults. Now, in our times, there is no harder proof to pass through than that of an army barracks for an intellectual, yet this feeble reflection of the ancient initiations must not frighten the Magister worthy of this title.

As much as the idea of universality and liberty should reign in a society which is hierarchically and magically organized, so too the idea of nationhood and necessity currently rule in our sick and disorganized society.

Therefore, as much as the duty of the Magister consists of devoting all his powers to the transformation of society towards a synarchic organization, so too his knowledge, *so long as this transformation hasn't been accomplished*, obliges him to obey the Laws of Fate imposed on his will by Providence, as compensation for his initiatory development.

The army is the living incarnation of Destiny in our Century.[152] Therefore, we should strive to transform this collectivity in the form of Providence, by destroying the reason for its existence: egotism and international hatred.

---

[151] The Serpent.

[152] The passage concerning the army and war is particularly poignant given the times (and let us not forget that one of his heroes, Louis-Claude de Saint-Martin, had also served as a commissioned officer in the Garrison of Foix a Century earlier). Europe was particularly unstable at this time, mainly because most of the countries had colonies of which they were fiercely protective, and a number of reciprocal treaties had been signed by countries surrounding, and potentially threatening France. It is sometimes forgotten that Hitler was not the first of Germanic descent to march down the Champs-Élysées in Paris, and in 1870, following the Siege of Paris, German troops had done exactly that, as well as annexing part of France – Alsace and Lorraine – during that war. The Triple Alliance between Germany, Austria-Hungary and Italy, and a hostile attitude towards England over her colonies in Africa, had further isolated France. German Field Marshal Alfred von Schlieffen was beginning to formulate his plans for invading France through neutral Belgium in the event of war, a plan which was finally put into action in 1914. So Papus was definitely writing this apparently out-of-place patriotic section to record the

But if the collectivity in which you were born, which has nourished you with its ideas, with its soul, with its generous aspirations and its genius, suffers one of these crises of fever called war in the common tongue; remember that your personality should disappear before the need to defend the collectivity: family, province, nation or race. Before Destiny you are nothing more than a cell like all the rest; so, have the strength of soul to sacrifice yourself in advance, and remember that the first three pieces of knowledge you possess can be summarized in these terms: to know how to suffer, to know how to abstain; and to know how to die. If your pride cannot bend to the intellectual brutishness of a non-commissioned officer, you are incapable of understanding and enduring an initiatory trial of a purely physical order, and you only merit employment as a eunuch, a valet or a lowly courtesan with all their analogical meanings.

So, fight militarism and reform its defective points in times of peace, if you feel this is your duty, since militarism is essentially the enemy of all intellectuality. But when Destiny inscribes its Laws and international brutality is unleashed, if your will was incapable of preventing that crime against humanity which is called a war, if Magic has been unable to provide you with the power to prevent the triumph of Power, then rejoin the body of combatants and, with your dynamism, increase the number of the national force. In doing so, you absolutely fulfill your duty as a Magister which Providence has placed in such a society and under such cruel Laws. If, on the contrary, you flee, you diminish you own people by your lack of contribution, and in the event of defeat, you have contributed to the annihilation of your own social body.

These teachings accord with those of all higher initiations, and if you doubt that for an instant, open a biographical dictionary and read about the life of Socrates, model and master of Magism in Greece. Did his genius, as translator of the divine mystery, prevent him from fighting for his country?

Here the great truth is affirmed, that fear of losing his carnal envelope at the hand of a thug or a madman has never stopped a true initiate. Plato accepted the status of slave without question, despite being an initiate, from which he was only freed by a miracle; and as for Socrates, read on:

"But in avoiding honors and offices, Socrates fulfilled the duties of a citizen in an inflexible manner, and none surpassed him in courage and justice, the two civic virtues *par excellence.*

---

existence of a potential threat, and perhaps also to cover himself in the event of war, in case the esoteric society used his name to say that they were above national wars, and claimed conscientious objection.

"As a soldier, we see him suffer without complaining of privation. He marched with bare feet, barely clothed, over ice. He endured hunger and fatigue better than Alcibiades himself and the other soldiers. He fought at Delium, at Potidaea, and at Amphipolis. He acted in battle as if he was in the streets of Athens, with superb demeanor and disdainful regard. In two of these campaigns, he saved the lives of Alcibiades and Xenophon.

"In Athens, Socrates only fulfilled a public function once. He was *prytanis* when the ten generals from the Battle of Arginusae were tried, and defended them before the people. Later, under the dominion of the oligarchy of the Thirty, he refused to go to bring Leon the Salaminian before them, whom they wished to put to death, despite his familial connections with them. Thus, Socrates defended justice against all the powers, against the people and against the tyrants."

PAUL JANET
Dict. Phil.

To those who preach moral or physical cowardice to you, or who demand proof and names, since Magic is *traditional*, its teachings are as ancient as the world, immutable as Truth, and the examples they provide are many and known. Occultism is not invented, and it is not modified according to the whims of caprice, any more than it changes over the course of days, months or years. It reveals or adapts: that is all.

———

Bibliography

To diagnose character:

DESBAROLLES………………………………*Chiromancy.*
POLTI ET GARY……..………………………*The Theory of Temperaments.*

To study the Macrocosm:

STANISLAS DE GUAITA…………………............*The Serpent of Genesis.*
JULES LERMINA..………………….................*Practical Magic*
                                      (The Elementals).
G. VITOUX…………………………………..*The Limits of the Unknown.*

To study the Microcosm:

PAPUS..…………….....................................*Methodical Treatise on Occult*
                                      Knowledge.
DR. BARADUC…………………………………*The Vital Force.*

CHAPTER XIV – THE MAGISTER AND THE MICROCOSM

MAGNETISM AND HYPNOSIS

Radiation – Esoteric Part

Those were the exoteric actions, those which the crowd and the ignorant can know. Let us now begin the personal work of the Magister and the description of his work of using astral radiation, which are esoteric actions, and which demand silence and contemplation.

Here we must summarize the processes of magnetic action on the Microcosm and the Macrocosm, the first effect of the radiation of will activated by the Magister.

We are going to look at:

1. The actions produced in man by hypnotism and magnetism, and the processes put into play to produce these actions.
2. The actions produced in Nature by incantation and conjuration, and the processes used to this end.
3. The actions produced by the combination of magnetic radiation and incantation, which allow us to comment on the preliminary elements of occult medicine.

Hypnotism and Magnetism

We already know, from what we said in the section on Theory, that any excessive excitation of one of the impulsive centers produces a break in the connections[153] which unite the impulsive being to the man of will.

---

[153] In French the term *rapport* has been used throughout. Though a word used in English as well, it was felt important to use an English word, and therefore the word 'connection' is used throughout. Here this is used in the sense of the relationship which is established between the hypnotists and his subject, which is of a psychological or mental nature. Indeed, a number of terms used in this section, including a reference to multiple personalities, prefigure mainstream psychology, and it is well known that the science of psychology draws its roots from magnetism and hypnosis.

From this arises certain mental states which manifest in the human being and also in animals, states which are classed under the general title of hypnotism and magnetism.

Magnetism, which uses the fluidic forces emanated by the human being, is one of the experimental branches of Magic, as Baron du Potet[154] clearly saw; but it isn't *the whole of Magic*, as an overly superficial study has claimed, since one can look in vain in his book "Magic Unveiled" for an even slightly serious description of the stars and the practical determination of their influence.

As has been clearly demonstrated by de Rochas, hypnotism forms a kind of transition between the state of being awake and the magnetic states designed by the aforementioned practitioner under the name of "profound states of hypnosis."

Leaving aside any theoretical discussions, we're going to look at the different practical means one can use to cause hypnosis in a human being.

We will class these practices in the following way:

1. Determining the subject's state of hypnotic receptiveness.
2. Hypnotizing the subject.
3. Determining the phases and deep states of hypnosis.
4. Review various procedures for waking the subjects.

1. State of Receptiveness

Despite the claims of certain medical schools, we can say that not all individuals are susceptible to being hypnotized. The percentages obtained in the hypnotherapeutic laboratories of La Charité is 40% for men and 60 – 70% for women.

Certain quick procedures permit one to obtain a preliminary idea of the influences which hypnosis can have on a subject.

---

[154] Jules Denis, Baron du Potet, (1796 – 1881) was a homeopath and mesmerist who lived in Paris and London. He was a member of the Theosophical Society and considered an adept by Mme. Blavatsky. He was also highly regarded by Lévi, who nonetheless didn't share Denis' belief that mesmerism cold be used to contact the dead and even disembodied spirits. Alarmingly, perhaps, his reputation was such that a man was convicted for murder and executed due to the sole testimony of "one of Dr. Potet's clairvoyants." In 1852 he published a book titled *La magie dévoilée et la science occulte* ('Magic Unveiled and Occult Science'), which is referenced here by Papus, though from his comments it is clear that he didn't see it as doing more than contributing to a part of the topic of Magic.

From among the numerous processes used to this end, we'll select the following:

1.   Attraction from behind (Moutin procedure).
2.   Attraction of the little finger.
3.   Suggestion in a state of wakefulness.
4.   Influence using a brilliant point.
5.   Influence using a rotating mirror.
6.   Influence using a magic mirror.

We will briefly describe each of these processes.

Attraction from behind – Place the subject in a standing position, with their two feet together. Then place your two hands flat on the subject's shoulder blades, standing behind them, and gently remove the hands after a few moments. If you are dealing with a very impressionable person, their shoulders will follow the movement of your hands and they will be attracted backwards, despite themselves. Mr. Moutin described this procedure in his book on "The New Hypnotism."

Attraction of the little finger – Ask a subject to give you their right hand after taking off their glove. Then position the hand with the palm facing downwards, and press the fingers gently with your left hand, leaving the little finger free. Then attract this little finger toward you by making small, slow horizontal passes over it with your right hand, and repeat these passes until it follows the movement of attraction. You can then give the verbal suggestion to the subject or to the little finger to remain separated from the others, in spite of everything, until the moment when you wish to end the phenomenon.

Suggestion in a state of wakefulness – Suggestion in a state of wakefulness is reached by staring fixedly at the subject in the eyes, and commanding them in a strong voice and with an air of authority to do such and such thing (close the eyes and you cannot open them, you can no longer open your mouth, etc., etc.). Subjects susceptible to this procedure are the most sensitive.

Influence using a brilliant point and a rotating mirror – If you have a subject focus on a brilliant point, either fixed or in motion, and after a few minutes the subject feels a heaviness in their eyelids or experiences an irresistible desire to fall asleep; then we can confidently proceed to hypnotic phases with such a subject.

Influence using a magic mirror – People whether normally hypnotizable or not who, if when placed in front of a magic mirror they see colors or forms, both types are capable of becoming excellent sensitives.

*
* *

We will leave aside those subjects who are resistant to these various procedures, and instead work with subjects who are more sensitive, in the subsequent experiments.

2.   Hypnotizing the Subject

Once identified as sensitive, the subject can be hypnotized.

Several methods can be used to this end, among which we will describe the following:

1.   Simple suggestion.
2.   Brilliant point.
3.   Rotating mirror.
4.   Gaze.
5.   Passes.

Simple suggestion – Gently gaze into the subject's eyes and, without being brusque, command them to close their eyes. Then command them, still with a gentle voice, to lose sense in their skin, and affirm to them at that moment, still without brusqueness, that they are falling asleep, that they are feeling sleep overtaking them more and more, which will be confirmed in a few moments with someone who has a moderately sensitive nature.

Brilliant point of light – This procedure is the most commonly known. It consists of having subject fix their view on a brilliant point (such as a nickel button, the blade of a lancet, a small mirror, etc.), placed at the level of the forehead before the two eyes. This position forces the subject to center their sight upwards and centrally, and achieves hypnosis very quickly.

Rotating mirror – The use of the rotating mirror of Dr. Luys is, in our opinion, preferable to all the other means for safety and speed. We particularly recommend the use of the mirror with a single head, and covered with nickel-plated copper. The manufacturer is Mr. Robillard, at 25 rue Notre-Dame de Nazareth, Paris. Place this mirror at the height of the subject's eyes, around .5 centimeters from them, making sure that the luminous scintillations pass properly in front of the eyes. The subject is seated in an armchair, with the head supported. Sleep is normally achieved at the end of twenty to thirty minutes by this process.[155]

Gaze – The use of a gaze as a means of hypnosis is a tiring method but has great power, and allows one to obtain good results when all the other means have failed. This is how it is done.

Have the subject sit facing you, their back turned towards the light. Then take the subject's two hands, holding the thumbs gently in your hands. Then, following the ritual outlined in the section about training the sight, stare steadily at the pupil of the subject's right eye. Sleep will be achieved all the more quickly if you add the use of suggestion to this procedure.

Passes – Begin as for the procedure for gaze, outlined above, but the subject's two thumbs should be brought together in the left hand of the magnetizer, who makes intense downward passes from the subject's head to the level of their stomach, for five or six minutes. Then place the subject's hands at their sides, and continues the passes with both hands. The sleep produced by this technique is of another order than the sleep produced by the preceding hypnotic procedures. We will speak further about this shortly, on the subject of profound states.

DETERMINING THE PHASES

I

In the first of the hypnotic phases, all the subject's members are limp. If you take an arm and let it drop, the arm will fall without resistance on the part of the subject, who is then deeply asleep and can perhaps be compared to someone who is dead-drunk. At this time, their respiration is deep and regular. This is the phase of LETHARGY.

---

[155] Dr. Luys also worked at La Charité hospital in Paris. This apparatus was also made with four arms which, when rotating at speed, was apparently capable of hypnotizing a roomful of people. Given the size of the apparatus (which may be seen on YouTube at: www.youtube.com/watch?v=SC2LRtYXdZs), with its long bars holding the mirrors, it seems that the instruction in the book to place it .5 centimeters from the eyes is unlikely, and it is rather more likely that the apparatus was placed at least half a meter from the subject, since having a quickly rotating instrument that close to the eyes would be extremely dangerous!

II

If, in this phase, you forcibly open the subject's eyes, or if you act in a different manner on them, the second phase will commence.

The members stiffen and keep the positions you give them, whatever their attitudes. The subject has fixed eyes (remember this well) and looks straight in front of them or at the spot where you direct their eyes. They don't hear you, however loudly you speak. They are completely *closed* to the exterior world. They are in CATALEPSY.

It is in this phase that one can place their head on one chair and their feet on another, with an empty space between these two points. It is also in this phase that *ecstasies* are produced.

III

If you now blow on the subject's eyes, or make passes, or if you stroke them gently on their forehead, the state changes completely.

The subject speaks and acts absolutely like a person who is awake. They can talk to you, but they aren't conscious of the surrounding environment, and take no account of where they are.

They are then in the third phase: LUCID SOMNAMBULISM.

In this state they manifest several specific characteristics which it is very important to know.

Firstly, they are *suggestible*. You can order them to see or to do such and such a thing, not only when asleep but also at a time when they are awake, and this vision will persist, and this action will be executed not only for days, but for months, and even a year, depending on the order given.

At the moment the subject completes the suggestion, they becomes *unconscious* and obeys their impulse without argument, and, a very important fact to note, they suddenly loses their feeling, only to regain it following the completion of the suggested action. Thus, the subject will see everything they have been ordered to see, and will execute everything they had been ordered to perform, but with exceptions[156] which we cannot study here.

In a somnambulistic state, another fact takes shape, and that is the possibility of a *change in personality*.

You say to a subject: you are not yourself, you are a Member of Parliament, and you are making a speech in the Chamber. You will then see the subject

---

[156] I am convinced that the subject's free will still endures, and can overtake action in an instant to combat a criminal suggestion. [PAPUS]

suddenly enter into the skin of the person you have just imposed on them, and take on the personality of the role you are making them play. In this way you can change the personality many times at will.

It is also in this state that *vision at a distance* can be produced in certain magnetized subjects.

So, to summarize all that we have said, here are the characteristics of the three states:

1. *Lethargy* – Deep sleep.
2. *Catalepsy* – Fixed stare. Stiff members.
3. *Somnambulism* – Suggestiveness. Change of personality. Vision at a distance.

We've described the principal phases. Doubtless, a great number of intermediate states and combinations of states exist, but there's no point in becoming tangled up in that question.

To finish, let's note that, according to hypnotizers, these phases always succeed one another in the following order:

1. *Wakefulness*; 2. Lethargy; 3. Catalepsy; 4. Somnambulism;
5. *Wakefulness*; 6. Lethargy; 7. Catalepsy; 8. Somnambulism;
9. *Wakefulness*, etc., etc.

So, one can draw this as a circle.

*
* *

These purely hypnotic phases hadn't been linked to the earlier work of the magnetizers prior to the recent work of Lieutenant-Colonel de Rochas, Administrator of the Polytechnic School. This researcher, the author of most inquiring experimental discoveries in this area, such as the very recent *Exteriorization of Sensibility*, and on its consequences from the point of view of enchantment, summarized his early works on the profound states in an article for *Initiation*, which, despite our desire to avoid citations, we felt obliged to reproduce in full, sending the reader to the author's work[157] for the supporting details.

---

[157] A. de Rochas – *Les Etats profonde de l'Hypnose* ("States of Deep Hypnosis"), Paris, in 8°, Chamuel, 1891. [PAPUS]

STATES OF DEEP HYPNOSIS

The three states of hypnosis described by Mr. Charcot have become classical, despite the School at Nancy, which either never worked with sufficiently susceptible subjects, or else didn't take all the precautions necessary to verify phenomena that they hadn't themselves discovered first.[158]

These states are: lethargy, catalepsy and somnambulism. I won't return to their specific characteristics, and I will limit myself to remarking that the doctors of Salpêtrière don't appear to have gone further than the somnambulistic state, since they have never indicated other phases than certain secondary states linking the principle stages which we have just named.

No doubt this arises from the fact that these practitioners, fearing a connection being made between their research and the practices of the magnetizers, limited themselves to producing hypnosis either through the use of very weak agents such as a sudden noise, pressure on the ocular globes or the top of the skull; or by procedures whose effect stops when an initial result is produced. An example would be using a fixed stare, which stops acting as soon as the subjects close their eyes.

Seeing that these subjects are more or less suggestible, one seems to come to the beginning of one phase or another of what is called the hypnotic state, and that within a few seconds.

The magnetizers act in a completely different fashion. With the aid of *passes*, they prolong their action on the subject for quarter of an hour, half an hour and sometimes longer. The don't concern themselves at all with what may be produced at the beginning, and they only stop when they recognize, with the aid of certain external signs, that the subject has attained the degree of *lucidity* they are seeking to obtain.[159]

---

[158] This comment reflects the strong rivalry which developed between the Nancy School and the Salpêtrière, or Paris School of Hypnosis. Essentially the Nancy School believed that anyone could be hypnotized, whereas the Paris School believed it was predominantly hysterics (which included men) who were susceptible. While the Paris School was initially in the ascendant, by the early 1890s the tide was turning, and the Paris School was accused of exhibiting their subject like a circus sideshow, eventually leading to their demise. However, in this instance Papus supports de Rochas in suggesting that both Schools were missing a major part of their studies by distancing themselves from the magnetizers, and that by adding passes and other magnetizing practices to the repertoire, both additional means of hypnotizing were made available and a broader range of hypnotized states could be identified.

[159] Moreover, to mold their subjects, they have a patience unknown among normal hypnotizers used to producing firstly the phenomena of suggestion, catalepsy, etc. They

Both imagine they have nothing in common. This is a mistake. I asked a magnetizer to induce his subject using the ordinary method, with which he took around twenty minutes to obtain an image with the eyes closed, and I stopped him at many points to try to determine the characteristics of sleep at each moment he paused.

From this, I have come to believe that the subject passes through all the states which I described in my book on the *Undefined Powers*, as follows:

1. State of credulity;
2. Lethargy[160];
3. Catalepsy;

---

only call *somnambulists* those who were already in the state which I have called a *state of connection*, and whose characteristics we will see later. [PAPUS]

"It is rare, said Charpignon (*Dr. of Magnetism*), to obtain somnambulism during the first session, lucidity even less, since it is possible to have somnambulism without there being clairvoyance.

"Sessions of magnetism repeated over several days, at the same time if possible, are necessary, for there is a law concerning the nervous system which leads it to periodically repeat sensations which have affected it, whereas the organism has already itself performed a part of the action woken by magnetization. This remark has raised the objection of imagination; but it is enough to dismiss that objection by remembering that nervous phenomena brought about through magnetization are also produced in people sleeping regularly, in infants at the breast, in people who aren't forewarned, and in circumstances completely different to those involving magnetization.

"The repetition of magnetizations is sometimes very long before leading to somnambulism. *It can take weeks, even months*, but finally crowns the magnetizer's patience with success. On other occasions, when one hoped for much from a cataleptic being and complete isolation, we waited in vain for whole months without obtaining any more results on the last day than on the first. For us, when the fifth magnetization had given nothing apparent concerning the nervous system, we stopped hoping for any phenomenon to occur. *When, on the thirtieth, a magnetically-induced sleep with isolation didn't become somnambulism, we no longer expected anything.* However, on one occasion we obtained a very lucid somnambulist at the fifth session." [PAPUS]

[160] I accept the dedicated term *lethargy* to indicate a state in which the subject presents an appearance of prostration a lot more accentuated than in neighboring states. This state or these states (for they are all a series) are quite hard to define: it is certain that hearing is not completely absent; speech isn't always missing; sight is absent, as it is in other hypnotic phases. When he is lethargic, the subject appears insensible, his members are inert, his head leans on his shoulders. When he comes out of it, he straightens his head and breathes deeply two or three times. Figures 1 and 6 in the list above represent Benoît in the lethargy which precedes the state of connection and that which follows; while figure 2 shows him at the moment where he is going into the state of connection. [PAPUS]

4.   Lethargy.
5.   Somnambulism;
6.   Lethargy;
7.   State of connection;
8.   Lethargy.

After this last stage, the magnetism lasts another dozen minutes, but it was impossible for me to detect any new changes in state, because I would ignore any phenomena which would have to be provoked in order to be characterized.

I have repeated this study since then, and have come to results which are sufficiently similar that I can, at least provisionally, formulate a Law.

I will first describe what happens with those subjects on whom I have experimented the most, and who can be considered as a type by the absolute regularity of the manifestations.

Then I shall point out the variations encountered with other sensitives.

Benoît is nineteen years old. He is a very intelligent boy, in good health and very sensitive to polarity.[161] He assisted with my research for three years, and I knew his constitution sufficiently well to avoid the majority of causes for error.

The agent used to administer hypnosis in this case was by placing the hand on the top of his head, so as to act at the same time upon the two cerebral hemispheres through polarity.

By placing my right hand on his forehead, I can determine firstly the state of credulity, then the lethargic state characterized by muscular contractibility, the cataleptic state with its two phases of rigidity and automatic imitation, a second lethargic state without muscular contractibility, and finally somnambulism.

After that, we enter into a period which has not yet been studied by the modern schools, which is a third state of lethargy. This lethargy (Figure 1

---

[161] There are subjects who are easily hypnotizable, but who are not at all sensitive to polarity. I use the term *sensitive to polarity* to indicate a person in whom I can produce effects determined by the application of certain agents, notably electrical agents, following the laws identified by Messrs. Dècle and Chazarain, as well as in my book on *Undefined Powers*. [PAPUS]

above)[162] appears to be nothing more than *normal sleep*[163], for if I surprise the subject during this sleep and diminish the hypnotic trance by placing the left hand on his head, I bring him to a state of somnambulism; and if on the other hand I use the right hand, I can determine the state of connection. In this lethargic state, the neuromuscular contractibility exists to almost the same degree as in the normal state.

State of Connection

The subject is only connected to the magnetizer, *whoever he may be.*[164] This state, like catalepsy, presents two phases.

---

[162] There are references to Figures 1 to 6, in the next paragraphs, but the images are missing both from this and at least the next edition. It is possible there were copyright concerns at the time, but since the images referred to those of Benoît in various states of hypnosis in de Rochas' book, they have been included here.

[163] As in ordinary sleep we find dreaming with the manifestation described. I have only been able to compose the identification of this lethargic state with ordinary sleep except in a single subject, Benoît. [PAPUS]

[164] If one brings the subject to this state by charging him with electricity either by a static machine, or a battery, or a magnet, he will see nothing different to a person in contact with the agent which produced the hypnosis.

For subjects who are very sensitive to polarity, they can be pushed into a state of connection using a positive part of their body (for example) by simple prolonged contact of this part with a gold object or a diamond. Then the hypnotized part only perceives the object which acted in it or an object of a similar kind. That area will not feel a prick made by a copper pin or rubbing with a piece of crystal. For a few moments, a true organic *touchstone* has been created.

This ability to bring some isolated part or other of the subject's body to a state of connection in order to produce this singular phenomenon of *multiple connection.*

Here is Benoît, who has been placed in a state of connection by A… through an ordinary procedure (the right hand placed on the head), and hears only him. Then B…, for example, placed his hand on his back. After a few moments the subject experiences heaviness, discomfort in the part touched, begins to understand, then understands B… completely, but only when he touches him on the back while speaking. He continues to understand A…, unless A… speaks while standing behind the subject's back, which is connected to B… If C… then places his hand on his side, he will produce a third effect of partial connection, similar to the preceding one, etc.

When the subject is waked, by the Operator A…, he feels an uneasiness in the places touched by B… and C… which don't vibrate in tune with the rest of the body. A few rubs make all of this go away.

In the first, the subject still perceived sensations coming from agents other than the magnetizer. But these sensations, of whatever nature they may have been, all appeared to be disagreeable, notably those coming from contact with animals. Asked about the nature of this suffering he felt when touching a dog, for example, Benoît replied that what he was touching wasn't constituted like him, and that it caused him confusion throughout his entire body.

In the second phase, the subject only perceived the magnetizer. If he played the piano, Benoît heard him; but Benoît didn't hear the sound of the instrument if it was another person playing; though for him to hear it in this case, it sufficed for the magnetizer to place his fingers against the subject's ear, so that the sound passed through his fingers before arriving at the ear.

In general, the subject doesn't perceive anything unless they are in contact with the magnetizer[165]: the regard of the latter is enough to establish contact, and it's probably this which explains, in most cases, how the old magnetizers found their subjects to be naturally connected with some people and not with others.

The phenomenon we have just discussed is analogous to that of *multiple personalities*, which can be obtained in the first states of hypnosis, where the subject is very suggestible.

We have already studied the phenomenon of double personality with one on the right and one on the left. David, one of the subjects known at La Charité, provided me with a striking example: I had given his right side the personality of Miss X..., and his left side that of Mr. Y..., her protector. David, who knew both people personally, had a domestic quarrel in our presence which was highly comical, where insults and blows rained down from one side to the other. With Benoît I was able to produce three personalities, A... on the right, B... on the left, and the third C... in the middle of the body. A dialogue could be entered into with the three individuals, who were constituted in the body with their own personality: each party responded when its name was called, C... from the middle of the lips, A... from the right side of the mouth, and B... from the left side. When A... wished to touch C... he touched the middle of the body, etc.

The experiment was exhausting, but is important in that it destroys the explanation of dual personality being created by suggestions being applied the one to the right lobe and the other to the left lobe of the brain. [PAPUS]

[165] The subject generally sees the persona of the magnetizer as if suspended in an empty space or on a greyish ground. [PAPUS]

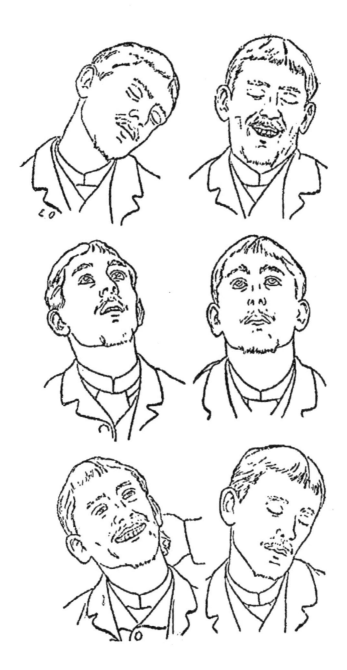

Figures 1 - 6: States of Hypnosis.

Any cutaneous excitation (pricking, pinch, etc.) produced by the magnetizer or by an object in contact with him is pleasant to the one magnetized, so long as it doesn't provoke too violent a pain. This same excitation, produced by a person not in connection with the subject, is not perceived at all, so long as it isn't too strong.[166]

A characteristic common to both phases of the state of connection is an extremely characteristic feeling of beatitude (Figure 2 above), seen in a majority of subjects, which almost always resists attempts to wake the subject or let them sleep again.

In the state of connection, psychic phenomena provoked by putting pressure on different points of their skulls, and what I will describe later, are produced with a very great intensity. Figure 3 shows ecstasy with a religious vision obtained by pressing the middle of the forehead. In Figure 4, Benoît is shown at the moment he experiences an attack of contrition under the influence of words he believes he is hearing; his eyes are filled with tears, and if he is asked what he is experiencing, he replies that the Blessed Virgin is reproaching him. Finally, in Figure 5, the vision has completely changed in nature under the simple influence of pressing point No. 18 corresponding to erotic thoughts. The eyes generally open as a result of pushing the head backwards. The subject objectivizes his vision externally, because he swerves his head away from the magnetizer's hand, when he places it in front of his face like a screen between his eyes and the apparition.

When the subject doesn't naturally have his eyes open in the state, it is enough to order him to open them to have him open them. Then he sees more or less clearly the *fluid* which escapes the eyes, fingers, nostrils and *ears of* the magnetizer, or the person with whom he has been put in connection. This fluid usually shows itself in the form of blue effluvium on the left side and red on the right side. For the subject, it also appears to come out of magnets, crystals, etc. Here I can only indicate a subject for study on which I have focused for many years, and because I will discuss it in a separate book.

Benoît, who in states of hypnosis is sensitive, for reasons which are still poorly understood, to the action of medicines which are brought in proximity to him, possesses this ability in a much more constant manner in a state of connection, provided it's the person who put him to sleep who is holding the

---

[166] When the subject who is sensitive to polarity is able to hypnotize himself by placing his right hand upon his head, he manifests restlessness and discomfort in the first phase, under the influence of the regard of spectators who he can still perceive a little. If one places oneself in connection with him by touching him, he manifests *by himself* that exclusive affection which the subject normally shows for the person who magnetized him. [PAPUS]

medicine. Ipecac makes him feel like vomiting; essence of cherry laurel contained in a phial with a ground stopper placed near the nape of his neck has provoked ecstasy. In the same conditions, essence of valerian firstly caused uneasiness: he felt himself transformed, with a longing to do something whose name he couldn't recollect, then looked like he was going to claw while making cat-like sounds.

When we push hypnosis beyond the state of connection, it leads to a new lethargy (Figure 6), where neuromuscular contractibility is suspended and where the pulse is slowed. Then follows a state of sympathy by contact.

State of Sympathy by Contact

The subject continues to be connected only to the magnetizer and the people who touch him; but what differentiates this state from the preceding one, is that it is sufficient for the magnetizer to experience a pain for the subject in contact with him to perceive it.

If I, as a magnetizer, hold Benoît's hand and a third person pricks me, pinches me or pulls my hair, Benoît perceives the same sensations as me and in the same places. If I am suffering pain or even a simple discomfort following an illness, Benoît also feels it. This phenomenon ceases when there is no further contact.

If I place Benoît's hand in contact with that of another individual and establish a connection while leaving my own hand in contact with the two others, Benoît doesn't feel the pricks or pinches which are done to this third person, and which are too light to affect his constitution, but he does feel the symptoms of illnesses and infirmities. It is by this means that he experienced a migraine by having contact with a woman was suffering from a migraine; that he became hard of hearing having contact with officer afflicted with this infirmity; that he could no longer speak when put in contact with a child whose tongue was paralyzed; to whom he had been led during his sleep; and had experienced a smarting pain on the neck of the bladder while touching a man suffering from chronic cystitis.

Many times, I have tried to make him feel the illness of an absent person, by having him touch an object belonging to that person, but I never succeeded. He felt the object carefully, but he always replied that he couldn't experience anything in particular.

He no longer saw the effluvium he perceived in the state of connection.

Following the state of sympathy by contact, then comes a period of lethargy when the subject is in a state of lucidity.

State of Lucidity

The subject, who continues to perceive the sensations of people with whom he has been put in contact, no longer sees the external effluvium as in the preceding state, but he now acquires a new property. He sees interior organs and those of people with whom he is in connection.

He describes them in terms which are familiar to him in a state of wakefulness, especially when these organs are diseased. Asked why he sees these better than others, he replies that it is because of the suffering or perturbation he experiences through sympathy concentrating his attention on them. These organs should be sufficiently deep in the body for him to perceive them. Thus, he only sees the digestive tract as far as the neck, and he cannot see the inside of the mouth. He sees the cerebral cells vibrating under the influence of thought, and he compares them to the stars which expand and contract successively.

When he's asked to touch a person and to examine them, he compares what he sees in that person to what he sees in his own body. For example, with the officer suffering with his ear, he said: "In the ear there is a small skin across it as in mine, but behind it I see a button which I don't have, and that button is suppurating." For cystitis, he saw an inflation all around the neck and the bladder, a little smaller than the little finger and full of blood, like inflated veins which just out from the Operator's hand, etc.

If you ask him what needs to be done to heal it, he either replies that he doesn't know, or he suggests remedies evidently coming from his memories of the state of wakefulness: thus, in a second experiment relating to cystitis, before he was put into a hypnotic state, the invalid falsely suggested to him that this ailment had a particular cause; then Benoît repeated the false assertion and recommended refreshing drinks.

In this state, the subject acquired yet another ability, which was to recognize the trace left by a contact, even from several days previously. On one occasion, wishing to assure myself whether I could get him to *travel* in *space* and *time* like some somnambulists, I led him in front of a cupboard where I couldn't find a particular object and I asked him if he could see where this object was and to identify who had taken it. He replied: "No", but on touching it, he added: "Here I feel contact with person other than you." Then I led him to several other pieces of furniture, which he also touched, with some feeling nothing, with others feeling an impression of the cupboard. Finally, I presented him with garments belonging to people in my house, and he recognized the contact in a pair of gloves belonging to a domestic. I haven't been able to verify the reality of the fact; many times I've obtained a counter-proof by making a person touch an object several times, and then have the person touched by the subject. The subject always finds the object touched.

State of Sympathy at a Distance

After numerous sessions, I managed to get Benoît to go beyond the lethargy which follows the state of lucidity. To get this result, I had to act not only on the head, but also on the stomach. Without this precaution the breathing stops, because it appears the subject is no longer *homogeneous*, and the chest no longer vibrates along with the head.[167] Therefore, I've been brought to adopt the procedures of the old Magnetizers, who worked by using passes which went down from the head to the trunk, or by pressing the thumbs.

In this new state, Benoît continued to only be connected with me, and to not see the external fluid, but he still saw the inner organs, and his sensitivity was so increased that I no longer needed to maintain contact for him to perceive my own sensations, so long as they were a little pronounced. Moreover, he localized these sensations, as occurred in the experiment by Havre, which we will examine in chapter 3.[168]

However, my attempts to obtain a mental suggestion were in vain: it was impossible to make him execute even the simplest movement through concentration and thought alone, both in this state as well as in the others.

Also, I have not been able to get him past this stage.

When the subject is *saturated*, so to speak, he cannot receive anything further, and seems to *shed* some of it[169] through radiation by returning little by little to a state of wakefulness.

By placing my left hand on his forehead and making some transverse passes to wake him completely, I gradually lead him backwards through all the phases which I've just described as being the most characteristic phenomena.

But these phenomena are not the only ones.

As a person progresses through the hypnotic states, remembrance of the waking states, particularly those concerned with personality, weaken little by little. The subject only retains with any clarity those phenomena which were produced in state similar to that in which he was when he was interrogated. When

---

[167] In the sense of being connected or controlled by the head (though in truth it is the parasympathetic system which controls the automatic functioning of organs such as the heart and lungs).

[168] Referring to de Rochas' book, from which these several pages are a long quote.

[169] De Rochas uses a non-existent word, '*dédoser*', to describe this process.

he arrives at the state of lucidity, there are only two people in the world: the magnetizer and him. He still knows neither their names nor any details about them.

The ability to accept suggestions begins at the state of credulity. It appears to reach its maximum at the instant of the phase of automatic catalepsy, then decreases gently during somnambulism, to disappear almost completely are the beginnings of the state of connection.[170]

The table below will better explain these modifications to memory which leave the ability for reasoning intact.[171]

[In the state of sympathy at a distance and in the deepest states, *connection* diminishes and memory returns little by little.

One may give very complicated suggestions during the period of lethargy which precedes somnambulism, where the subject appears to see nothing, nor hear anything.

If one touches the subject on the skin or clothes, either during this state or in one of the consecutive states of lethargy, in order to have him remember that physical contact on waking, it is sufficient either to tell him to do so; or even, for the majority of subjects, by putting pressure on a point in the middle of the forehead, to cause the memory which I term *somnambulized*, because it covers all the states of hypnosis.

Thus, the *me* persists despite his apparent changes in state; but, in periods of lethargy, the sensory nerves continue their activity to bring impressions from the periphery to his knowledge, whereas his motor neurons, paralyzed for the time being, are incapable of fulfilling their normal duty.

This is a phenomenon analogous to that produced in the case of poisoning by curare.

"Intelligence, sensibility and will are not overtaken by the poison, but they successively lose the instruments of movement which refuse to obey them. The most expressive movements of our abilities disappear first, initially the voice and speech, and then the movement of the members, those of the face and the thorax, and finally the movements of the eyes which, like the dead, persist till the end.

---

[170] From this moment, if the influence of the magnetizer over the magnetized subject is only exercised by suggestion, it is no less extremely powerful, because the affections of the magnetized subject are focused on the magnetizer, to whom he seeks to be nice by every means possible, provided that they weren't offended either by his instinct or his resolutions at the moment of his falling asleep. [PAPUS]

[171] There is a most interesting study to be undertaken to explain how the subject can retain a memory, outside of the ability to reason, of words clear enough to understand questions and reply without hesitation, whereas he has completely lost the memory of people, places, figures, etc. [PAPUS]

Can one imagine a suffering more horrible than that of an intelligent being witnessing thus the successive subtraction of all the organs which, according the expression of de Bonald, are destined to serve, and find themselves in a way enclosed, completely alive, within a cadaver." (*Larousse Encyclopedia*, V°, *Curare*).][172]

I have experimented on several other subjects, but unfortunately, it hasn't always been possible for me to do this with all the precision I wished. One must practice on one's instrument many times and understand its degree of responsiveness, before being able to play it with precision, and time was lacking to accomplish this. Nevertheless, here are some more or less summarized observations:

Joseph, a boy and hairdresser, 18 years old, extremely sensitive to polarity, regularly passed through all the states described above[173], and even went beyond them. With several repetitions, I determined three of four states of apparent lethargy and wakefulness, following the state of sympathy at a distance. But, not knowing the phenomena which characterized them, I was unable to place them in evidence. I was limited to seeking mental suggestions, and on one occasion I obtained one of the extreme states. I *thought*: "Raise your right arm", and he slowly raised his right arm. "Embrace me": he rounded his arms, but didn't reach me and embraced the air. "Stand up": he stood up progressively, like an automaton.

All this happened with a delay of one or two minutes, and the subject, when asked later about what he has perceived at the mental level, replied that he hadn't been conscious, but he had felt his muscles stiffen little by little in order to accomplish certain movements.

Joseph also perceived illnesses in people with whom he had been put in connection. He imagined he felt them himself at this point, and lamented his sorry state; and him so young!... He willingly suggested the most extraordinary remedies and argued for them by amalgamating fragments of consultations he had witnessed. For the cystitis he had been asked about, he made inferences on the position of the organ and prescribed mercury.

One day, a doctor brought him the bonnet of a sick woman I didn't know at all, and he appeared to precisely describe the symptoms of the woman's illness. He kindly added that the person in question suffered in the head, and that the

---

[172] The six paragraphs enclosed in [] were omitted from Papus' book. However, since they are an integral part of the book by de Rochas being quoted *in extenso*, they have been added back in this translation.

[173] In the state of connection, phenomena of religious and sensual ecstasy were produced by pressing the corresponding points; the head fell backwards, but the eyes didn't open and the subject described his visions. [PAPUS]

bonnet could have launched his imagination to focus on this part of the body. The experiment has never been repeated.

R..., 25 years old, blacksmith, a former foot soldier, passed distinctly through all the states up to sympathy, and never progressed beyond that. He was only worked on twice, and the experiment, which was performed separately by two different people, gave the same results: in the state of sympathy he felt the pricks made to the magnetizer, but he didn't perceive illnesses.

Clotilde, 20 years old, a glovemaker, and Mrs. D..., a widow aged 25. Identical observations for both, as far as the state of sympathy. In both women waking up took place very quickly, and it was very difficult to follow the phases of return, whereas the phases of being hypnotized only took place slowly and without the deep inhalations which clearly marked the changes of states in Benoît.

Louise and Maria, 19 years old, linen seamstresses. The same observations, with the difference that the sensitivity was so great, it was necessary to pay great attention and pay close attention to recognize the phases, both going in and coming out.

Mrs. X..., 35 years old, a mother of a family, in excellent health, used to foot-races and horse-racing, of a superior spirit, who had tried hypnotism once without success from her doctor, but fell asleep very easily the moment I had touched her.

In a state of somnambulism, she had her eyes open without being fixed. We needed to check her sensitivity and test her suggestibility to be certain that she wasn't in fact completely awake.

Perhaps she was pushed too far, and in all the states other than lethargy, her eyes were open, but she only saw the Operator and or objects with which he put her in touch. The specific characteristics of the state were only determined with precision up to the state of *sympathy at a distance*. In this state, like the following, when I had a strong thought, she sensed a congestion in the head, but couldn't divine what I was thinking. However, I obtained on one occasion, *one only*, the communication of a very characteristic thought with this lady from a distance of several kilometers, which I shall return to in chapter 3.

Although, as with all the other subjects, once in a state of connection she only knew the magnetizer, for whom she witnessed a very strong affection, having forgotten her husband and children completely, she retained her will, and it was impossible for me to make her execute an action which she had been determined, and at my request while she was still awake, not to undertake. However, I was able to overcome her resistance by subterfuge, when her vitality was at a low ebb.

Questions	Responses		
	State of Connection	**State of Sympathy**	**State of Lucidity**
Do you feel OK? What is your name?	Yes! (With some hesitation) Benoît.	A little dull. (With a lot of hesitation) Benoît.	Quite well. I don't know, it's all the same to me.
What is the baptismal name of your father?	(With a lot of hesitation) Théophile.	I don't know.	I don't know.
What is my name?	Commandant de Rochas.	Commandant…I don't know the rest any more.	I don't know.
How many children do I have?	Three (I have four).	I don't know if you have any.	Don't know.
What are their names?	He thinks and gives names close to the same consonances as my children, who he knows well.	Don't know.	Don't know.
In what town do you live?	In Blois (he used to live in Blois and now lives in Grenoble).	(He thinks). I can't remember.	I don't know at all.
What is your profession?	Accountant.	I don't have one.	I don't know.
Count: one, two, three, etc.	One, two, three, four…six…	One, two, four…I can't remember any more.	One, two… I don't know any more.
What is two plus three?	(with a lot of hesitation) Five.	Two and three… seven.	… I don't know.
What can't you can't remember?	– see right –	– see right –	There are certainly things which I cannot remember, above all those concerning people and places.

You feel an itching on your nose (I stress this with emphasis several times).	No! Oh, yes, a little.	I don't feel anything.	I don't feel anything (I scratch my own nose), but it is you who feels an itch on your nose, not me.
Do you still wish to sleep?	I don't want to. Leave me alone, I'm fine like this.	I don't want to. What you say means nothing.	What you are saying is pointless. You aren't putting me to sleep at all. I feel that this is tiring me out.
On waking, you will do something.	(The suggestion is only partially executed).	(The suggestion isn't executed).	(The suggestion isn't executed).

Miss. K…, a young woman of 30 years, intelligent, well educated, who had never been magnetized except by me (with the exception of two or three attempts in which she was only out for a few seconds) had an extreme sensitivity to all the phenomena which characterize these first states, except for suggestions about hearing which she only entertained with difficulty. It took me several sessions to bring her to the state of connection, where she continued to hear everybody[174], but she only saw me, for whom she then experienced the usual exclusive affection.

It took me many sessions to lead her to sympathy of contact, when she experienced my sensations without being able to localize them. In return she experienced my emotions, even at a certain distance, smiling when I smiled behind her, becoming sad when I became sad.

Even after a dozen sessions I was never able to get beyond that state, and I attribute this difficulty on the one hand to her extreme vivacity, and on the other

[174] The condition of isolation isn't completely indispensable for we have come across very good somnambulists who hear everything and whose hearing had still become very keen. This anomaly is thorny, and should put the magnetizer on his guard: one should always seek to destroy it, and with patience, one can succeed after several sessions.

"It is the same for forgetfulness on waking, a circumstance which we consider to be very important; for, without these two characteristics, the isolation of all that it not the magnetizer and forgetfulness on waking, what serious guarantees can we have with regard to somnambulism?" (Chaporgnon, Physics of Magnetism, p. 70). [PAPUS]

to external distractions coming from the fact that her hearing could not be put to sleep.

Mrs. K…, like Miss. X…, having only been magnetized by me, and on a regular basis, went to sleep simply by pressing their thumbs, and woke up on command by passing very quickly through all the phases both in falling asleep and in waking up.[175]

Anna, a longtime subject of R…, had been worked on for a long time to reach the stage of lucidity. She demonstrated the ordinary phenomena of suggestibility at the beginning, of sensitivity and forgetfulness on waking, slept deeply under the influence of passes, but didn't show any of the other characteristics of the state described earlier. In her sleep she had visions which, it appears, are sometimes met with previsions.

Miss. V…, a professional subject, well-known in Paris, very clearly polarized, passes, like Benoît, through all the phases described with extreme regularity, and moreover, through phases which I have not yet been able to determine, as far as fainting.

If, instead of placing the right hand on her head, you use the left hand (heteronomic imposition), one first sees excitation, as in other subjects, then a torpor, and finally a general paralysis presenting symptoms so close to those of death, that I have never dared to continue these experiments.

One may wonder whether, by prolonging this action, one wouldn't get a series of states separated by lethargies and possessing special properties. The state of wakefulness would therefore only be a specific and habitual phase of the many modalities with which the brain is endowed, and would constitute the median part of the intellectual keyboard.

---

[175] In some of these subjects, the aptitude for suggestibility begins after being woken up. These are naturally *credulous* people, and this aptitude continues with a certain intensity up to during the state of connection. Mrs. X…, R… and Maria could only get up from their chair with great difficulty after being woken, when, during the state of connection, they received the order that they couldn't stand up.

These variations in suggestibility are expressly important to note. It means, indeed, that one can generally produce or end hypnosis with a simple command in the state of connection, but when one wishes to go further, one must employ physical agents. The action of these agents in deep states clearly shows that, in the lesser states, they also work, and that the theory of auto-suggestion to explain their effects is not admissible in an absolute manner.

We can also see, by the differences shown by my subjects, that the characteristics which I have described for the states of hypnosis are not the result of education. It is wrong, as some superficial observers claim, to say that one can fashion these subjects to do what one wants. One is developing their natural abilities to a greater or lesser extent; that is all. [PAPUS]

Who knows what the future holds for us?[176]

Waking the Subject

One must never experiment with putting a subject to sleep unless trained in the practice of various procedures for waking them up. Indeed, this is the moment most subject to surprises, and the one which most leads beginners and Operators, who can easily lose their composure, astray.

One can wake a subject by many procedures, among which we will describe the following:

---

[176] As we come to the end of what is in effect the entire first chapter of Albert de Rochas' book, which is probably included courtesy of the fact that he and Papus worked together, one can't help commenting on several aspects of this section from a scientific and for that matter a moral point of view. Firstly, in a trait in common with early psychology and psychoanalysis, both practices suffered from being held in contempt by mainstream science, primarily because the basic tenets of scientific method include, among others, the fact the experiments are repeatable with identical results obtained; and that a large population is used to avoid individual variations in what is observed, with statistics used to analyze the results. Both are missing in the case of psychological studies, magnetism and hypnosis. Indeed, we see in the text that hypnosis, while hardly an accepted science itself even then, and not above debasing itself on occasion to the level of Vaudeville entertainment (indeed, one is reminded of the visits to Bedlam – or Bethlem Royal Hospital in London – to gawk at the mentally disturbed inmates for entertainment, which appears to have mirrored the 'carnival' atmosphere at the Salpêtrière School's public exhibitions), nevertheless sought to distance itself from magnetism, with its touches and passes, and its claimed psychic phenomena in terms of out-of-body experiences, seeing at a distance, somnambulistic diagnosis, etc. While psychology later attempted to address accusations of small samples by creating new statistical measures for small populations, we can see from the excepts of de Rochas' book that most of their findings were anecdotal at best. A second concern is the age of the participants. Nobody under the age of 31 is mentioned, and the majority are in their teens. Despite de Rochas' final footnote comment, it is hard to be absolutely and irrefutably convinced that these young subjects, often in menial positions of work, might not find it easy to fake the conditions so eagerly sought by de Rochas and his contemporaries, especially as the physical 'signs of affection' he so often refers to could also indicate a delight in being taken seriously and receiving personal attention, in a society where they were more often than not forgotten and ignored. Finally, the very nature of the experiments would, one feels, raise an eyebrow nowadays with all the 'touching' and 'stroking' and 'passes' of young men and women, no doubt without a chaperone!

1. Waking by simple suggestion, or command.
2. Waking through breath.
3. Waking through passes.
4. Waking without suggestion, by gaze.
5. Waking with a combination of some of these various procedures.

Waking by command – With the subject in the somnambulistic phase, they are ordered to wake, completely released, in a minute. One can also order them to wake when someone has tapped on their hands three times, or by another completely different variety of suggestion. This procedure should be used in preference in the somnambulistic phase; but it also succeeds very often if the subject is in the lethargic phase, although less rapidly.

Waking through breath – By breathing strongly between the subject's eyes, one can wake them and release them at the same time.

Waking through passes – One of the best procedures, above all in deep states, when it must *always* be used. Make horizontal passes and repeat with both hands, firstly at the level of the chest, then at the level of the subject's head. The waking so produced take a long time to obtain; but one is assured of never having to fear any later accident, since the subject is completely released.

Waking by gaze – Used when the subject, for one reason or another, resists suggestion. In this case, stare at the subject fixedly between the two eyes, at the height of the middle of the forehead, and you will see the subject wake soon, totally and without having to have said a single word.

Combined waking – The best results are obtained by waking a subject by the following process, resulting from the combination of a majority of the other procedures:

1. The suggestion is given in the somnambulistic phase, and when one blows between the two eyes, a complete awakening should soon take place;
2. Once that is done, blow on the same place, at the same time quickly releasing the forehead by means of passes;
3. End by blowing a final time when the subject is completely awake.

When one has the situation of facing a difficult case, such as that of a subject in a deep lethargy who refuses to obey the suggestion, one firstly seeks to lead them to any phase of hypnotism, be it catalepsy or somnambulism, then give the suggestion that it will end after a specified period (a half-hour or an hour) preceded by the breaths and passes mentioned above.

WITCHES AND MAGNETISM

We've taken the time to describe in minute detail the phenomena of hypnosis, since it's connected with procedures currently used by village sorcerers, and by all those who pass more or less for Adepts of Magic.

Magic doesn't consist of the practice of magnetism alone, any more than it is only the practice of evocations, or the gathering of herbs for "simples", or the erection of a horoscope for an Operation; but it is in fact the coming together of all these applications.

Nevertheless, knowledge of the magnetism of the earth, that intelligent and mysterious force called "Astral Light" by the Adepts, is a powerful aid to the Magister. It is through studying self-hypnosis, and learning meditation and ecstasy that one becomes conscious of this force, whose use has never been completely forgotten. This is the secret of "Enchantment"[177], and we only need to give the following two cases as proof: 1. Two healings obtained at the Hospital La Charité by the author; 2. The very curious facts of Cideville, which were produced well in advance of modern spiritualism and which are of a purely magical kind. In his remarkable book *Le Serpent de la Genèse* ("The Serpent of Genesis"), Stanislas de Guaita gives a minute analysis of it. The summary which we are publishing from a contemporary magazine is drawn from *Fragments occultes* by Marcellus Leloir (Bordeaux, 1890). But firstly, let us give the following interesting note:

---

[177] Most dictionaries translate *envoûtement* as "spells" or "casting spells". However, this is a rather general term, so the word "enchantment" has been used throughout. This lends a more personal element to the word, since it refers to the actions of one person over another, normally as a means of control. The word itself, *envoûtement*, has its root in *voûte* or "vault", giving a sense of entombment or enclosing. Another word sometimes used is "fascination", which in its magical sense refers to a person taking control of another's emotions, normally to make them love the sorcerer. In his book 'Mastering Witchcraft' (pub. Corgi, 1970), Paul Hudson gives a comprehensive description of the process, which incorporates much of what is included in this section of Papus' book (indeed, he defines it as the: 'process of casting a spell upon someone using only the projection of witch power in close personal proximity'), including mind games, focusing on the person's eyes, touching, etc. The close connection between 'fascination' or 'enchantment' and hypnosis or magnetism certainly explains why Papus devoted so much space in his book to the studies then being undertaken in Paris. Finally, despite the apparent lack of scientific method in these experiments, one should remember that this field of study (including photography, which Papus discusses later) were all in their infancy at that time.

The *Annals of Psychic Science* (September/October) relate a series of experiments made in 1888 by Dr. A. Gibotteau, and which have very close connections to magical actions. His subject, B…, was from a family of peasants from Champagne which produced wiches. Among other things: "she knew, as I've proved, how to make someone *lose their way*, by making them confuse their right with their left (a hallucination in terms of space). She said that, as a little girl, she had gone into the woods with her mother to gather strawberries. When she got bored and wanted to go home, she played at *circling* her mother to make her lose her way. In our countryside, this power is usually attributed to witches. In Cuba, the negro sorcerers claim to do the same. There is interesting research to be done on this practice which, from experience, I believe would prove its reality.

"Another time, Berthe taught me how what one had to do in order to *make a person fall over*. The method is remarkably logical. Firstly, she had to get to know the person, talk to her, affect her as much as she could, and make her fear her. When that person was on the road, she followed behind her, carefully imitating her walk, and *encumbering* her (this was the word she normally used to mean to mentally impair someone's thoughts and making them a little drowsy, a process which was familiar to her). Then she would visualize a cord stretched across the road a few steps ahead. She closely matched the movements of the person and, at the moment she came to the cord, she herself voluntarily made a misstep: then the person was forced to fall.[178]

"Here, then, was a means of making an enemy hang himself: follow his steps and his thoughts, and each day *show* him a tree in a lonely place. Make him think that he is unlucky, that his livelihood is irretrievably ruined, and, each day, show him the same place, etc."

---

[178] This technique is remarkably similar to the oft-repeated story about Aleister Crowley, in which he accomplishes much the same result by following a person (in this case a complete stranger) down 5th Avenue in New York, copying the person's gait and speed, then finally stumbling deliberately but recovering at the last moment, leaving the person with whom he had sympathetically identified to fall over. The only thing missing from Crowley's version was the visualization of a cord across the road.

VILLAGE WITCHES AND SUGGESTION

BY GÉRARD ENCAUSSE[179]
Head of the Laboratory of Hypnotherapy at La Charité

Among the illnesses treated at the laboratory of La Charité, there are two rather interesting cases which reveal the influence which certain country folk can have over somewhat emotional subjects.

When we talk about these village witches, the bonesetters, the old wives, representatives of occult knowledge which is nowadays almost forgotten, the first tendency is to laugh and to take no notice of the thousand facts spread from cottage to cottage, and embellished by the narrators' imaginations.

There would, however, be an interesting study to be made of these suggestions, accompanied by bizarre words, which are the true cause of the majority of results from these pale imitations of Magicians. These suggestions only have an effect on emotional beings, and anyone who laughs at the "witch" overlooks the fact of her influence, though partisans will defend to the death any suggestion of the state of wakefulness, and of their universal action.

The two invalids we'll discuss are both hysterics, who had never admitted to any accident taking place prior to the time the suggestion had been given.

The first of these invalids, Elisa C..., was brought to us on December 11th by a parent who had consulted numerous doctors on this subject, who had prescribed various treatments, none with any success.

The sick person, 18 years old, had a persistent contraction in her right arm, of purely hysterical origin.[180]

Placed before the rotating mirror, she wasn't long in being fascinated, and from that time we were able to combine treatment by transference with treatments by suggestion. Under this dual influence the contractions of the arm disappeared at the end of the fourth day of treatment.

But the night of the 4th or 5th day, the invalid suddenly became dumb. We thought we could easily end this muteness through suggestion, but for the next two days we attempted many procedures of suggestion in vain. All of them failed.

It was then that the thought came to us that the invalid might have been dominated by a previous suggestion unknown to us, and which would gradually

---

[179] *Ann. De Psychiatrie*, N°. 6 (June 1891). [PAPUS]. It's worth noting, perhaps, that since this book was published under the name of 'Papus', the quotation from a 'Dr. Gérard Encausse' was intended to be read as a paper contributed by a dispassionate author!

[180] Or what might nowadays be called 'psychosomatic'.

destroy our actions concerning the results obtained. Persistent mutism prevented us from interrogating the invalid. We had to have recourse to an experimental subterfuge.

Being certain that all suggestions were being carried out by the invalid, with the exception of those to do with her illness itself, when the subject was in a period of lucid somnambulism, we suggested that the person who had *done her harm* was there in front of her, and at the same time we showed her one of the students in the laboratory.

Her face took on a very strong expression of anger, and it was with only great difficulty that the presumed author of the subject's present state was able to approach and command the young girl in a strong voice to be cured immediately, which did indeed take place on the spot.

From the dialogue between the two of them, we were able to deduce the following facts: the young girl was the daughter of a man considered in the village to be something of a sorcerer. The day that she came to Paris, brought by her teachers, her father flew into a rage and cursed her, saying:

"From today, you will always be ill, and nobody but me will be able to cure you."

Until that time she had never been ill, and had never had any hysterical crises or neuropathological concerns of any kind. This event, as one might expect, had affected her deeply. She had departed, and a few hours later the contraction of her arm had appeared.

One may easily understand how, when this contraction had been cured, another affliction made itself known. Her father's words had acted like a genuine hypnotic suggestion.

Knowing this story, it was easy for us to make it stop. The 'pretend' father, created by our act of suggestion, declared an end to the curse and pardoned his daughter. He repeated this pardon when the subject was woken, and from that moment all the afflictions ceased.

*
* *

The story of another invalid also falls into the same category.

Adolphine F…, 27 years old and married from the age of 18, was brought to us on September 7th, 1890.

She had suddenly been subject at her home by neuropathological afflictions, choking fits, sudden pains, attacks of hysteria, etc., etc.

She had been treated with bromide, even in high doses; with valerian, chloral, etc., but nothing had worked.

Treatment by transference alone was the correct treatment for all these ailments, and less than fifteen days following the commencement of this treatment, the lady returned home, completely cured. Despite all our questioning, it had been impossible for us to find the cause for the illness, for while we had good reason to believe her to be of a nervous disposition, even a little emotional, this wasn't sufficient to establish the origin of such sudden afflictions.

On December 11th, 1890, the lady came to see us, once again afflicted by the same symptoms. A detailed interrogation led her to confess that she had been treated in her own country by a woman who passed as a *witch*. One day, in a moment of anger, this woman had told her that she would always be ill from that moment, and no doctor had been able to heal her. The witch's anger had been caused by the invalid refusing to give her a small sum of money. We had witnessed the results of this genuine suggestion.

A new treatment using suggestion, appropriate to this singular origin, worked on the illness which his now completely cured – to the great shame of the witch, it turns out.

*

* *

In conclusion, this is an issue which is often passed over with disdain.

The recent works of our Master, Dr. Luys, freshly clarifies the actions of these so-called charlatans, whose suggestion can perhaps be sustained in various objects (talismans, pacts, etc.), just as a neurological state may be sustained by a magnetic crown.[181]

There would be a good reason to differentiate between cases where these village hypnotizers perform good works, from those who should be liable to punishment set by the law for extorting money from their victims by menace.

These two observations also show the use of *etiology* [182] in neuropathological afflictions which suddenly appear in subjects who, up to then, were in perfect health or barely emotional.

---

[181] In 1894, Dr. Jules Luys delivered a paper at the February 10th meeting of the Biological Society in Paris, titled: *De l'emmagasinement de certaines activités cerebrales dans une couronne aimantée* ("Retention of certain brain activity in a magnetic crown"). While there appear to be no images of this contraption available, one may imagine it looked not dissimilar to the metal bands with wires commonly used in contemporary studies of the brain's activities.

[182] The study of causation, or the source of effects or events.

Let me quote an extraordinary case of enchantment which played out in front of the tribunals, and whose description was inserted by Montet in the journal *la Patrie* ("Fatherland") on May 26th, 1853.

Here is the text of the article:

"We must bring to the attention of the readers of this Bulletin some facts of a nature so singular, so unbelievable, so inadmissible for people raised as all of us have been, to a greater or lesser extent, on the skeptical philosophy of the 18th Century, which requires all the evidence resulting from a two-sided debate conducted before the tribunals – where more than twenty witnesses were heard and were unanimous in their depositions – for us to take upon ourselves the task of giving publicity to facts which took place in the middle of the 19th Century, and which go back four hundred years... They prove once again that modern science and philosophy, which completely denies the facts of Magic and Witchcraft, which has filled the history of all peoples through all ages, is wrong; and that those simple in spirit, those good people who believed what they had seen, despite the things they had seen being called absurd, were in fact correct."

Here, now, is the documentation of the facts which took place in the present day, in 1850 in Normandy, in the village of Cideville, District of Yvetot, of which a summary, itself very long, is currently being published by Vrayet de Surcy.[183]

.   .   .   .

"Around the first days of the month of March 1840, Mr. Tinel, vicar of Cideville, met in the home of one of his sick parishioners an individual called G..., who the local region had for a long time accorded a reputation as a healer and a sorcerer. The vicar gave the sorcerer a sharp reprimand, and sent him on his way. For its part, justice laid its hand on G..., who spent one or two years in prison.

"G... promised revenge on the vicar, to whom, for right or wrong, he attributed his legal problems, and chose the shepherd Thorel, his disciple and friend, as instrument for his vengeance.

---

[183] Following the article published in 1853, a book by Jules de Mirville, titled *Des Esprits et de leurs manifestations fluidiques* ("Of Spirits and their Fluid Manifestations"), containing the story of Cideville, was indeed published in 1858 by Vrayet de Surcy, Paris.

"Two children were being raised in the presbytery at Cideville. One was twelve years old and called Gustave Lemoniers. The other, called Clément Aunel, was fourteen. The education of these children was, for the vicar, both an agreeable occupation and a source of comfort. It is in the person of one of these children that, according to the general opinion of the witnesses, the sorcerer struck at the priest.

"One day during a public sale, young Gustave was accosted by the shepherd, and a few hours later the events began. Almost immediately following the return of that child, a kind of whirlwind came and burst on the presbytery. Then, following this squall, blows which sounded like the blows of a hammer were continually heard in all parts of the house, which felt as though it wanted to fall into ruins.

"The blows were so loud that they could be heard two kilometers away, and a large number of the inhabitants of Cideville, one hundred fifty people it is said, went to the presbytery, surrounded it for many hours, and explored it in every way possible without being able to discover the cause.

"While these mysterious noises continued their incessant concert, and reproduced the exact rhythm of any air requested, the flagstones broke in every sense, objects were agitated, tables were violently thrown over or moved by themselves, knives, brushes, breviaries flew out one window and returned through the opposite window; shovels and tongs left the hearth and moved on their own across the room; hammers flew through the air and fell with the gentleness that a child's hand would give to a feather, enormous desks shook and broke; even more, one of them, filled with books, came violently and horizontally up to the forehead of a witness, and there, without touching and contrary to all the laws of gravity, fell perpendicularly at his feet.

"Another witness, a landowner from fourteen kilometers away, was transported unawares to the presbytery at Cideville and settled in the children's room.[184] He interrogated the mysterious noise, he knocked in all the corners of the room, and established the conditions for a dialogue. One knock, for example, came to mean *yes*, two knocks *no*, and then the number of knocks signified the number of letters, etc. This having been agreed, the witness had it knock all the letters which composed his first and last names, those of his children, his age and theirs, by year, month and day, the name of his town, etc., all of which was executed with an accuracy that was irreproachable.

---

[184]The text is not absolutely clear as to whether he was 'magically' transported, or whether he found himself strangely compelled to go to the presbytery. One would assume the latter.

"A priest, a vicar from Saint-Roch, Father I…, finding himself in transit through Yvetot by chance, went to Cideville and interrogated the mysterious knocker. It told him the ages and first names of his mother and father; but he had forgotten them or had never known them. No matter: he noted them down, and on his return to Paris, he rushed to the Town Hall, consulted the Civil State Registries, and found a direct correspondence between them and the revelations of Cideville.

"As for the state of the child who was the object of this obsession, he presented extremely remarkable symptoms. There was a complete invasion of the nervous system, an unprecedented weight pushed down his shoulders and compressed his chest. Moreover, that child saw the shadow of a man always behind him wearing a smock he said he didn't recognize, until the day that, standing before Thorel, he cried out: 'This is the man!'

"One day, this child indicated a most singular hallucination. He saw a black hand descending from the chimney, and exclaimed that it had given him a slap in the face, and one could see his cheek become and remain red. In his naivety, the child rushed outside, believing he would see this hand come out of the top of the chimney.

"One evening, the vicar of Cideville and come of his colleagues discussed the means to use in order to free this child. One of the priests said he remembered reading in an old tome that spirits feared iron points. At the risk of sliding a little into superstition, our brave ecclesiastics armed themselves with iron points and began to fence in the emptiness, each more than the other, everywhere that the noise was heard. After some time had been spent doing this exercise, a boot which appeared to have been thrown, caused a flame to shoot forth, followed by smoke which was so thick, the windows had to be opened to avoid asphyxiation. They continued, a groan was heard, then inarticulate cries, in the midst of which they distinguished the word 'forgive'. 'Forgive', replied the priests. 'We forgive you and we pray God that He will forgive you, too, but on condition that you will come yourself to ask forgiveness of this child.' 'You forgive all of us?' 'So, there are several of you?' 'There are five of us, including the shepherd.' 'We forgive all of you.' Silence now returned to the presbytery.

"The following afternoon, there was a knock at the presbytery door. It was opened and Thorel stood there. His attitude was humble, his language embarrassed and, and he sought to hide the bloody grazes which covered his face with his hat. The child perceived him and cried out: 'This is the man who has been haunting me these past fifteen days.' 'What do you want?', the vicar asked him. 'I have come…I have come on behalf of my Master to fetch the little organ you have here.' 'No, Thorel, no. Nobody gave you such an order. Once again, this is not the reason you came here. What do you want? But firstly, where did these wounds come from? Who gave them to you?' 'That is none of your business. I cannot tell you.' 'Then say what you want. Be frank, and tell us that you are here to ask forgiveness of this child. Say it, then, and go down on your knees.' 'So be it. Forgive me', said Thorel, falling on his knees. And while asking for forgiveness, he crawled forward and sought to seize the child by his smock.

"He succeeded in doing so, and witnesses say that from that moment the sufferings of the child and the mysterious noises in the presbytery increased. Immediately the vicar persuaded Thorel to go to the town hall. He went, and there, in front of witnesses, without anyone asking him to do so, he fell to his knees three times and again asked for forgiveness. 'What are you asking me forgiveness for?' the vicar asked him. 'Explain yourself.' And Thorel continued to kneel. But while asking for forgiveness, as he had in the presbytery, he crawled forward and sought to touch the vicar as he had done with the child. 'Don't touch me!', cried the vicar. 'In the name of Heaven, don't touch me, or I will hit you!' An empty threat, perhaps, and Thorel still edged forward, until the vicar, forced into a corner of the room, was forced, in his legitimate defense, to deal him three blows on his arm with his cane.

"It was these three blows with the cane which had been the reason behind the lawsuit which was being tried before the Justice of the Peace in Yerville, where al the facts we have just given in summary form were stated in minutest detail by the many witnesses, who never varied in their testimonies. The Judge of Yerville, having heard the depositions of the witnesses and the parties' respective pleas, on February 5th, 1851, rendered a definitive judgement, by which Thorel's claim for 1,200 francs in damages for the blows of the vicar's cane was rejected, and he was ordered to pay all expenses."

Such was the juridical end to this singular affair. As to the material issue, we can say that these episodes and a thousand others, which were produced daily and without interruption from November 26th, 1850 till February 15th, 1851, only ended when, by order of the Archbishop of Rouen, the two children were removed from the presbytery at Cideville and give in charge of another priest in Rouen, who continued their education.

"When the air is condensed through an electrical build-up[185], and this electricity is drawn off with a metallic point, it produces a strong spark, then all the appearances of dense smoke. It is enough to state that the point had dissipated a knot of astral light coagulated by a larva."

---

[185] Eliphas Lévi, *History of Magic*. [PAPUS]

This is the phenomenon which was produced in the preceding story.

As we described above, the instrument of enchantment is a powerful magical agent, or, in more contemporary terms, magnetic power directed by a perverse will.

"What sorcerers and necromancers sought above everything else in their invocations of impure spirits, was that magnetic power which is the purview of the true Adept, and which they wished to usurp for unworthy abuses.

"The madness of the witches being an evil madness, one of their primary aims was to gain the power of enchantment or deleterious influence."

.   .   .   .

ENCHANTMENT

All these stories attract the attention of the seeker after these ancient practices of enchantment which were believed to be fabulous, and had disappeared forever from the history of the sciences. Now, the powerful experiments undertaken by Colonel de Rochas since 1891, and concerned with the *externalization of sensitivity* in deep states of hypnosis have renewed a remembrance of these strange facts and the magical domain.

Since the treatise we are writing isn't a book about witchcraft but rather a book about Magic, we haven't given details of these practices, which are so dangerous in the service of an evil will. We are simply emphasizing a "scientific possibility" behind these phenomena, and to this end we will continue to lend our best efforts to these very recent works which we have been called on to verify experimentally in the laboratory of La Charité.

To proceed in order, we will firstly relate the first experiment as published in the daily journals in the month of August 1892.

ENCHANTMENT

THE EXPERIMENTS OF DE ROCHAS

From *Justice* (August 2nd):

These experiments took place yesterday in the presence of two doctors, members of the Academy of Sciences, and a well-known mathematician.

De Rochas tried to dissipate the sensitivity of a subject in a photographic plate.

He placed the first of these plates in contact with a subject who was wide awake: the photograph thus obtained of the subject didn't show any image of him.

A second, taken from the front in contact with a sleeping subject, gave an image which was barely perceptible.

Finally, a third, which had been placed in a camera had been strongly charged with the image of the sleeping subject, produced a photograph which exhibited the most curious characteristics.

Every time the Operator touched the image, the subject felt it. Finally, he took a pin and scratched the photographic film on the plate twice, in the placed the subject's hand was shown.

At that moment, the subject completely lost consciousness in contraction. When he was woken, we found two red stigmata on his hand beneath the epidermis, corresponding to the two scratches made on the photographic film.

De Rochas came to believe that this demonstrated the "enchantment" of the ancients very clearly.

In the most mysterious realm of these facts, we would like to limit ourselves to nothing more than a sincere narrative, which is not concerned with belief or non-belief here. We're stating what we saw, and that's all.

Let's now see the details given by the author about this discovery in *Initiation* (Vol. 17, N°. 2, November 1892):

Most subjects, when their eyes are made overly sensitive by means of certain maneuvers, see glimmers escaping from animals, plants, crystals and magnets, which could have a direct connection with these radiations. That is what was discovered for the first time fifty years ago through many experiments, by a wise Austrian chemist, Baron Reichenbach.

In humans, these effluvia come from the eyes, nostrils, ears and the ends of the fingers, while the rest of the body is simply covered with a layer like a luminous duvet. When the image of a subject was externalizing, the *seer* subject saw this luminous layer leave the skin and float directly over him, and one can directly verify the patient's image through touch or pinching it.

By continuing the maneuvers necessary to produce externalization, I recognized, with the help of these various procedures, that it produced a successive series of sensitive layers which were very thin, concentric, and separated by insensitive zones, up to several meters from the subject. These layers were spaced approximately 5 to 6 centimeters apart, and the first was separated from the insensitive skin by half that distance.

According to wave theory, which is used nowadays to explain the propagation and properties of light, sound and even electricity, it could be assumed that these sensitive and insensitive layers were due to the interference between waves producing maximums and minimums, and it was natural to try and see if the waves of different speeds and directions needed to produce these interference patterns, were not due to the two great rhythmic movements of the human body, heartbeats and respiration.

I have thus been led to try to determine whether these waves, to which I will give the name of *Od*, as Reichenbach did[186], enjoy the properties of reflection and refraction, as do other waves studied in Physics.

Using a plate glass prism of 0.30 meters on the side, I performed quite a number of experiments, in which I varied the conditions, but the principal phenomenon was complicated by additional peripheral phenomena, and all I believe I can conclude from my observations is that the prism permits the waves to pass through while bending them, in accordance with a Law I've still not been able to identify.

What I consider as clearly established is that liquids, in general, not only stop the Od, but dissolve it; that is to say that, for example, by moving a glass of water through one of the closest sensitive layers to the body, an *Odic shadow* was produced, with the following sensitive layers disappearing behind the glass to a certain extent, Moreover, the glass of water became completely sensitized, and after a period of time even emitted (probably because it was saturated) sensitive vapors with rose vertically from the upper surface. Finally, if one

---

[186] Baron Dr. Carl von Reichenbach (1788 – 1869) was initially a highly-respected scientist, contributing important findings in a number of fields, including geology, chemistry, engineering and industry. However, in his later years, while having no training at all in psychology or anatomy, he became obsessed with the human nervous system, focusing on those affected by hysteria, phobias and somnambulism, believing that those who were particularly affected possessed unusually highly developed sensory abilities, whom he called 'sensitives'. He believed he had found a new vital force which he called 'Od' or the 'Odic Force', after Odin, the Norse god, similar to magnetism, and spent the rest of his life trying to prove this life force, which he believed permeated all living things, as well as crystals and magnets, to a skeptical scientific community. Even in the late 19th Century it was considered unproven, and a clear example of 'pathological science', where an investigator becomes so obsessed with his study he ignores any results which contradict his passionately-held belief. Given this, it is perhaps surprising that de Rochas continued to embrace a theory which had been largely discredited. A very detailed article on 'Odic Force' may be found here: http://customers.hbci.com/~wenonah/history/odenergy.htm.

moved the glass away, the water it contained remained sensitized up to a certain distance, beyond which the link which joined it to the subject's body seemed to gradually weaken. Up till then, the subject felt on the part of his body closest to the place where the water was when it was charged with his sensitivity, any touches which the magnetizer made to this water, even though the intervening space from which the glass had been moved no longer contained any sensitized parts, outside of this glass.

III

The similarity this phenomenon has to stories of people who murder at a distance, by wounding a figure of wax modeled in the victim's image, was obvious. I experimented to see if wax, like water, also possesses the property to store sensitivity, and I discovered it possesses it to a high degree, as do other fatty, viscous or velvety substances, such as cold cream and woolen velvet. A small statuette made of modeling wax and sensitized through a period of a few moments facing, and a short distance from, a subject, reproduced the sensation of pricking when I pierced it: toward the top of the body if I pricked the statuette in the head; towards the bottom if I pricked it in the feet (that is to say, the prick was felt in a more or less general manner in the regions which had most directly emanated their effluvia). However, I managed to localize the sensation precisely, by following the witches of old, and implanting a piece of hair cut from the nape of the subject's neck while they were asleep, into the head of my figurine. This was the experiment which our collaborator from the *Cosmos* witnessed, and even participated in. He placed the statuette thus prepared behind the pigeon-holes of a desk, where neither the subject nor me could see it. I woke Miss. L... who, without leaving her place, began to chat with him, until the moment when, turned suddenly and putting her hand behind her head, asked laughing who was pulling her hair. It was very instant when Mr. X... had, without my knowledge, pulled the hair on the statuette.

The effluvia appear to refract in a way similar to light, which could perhaps link them to her, I thought that if, using a lens, one projected the image of a person who was sufficiently externalized onto a viscous layer, one might localize precisely the sensations transmitted from the image to the person. A plate charged with gelatinous bromide and a camera allowed me to accomplish this experiment with ease, which only worked completely when I took care to charge the plate with the subject's sensitivity before placing in the camera. But, after doing this, I obtained a portrait where, if the magnetizer touched any point of the figure or hands on the layer of gelatinous bromide, the subject felt the prick at the point corresponding exactly; and this not only immediately after the Operation, but even three days later, after the portrait had been fixed[187] and brought close to the subject. The latter seems to have felt nothing during the Operation of fixing, which had been done far away from her, and she didn't feel anything much when, instead of the gelatinous bromide, we touched the glass plate which supported it. Wanting to push the experiment as far as possible, and taking advantage of the fact that a doctor was present, I violently pricked the image of the right hand of Miss. L… twice with a pin, without warning, and she cried out in pain and lost consciousness instantly. When she came to, we saw two red subcutaneous lines on the back of her hand which she didn't have previously, and which corresponded exactly to the two abrasions that my pin had made, sliding across the gelatinous layer.

Those are the facts which took place on August 2nd, not in the presence of members of the Academy of the Sciences and the Academy of Medicine, as has been related, but in the presence of three officials of the School. They would, it is true, become academics later on, but they weren't yet, and on that day, they came together by chance in my study, after going to receive their salaries from the bursar. The same evening I left for Grenoble, and couldn't repeat the experiment, but I am convinced that I would obtain once again the exact location of the sensations.[188] With respect to the stigma, I dare not hope to repeat that,

---

[187] Here fixed refers to the process of stopping the development of the photograph by removing any silver halide remaining, thus preventing any further development of the photograph, thus preserving it for posterity, normally using a thiosulfate solution.

[188] On my return from Grenoble, I found Mrs. L…, and I was able to repeat the experience of the photograph, which succeeded without any issue, following the mode of operation recognized as successful on August 2nd.

The image was immediately fixed, and I then made a smooth tear on the layer of collodion with a pin at the location of hands crossed on the chest. The subject swooned and cried, and two or three minutes later the stigmata appeared and gradually developed in front of our eyes on the back of one of her hands, at the place corresponding exactly to the tear.

The snapshot was, moreover, sensitive to my touch alone. The handling by the photographer was only perceived when I established a connection by touching her person, either on the foot or elsewhere.

On October 9th, proof having been concluded on paper, I proved that this test only had a confused sensitivity, that is, that the subject perceived general sensations which were pleasant or unpleasant, depending on the way in which I touched him, but without being able to locate them. Two days later, any sensitivity had disappeared both in the plate and in the subject.

since the person on whom they were produced possessed an ability in this regard which we find only very rarely and which, even for her, is very unusual.[189]

*

* *

THE SYMPATHETIC ALPHABET

This kind of Operation consists of tracing some letters on one's arm by means of a needle, and introducing the blood of a friend into the wound you have just made.

Dr. Luys told me that, during my absence, he had tried to reproduce the phenomenon we had discussed with him, and he had been able to obtain a transmission of sensitivity at 35 meters, a few moments after the sitting.

Finally, someone has just sent me the following extract from an article which appeared in Brussels on October 12th, in the journal Paris-Brussels, under the signature of ARSAC. "We have seen the experiment with the sensitized photographic plate repeated. The connected phenomena occurred each time the pinpricks were administered by the practitioner, by the person who had put the subject to sleep. In the hypnotist's absence, nine times out of ten the portrait could be pricked without the hypnotized subject feeling any pain. Never has the subject testified to the slightest pain when the photographic plate was pricked by a person who was completely ignorant of the purpose of the experiment. "So, we were inclined to conclude that what has been taken to be the phenomenon of enchantment is really only a phenomenon of suggestion. Enchantment is possible; but, for now, we can only reproduce it under certain conditions that have been clearly defined...

"What should be retainedt from the experiments of de Rochas, is that the externalization of sensitivity is now an established fact."

The observation of Mr. Arsac on the need for a connection confirms mine, but it doesn't prove there is a phenomenon of suggestion, or, to state it more precisely, a transmission of thought. I always pricked, without looking, in the area of the hands, and the subject didn't know, any more than me, where the tear which impacted the epidermis was going to occur. Indeed, I have never, as I said in the body of the article, been able to produce any transmission of thought with Mrs. L... The only auto-suggestion admissible is that which would relate to the production of stigmata under the influence of the imagination, to the point where the patient felt the pain.   Paris, October 15th, 1892. [PAPUS]

[189] We have sometimes been able to identify the phenomenon of *dermography* with the subject, which is the swelling of the skin through the simple passing of a blunt point over it. [PAPUS]

This Operation should also be practiced on the individual with whom one needs to enter into correspondence, and then, however far apart the two are from each other, one can be warned about certain events by means of a prick lightly applied to certain letters. This is immediately felt by the person to whom one wishes to address the message.

*

* *

Despite our desire not to include long quotes in this elementary treatise, we were led to summarize the experiments performed at length. These quotes were indispensable to show the reader the reality of these facts of Magic, which have always been put on the list of deceptions and the effects of the "evil eye", along with and the magnetic action of one man on another, or of the will in the Macrocosm, as we say in Occultism. We can now continue our study and begin to detail the actions of the human will over the intelligent forces of Nature.

Let us simply remember that when we need to use the magnetic force, the primary rule to observe is that it is always necessary to act for good, never to attack anyone, and to devote all one's powers to the defense of the weak and the uninformed. This is indeed the only "Right Path". All the others only lead to madness and suffering, if not to *eternal death*. To him who understands this, we salute you.

Bibliography

STANISLAS DE GUAITA.....................*The Serpent of Genesis.*
MARCELLUS LELOIR...........................*Occult Fragments.*
G. VITOUX....................................*The Limits of the Unknown.*
MOUTIN.....................................*The New Hypnosis.*
A. DE ROCHAS.............................*Enchantment.*

Annals of Psychic Sciences. (October 1892)
Annals of Psychiatry and Hypnology. (1890)

CHAPTER XV – THE MAGISTER AND THE MACROCOSM

EVOCATIONS

The radiation of the Magister's will extends over the physical world, which he must modify in its mediate forms and over man, whose magnetism makes him Master in part. Exercising composure can still open a new field of action to the seeker. It concerns invisible Nature, that plane we call "astral" the receptacle of future forms and images from the past, as well as the most active and the most hidden powers permitted to man to use. This is a garden of the Hesperides[190], where only the navigator who is audacious and contemptuous of death and danger may come.

In our visible world, man has learned how to make himself the Master of physical forces, and he has also learned how to subdue and use several animals. A similar field of activity opens to the will in the astral plane.

We know the forces which must be used: they emanate from the stars and we know their character, but the *beings* over which we can have an effect are as yet unknown to us. Authors who have spoken of them always make a great mystery of them, and lead the reader's attention astray by using different names, which they attribute to these beings. Along with the Kabbalah, we will call them ELEMENTALS, carefully remembering that they are also called *elementary spirits, princes of the elements, mortal demons* (δαιμων), etc., etc. We will come to see why there are so many names.

Their role is similar to that of animals in the visible world: they relieve the Operator of a large part of his labors, provided that they are directed and have no responsibility for their actions.

So it is that, for man's work, the dog is a precious help, attached to its master, but having no concern about the moral character of the works which the master has him perform. So, a smuggler's dog will throw itself at the Customs Officer, because he has been trained to perform this action for which he is not responsible; whereas a guard dog of an honest farmer will jump at the calves of young scamps who come to steal apples. A robber's dog or a policeman's dog: in both cases the animal is only a simple assistant, a tool in the hands of his master who alone is responsible for the beast's actions. It is exactly the same

---

[190] The Greek mythical orchard of Hera in the West, containing one tree bearing golden apples, guarded by the Hesperides nymphs, and also Ladon, a hundred-headed dragon, which granted immortality to the consumer.

with the Elementals, who begin their work in the currents of psychic force projected by him who has subjugated them, without inquiring about the intimate character of the action they have been made to undertake.

The Magister's action over the Elementals on the astral plane is directly comparable to the action of a hypnotizer on the nervous cells which preside over the incessant repair of the human body: to command the production of stigmata on a fixed day or make a birthmark disappear, which is exactly the same thing as commanding a slight atmospheric disturbance or discovering a spring. Only the plan of action and the intimate character of the beings put into play are different. In the first case it concerns man, that is, on the microcosmic plane and by means of nervous cell and embryonic cells; in the second case it concerns Nature, that is, the macrocosmic plane and by means of astral beings and Elementals.

But what we should remember is that animals only obey the person who tamed them, and that the person who doesn't have sufficient knowledge, sufficient courage and sufficient experience and composure, yet wishes to act on these astral beings 'for his amusement', is like the idiot who throws himself into the middle of a pack of furious hounds who do not know him. We would prefer to see someone laugh at these experiments a thousand times over, than risk training a rash person in studies in which he might lose his health, if not his mind and even his life. We would therefore charitably counsel the intelligent worldly person to try table-rapping, or to turn their impulsive side to automatic writing and receive sentimental 'communications' from Victor Hugo or Plato: it's not very dangerous, it suits all levels of courage and intelligence, and it makes a long evening go quickly in a pleasant manner. But just as you don't give a microscope showing the intimate actions of organic cells to a child or an uneducated person, you do not place the Elementals at the level of the first experiment.

We can define the Elementals as: *instinctive and mortal beings which are intermediaries between the psychic and material worlds*. This definition agrees with the teachings of tradition which tells us through Porphyry and Iamblichus initially, then Paracelsus and Agrippa, and finally Eliphas Lévi and the Kabbalah, that the spirits are divided into: mortal spirits or spirits of the elements (Elementals), and immortal spirits or human spirits (Elementaries) at different stages of evolution.

The essential characteristic of Elementals is being able to animate instantly all forms of astral substance which condenses around them. They will also appear sometimes as a crowd of eyes fixed upon an individual, sometimes like small luminous and points of brilliant light surrounded by a phosphorescent substance which obey the orders of human speech, and sometimes like strange animals, unknown on earth, and like unusual combinations of animal and human forms, whose reproductions we will see in a moment. For now, it is enough to remember that the Elemental has nothing bad in him, and is just as inoffensive as a poor animal when it is left alone.

To come in contact with the Elementals, one must enter into the astral plane. One can accomplish this either personally through psychic training and meditation, or by means of an intermediary using a somnambulistic subject.

But you should know that every human being enters into a close relationship with the astral world immediately before falling asleep and immediately before waking, that is to say, that the connection between the impulsive being (the astral body) and the conscious being undergoes some kind of change. This relationship between the two planes also happens at the moment of a sudden joy or fear, and also at the instant of a grave foreboding. The progressive disequilibrium of the human being, going under the name of *"transemotional impulse"*[191] because of the vision, hearing or incarnation, also allows entering into a connection with the astral plane, and as a result with the Elementals.

That is why many people, as the moment of falling asleep and when their eyes are closed, see strange heads and bizarre shapes advancing towards the bed at an incredible speed, which vanish only to be replaced by others. Those strange nightmares, visions and profanations which precede sleep may be the result of organic problems, or also due to Elementals, depending on the situation.

Also, the existence of these beings can only be affirmed by those who have seen them, and with their personal assurance. Without wishing to describe our own works, which are still unfinished concerning such an interesting point of Magic, we will report on some drawings made by two principle subjects, and the facts of some very special circumstances.

The first of these designs was obtained with a subject placed in front of a magic mirror of carbon.[192] This subject (a society woman) had never been hypnotized and hasn't been since. She didn't know how to draw and was content to quickly outline the contours of the forms she saw appear in the improvised magic mirror.

---

[191] *Entraînement médianimique* – no English translation could be found for this term.
[192] Being improvised, one may assume it was made out of a plate of glass held over a candle so that carbon was deposited on the back to create the mirror.

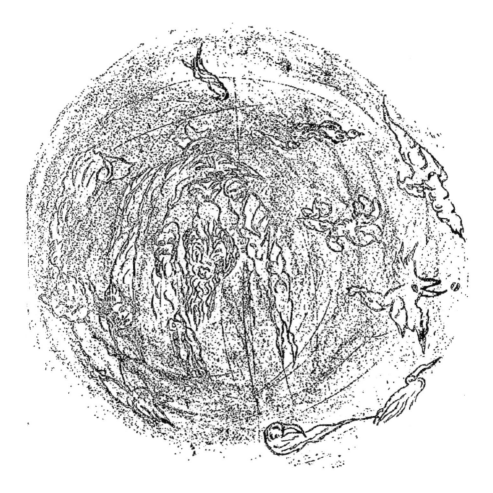

We have some photographs in our possession of this vision, but the necessities of printing have obliged us to reproduce this most curious plate very roughly. In this image, the most disparate forms carried in the whirlwind of astral forces can be perceived. This agrees on all points, not only with our personal research, but also with the accounts of all those who have also perceived these beings which are unknown to all except magicians.

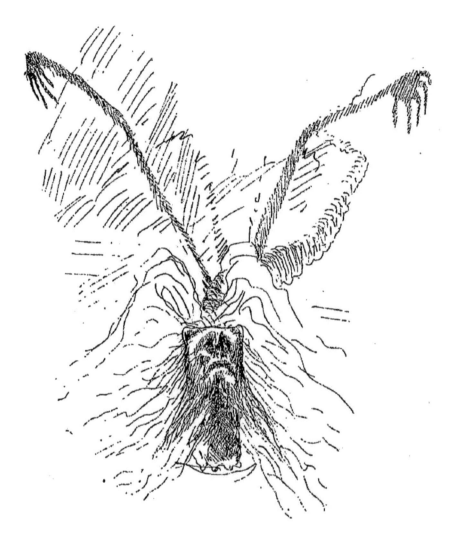

The second series of drawings were obtained by one of our friends, C. de P., who is very sensitive to telepathic experiments at a distance, and under unusual conditions. C. de P. was seated at a table one afternoon around 4:00 o'clock in the afternoon, and had several sheets of white paper in front of him. Suddenly, he was seized with a violent fit of sadness, without the least cause, and this during a conversation he was having with two people present. It seemed to him as though a veil had been torn in front of him, and he suddenly had a perception of beings and strange forms for four to five minutes. It was then that he made these drawings, copying his vision precisely, he said. If our memory is accurate, our friend has never seen the results of our previous experiments, we were absent at the time, and it was only two hours later, when we returned, that we saw the drawings. Moreover, his sincerity and honesty are above any suspicion, and the agreement of these later drawings with our first one, and their similarity to the so-called images of the old Grimoires will strike any conscientious observer. Here, then, are the drawings obtained during this second experiment which were so unexpected.

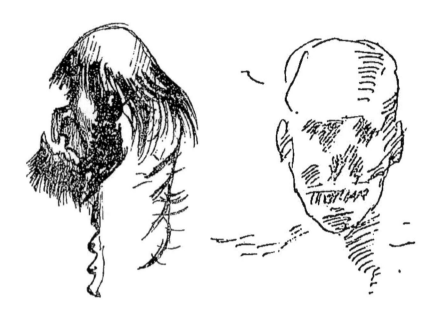

Now that we have described as clearly as possible all that Occult Science teaches concerning Elementals, we will begin a study of the various means used to act on these being and direct them.

To understand these means properly, one should know that these beings are theoretically divided into four great classes corresponding to the four elemental forces and to the four letters of the Tetragrammaton.

To these four classes of Elementals are given respectively the names of Gnomes (Earth), Salamanders (Fire), Sylphs (Air), and Undines (Water). These divisions have no other purpose, we know, than the modifications which the astral substance undergoes, depending on the various environments in which it is manifested. However, it is no less true that these modifications determine the use of the various implements, Kabbalistic words, prayers, conjurations, etc., being used. We have put together a Table of Concordances based on Eliphas Lévi, which itself is a summary of the IVth Book of Agrippa (not yet translated) on Practical Magic. An attentive reading of this table will provide the preliminary instructions necessary.

To conjure Air Earth, Water and Fire, refer to what we've said in the first chapter of this third part, as well as the prayers, adding the following instructions which complete certain points which were left incomplete till now.

TABLE OF CORRESPONDENCES OF THE MAGICAL QUATERNARY[193]

(taken from Eliphas Lévi (1861). Ritual p. 86.

	ELEMENT	KING	CARDINAL POINT	TEMPERAMENT	HIEROGLYPH	MAGICAL IMPLEMENT
GNOMES	EARTH	GHOB	NORTH	MELANCHOLIC (Pessimist)	TAURUS	SWORD
SALAMANDERS	FIRE	DJIN	SOUTH	SANGUINE (Active)	LEO	WAND (Trident)
SYLPHS	AIR	PARALDA	EAST	BILIOUS (Ambitious)	EAGLE	TALISMANS (Pantacles)
UNDINES	WATER	NICHSA	WEST	PHLEGMATIC (Tranquil)	AQUARIUS	CUP

EXORCISM OF AIR

(Prayer)

Spiritus Dei ferebatur super aquas, et inspiravit in faciem hominis spiraculum vitae. Sit MICHAEL dux meus, et SABTABIEL servus meus, in luce et per lucem.

Fiat verbum halitus meus ; et imperabo spiritibus æris huius, et refrænabo equos solis voluntate cordis mei, et cogitatione mentis meæ et nutut oculi dextri.

Exorciso igitur te, creatura æris, per Pentagrammaton et in nomine YOD-HEH-VAV-HEH, in quibus sunt volunta firma et fides recta. *Amen.*[194]

---

[193] The Table, together with most of the section, is asembled from Eliphas Lévi's book on Ritual Magic. One amusing misprint which persisted from the first edition of Papus' book at least until the 1906 version, was the name of the King of Earth Elementals, which was given as 'Bob'! The reader will also note some points which differ from contemporary attributions. Firstly, the second column title is 'Genius' rather than 'King', although Lévi's book clearly calls them the sovereigns of each element. Secondly, it is worth noting that in magic the Eagle and Scorpion are often interchangeable, and Aquarius stands in for Man: thus, the Hieroglyphs also equate with the four beasts of the Merkabah. Finally, note that the magical implements listed in Lévi's book differ from those now equated with the four Elements, in that Earth is represented by Pantacles and Air by Swords. These would seem more logical, since the Gnomes are associated with wealth and therefore gold and coins; while swords and knives are used to cut through Air.

[194] "The Spirit of God moved upon the waters, and breathed the breath of life into the face of man. Let Michael by my leader, and Sabtabiel my servant, in light and by light.

EXORCISM OF EARTH

The earth is exorcized by the sprinkling of water, by breath and by fire, with incense appropriate to each day, and the Prayer of the Gnomes is said.

*
* *

The Magister's action over the Elementals should begin with exervcising full sovereignty of will over the physical world.

Eliphas Lévi summarized the detail of this action in his ritual, and as a reminder we should remember that he who has vertigo will never command the Gnomes; he who fears the tempest will always be conquered by the Undines; the Salamanders will laugh at him who is scared of fire; and the Sylphs at him who is terrified of thunder and storms.

It's through prayer, as we've said, by aljusting the ritual prayers according to the four Cardinal Points according to the correspondence of the implements, that one can command the Elementals. One should always remember that any practical study to this end should be done in the middle of a Magic Circle. This way one is completely isolated, and safe from any deceit by the powers of the Astral.

Meditation in darkness, with isolation aided by wood and the discretionary use of a sword, allows one to see the Elementals quickly.

By way of an extension, we give here the three great magical conjurations which are quioted by Eliphas Lévi.

CONJURATION OF THE FOUR

Caput mortuum, imperet tibi Dominus per vivum et devotum serpentum. – Cherub, imperet tibi Dominus per Adam Jotchavah! – Aquila errans, imperet tibi Dominus per alas Tauri! – Serpens, imperet tibi Dominus tetragrammaton per Angelum et Leonem!
Michaël! Gabriël! Raphaël! Anaël!

Let the Word be my breath, and I will command the spirits of Air thereby, and I will breathe the horses of the Sun with the will of my heart, and the thoughts of my mind and the commandment of my right eye. Therefore, I exorcise thee, O Creature of Air, by Pentagrammaton and in the name of Yod-Heh-Vav-Heh, in which are firm will and true will. Amen."

Fluat udor per spiritum *Elohim.*
Maneat terra per *Adam-Iotchavah.*
Fiat firmamentum per *Iahuvehu-Tzabaoth.*
Fiat judicum per ignem in virtute *Michaël.*[195]
O angel with the dead eyes, obey or be drowned in this holy water.
O Winged bull, work, or return to the earth, if you do not want me to pierce
you with this sword.
Chained eagle, obey this sign, or retire before this breath.
Stirring serpent, crawl at my feet, or be tormented by the sacred fire, and
dissipate in the incense which I burn here.
May the water return to water; may the fire burn; may the air flow; may the
earth fall upon the earth by virtue of the Pentagram, which is the morning
star, and in the Name of the Tetragrammaton, which is written in the
center of the cross of light. *Amen.*

CONJURATION OF THE SEVEN

In the name of Michaël, may Jehovah command you and drive you far from
here, Chavajoth!
In the name of Gabriël, may Adonaï command you and drive you far from
here, Belial!
In the name of Raphaël, disappear before Elohim, Sachabiel!
By Samaël Tzabaoth and in the name of Elohim Gibor, be far from here,
Adramelech!
By Zachariël and Sachiël-Melech, obey Eloah, Samgabiel!
In the divine and human name of Shaddaï, and by the sign of the pentagram
which I hold in my right hand, in the name of the angel Anaël, by the

---

[195] Death head, may the Lord command thee by the living and consecrated serpent.
Cherub, may the Lord command thee by Adam Jotchavah! Wandering eagle, may the
Lord command thee by the wings of the Bull! Serpent, may the Lord command thee by
the Angel and the Lion! Michael! Gabriel! Raphael! Anael! Let liquid flow by the spirit
of Elohim. Let the earth stand by Adam-Iotchavah. Let the firmament endure by
Iahuvehu-Tzabaoth. Let justice endure by fire in the power of Michael.

power of Adam and Eve[196], who are Iotchavah, leave this place, Lilith. Leave us in peace, Nahemah![197]

By the holy Elohim and the names of the geniuses Cassiël, Sehaltiël, Aphiël and Zahariël, by the command of Oriphiël, turn from us, Moloch! We shall not give you our children to devour!

INVOCATION OF SOLOMON

Powers of the kingdom, be beneath my left foot and in my right hand!

Glory and Eternity, touch my two shoulders, and lead me in the paths of victory!

Mercy and Justice, be the balance and splendor of my life!

Intelligence and Wisdom, give me the crown!

Spirits of Malkuth, lead me, between the two pillars upon which the whole edifice of the Temple rests!

Angels of Netzach and Hod, establish me upon the cubic stone of Yesod!

O Gedulaël, O Geburaël, O Tiphereth, O Binaël, be my love!

Ruach Chokmaël, be my Light!

Be what you are and what you shall be, O Ketheriël!

Ischim, assist me in the name of Shaddaï!

Cherubim, be my strength in the name of Adonaï!

Beni Elohim, be my brothers in the name of the Son, and by the virtues of Tzabaoth!

Elohim, fight for me in the name of Tetragrammaton!

Malachim, protect me in the name of Yod-Heh-Vav-Heh!

Seraphim, purify my love in the name of Eloah!

Chasmalim, enlighten me with the splendors of Eloï and of the Shekinah!

Aralim, act; Ophanim, revolve and be resplendent!

Chayoth ha-Kadosh, cry, speak, roar, bellow: Kadosh! Kadosh! Kadosh!

---

[196] In the original this is *Heva*, which is the Hebrew pronunciation of 'Eve'. In modern French bibles Eve is written as *Éve*. Now, a number of Kabbalistic commentaries point out that if the first 'H' is aspirated (if silent the names would sounds like 'Eva', this forms 'Cheva', which allegedly in Phoenician and Aramaic refers to 'serpent'.

[197] In many traditions Lilith was Adam's first wife, who was sufficiently confident in her equality that she refused to lie beneath Adam. Therefore, the more compliant Eve was formed. In the Zohar, Naamah is sister to Lilith, demons who visit Adam and bear demonic children from his seed when he separates from Eve for a time, following Abel's murder.

Shaddai! Adonai! Iotchavah! Eheieh Asher Eheieh!198
Hallelujah! Hallelujah! Hallelujah! Amen.

It's to the knowledge of the Elementals and their actions, that the various practices concerning the evocation of astral forms are associated:

1. This evocation should be performed in the following manner, when the Operator is satisfied with his psychic training and dietary habits.
2. Trace the Circle according to the planetary correspondences.
3. Give a magical prayer in the Circle following the ritual indicated, during which burn an appropriate perfume on the altar, with the light illuminating the smoke of the perfume before the magic mirror.
4. Recite the Prayer of the Gnomes, Sylphs, Undines or Salamanders, depending on the case.
5. Perform   the   Conjuration   (following   the   planetary correspondences).
6. After their appearance in the mirror, send them on their way.

All the details concerning the implements, the Circle, etc., may be found in the last chapter of this part of the book.

We will give the two first evocations *by virtue of curiosity*, and a final one taken from Eliphas Lévi, as a preliminary opening to the ritual of evocation which we will analyze in a later chapter.

EVOCATIONS FROM THE GRIMOIRES

TO MAKE A GIRL COME TO YOU, HOWEVER MODEST SHE MAY BE;
EXPERIENCE A MARVELOUS POWER OF THE SUPERIOR INTELLIGENCES.

During the waxing or waning Moon, look for a star between the hours of eleven and midnight; but before beginning this process, do what follows:

Take virgin parchment, and write on it the name of the girl you wish to come. On the other side of the parchment, write the words: Melchiael, Barechas,

---

[198] This last name appears in Lévi as *Eieazereie* and Papus as *Eiazerie*. It seems clear that Lévi was trying to say *Eheieh Asher Eheieh*, meaning 'I Am That I Am', the name God gave to Moses at the burning bush. Papus apparently mistyped the name.

then put the parchment on the earth, with the person's name next to the ground, with the right foot upon it and the left knee upon the ground. Then look at the most brilliant star, and holding a taper of white wax, sufficiently large to burn for one hour in your right hand, say the following salutation:

Conjuration.

I hail thee and I conjure thee, O beautiful Moon and beautiful Star, brilliant light which I hold in my hand. By the air that I breathe, by the air which is upon me, by the earth that I touch, I conjure thee, by all the names of the spirit princes which live within you, by the ineffable name ON, which created all, by thee, resplendent angel Gabriël, with the prince Mercury, Michaël and Melchidaël.

I conjure thee again by all the Divine Names of God, that thou mayest send down power to beset, torment and trouble the body, soul and the five natural senses of N…, whose name is written here, so that she may come to me and accomplish my will; and may she not have love for anybody in the world, especially for N…, so long as she is indifferent to me, and may she be unable to endure, may she be obsessed, suffering and tormented. Go, then, at once, Melchidaël, Baresches, Zazel, Phiriel, Malcha, and all those who are with thee! I conjure thee by the Great Living God to send her promptly to accomplish my will, and I, N…, promise to satisfy you.

When this conjuration has been said three times, burn the parchment with the taper. On the following day, take the ashes from the parchment and place it in your left shoe, and leave it there until the person for whom you performed the Operation comes to seek you out. In the conjuration you must specify the day you wish her to come, and she will not fail.

To Make Three Ladies or Three Gentlemen Appear in Your Room After Supper.

It is necessary to be chaste for three days. On the fourth day, clean and prepare your room in the morning, as soon as you have dressed, while still fasting. Make preparations so that your room will not be disturbed for the rest of the day, and note that there should be nothing hanging in it nor anything on hooks such as tapestries, clothing, hats, bird cages, bed curtains, etc. Above all, put white sheets on your bed.

The Ceremony.

After supper go confidently to your room, prepared as above. Light a good fire, place a white cloth on the table, and three chairs around it. In front of each place, put a wheat roll and three glasses filled with clear and fresh water. Then place a chair or armchair by the side of the bed, and retire, saying the following words:

Conjuration.

Besticitum consolatio veni ad me vertut Creon, Creon, Creon, cantor laudem omnipotentis et non commentur. Stat superior carta bient laudem omviestra principiem da montem et inimicos meos ô prostantis vobis et mihi dantes que passium fieri sincisibus.[199]

The three people having arrived, will sit by the fire, eating and drinking, and will then thank the person who has entertained them. If it is a woman who has done this ceremony, three young men will come; and if it is a man, three girls will come.

Then the three will draw lots to determine who will stay with you. The person who wins will sit in the armchair or chair which you placed by the bed, and will stay and talk with you until midnight.[200] At this time the person will leave, along with her companions, without needing to dismiss them. With regard to the two others, they will stay by the fire while the first entertains you; and while that person is with you, you can interrogate them about any art, science or subject you wish, and they will immediately answer you in a positive manner. You may also ask them if they know of any hidden treasure and they will tell you the spot, and the best time and place to dig it up, and even to find it with his or her companions in order to defend you against the attacks of the infernal spirits which have it in their possession. And on departing, he or she will present you with a ring which will make you lucky in games of chance when you wear it on your finger; and if you place the ring on the finger of a woman or a girl, you will get to enjoy her immediately.

NOTE: You should leave the window open so that he or she can enter. You can repeat this ceremony any time you wish.

---

[199] There are several mistyped words in Papus' version. Any discovered have been corrected.

[200] One gets the impression that talking is not the first order of business…

EVOCATION OF LOVE
ACCORDING TO ELIPHAS LÉVI

(Ritual on p. 185 et seq.)

Firstly, you must carefully recollect every memory of him or her you wish to see again, the objects they used, and which have retained an imprint, and hang a room which the person inhabited while alive, or a similar place, with their portrait, veiled in white, in the midst of flowers which that person loved and which should be replaced each day.

Then you must observe a precise date, a day of the year which was either their birthday or the happiest day for your affection for one another, a day whose memory you believe that, however happy they are now, their soul could not have forgotten. It is that precise day you should choose for the evocation, for which you will prepare for the preceding fourteen days.

During that time, you must be sure not to give the same tokens of affection to anyone else which the deceased had the right to expect from you. You must observe a strict chastity, live in retreat, and only have one modest meal, and one light snack each day.

Every evening, at the same time, you must close yourself off with a single, dim light, such as a small funerary lamp or candle, in the room set aside to the memory of the deceased person. Place this light behind you, then uncover the portrait, in whose presence you remain in silence. Then cense the room with a little good incense, and leave by walking backwards. On the day set aside for the evocation, you must dress up from the morning as if for a celebration. Do not speak first to anyone the entire day, and only have a single meal of bread, wine, and roots or fruits. The tablecloth should be white, and you will set the table for two and break off a portion of the bread, which should have been served whole. You will also put a few drops of wine in the glass of the person you wish to evoke.

This meal must be eaten in silence, in the room of evocation, in the presence of the veiled portrait. Then remove everything used for the meal, with the exception of the deceased's glass and serving of bread, which will be placed before their portrait.

In the evening, at the time of the usual visit, go into the room in silence, and light a bright fire with cypress wood, and throw incense seven times upon it, while pronouncing the name of the person you wish to see again. Then extinguish the lamp and let the fire die out. On this day do not veil the portrait again. When the fire has gone out, place incense on the coals and invoke God following the formula of the religion to which the deceased person belonged, and in accordance with the ideas they themselves had of God.

When saying this prayer, you must identify yourself with the person being evoked: speak as they would have spoken, believe in the same way they had believed. Then, after a quarter of an hour of silence, talk to them as though them were present, with affection and faith, while praying them to show themselves to you. Repeat this prayer mentally while covering your face with both hands, then call out to the person three times in a loud voice. Wait, while kneeling and with your eyes closed or covered for a few minutes, while speaking to them mentally; then call out three times to them once again in a soft and affectionate voice, and slowly open your eyes. If you see nothing, you will have to try the experiment again in a year's time, and up to three more times. It is certain that by at least the third time you will obtain the desired appearance, and, the longer they took, the more visible they will be, and strikingly real.

*

* *

As one can see, in these variations of astral forms, all the power used is exclusively drawn from the Operator. In modern séances, the spirits or the gifts of magic are completed corrupted, and it is a human in a state of hypnosis, called a *medium*, who provides the necessary power, and whose psychic power is drawn in voluptuously by the Elementals present. It is indeed thanks to this vital force that the entities can manifest themselves, and the ancients used the blood of victims to this end, as one can see in Homer.

In difficult experiments, we add to the burning of perfumes the action of the astral body of some animal, usually a batrachian (most often a frog).

Bibliography

ELIPHAS LÉVI.. *Ritual of High Magic.*
STANISLAS DE GUAITA........................... *The Serpent of Genesis.*
JULES LERMINA................................. *Practical Magic.*
DURVILLE.. *Practical Treatise of Magnetism.*

Grimoires attributed to Albertus Magnus. – Keys of Solomon. – Grimoire of Honorius.

CHAPTER XVI – HERMETIC MEDICINE

ALLOPATHY – HOMEOPATHY – HERMETISM

The characteristics and healing of obsessions

Healing is one of the principle aims offered by initiation to the Magister. Therapeutic science is threefold, and can focus on the body, the astral body and the psychic being. To each of these divisions corresponds a special medicine.

The physical body is affected by the actions of material substances gives in high doses. This is materialist medicine, Allopathy, the medicine of contraries, the only one known to and accepted by the majority of contemporary people prejudiced by narrow positivism.

The astral body is affected by fluidic substances supported by minute doses of matter. This is Homeopathic medicine and the action of similar branches, the first application of Magic to the Microcosm.

The psychological being is affected by the action of ideas vitalized by the will of the Magister. From this comes magnetic medicine and the action of the psychic forces.

Finally, the management of the psychic fluids, linked to the knowledge of astral dynamics, brings together all these actions and constitutes Hermetic medicine, known to only a few Adepts.

It is a lack of understanding of these basic divisions that lead people to make such rash judgements about the therapeutic art, which is however so useful to every student who desires to practice the teachings of Esotericism.

Also, although the teachings we are going to cover are concerned on the one hand with man's action on the Microcosm, and on the other hand with the action of Nature on this Microcosm, we have preferred to give a focus which is particularly aimed at those interested in medicine, and who wish to understand the connections which Magic has to the various schools of medicine.

Above all, it is essential to remember the theories of Magic concerned with the endless development of the human organism.

The physical body is manufactured by the astral body, which itself only realizes the general principles or the original ideas of all material form. This concept is summarized in the Law which states: *the Visible is but the manifestation of the Invisible*.

Now, since all afflictions are the result of some trouble in the action of the generating elements, be they physical, astral or psychological, there are three means, three points of different departure, which lead to equilibrium being destroyed.

One can act on the physical body by means which are purely physical, focusing primarily on the sick organ and calming the symptoms by removing it. This is the *medicine of opposites*, or physical medicine, the most used in the official schools and the fundamental basis of Allopathy.

One can act on the astral body by more subtle means, by supporting a considerable dynamism with a minute piece of matter. In this case one reinforces the astral organ responsible for restoring the equilibrium which has been destroyed. This is the *medicine of similarities*, or astro-magnetic medicine, the most unknown of the official schools, and the fundamental basis of Homeopathy.

Finally, one can act on the psychological being through purely magical means, by stimulating the creative ideas which modify all material forms. This is the *medicine of correspondences*, or Hermetic medicine, which official school believe goes under the title of *hypnotherapy*, but whose complete development leads to sacred therapeutics.

These, then, are the three fundamental divisions of the Schools of Medicine across the ages. We are now going to study those facts which are most important to know.

The afflictions which the human being is capable of suffering are also classed according to the center especially being attacked. These afflictions can affect the physical body, the astral body or the psychological being; but never the spirit, which can only by troubled in its connection with the organism, but not in its essence.

Thus, Allopathy finds its application in illnesses originating in the physical body.

Homeopathy, on the other hand, gives excellent results in afflictions coming from the astral body, such as illnesses of the chest, cancer, and certain forms of nervous ailments (St. Vitus's dance, shaking paralysis, etc.).

Hermetic medicine is used in psychological afflictions, such as those cases of obsession or vampirism so little understood by current doctors, who confuse them with madness.

As we cannot give a treatise on medicine in a few pages, we will indicate the principal means placed at the Magister's disposal for his therapeutic activities.

When you find yourself in the presence of someone who is ill, the first rule to observe is to determine the planetary influence which governs that human being.

If you don't have sufficient knowledge of the astral signatures, it is enough to know the month and day of birth. The table we give below indicates the planetary influence which one may consider to be the principle one.

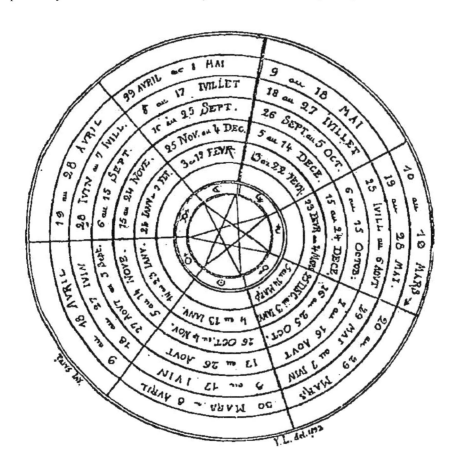

Table of Planetary Influences

Then one should revisit our chapter on Realization in Nature (in the second part), where you will find the Table of Correspondences necessary for determining the inclination of the invalid towards such or such illness, according to the planetary correspondences.

Finally, verify the connections of the Zodiacal Signs presiding over the birth with the corresponding organs. It would also be a good idea to draw up a quick horoscope for the Magical Operation, to see the relative planetary positions in the heavens on the date of birth of the invalid in question.

But, in current practice, indications taken from the following table alone will suffice to give a preliminary idea of the planetary influences in play. Once this initial result has been obtained, how do we effect a cure?

If the illness is connected with the physical body, the use of alcohol and plants which fortify the invalid's good planetary influences will suffice. You can find a list of these plants together with their connections in our chapter on Natural Astrology. You can also find important entries on this subject in the Little Magical Dictionary in the Appendix, either under the names of the planets or the names of the illnesses.

If the affliction has an astral origin, the use of perfumes connected with magnetism will be of great help. In this case you can also make talismans under influences favorable to the healing of the illness. Homeopathy, enlightened by study of the Astronomical correspondences, is also very useful in this type of affliction.

Finally, in illnesses which affect the connections of the nervous force uniting the psychological being with the spirit, or which overtake the psychological being itself at its core, the Magister can make use of *music*, managed according to the principles explained in the Realization of Man (2nd Part); then the *power of the word* acts through persuasion, a procedure which have given marvelous results in America to initiates of "Christian Science", magnetism united with magical formulas allowing them to achieve a great number of successes.

However, we need to give some information about the healing of obsessions.

Obsession

The human being in certain conditions of nervous irritability, under the influence of great fear, remorse, violent hatred, etc., etc., generates particular entities in his astral atmosphere called *larvae* in Occultism, which are nourished by the astral substance of the incautious person who has given birth to them. This is the great danger of psychic experiments, and we have already warned our readers on this topic.

Now, a person who fears being hated by another, and who believes himself to be persecuted, creates a larva which is brought into being by this idea like a soul, and by his own vital force like an astral body. Little by little this larva penetrates the substance of the obsessed person; soon madness breaks out, and it becomes necessary to confine that person, who was too weak to be able to conquer the impulse of terror coming from his psychological center.

It is the same with the creation of remorse, which haunts the astral of murderers to the point of bringing them to confess their offense, or to seek relief to this horrible suffering in death. The larva of this latter type is so much more terrible because it is partly constituted by the astral body of the victim. The practice of mediumship can also lead to these obsessions, and we can personally name several mediums afflicted with this dangerous condition and who have come to ask for our help in this regard.

So, it is very important to let the official doctors treat lunatics and invalids, and to heal those who are possessed by Magic; but it is important to know how one can remove an obsession.

To this end, two main procedures can be used:

1. Indirect action, based on the correspondence between the physical and the astral, which requires the subject to be in a profound hypnotic state.
2. Direct action, based on Ceremonial Magic and which ordinarily only requires the use of the sword in the Operation.

The first procedure will be sufficiently described by the following commentary.

While in London, we had the opportunity to get to know a famous mystic who believed herself to be persecuted by an enemy considered, rightly or wrongly, to be quite expert in Practical Magic. The obsession had become sufficiently violent to lead to two attempts at suicide, stopped in time by witnesses who arrived unexpectedly. This idea of suicide was normally stronger when the invalid (I never considered her as anything else) went to a specific corner of her bedroom. Brought up-to-date with the situation, we tried the following experiment: among the people who came to visit the house, we noted a woman who was quite nervous and who had never been hypnotized. At our request this woman, who was ignorant of that was going on, agreed to lend herself to a hypnotic attempt, and was asleep within a few minutes. Slow passes soon confirmed a state of hypnosis deep enough for the subject to describe to us a kind of fluidic noose situated in the corner of the bedroom. We drew the noose, guided by the subject's description, on a piece of paper recently consecrated and censed. Once the drawing was finished, a formula and a prayer placed the physical image in communication with the astral image. It was then that, with a long steel blade, we divided the drawing into several portions which, according to writings on the topic, immediately connected with the fluidic object, which then also went to pieces.

Whether through suggestion or for another reason, the desire to die by strangulation immediately left the sick woman, who has been fine ever since (in fact, it has been two years).

In sum, this procedure consisted of repeating astral images in the physical world, to establish a magical link between the drawing and the image, then to execute upon the drawing those changes one wished to carry out on the astral image. A subject who is electrically isolated is needed for this experiment.

The second procedure is more active and is used in cases where obsession has taken on a particularly grave character.

It is based on the fact that Elementals and larvae are nourished by the astral substance, and that blood contains the most of this substance.

Now, supposing a person is violently obsessed, one operates as follows:

Take a lock of hair from the person in question, and cense this lock, consecrating it following the usual procedure.

Once this has been done, go to the invalid, and soak the hair in the blood of a pigeon or a guinea-pig in front of him, which has also been consecrated under the influence of Jupiter or Apollo, pronouncing the Great Conjuration of Solomon. For this Operation the purified officiant will be dressed in white.

Then place the lock of hair soaked in blood on a small board and trace a circle around the lock with a mixture of pulverized charcoal and lodestone.[201]

Once this has been done, write the four letters of the sacred Tetragrammaton at the four cardinal points within the circle.

Then, with a magical sword (or at a pinch with the point of an ordinary piece of steel terminating in an isolating sleeve of varnished wood), firmly pierce the lock of hair soaked in blood, while commanding the larva to dissolve.

It is rare for this experiment, repeated three times at seven-day intervals, not to give very satisfactory results. This ritual was created in broad outline by François-Charles Barlet, and we have only modified its details.[202]

This Ceremony has given us wonderful results on several occasions when there was an immediate need to confine the invalid. Rereading the facts

---

[201] This powder may be obtained by pulverizing a piece of lodestone. In Paris, opposite Notre Dame, there is a merchant, a vendor of Physics equipment, who sells natural lodestone. [PAPUS].

[202] François-Charles Barlet was the penname of Alfred Faucheux (1838 – 1921), a friend of Papus. In 1885, he joined the Hermetic Brotherhood of Luxor; and he was one of the co-founders of the Ordre Kabbalistique de la Rose-Croix in 1881, along with Joséphin Péladan, Papus, Stanislas de Guaita, Paul Adam and Charles Melinge.

surrounding Cideville, one may easily reconstitute a comprehensive theory of the steel point, and how it worked with regard to the electrical agglomerations.

*
* *

This question concerning obsession asks for particular attention on the part of the Magister, and this is why we have devoted a special study to it, which has allowed us to say a few words about medicine and its divisions from the point of view of Occult Science.

We can now return finally combining all the Operations we have talked about till now. But first, we will end this chapter with some interesting traditions from Folk Magic.

Hermetic Medical Traditions Preserved in the Countryside

To know whether an invalid will live or die.

Many are the judgements made by people if an invalid should live or die: but I will publish the present infallible sign which can serve a person to give a firm judgement.

Take a nettle and place it in the urine of the incontinent invalid, after the invalid has passed it, and leave the nettle in the urine for the space of twenty-four hours, and afterwards, if the nettle is found to be dry, it is a sign of death, and it is found to be green, it is a sign of life.

To protect against gout.

This illness is caused by Saturn[203]. At the hour of Mars or Venus take the herb called Marica, crush it and mix it with the yellow of an egg into the shape of a match, and eat it on an empty stomach: this will protect you from gout.

---

[203] Instead of these herbs, which are mainly unknown, one can name those which we listed in our chapter on Natural Astrology, according to their planetary correspondences. [PAPUS].

For fistulas.

This ailment is caused by Mars. At the hour of Saturn or Jupiter, his enemies, take the root of Lirios in powdered from, and mix it with the ashes of boiled oysters and pig-bread, and apply it to the fistula.

To wash away the spots from smallpox.

This ailment is caused by Mars. At the hour of the Moon, Mercury, Saturn or Jupiter, his enemies, take Litharge, the root of dry reeds, corn flour and rice flour. Crush and mix it with sweet almond oil and the liquified fat of mutton, and anoint the face, leaving it on throughout the night and morning, then wash it off with warm water.

For kidney stones.

This illness is caused by the Moon. At the hour of Mars or Mercury, take scorpions, and place them in an earthenware pot with a narrow mouth, and place it in an oven which isn't too hot for a period of six hours, then take it out and quickly crush it.

For colic pains.

This illness is caused by the Moon. At the hour of Mars or Mercury, her enemies, take laurel fruits and make a powder of them, and give two grams to be drunk in aromatic wine. This will relieve the pain.

For difficulty urinating.

This ailment is caused by the Moon. At the hour of Mars or Mercury, her enemies, take the seeds of triolet and the seeds of Alsabanus, and boil them in water. From this concoction add a cantharides beetle with the head, feet and wings removed, ground to a powder, and drink a spoonful. This will allow urination.

For dropsy.

This illness is caused by Saturn. At the hour of Mars or Venus, his enemies, take a pheasant. Kill it and take the blood. Give this in two glasses to drink, and the invalid will be invariably cured.

For stomach pains.

This illness is caused by Saturn. At the hour or Mars, Mercury or the Moon, his enemies, take a chicken and kill it. Take out the rough part of the small stomach and crush it to a powder. Give it to drink with wine: it is a good remedy.

Chapter XVII – Bringing It All Together

THE GREAT OPERATION

We have followed the Magister in his training which allows him to appropriately dynamize his will. We have seen him magnetize, concentrate and then radiate the psychic force outside him in various Operations. He must now begin the study requiring the greatest effort which can be asked of human nature: the Great Evocation and the Externalization of the Astral Body.[204]

The Great Evocation, which brings together all the magical teachings into one Ceremony, is described in a few manuscripts published under the name of "The Clavicles of Solomon." It comprises the truly esoteric part of Practical Kabbalah, and we are going to expose its elements as clearly as possible by summarizing, in a few pages, the most serious and most authentic practices of all those ancient Grimoires. However, we will respect so far as possible the style and even the faults in Latin in these ancient manuscripts, the better to state precisely the purely archeological character of our reconstitution.

We said that this practice constituted the bringing together of all magical teachings; and we also find in the Clavicles, or Keys, a mountain of teachings concerning the planets and the correspondences which would be superfluous for a reader in possession of this treatise.

However, we are going to transcribe a summary of the theory of the invisible world titled: "Discourse of Solomon to Rehoboam, his son", and which will certainly receive the appreciation it deserves. We transcribed this passage from the exemplar in the National Library.

---

[204] *la grande évocation er la dédoublement* – in the book, Papus in fact writes 'the Grand Evocaiton and Splitting in Two' or 'Doubling'. It is odd that at this climax to the book, when he announces with a fanfare that the reader is finally going to learn how to do Magic, this previously clear and unambiguous author would cloud his grand announcement with this bizarre addition. Since it completely ruins the flow and the gravity of the announcement, it has been omitted, and only included in this footnote for the sake of completeness. However, the section on the Astral Body comes after the section on Solomonic Magic in this book

DISCOURSE OF SOLOMON TO REHOBOAM, HIS SON

O my Son Roboam! seeing that of all Sciences there is none more useful than the knowledge of Celestial Movements, I have thought it my duty, being at the point of death, to leave thee an inheritance more precious than all the riches which I have enjoyed. And in order that thou mayest understand how I have arrived at this degree (of wisdom), it is necessary to tell thee that one day, when I was meditating upon the power of the Supreme Being, the Angel of the Great God appeared before me as I was saying: *O quam mirabilia opera Dei*, O how wonderful are the works of God. I suddenly beheld, at the end of a thickly-shaded vista of trees, a Light in the form of a blazing Star, which said unto me with a voice of thunder: "Solomon, Solomon, be not dismayed; the Lord is willing to satisfy thy desire by giving thee knowledge of whatsoever thing is most pleasant unto thee. I order thee to ask of Him whatsoever thou desirest." Whereupon, recovering from my surprise, I answered unto the Angel, that according to the Will of the Lord, I only desired the Gift of Wisdom, and by the Grace of God I obtained in addition the enjoyment of all the Celestial treasures and the knowledge of all natural things.

It is by this means, my Son, that I possess all the virtues and riches of which thou now seest me In the enjoyment, and In order that thou mayest be willing to be attentive to all which I am about to relate to thee, and that thou mayest retain with care all that I am about to tell thee, I assure thee that the Graces of the Great God will be familiar unto thee, and that the Celestial and Terrestrial Creatures will be obedient unto thee, and a science which only works by the strength and power of natural things, and by the pure Angels which govern them. Of which latter I will give thee the names in order, their exercises and particular employments to which they are destined, together with the days over which they particularly preside, in order that thou mayest arrive at the accomplishment of all, which thou wilt find in this my Testament. In all which I promise thee success, provided that all thy works only tend unto the honor of God, hath given me the power to rule, not only over Terrestrial but also over Celestial things, that is to say, over the Angels, of whom I am able to dispose according to my will, and to obtain from them very considerable services.

Firstly. It is necessary for thee to understand that God, having made all things, in order that they may be submitted unto Him hath wished to bring His works to perfection, by making one which participates of the Divine and of the Terrestrial, that is to say, Man; whose body is gross and terrestrial, while his soul is spiritual and celestial, unto whom He hath made subject the whole earth and its inhabitants, and hath given unto Him means by which may render the Angels familiar, as I call those Celestial creatures who are destined: some to regulate the motion of the Stars, others to inhabit the Elements, others to aid and direct men, and others again to Sing continually the praises of the Lord. Thou mayest then, by the use of their seals and characters, render them familiar unto thee, provided that thou abusest not this privilege by demanding from them things which are contrary to their nature; for accursed be he who will take the Name of God in vain, and who will employ for evil purposes the knowledge and good wherewith He hath enriched us.

I command thee, my Son, to carefully engrave in thy memory all that I say unto thee, in order that it may never leave thee. If thou dost not intend to use for a good purpose the secrets which I here teach thee, I command thee rather to cast this Testament into the fire, than to abuse the power thou wilt have of constraining the Spirits, for I warn thee that the beneficent Angels, weaned and fatigued by thine illicit demands, would to thy sorrow execute the commands of God, as well as to that of all such who, with evil intent, would abuse those secrets which He hath given and revealed unto me. Think not, however, O my Son, that it would not be permitted thee to profit by the good fortune and happiness which the Divine Spirits can bring thee; on the contrary, it gives them great pleasure to render service to Man for whom many of these Spirits have great liking and affinity, God having destined them for the preservation and guidance of those Terrestrial things which are submitted to the power of Man.

There are different kinds of Spirits, according to the things over which they preside; some of them govern the Empyrean Heaven, others the Primum Mobile, others the First and Second Crystalline, others the Starry Heaven there are also Spirits of the Heaven of Saturn, which I call Saturnites there are jovial, Martial, Solar, Venerean, Mercurial, and Lunar Spirits there are also (Spirits) in the Elements as well as in the Heavens, there are some in the Fiery Region, others in the Air, others in the Water, and others upon the Earth, which can all render service to that man who shall have the good fortune to understand their nature, and to know how to attract them.

Furthermore, I wish to make thee understand that God hath destined to each one of us a Spirit, which watches over us and takes care of our preservation; these are called Genii, who are elementary like us, and who are more ready to render service to those whose temperament is conformed to the Element which these Genii inhabit; for example, shouldest thou be of a fiery temperament, that is to say sanguine, thy genius would be fiery and submitted to the Empire of Baël. Besides this, there are special times reserved for the invocation of these Spirits, in the days and hours when they have power and absolute empire. It is for this reason that thou wilt see in the following tables to what Planet and to what Angel each Day and Hour is submitted, together with the Colors which belong unto them, the Metals, Herbs, Plants, Aquatic, Aërial, and Terrestrial Animals, and Incense, which are proper to each of them, as also in what quarter of the Universe they ask to be invoked. Neither are omitted, the Conjurations, Seals, Characters, and Divine Letters, which belong to them, by means of which we receive the power to sympathize with these Spirits.

*

* *

Such is the summary put into the vulgar language by Monseigneur Barault, archbishop of Arles [205] , concerning the magical theory of spirits and correspondences.

Now let us look at the practice.

The first condition to be fulfilled consists of carefully preparing all the objects necessary for the Grand Evocation. These objects, purchased or prepared under the appropriate planetary auspices, will be enclosed in the special receptacle placed to the left of the Magic Altar, as we explained *a propos* the Laboratory.

Here is the complete list of these objects:

Objects Necessary for the Operations of the Art

A box of olive or hazel wood
Another box of wood lined with
new white cloth
A cap
White pants/trousers   New for important Operations
Light shoes
White stockings
A writing-desk
Clean crow's feathers
A white-handled penknife
A steel stylus for engraving
A pair of good scissors
A white earthenware inkstand   (new ink and cotton)

In the olivewood box:

A *small box* with the utensils required to make fire with a tinderbox (sulfur being dedicated to Saturn).[206]

---

[205] In this book, as far as possible, we will use the excellent translations of *The Key of Solomon the King* made by S.L. McGregor-Mathers in 1888, and, where his translation is missing a section, we will refer to *The Magus*, by Francis Barrett in 1801, which also includes extensive tracts of the *Key*.

[206] A lighter could be substituted by a box of matches, tinderbox, etc. However, most Operators avoid the use of sulfur in lighting a candle or charcoal for incense. The two most common methods used are firstly, to light a 'profane' or votary candle such as a night light, then light the blessed candles and charcoal using this candle (which is then extinguished with a snuffer), thus avoiding the sulfur in a match head. The other method

A candle of virgin wax.

A container filled with lustral water (made at the Paschal Vigil on Holy Saturday).

Three knives: – one pointed with a white handle.

                 – one cutlass (large kitchen knife) with a black handle.

                 – one in the form of a sickle with a black handle.

A large pair of compasses.

In the lined box:

A hazel stick the length of the box (thickness and roundness of a thumb)

A small wand around the same length

An asperser made from the hair of a young white horse or foal

Small packets of incense.

Earthenware censer, fresh charcoal

A small ball of new cord (to draw the great circle)

The different between a Witch and a Magician is that the former blindly follows the teachings of the Grimoires, while the latter *adapts* these teachings to his age.

The assiduous reader will find in our study about the realization of gesture how to adapt the wand and the magical sword to our era. Also, with regard to talismans, we describe adapting the ink and goose feathers and transforming them into colored pencils. We don't feel it's necessary to go into detail about the vestments and how to adapt them to our modern clothing, the tinderbox, and other details which the wise reader will understand without difficulty.

All these objects should be consecrated following the ordinary ritual. Here are the conjurations and prayers used by the "Clavicles" on this subject.

---

is to use 'New Fire', which is normally done by holding a convex lens above tinder in sunlight, thus using the sun to create the fire necessary for the Operation. As a rule of thumb, never blow out a candle – always snuff them with fingers or a snuffer – since the fire from them is considered to be sacred, associated with the Elmenetal forces in Magic, and angels in Theurgy.

TABLE OF IMPLEMENTS[207]

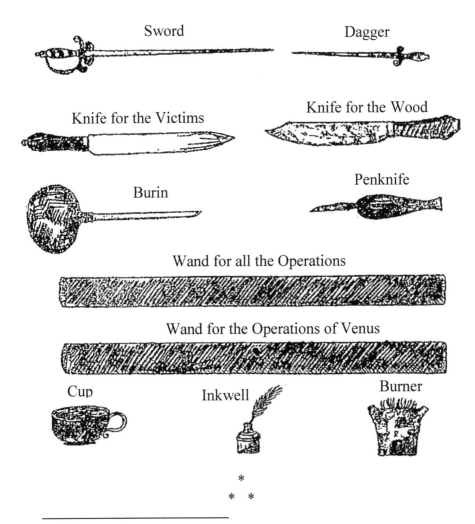

Sword

Dagger

Knife for the Victims

Knife for the Wood

Burin

Penknife

Wand for all the Operations

Wand for the Operations of Venus

Cup

Inkwell

Burner

*

*   *

---

[207] In the following text some of the sections have been rearranged to flow more logically. For example, Papus will often give half the instructions, then refer to a prayer several pages later. In this translation, the prayers have been restored to their logical locations. In addition, the diagrams from the original book have been used so far as possible, even if their poor reproduction in the original book meant that parts of lines or words are missing. Any serious student knows that many fine reproductions of the texts and the diagram have been published since 1893: the intention here was to keep to the spirit of the original book as closely as possible.

Blessing of the Ink Bottle[208]

It doesn't matter what it is, so long as it is new and clean. It will suffice to bless it and cense it as usual, saying:

"Hamiel, Hamiel, Hel, Miel, Ciel, Joviel, Nas, Nia, Magde, Tetragrammaton. Almighty God, grant the prayers of those who invoke you, and bless this small bottle prepared in Thine honor for all Thy works. Amen."[209]

Having set it aside until needed, you will put in it whatever ink you wish, provided that it is censed and of the planetary color.

Exorcism for the Cup into which one puts the Blood

One must have a cup in which to put a little of the victims' blood, to use when printing or writing, which must be made of unvarnished earthenware, and new like all the other implements, which, being washed thoroughly and censed, you will exorcize similarly to the ink bottle, saying:

"Hamiel, Hamiel, Hel, Miel, Ciel, Joviel, Nas, Nia, Magde, Tetragrammaton. Almighty God, grant the prayers of those who invoke you, and bless this vessel prepared in Thine honor for all Thy works. Amen."

After which you will set it aside until needed.

Exorcism of the Wand[210] for the Operations of Venus

You must cut a wand from a branch of elder, two feet long, on the day and hour of Venus, and after scraping it, you will make a small opening in all the spaces between the knots, into which you will insert a small piece of copper, on which you

---

[208] Note: Papus' font size changes have been followed here, as he put all quotations from the Clavicles in a slightly smaller font to distinguish them from his annotations and commentaries, which are in usual font size.

[209] In these and in the subsequent orisons, the reader will note that there are none of the usual 'cross' signs (✠) so popular in works of this kind, and in any church blessings. This is probably simply because the practitioner of the times would have known when to make the Sign of the Cross, and the authors didn't think it necessary to add them. Be assured that liberal addition of the Sign of the Cross throughout can only be efficacious.

[210] The text in fact refers sometimes to a rod or wand, and sometimes to a staff. However, the images show both to be the same length, and if they are to fit in a reasonably-sized box, we may assume they are both two feet or slightly less in length.

have engraved or had engraved the character which follows, on the same hour and day of Venus, and after reclosing the opening with new, yellow wax, cense it, saying:

"Founder of the Universe, Creator of the heavens, Puissant Being Pentagrammaton, Eye, Eye, Eye[211], Ischyros, Come, Almighty Sanctifier, Eternal God, and purify this wand, by Thy Name which is Holy, and through Thy angels. Amen."

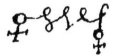

Manner of cutting the other Wand to be used in all other Operations

You must cut a wand of elder of the same length as the first, which should have a uniform bark, and, on the night of the new moon, take the wand in your right hand after midnight, turning towards the East, throw it into the air, and catch it without letting it fall to the ground, and say:

"Yea, though I walk through the Valley of the Shadow of Death, I will fear no evil, for Thou art with me: Thy rod and Thy staff, they comfort me." (*Psalm 23:4*)

Repeat the ceremony, together with these words, three times; then keep the wand to be used when needed.

Exorcism of the Place intended for doing the Operations

Since it is necessary to choose a clean and suitable place for the Operations, all places are good provided that they have been purified, and to this end the one you select should not have been inhabited by any person, particularly by a woman, for at least seven days. After this, you will hang the walls with cleaned white cloth, then exorcize it, saying:

"Eternal God, wise, strong, powerful Being of beings, come into this place and sanctify it by Thy presence and Thy majesty, so that purity, chastity and the fulness of Thy law may abide here. And as the smoke of this incense rises up to Thee, may Thy virtue and Thy benediction descend into this place. O ye angels and spirits, be present at this consecration through the true, living and eternal God, Who hath

---

[211] In his translation of *The Veritable Clavicles of Solomon* © 2001, Joseph H. Peterson has suggested that 'Eye, Eye, Eye' or rather 'Ye, Eye, Ye' should be *Eheieh*, or אהיה.

created you and me from nothing, Who can plunge me back with you into nothingness by His wisdom. Amen."

After censing it during this prayer, shut the place up, taking care that none enter it except you and those you need for the Operations; and leave a lamp burning there, day and night, for forty days.

Exorcism of the Vestments

You should make a vestment of white linen, in the form of a large shirt, which only has an opening for the head to pass through, and which extends down to the feet, a little wider at the bottom, having two sleeves of the same cloth which narrow towards the wrists. The vestment should be extremely white. You should also have small underwear of the same material. The vestment should be exorcised, saying:

"O Amiable Father, Creator of the stars, Infinite Wisdom, deign to sanctify through all Thy powers and virtues this vestment prepared in Thine honor. I exorcise Thee by the True Living and Eternal God, who hath made all things from nothing, that there may be nothing impure in this, my Operation, but only that which is filled with virtues. Amen."

And after censing them as usual, set them aside until needed.

The Victim

As with all Operations, there must be a victim. It must be pure and unpolluted; and having washed it and censed it with the planetary incense, you should cut a little piece of fur or feathers from the head, which you will exorcise with sea salt, saying:

"Almighty and Eternal God, Who holds all the earth in Thy power, sanctify and purify this victim by Thy virtue, so that the shedding of blood may be agreeable to Thee, and as by Thy grace Thou hast given me the power to kill it, if I will or not, so bestow upon it Thy benediction. Amen."

After which you will slit the victim's throat, and sprinkle part of its blood around the room, or the place intended for the Operation, saying:

"Almighty and Merciful God of Moses, God of Abraham, and God of Jacob, sanctify this place, and by the shedding of this pure victim's blood; and you, all the angels and spirits come and collect this blood to offer to the Most High God of all things. Amen."

Consecration of the Book

You must create a small book containing the prayers for all the Operations, the names of the angels in the form of litanies, their seals and their characters, which should be written in the blood of a dove on virgin parchment. Once this has been done, you will consecrate it to the Supreme Divinities, that is to say, to the Great God and to the spirits, in the following manner:

In the intended place you will place a small table covered with a white cloth, on which you will place the book open at the page of the Great Pantacle, which should be on the first page of this book. After lighting a lamp which will be suspended above the center of the table, you will surround the table with a white curtain. Then you will clothe yourself in the vestments and, taking the open book, you will say the following prayer with great attention and simplicity[212]:

"Adonaï, Elohim, El, Ye, Eye, Ye[213], Prince of Princes, Being of Beings, have pity on me, and cast Thine eyes upon Thy servant who invokes Thee most devotedly and beseeches Thee, by Thy Most Holy and Terrible Name, Tetragrammaton, to be favorable unto me in my Operations, to command Thine angels and spirits to come and establish their abode in this place. O ye angels and spirits of the stars, O all ye angels and elementary spirits, O all ye spirits who are present before the Face of God, I, the minister and faithful servant of the Most High conjure ye; God Himself, the Being of Beings, the Tetragrammaton conjures ye to come and be present at this Operations, I, the servant of God most humbly entreat ye. Amen."

Then you will cense the aforesaid book on the aforesaid table with the incense appropriate to the planet of the day, taking care that the lamp burns perpetually during the Operation; and after closing the curtains, you will perform the same ceremony for seven days, beginning on the Saturday, censing it each day with the incense appropriate to the dominating planet of the day, at the hour of the sun, taking care that the lamp burns day and night, after which you will close the book and put it away in a small drawer under the table until you need it, at which time you will take the habit and vest yourself, light the lamp, and on your knees you will open the drawer, while saying the prayer *Adonaï, Elohim, etc.*, as before.

It is also necessary, while consecrating the book, to call upon all the angels who are written in the book in the form of litanies, which you will do with devotion, and even if the angels and spirits do not appear while you are consecrating the book, do not be surprised, since they are of a pure nature, and because of that they are scarcely able to become intimate with men who are inconstant and impure. But, with perseverance, ceremonies, and characters drawn with devotion, they are compelled to come to us, and because of this, from the first evocation you can see them and

---

[212] Most versions of the *Clavicles* add the rubric: while kneeling.

[213] Or *Eheieh* (אהיה) – see previous footnote.

communicate with them; but I recommend that you undertake nothing needless or impure, because the importunity, far from attracting them, will only make them flee, and it would then be very difficult to call them back on profitable, holy and necessary occasions.

Exorcism of the Dagger

As you cannot do without a dagger in the Operations, have someone make one from very fine steel, whose handle is of the same nature, which you will wash as you did with the sword, and after cleaning it, set it on its point on a small pedestal of boxwood, and say this prayer over it:

"Aglo, On, Pentagrammaton, On, Athanatos, Agraton, Tela, Tutus, Tamon. God of Abraham, God of Isaac, God of Jacob, cast Thine eyes upon Thy servant, N..., who wishes to do battle on Thy behalf. Grant that Thine angels may assist me, and that they do not abandon me in my undertakings, and through Thee, O Theos, Athanatos, Agios, Agios, Agios, Agios, Agios, Alpha and Omega, the Angels Cassiel, Sachiel, Samaël, Anaël, Raphaël, Michaël and Gabriel, come and grant me support in all my Operations, let them never abandon me, and by the power of the art which Thou hast revealed unto my father, grant that they be faithful and obedient unto me through Thy Name Tetragrammaton. Amen."[214]

And afterwards, as on the sword, you will engrave or have engraved the following characters:

Once these characters have been engraved, you will cense them and say the following prayer:

"Hel, Ya, Yac, Va, Adonaï, Kadosh, Kadosh, Aborel, Elohim, Agla, Agiel, Asel, Sadon, Esul, Eloha, Elohim, Yeny, Del, Hagios, Hagios, Hagios, Raraël, Raraël, Raraël. Almighty Lord God, Who hath created everything from nothing, do

---

[214] There is a misprint in the 1893 edition, which still appears in the 1906 edition. Papus jumps directly from consecrating the Book to consecrating the Dagger, omitting the consecrations of the Sword, the two Knives and the Burin. This is clearly an error, since in the prayer over the Dagger, he says: "...and say this prayer over it: *"Aglo on Pentragrammaton, etc."*, clearly referring to the full prayer over the Sword (which has been included *in extenso* for completeness' sake). The reader is encouraged to refer to more modern editions of the Clavicles for the missing prayers.

not scorn Thy servant who addresses his humble prayers to Thee, and may it please Thee to bless, purify and sanctify this knife, so that it may be worthy and proper to execute my Operations. Grant also Thy saints and angels to come and be present at this my Operations. O Almighty Lord, remember my father to whom Thou hast granted the knowledge of all things, by the virtue of his teachings, grant that these knives become pure and agreeable unto Thee, through Thy Name which is the Holy Tetragrammaton. Amen."

Afterwards, you will engrave or have engraved, at the same hour as stated above, the following characters[215]:

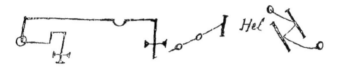

The aforesaid characters being engraved, you will cense them, saying the same prayer: "*Hel, Ja, Jac, etc.*", then you will wrap it in a new piece of red taffeta to use when required.

The Book

Let is draw the Operator's attention to the *Book*, which every practitioner should make himself, while focusing as much of his will as possible.

Ideally, he should make each of the pages himself with commercial paper paste. Then you would have paper made on a particular day, where every leaf would have been magnetized by the desired planetary influence.

If this isn't possible, it's fine to make the Book from fine paper or parchment.

Those who want to know how to consecrate the Book in such a way that the spirits will appear when you open it, should study the Latin editions of Book IV

---

[215] In his book, Papus has reversed these two sets of characters. However, for accuracy I have followed the commonly accepted version. While it is only conjecture, it is probably because Papus was taking notes from the library copy of Rabbi Abognazar's version, which he tells us elsewhere is in fact a French translation of the original. Thus, there are several opportunities for images and prayers to be reversed, or even sections omitted. Nevertheless, we must remember that this was the first time these texts had been seen in this level of detail in a published book: even McGregor-Mathers' version published in England in 1888 omitted significant parts, especially the consecrations of the implements.

of Agrippa's "Occult Philosophy", which is believed to be apocryphal, but which contains the entire ritual needed for this.

But let us remember the fact that the Book of Conjurations has no value, unless it is written entirely in the Operator's handwriting.

At the front of this book is put the Great Pantacle of Solomon, whose reproduction appears below. The Cross, explained by Eliphas Lévi, is put at the very front of the book, and the double triangle put at the top of all the pages devoted to talismans.

Now that the preparations of the objects are ended, let us talk about the circles and the personal preparations.

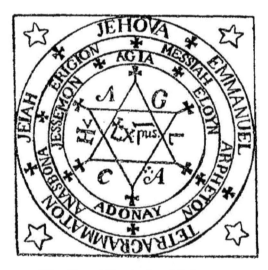

The Great Pantacle of Solomon

The Magic Circle

Every magical Operation must be performed within the area of a Circle, which symbolizes the will of the Operator, and which isolates him from all external evil influences. This is the very basis for Ceremonial Magic.

This Circle can be drawn with a Magic Sword alone in urgent cases, or with a mixture of pulverized charcoal and powdered lodestone, or with carbon, which is an excellent magnetic isolator in itself.

To avoid our readers having to immerse themselves in lengthy studies, we are going to give detailed descriptions on how to create a magic circle and will follow this description with seven figures representing each of the Circles corresponding to a specific planetary influence. A close reading of our Chapter on Kabbalistic Astrology will provide all the other clarifications necessary.

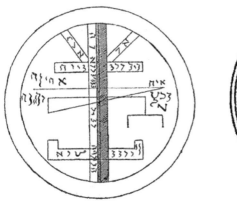

The Secret Seal I (Papus)

The Secret Seal II (Lansdowne MS.)

The Secret Seal III (McGregor-Mathers)

THE GREAT PANTACLE & SECRET SEAL OF SOLOMON[216] THE CIRCLE

Three circles a width of 9 feet, and the palm of the hand between each of them.

A. Write in the *Middle Circle*:
    i.   Name of the hour of the Operation.
    ii.   Name of the angel of the hour.
    iii. Seal of the angel of the hour.
    iv. Name of the angel and the ministers of the day.
    v.   Name of the current time.
    vi. Name of the presiding spirits.
    vii. Name of the reigning spirit.
    viii. Name of the each according to the season.
    ix. Name of the sun and the moon at this time.
B. *Outer circle.* In the four angles the names of the angels of the air for that day.
C. *Inner circle.* The four Names of God separated by crosses.
D. *Outside the circle.* At each angle, a pentagram.
E. *In the area of the circle.* At the East 'α' (or **Alpha**), at the West 'ω' (or **Omega**).

(See the following pages for diagrams of the seen circles to be used for eaxch of the planets).

---

[216]According to Dr. Stephen Skinner in *Techniques of Solomonic Magic*, pub. Golden Hoard Press (2015), ISBN 978-981-09-4310-3, this is referred to as the Secret Seal of Solomon, whose function is to stopper the bottle in which a spirit or genii has been imprisoned (pages 204 – 206). Curiously, it also featured regularly in 18th Century French Masonic Rituals, particularly some of those written by Jean-Baptiste Willermoz, and in the Ancient Accepted Scottish Rite, but with very different interpretations regarding moral lessons and balance, from which it gains its alternative title of 'Scales of Solomon'. Skinner says: "Mathers could not resist 'restoring' the figure by erroneously adding in Kabbalistic words corresponding to the ten Sephiroth…and rather unimaginative is the string of Hebrew letters running anti-clockwise round the figure from the top." It is clear from the three versions shown above (only the first appears in Papus' book) that Papus took his drawing from the Rabbi Abognazar copy in the National Library in Paris (there are no Sephiroth or letters around the outer circle). The last is McGregor-Mather's version, replete with 'erroneous' Hebrew. The middle one seems to be an intermediary step, which features in Joseph H. Peterson's article, labeled as being from the British Library, Lansdowne MS. 1203. These are provided for comparative purposes.

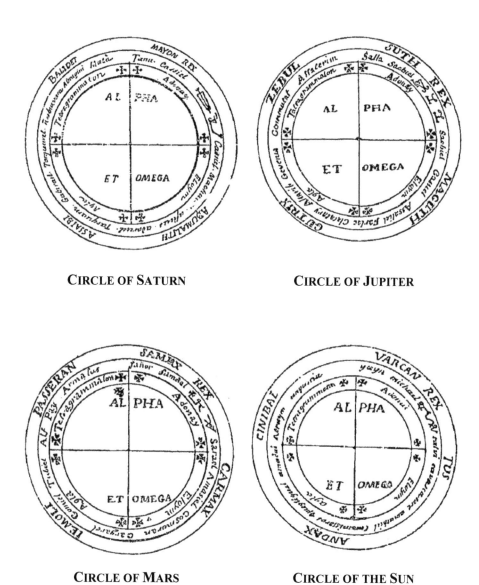

CIRCLE OF SATURN

CIRCLE OF JUPITER

CIRCLE OF MARS

CIRCLE OF THE SUN

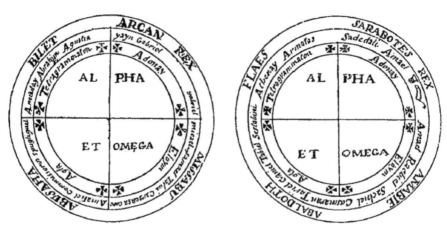

CIRCLE OF VENUS   **CIRCLE OF MERCURY**

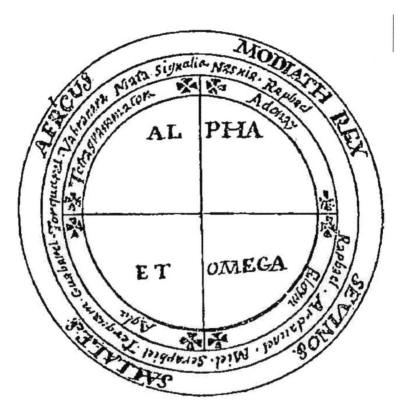

CIRCLE OF THE MOON

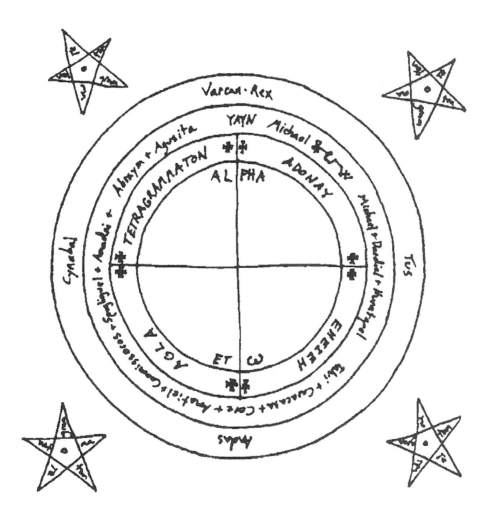

SOLAR CIRCLE IMAGE FROM FRANCIS BARRETT – THE MAGUS (1801)
Note: Not in the Original Papus Book[217]

---

[217] While this figure is not in the original book by Papus, if was felt imperative to include it to show the full image as described by Papus, including the four pantacles in D. of his description of the circle. This diagram comes from *The Magus* by Francis Barrett, published in England in 1801. The images apparently drawn or found by Papus for each of the seven planetary days are almost illegible, which is odd for a book which purports to provide the serious student with everything he or she needs to practice Ceremonial Magic. While it is indeed true, as Papus himself says, that all the words required to construct these circles can be found in his Chapter on Kabbalistic Astrology, the work required to do so would most likely lead to errors. So, since this book is a translation of

Personal Preparation

The Operator can act alone. For the common Circle one may use only one Assistant, but for great evocations three are needed: either the Operator and two trained and initiated Assistants, or three living beings of which two should be human and one well-trained dog, who should never leave the Circle, whatever takes place. One can tie the dog to a leash if needed.

These Assistants should all be blessed and exorcised following the usual rituals, by earth, air and fire. They should each wear a talisman which in this case will be the Great Pantacle of Solomon.

While consecrating the Disciples by water, say:

"Renovati toti mundati sitis, in nomine sanctæ et individuæ Trinitatis Patris et Fili et Spiritu Sancti; ab omnibus peccatis vestris, verbumque Altissimi descendat super vos et maneat semper. Amen."

If you are using a dog, you must first plunge it into holy water and say to it:

"Conjuro te creatura canis, per eum qui to creavit in monine sanctissimæ Trinitatis, ut sis mihi in hac Operatione et in quacumque alia quam facere intend, fidelis socius and amicus."

It is only after these Operations and censing with blessed incense that the Disciples are admitted to the place of the Operation which, in the present case, will be the Magical Laboratory.

Papus' book, and cannot therefore stray too far from its mandate, the serious student who wishes to understand precisely how to construct these circles is referred to *The Magus*, *Book II, Part III* by Francis Barrett, where they will find a comprehensive list of all the names, angels, seasons, etc. to be used to construct all the circles. The same information in an easier to read format can also be found in the excellent book *Secrets of the Magical Grimoires* by Aaron Leitch, pub. Llewellyn (2003), ISBN 0-7387-0303-6, pages 408 – 412. This – and the following prayers for the days of the week – would indicate quite clearly that Papus had had access to Barrett's book. Barret's source was almost certainly the Heptameron, which covers Operations over the days of the week, and whose circles changed from day to day. While outside the scope of this book, the serious student is strongly referred to *Techniques of Solomonic Magic* by the renowned scholar Dr. Stephen Skinner, pub. Golden Hoard Press (2015), ISBN 978-981-09-4310-3, particularly pages 167 – 171.

Diet

Nine days before the Operation, all those who are taking part should follow a strict vegetarian diet.

Moreover, the magical prayers should be done together, in the morning and twice in the evening, following the ritual previously given.

On the last three days, the diet will be solely composed of bread, water and vegetables cooked in water.

Finally, on the eve and the day before the eve of the Operation, each will say the Confession, whose following simple citation indicates the general character, which should be modified by each Operator according to his or her needs.

Confession

Confiteor omnipotenti Deo cœli et terra visibilium et invisibilium sanctisque omnibus angelis suis cunctisque creaturis cœlis et terra, coram sacro altari tuo et majestate tua quod ex peccatis conceptus sum, et in pecatis ic usque ab uro, conversatus sum. Confiteor tibi sanctissime pater omnia peccata mea quia peccavi in superbia, tam cordis quam oculorum, in vana gloria, in excellencia mentis meæ, invidia, in odia, in avaricia tam honorum quam pecunia, in insitia, in commestionibus, ebrietatibus, in fabulis et verbis, iniosis, osculi in amplexibus in tactu immondo in femoribus, in genitalibus meis, et in omni generare fornicationis et adulteris, in sacrilegiis et parjuriis, infurtis et rapinis in homicidis; pevccavi contrafidem, spem, et charitatem in exhortionibus moliigis, in blanimentis, in ignorantia, in negligentia, in suspectione, in recipiendis muneribus injuste in comtenedo pauperem et hospitalitem denegando in non visitando informos in non potando sitientes, in locutione maligna, in non elargiendo pauperibus elemosinam, no rectifiendo esurientes nec sitientes, sobrie et pie non vivendo, confectiendo suadendoque malum nocendo potius quam adjuvando, opem nonferendo potentibus pauperem clamares non libenter audiendo, mala amicis et propinquis meis inferendo et desiderando benefactoribus meis, pacem non referendo, necfidem eis servando, debita obsequia majoribus meis non præstando animalium occulo immuando vivendo, templum Dei rarissime intrando, colloquia immunda et vana in eo preferendo, res sacras manibus immundis tengendo. Peccavi partier in judicis cogitationibus malignis, in meditationibus perversis, in parjuriis in judicis temeraris, in malino imgressu impiorum, in concupiscentia carnis, in delecationibus immundis, in verbis luxuriosis et in contumeliis in mandaciis et falcitatibus in detractionibus, in rixis et discordiis seminando in malignitate ac malevolentia, in blasphemis ac insultationibus in transgretione preceptorum Dei in negligentia boni præpositit, peccavi in omnibus meis sensibus in visu, auditu, gustu, odoratu, factu, et tandem in omni modo corde ac voluntate et opere in his igitur et omnibus aliis vitiis quibuseumque humana fragilitas, vel malitia, contra Deum creatorem suum aut cogitando, aut loquendo aut operando aut suadendo, aut delectando, aut cucupiscendo peccare.

Potest in omnibus me pateor peccasse et reum in conspecutu Dei et super omnes homines peccatorem me esse Confiteor. Ideo suplex exoro vos omnes angelos et sanctos Dei in quorum conspectu hæc omnia confessus sum, ut mihi testes sitis in die judicii contra diapolum hostem et inimicum humani generis me hæc omnia puro et sincero corde confessum fuisse ita ut non gaudeat inimicus meus, et non glorietur adversum me in ide turbidinis et caliginis delicta mea vacuisse neque ad Deum creatorem meum confessum non fuisse."[218]

Having said that three times with a pure and contrite heart, lying prostrate on a place which is purified and far from the mundane world, the Master should wash his face with water and hyssop, saying:

"Asperges me, Domine, hysopo et mundabor, lavabis me et super nivem dealbaor."[219]

---

[218] This ancient, and extraordinarily comprehensive confession is probably simply Papus making a point. While the Tridentine Mass was still in full operation at that time (i.e. the entire Mass was said in Latin), this is not the confession normally used at Mass, which was – and is – considerably shorter; and the majority of the public were not well-educated in the Latin language outside of that environment. Given Papus' earlier hostile comments about formalized religion and particularly its priests, and the fact that he had stated earlier that the most powerful prayers are those created by the Magister himself, it is very possible he included this lengthy Latin prayer to emphasize the point that it should be ignored, and that the Operator should create his own, more personalized prayer in the vernacular. That said, this confession is almost gruesome in its list of faults – a majority being of the sexual variety, of course, and a significant emphasis on the sins of not looking after the poor, or attending church – so it could perhaps be used as a kind of checklist, prior to writing one's own personal prayer. That said, the wording of this confession is close to the wording used in McGregor-Mather's translation, but while it broadly adhered to Papus' version in this text, key sections are omitted, possibly because of their florid Catholicism, and because or simple prurience. An example of a missing section would be: "[I have] immodestly touched my thighs and my genitals (*in tactu immondo in femoribus, in genitalibus meis*) which has been delicately reduced to "all kinds of sins of the flesh…"

[219] The *Asperges* is the first part of the Mass after entering, when the priest sprinkles himself, the servers and the congregation with water infused with hyssop, while intoning the words of Psalm 51:7, "Thou shalt Purge me, O Lord, with hyssop, and I shall be clean: wash me, and I shall be whiter than snow."

Then he will wash himself with holy water and put on his vestments, which he had taken off, and fumigate all around about himself. Then, he will go to the prepared place with his companions and the necessary implements and draw a Circle, and on entering it, will invoke the spirits with the sign of penitence, and each will kiss the ground and do exactly what I have said.

The Baths

During the entire period of preparation, it is essential to take a bath every morning.

The bathwater will be blessed before entering it, and certain rituals suggest the Psalms which should be pronounced in the bath. These Psalms are the following[220]:

When entering the water, say the following: 26 (27), 13 (14), 38 (39), 68 (69) and 105 (106).

When washing with the water, say the following: 50 (51) and 23 (24).

When getting out of the bath, say the following: 142 (143), 4 (4), 137 (138), 125 (126) and 138 (139).

Each bath should contain a handful of blessed salt, which is thrown into the water while saying:

"Ismael, Imamon, Amason, Inerobimeum, Danayon, Zaton, Satimon, Vagran, Coriston, Zagueron, Momeston, Saniteon, Mamon, Zarinazon, Felicion, Sermion, Metron."

It is obvious that a well-instructed Magister could replace these prayers with magical prayers and formulas in enunciating the ten great Divine Names.

---

[220] Papus was using the Vulgate numbering. Briefly, the Greek Bible known as the *Septuagint* was translated towards the end of the 4th Century under the guidance of St. Jerome into Latin, which is called the *Vulgate*. This Bible was revised in 1592, and became the official translation of the Roman Catholic Church. However, the numbering of the Psalms differs between the Vulgate and other translations, mainly because the Greek source split some Psalms into two, and vice versa. Therefore, the Psalms listed are almost always one number different. The Psalm numbers from a non-Vulgate Bible have been added in parentheses after the numbers in this translation, to guide the reader.

The Operation

Once in the circle, before the Magic Altar, the Operator will first say as fervent a prayer as he can to the Principle of all creation.

Then he will say the Conjuration of the Four, then the Conjuration of the Seven, and finally the Great Invocation of Solomon.

This is the most elevated version. There are a host of variations, from which we have selected the following (from Peter Abano), which will serve to guide the Magister in his choice of adaptations. As in the original, we will give the prayers in Latin and in French.

On the manner of performing the Operation

Let the Moon be increasing and equal, if it can be conveniently done then; but it should not be enflamed, and the Operator should be clean of all stain for nine days before undertaking the work. He should have confessed and communed. He should also have ready the incense specific to the day when he performs the Operation; and he must have water blessed by a Priest, and a new earthenware vessel, filled with burning coals, the vestment and the Pantacle, as we have said. And finally, when everything has been consecrated as required, let one of the disciples carry the earthenware vessel filled with coals and the incense, and let the second carry the Book, and the third vestment and Pantacle; and let the Priest or Master himself carry the sword, over which has been said the Mass of the Holy Spirit: and on which will be engraved on one side of the sword *Agla* ✠ , and on the other side, *On* ✠, and while they are on the path which leads to the place where the Operation will take place, the Master says the litanies, and the disciples respond. When they have arrived at the place where the Circle will be drawn, let the Master draw it in the manner we have described above, and sprinkle the same with holy water, and once done, he must asperge it with holy water, saying: *Asperges me, Domine*, etc. The Master who will perform the ceremony, being prepared with three days of fasting and abstinence; being clothed in his white vestments, with the Pantacle, the incense and the other necessary things, will enter the Circle, and then he will call from the four parts of the earth, the angels who preside over the seven planets, the seven days of the week, the colors, and the metals, and will bend his knees to invoke the angels, and will say, calling each of them by their name:

"O angeli supra dicti, estote adjutores maæ petitioni, et in adjutorium mihi in meis rebus et petitionibus."

Translation: *O aforementioned Angels, be my help with my petitions, and help me in my affairs and my petitions.*

Then he will invoke from the four parts of the world, the Angels which will rule over the air of the day that he performs this Operation; and after having especially implored them, and having drawn their names in the Circle, he will say:

"O vos omnes, adjuro atque contestor per sedem Adonaï, per Hagios, o Theos, Ischyros, Athanatos[221], Paracletos, Alpha et Omega, et per hæc tria nomina secreta, Agla, On, Tetragrammaton, quod hodie teneatis adimplere quod cupio."

Translation: *I adjure and call you all forth, by the seat of Adonaï, and by Hagios o Theos, Ischyros, Athanatos; Paracletus, Alpha and Omega, and by these three secret names: Agla, On, Tetragrammaton, that you will fulfill on this day what I desire.*

After finishing this prayer, he will read the specific conjuration for the day he performs the Operation (they will be found below). If the Demons are refractory or stubborn, and will not render themselves obedient to the conjuration of the day, then use the following exorcisms and conjurations:

Exorcism of the Spirits of the Air

"Nos facti ad imaginem Dei, dotati potentia Dei, et ejus facti voluntate, per potentissimum et corroboratum nomen Dei El, forte, admirabile, vos exorcisamus (*here he will name the Spirits he would have appear, of whatever order they may be*), et imperamus per eum qui dixit et factum est et per omnia nomina Dei, et per nomen Adonaï, El, Elohim, Elohe, Tzabaoth, Elion, Escerchie, Yah, Tetragrammaton, Shaddai, Dominus Deus, excelsus, exorcizamus vos atque potenter imperamus, ut appareatis statim nobis hic, juxta circulum in pulchra forma, videlicet humana et sine deformitate et tortuositate aliqua. Venite vos omnes tales, quia vobis imperamus, per nomen Y et V quod Adam audivit, et locutus est: et per nomen Dei Agla quod Loth audivit, et factus salvus cum sua familia: et per nomen Joth, quod Jacob audivit ab Angelo secum luctantes, et liberatus est de manu fratris sui Esau:

---

[221] These words, which often appear in conjurations, are the *Trisagion*, or 'Thrice Holy', and are some of the oldest words in Christianity, dating at least from the earliest days of the Byzantine Empire. The Greek transliterated words are: *Hagios o Theos, hagios ischryos, hagios athanatos, eleison imas*, meaning: "Holy God, Holy Strong, Holy Immortal, have mercy on us." The second reason they are considered to be powerful in invocations is because of the *Improperia*, or the Reproaches which initially appeared around 850 C.E.. These are the remonstrances of Jesus towards His people, and include the *Trisagion*. They begin: "O my people, what have I done to thee? How hath I offended thee? Testify against me. I led thee out of Egypt from slavery to freedom, but you led your Savior to the cross. Hagios o Theos, Hagios ischryos, Hagios athanatos, eleison imas." As one may imagine, words allegedly spoken by the Operator's avatar while *in extremis* were considered to be exceptionally powerful.

and by the name Anephexeton, quod Aaron audivit, et loquens, et sapiens factus est: et per nomen Zebaoth, quod Moses nominavit, et omnia flumina et paludes de terra Ægypti, versæ fuerunt in sanguinem: et per nomen Ecerchie Oriston, quod Moses nominavit, et omnes fluvis ebullierunt ranas et ascenderunt in domos Ægyptiorum, omnia destruentes: et per nomen Elion, quod Moses nominavit, et fuit grando talis, qualis non fuit ab initio mundi: et per nomen Adonaï, quod Moses nominavit, et fuerunt locusta, et apparuerunt super terram Ægyptiorum, et comederunt quæ residua erant grandit: et per nomen Schemes amathia, quod Joshua vocavit, et remoratus est Sol cursum: et per nomen Alpha et Omega, quod Daniel nominavit, et destruxit Beel, et Draconem interferit: et in nomine Emmanuel, quod tres pueri, Sidrach, Misach et Abednago, in camino ignis ardentis, cantaverunt, et liberati fuerunt: et per nomen Hagios, et sedem Adonaï, et per o Theos, Ischyros, Athanatos, Paracletus; et per hæc tria secreta nomina, Agla, On, Tetragrammaton, adjuro, contestor, et per hæc nomina, et per alia nomina Domini nostri Dei Omnipotentis, vivi et veri, vos qui vestra culpa de Coelis ejecti fuistis usque ad infernum locum, exorcizamus, et viriliter imperamus, per eum qui dixit, et factum est, cui omnes obediunt creaturæ, et per illud tremendum Dei judicium: et per mare omnibus incertum, vitreum, quod est ante conspectum divinæ majestatis gradiens, et potestiale: et per quatuor divina animalia T. aniè sedem divinæ majesta is gradientia, et oculos antè et retrò habentia: et per ignem ante ejus thronum circumstantem: et per sanctos Angelos Cælorum T. et per eam quæ Ecclesia Dei nominatur: et per summam sapientiam Omnipotentis Dei viriliter exorcizamus, ut nobis hic ante Circulum appareatis, ut faciendam nostram voluntatem, in omnibus prout placuerit nobis: per sedem Baldachiæ, et per hoc nomen Primeumaton, quod Moses nominavit, et in cavernis abyssi fuerunt profundati vel absorpti, Datan, Corah et Abiron: et in virtute istius nominis Primeumaton, tota Coeli militia compellente, maledicimus vos, privamus vos omni officio, loco et gaudio vestro, esque in profundum abyssi, et usque ad ultimum diem judicii vos ponimus, et relegamus in ignem æternum, et in stagnum ignis et sulphuris, nisi statim appareatis hic coram nobis, inte Circulum, ad faciendum voluntatem nostram. In omnibus venite per hæc nomina, Adonaï Zebaoth, Adonaï, Amioram. Venite, venite, imperat vobis Adonaï, Saday, Rex regum potentissimus et tremendissimus, cujus vires nulla subterfugere potest creatura vobis pertinacissimis futuris nisi obedieritis, et appareatis ante hunc Circulum, affabiles subito, tandem ruina flebilis miserabilisque, et ignis perpetuum inextinguibilis vos manet. Venite ergo in nomine Adonaï Zebaoth, Adonaï, Amioram: venite, venite, quid tardatis? Festinate, imperat vobis Adonaï, Rex Regum, El, Aty, Titeip, Azia, Hyn, Ien, Minosel, Achadan: Uay, Vaa, Ey, Haa, Eye, Exe, Exe à El, El, El, à Hy, Hau, Hau, Hau, Va, Va, Va, Va."

Translation: We being made after the image of God, endowed with His power, and created by His will, do exorcise you by the Almighty and Powerful Name of God, El, (here he will name the Spirits he would have appear, of whatever order they may be), *and we command you by Him who spoke the word and it was done, and by all the names of God, Adonaï, El, Elohim, Elohe, Tzabaoth, Elion, Eserchie, Yah, Tetragrammaton, Shaddaï, the Lord God Most High: we exorcise you, and powerfully command ye, NN..., that you appear unto us visibly forthwith, here before this circle in a fair human shape, without any trouble, any ugliness or deformity; come ye all such NN..., because we command you by the name Y and V, which Adam heard and spoke; and by the name of God Agla, which Lot heard, and by virtue of which he was saved with all his family; and by Yod, which Jacob heard from the angel wrestling with him, and was delivered from the hand of his brother Esau; and by the name Anaphexeton, which Aaron heard, and which made him loquacious and wise; and by Tzabaoth, which Moses pronounced, and immediately all the rivers and marshes of the land of Egypt were turned to blood; and by Eserchie, Oriston, which made all the rivers boil and bring forth frogs, which ascended into the houses of the Egyptians, spreading destruction everywhere; and by Elion, which Moses pronounced, which made fall a great hail, such as had not been since the beginning of the world; and by Adonaï, which Moses named, and there immediately came up locusts, which devoured all which had escaped the fury of the same hail; and by Schema Amathia, which Joshua pronounced, and the sun stayed its course; and by Alpha and Omega, which Daniel pronounced, which destroyed Bel and slew the Dragon; and in the name Emmanuel, which being heard by the three children, Sidrach, Misach, and Abednego, they sung in the midst of the fiery furnace, and were delivered; by Hagios; and by the throne of Adonaï; and by o Theos, Ischyros, Athanatos, Paraclete; and by these three secret names, Agla, On, Tetragrammaton, I conjure you by these names, and by all the other names of our true and living Lord God Almighty, you who by your fault were thrown from the highest heavens to the deepest infernal abyss, I exorcise and command you powerfully, by Him who spoke the word and all was created, to whom all creatures are obedient because of the dreadful and redoubtable judgment of God ; and by the floating and transparent sea of glass, which is before the presence of the divine Majesty, being in strong and continual movement; by the four divine Animals T. which come and go before the Throne of the Divine Majesty, having eyes before and behind; and by the holy fire round about his Throne; and by the holy angels T. who are ever in the presence of God, by this same Majesty who is recognized in His Church, we do powerfully exorcise you, that you appear here before this circle to fulfil our will in all things, which shall seem good unto us; by the Throne of Baldachia, and by this name Primeumaton, which Moses pronounced, and by virtue of which the earth opened and swallowed up Dathan, Corah and Abiram in the frightful pit of the abyss, and by virtue of which the whole of the heavenly, earthly and infernal Militia tremble, are confused and throw themselves down: that if you do not appear here immediately before this circle to fulfill our will in every way, we curse you, and deprive you of your office, joy, and place; we condemn you to burn for eternity in your lair, in the lake of fire and brimstone: therefore come in the names of Adonaï, Tzabaoth,*

Adonaï, Amioram; come ye, come ye, Adonaï, Shaddai, the most mighty and terrible King of Kings commands you, whose power no creature is able to endure nor resist; which is why, unless ye obey, and forthwith appear immediately before this circle, gently and affably, and ready to execute my will, He will be forever inflexible before you, and will punish you in the eternal fire; therefore come ye, come ye, in the name of Adonaï Tzabaoth, Adonaï, Amioram; come, come: why tarry you? Who prevents you? Hasten! Adonaï, Shaddai, the King of Kings commands you: El, Aty, Titeip, Azia, Hyn, Ien, Minosel, Achadan, Uay, Vaa, Ey, Haa, Eye, Exe, à El, El, El, à Hy, Hau, Hau, Hau, Va, Va, Va, Va.

PRAYER TO GOD

Said in the Circle, towards the four parts of the Wortd

"Amorule, Taneha, Latisten, Rabur, Taneha, Latisten, Escha, Aladia, Alpha and Omega, Leyste, Oriston, Adonaï, clementissime Pater mi Cœlestis, miserere mei licet peccatoris, clarifica, in me, hodierno die, licet in digno filio tuo, tuæ potentiæ brachium, contra hos spiritus perticinacissimos: ut ego, te volente, factus tuorum divinorum operum contemplator, possim illustrari omni sapientia, et semper glorificare et adorare nomen tuum. Suppliciter exoro te et invoco, ut tuo judicio, hi spiritus, quos invoco, convicti et constricti, veniant vocati et dent vera responsa, de quibus eos interrogavero: dentque et deserant nobis, ea quæ per me vel nos præcipietur eis, non nocentes alicui creaturæ, non lædentes, non frementes, nec me, sociosque meos, vel aliam creaturam lædentes, et neminem terrentes: sed petitionibus meis, in omnibus quæ præcipiam eis, sint obedientes."

Translation: *Amorule, Taneha, Latisten, Rabur, Taneha, Latisten. Escha, Aladia, Alpha and Omega, Leyste, Oriston, Adonaï: O my most merciful Heavenly Father, have mercy upon me a sinner; deign today to spread over Thy unworthy servant thy holy benediction, and extend Thine Almighty Arm against these obstinate and rebellious Spirits, that by Thy will I may be made a contemplator of Thy divine works, and may be endowed with all wisdom, and always worship and glorify Thy Name. I humbly invoke Thee, O My God, and beseech Thee from the depths of my heart, that these Spirits which I call by Thy power, may immediately be bound and constrained to come, and give true and perfect answers to those things which I shall ask them, and that they may declare and shew unto us those things which by me or us shall be commanded them, not hurting any creature, neither injuring nor terrifying by noise or murmurings me or my associates, nor hurting any other creature, or causing any kind of fright or terror to any man; but let them be obedient, resigned and completely submissive to my requests, in all these things which I command them.*

Then, standing in the middle of the Circle, holding the Pantacle in his hand, he says:

"Per Pentaculum Salomonis advocate, dent mihi responsum verum."

Translation: Through the Pantacle of Solomon I call you, that you may give me a true answer.

Then he says:

"Beralanensis, Baldachiensis, Paumachiæ et Apologiæ sedes, per reges potestatesque magnanimas, ac principes, præpotentes, Genio, Liachidæ, Ministri Tartareæ sedis: Primac, hic princeps sedis Apologiæ nona cohorte: ego vos invoco, et invocando vos conjure, atque supernæ majestatis munitus virtute, potenter impero per eum qui dixit et factum est, et cui obediunt omnes creaturæ, et per hoc nomen ineffabile, Tetragrammaton cum Jehovah, in quo est psalmatum omne seculum, quo audito elementa corruent, aer concutitur, mare retrograditur, ignis extinguitur, terra tremit, omnesque exercitus cœlestium, terrestrium, et infernorum tremunt, turbantur, et corruunt: quatenus cito et, sine mora et omni occasione remota, ab universis mundi partibus veniatis, et rationabiliter de omnibus quæcunque interrogavero, respondeatis vos, et veniatis pacifice visibiles, et affabiles, nunc et sine mora, manifestantes quod cupimus: conjurati per nomen æterni, vivi et veri Dei Helioren, et mandata nostra perficientes, persistentes semper usque ad finem, et intentionem meam visibiles nobis et affabiles, clara voce nobis intelligibili, et sine omni ambiguitate."

Translation: Beralanensis, Baldachiensis, Paumachia, and the Throne of Apologia, by the most magnanimous Kings and Powers, and the most powerful Princes, Genio, Liachidæ, Ministers of the Infernal Empire: Primac, Prince of the Throne of Apologia, in the Ninth Legion: I invoke you, and by invoking you by virtue of the supreme Majesty, with which I am armed, I conjure and command you most strongly, by Him who spoke and it was done, and to whom all creatures are obedient; and by this Ineffable Name, Tetragrammaton Jehovah, which being heard the ages dissolve, the Elements are overthrown, the air is shaken, the sea runneth back, the fire is quenched, the earth trembles, and all the Celestial, Terrestrial and Infernal Hosts do tremble together, and are troubled and confounded: wherefore, forthwith and without delay, do you come from all parts of the world, and make rational answers unto all things I shall ask of you; and come in peace, visibly and affably, manifesting in good will, as we desire it, being conjured as you are by the name of the True, Living and Eternal God, Helioren, to fulfil our express commands, and persist unto the end, and according to our intentions, answering us with a clear and intelligible voice, and without any ambiguity.

Visions and Apparitions

After that is said, you will see phantoms filling the air with noise, in order to frighten the Assistants in the Circle, and make them flee; and you will see armies of arrows, and an infinity of horrible beasts, but nobody should have any fear because the Master, against whom they can do nothing, will contain them by saying, with his hand upon the Pantacle:

"Fugiat hinc iniquitas vestra, virtute vexilli Dei."

Translation*: Flee with your iniquities, by the virtue of the banner of God.*

Then, still holding his hand upon the Pantacle, he says:

"Ecce Pentaculum Salomonis, quod ante vestram adduxi præsentiam, ecce personam exorcizatoris, in medio exorcismi, qui est optime a Deo munitus, intrepidus, providus, qui viribus potens vos exorcizando invocavit, et vocat. Venite ergo cum festinatione in virtute nominum, Aye, Saraye, Aye, Saraye, Aye Saraye, ne differatis venire per nomina æterna Dei vivi et veri Eloy, Archima, Rabur: et per hoc præsens Pentaculum, quod super vos potenter imperat, et per virtutem cœlestium Spirituum, dominorum vestrorum, et per personam exorcizatoris conjurati, festinate, venite et obedite præceptori vestro, qui vocatur Octinomos."

Translation*: Behold the Pantacle of Solomon, which I have brought into your presence; behold, too, the person of the Exorcist in the midst of the exorcism, who, armed by the aid of God, is without fear and well provided, who is powerful and invokes and calls you by exorcising you. Come, therefore, with speed, by the virtue of these names; Aye, Saraye, Aye, Saraye, Aye, Saraye, and defer not to come here by the Almighty and Names of the living and true God, Eloy, Archima, Rabur, and by the Pentacle of Solomon here present, which commands you and impels you; and by the virtue of the celestial Spirits, your Lords; and by the person of the Exorcist, in the midst of the exorcism which has conjured you, make haste, come and obey your Master, who is called Octinomos.*

Then he blows towards the four parts of the Earth, and immediately you will see great movements, and then say:
"Quid tardatis? Quid moramini? Quid factis? Præparate vos, et obedite præceptori vestro, in nomine Domini Bathath, vel Vachat super Abrac ruens, superveniens Abeor super Aberer."

Translation: Why do you stay? Why do you delay? What are you doing? Prepare yourselves, and obey your Master in the name of the Lord Bathath, or Vachat rushing upon Abrac, Abeor coming upon Aberer.

Then they will immediately come in their regular and natural forms; and when you see them before the Circle, show them the Pantacle covered with fine linen; uncover it, and say:

"Ecce conclusionem vestram, nolite dieri inobedientes."

Translation: Behold your condemnation, if you refuse to be obedient!

After that, you will see them peaceful in their natural forms, and they will say: "*command and ask what you desire, because we are here ready to do everything, because Almighty God commands us.*"

And when they have appeared, say to them:

"Bene veneritis Spiritus, vel Reges nobilissimi, quia vos vocavi per illum cui omne genu flectitur, coelestium, terrestrium et infernorum, cujus in manu omnia regna Regum sunt, nec est qui suæ contrarius esse possit majestati. Quatenus constringo vos ut hic ante circulum visibilis, affabiles permanteatis tam diu tamque constantes, nec sine licentia mea recedatis, donec meam sine fallacia aliqua et veredice perficiatis voluntatem, per potentiæ illius virtutem, qui mare posuit terminum suum, quem præterire non potest, et lege illius potentiæ non pertransit fines suos, Dei scilicet Altissimi, Regis, Domini, qui cuncta creavit, Amen."

Translation: Welcome spirits, or most noble princes, because I have called you through Him to whom every knee doth bow, both of things in heaven, and things in earth, and things under the earth; in whose hands are all the kingdoms of kings, neither is there any able to contradict his Majesty. Wherefore, I bind you, that you remain affable and visible before this circle, so long and so constant; neither shall you depart without my license, until you have truly and without any fallacy performed my will, by virtue of his power who hath set the sea her bounds, beyond which it cannot pass, nor go beyond the law of his providence, that of the Most High God, Lord, and King, who hath created all things. Amen.

Then you ask them what you desire, and they will satisfy you; and after you have obtained what you wished for, you will send them away as follows:

"In nomine Patris ✠, et Filii ✠, et Spiritus Sancti ✠, ite in pace ad loca vestra, et pax sit inter nos et vos parati sitis venire vocati."

Translation: *In the Name of the Father* ✠, *and of the Son* ✠, *and of the Holy Spirit* ✠, *depart in peace to your habitation, and let there be peace between us and you and be ye ready to come again when you are called.*

THE CONJURATIONS FOR THE SEVEN DAYS OF THE WEEK

Conjuration for Sunday

"Conjuro et confirmo super vos Angeli fortes Dei et sancti, in nomine Adonaï, Eye, Eye, Eye, qui est ille, qui fuit, est et erit, Eye, Abiaye, et in nomine Shaddaï, Kadosh, Kadosh, Kadosh, alte sendentis super Cherubin, et per nomen magnum ipsius, Dei fortis et potentis exaltatique super omnes Cœlos, Eye, Saraye, plasmatoris sæculorum, qui creavit mundum, coelum, terram, mare et omnia quæ in eis sunt, in primo die, et sigillavit ea sancto nomine suo Phaa: et per nomina sanctorum angelorum, qui dominantur in quarto exercitu, et serviunt coram potentissimo Salamia, angelo magno et honorato, et per nomen stellæ, quæ est sol, et per signum, et per immensum nomen Dei vivi, et per nomina omnia prædicta, conjuro te, Michael angele magne, qui es præpositus diei dominicæ: et per nomen Adonaï, Dei Israel, qui creavit mundum et quicquid in eo est, quod pro me labores, et adimpleas omnem meam petitionem, juxta meum velle et votum meum, in negotio et causa mea."

At this point one may demand what you desire.

Translation: *I conjure and confirm upon you, ye strong and holy angels of God, in the name of Adonaï, Eye, Eye, Eye, which is He who was, and is, and is to come, Eye, Abray; and in the name Shaddaï, Kadosh, Kadosh, Who is seated upon the Cherubim, and by the great name of God himself, strong and powerful, Who is exalted above all the Heavens, Eye, Saraye, the Master of Ages, Who created the heaven and the earth, the sea, the universe, and all the things which were on the first day, Who sealed them with his Holy Name Phaa. I conjure you also, and by the names of the holy angels who command the Fourth Legion, and who serve before the most mighty and illustrious Salamia: by the name of the star, which is the Sun, by his sign, by the adorable and terrible Name of the Living God, and by all the names which have previously been professed, I conjure thee, O Holy Angel Michael, you who presides over the day of Sunday through the adorable name of Adonaï, God of Israel, Who created the whole universe and all that it contains, that you give me aid, and fulfil all my petitions according to my will and desire, both in my business and in my fortune, and in general in all things which are useful and necessary to me.*

Here you specify the purpose of your business, and the reason for your conjuration.

Their power is to give gold, pearls, carbuncles, riches, to cause the favor of the great, to cease enmities and procure honors, to cause or heal ailments.

Forms under which these Spirits of the Sun or of Sunday are accustomed to appear

They are accustomed to take a large and great body, sanguine, and proclaim their arrival with an inflammation of the sky, and their sign is to make him who invokes them sweat.

Their particular forms are:

A king carried upon a lion, carrying a golden scepter in hand; a crowned cockerel; a yellow habit.

A queen with a scepter; a bird; a scepter; a lion; a man with a tail.

Conjuration for Monday

"Conjuro et confirmo super vos, Angeli fortes et boni, in nomine Adonaï, Adoney, Adonaï, Eye, Eye, Eye, Kadosh, Kadosh, Kadosh, Achim, Achim, Achim, Ia, Ia; qui apparuit in monte Sinaï, cum glorificatione Regis Adonaï, Shaddai, Tzabaoth, Amathay, Ya, Ya, Ya, Marinata, Abim, Ieia, qui maria creavit, stagna and omnes aquas in secundo die, quasdam super cœlos, and quasdam in terra. Sigillavit mare in alto nomine suo, and terminum, quem sibi posuit, non præterbit: et per nomina angelorum qui dominantur in primo exercitu, qui serviunt Orphaniel angelo magno, pretioso and honorato: et per nomen stellæ quæ est in Luna: et per nomina prædicta super, te conjuro scilicet, Gabriel, qui es præpositus diei Lunæ secondo, quod pro me labores et adimpleas, etc."

Here, as on Monday, you specify what you desire.

Translation*: I conjure and confirm upon you, ye strong and good angels, in these names Adonaï, Adonaï, Adonaï, Eye, Eye, Eye, Kadosh, Kadosh, Kadosh, Achim, Achim, Achim, Ia, Ia, Ia, who appeared on mount Sinaï with all His sovereign glory, Adonaï, Shaddaï, Tzabaoth, Amathay, Ya, Ya, Ya, Marinata, Abim, Icia, who created the sea, the rivers and all the waters, on the second day, even those which are above the Heavens and in the earth, and sealed the sea in His High Name, and gave it its bounds beyond which it cannot pass. I conjure you, strong and good Angels, by the names of those who command the First Legion, and who serve the great and honorable Orphaniel: by the name of his star which is Luna, and by all the names* *aforesaid pronounced. I conjure thee, O Gabriel, who presides over the Second Day dedicated to the Moon, that you come to my aid and accomplish all my desires."*

Their power is to give silver, to transport things from one place to another, to make horses swift, to disclose certain secrets, present or past.

Regular form of the Spirits of the Moon or Monday

Their bodies are normally large, great, phlegmatic; their color is that of a dark and shadowy cloud: they have a swollen face, red eyes, full of water, a bald head, teeth like a wild boar. Their movements are like those of a violent tempest, their sign is abundant rain which they make fall outside the Circle.

Their particular forms are:

A king, bow in hand, upon a fallow deer; a young child; a woman hunter with a bow and arrows; a cow; a goose; a little doe; a green or silver-colored habit; an arrow and a man with many feet.

Conjuration for Tuesday

"Conjuro et confirmo super vos, Angeli fortes et sancti, per nomen Ya, Ya, Ya, He, He, He, Va, Hy, Ha, Ha, Ha, Va, Va, Va, An, An, An, Aie, Aie, Aie, El, Ay, Elibra, Elohim, Elohim; et per nomina ipsius alti Dei, qui fecit aquam aridam apparere, et vocavit terram, et produxit arbores et herbas de ea, et sigillavit super eam cum precioso, honorato, metuendo et sancto nomine suo: et per nomen angelorum dominantium in quinto exercitu, qui serviunt Acimoy angelo magno, forti, potenti et honorato: et per nomen stellæ, quæ est Mars: et per nomina prædicta conjuro super te, Samael, angele magne, qui præpositus es diei martis: et per nomina Adonaï Dei vivi et veri, quod pro me labores et adimpleas, etc."

Translation: *I conjure and call upon you, ye strong and good Angels, by the sacred names Ya, Ya, Ya, He, He, He; Va, Hy, Hy, Ha, Ha, Ha; Va, Va, Va; An, An, An; Aie, Aie, Aie; El, Ay, Elibra, Elohim, Elohim; and by the other names of the High God, Who hath made appear the sea and dry land, and by His word hath made the earth, and produced trees and grass from it, and hath seales His holy, precious, adorable and redoubtable Name upon the planets, and by the name of the Angels governing in the Fifth Legion, who serve the great angel Acimoy, by the name of the star which is Mars, I call upon thee, O Samael, who presides over Tuesday, by the aforementioned names, by the name Adonaï, the Living and True God, to come to my aid to accomplishing all my labors.*

This power concerns battle, fire, the dead, providing ten thousand soldiers when required, to make healthy or ill.

Regular form of the Spirits of Mars or Tuesday

Their body is tall, of a blackish color, drawn in a reddish color, their aspect is hideous; they have horns on the head, quite similar to those of stags, their claws are like griffins'. Their movement is a noise like fire burning, and their sign is lightning around the Circle.

Their particular forms are:

An armed King, riding on a wolf; a red habit; an armed man; a woman wearing a buckler on her thigh; a piece of wool; a horse; a man with several heads.

Conjuration for Wednesday

"Conjuro et confirmo vos angeli fortes, sancti et potentes, in nomine fortis, metuendissimi et benedicti Adonaï, Elohim, Shaddaï, Shaddaï, Shaddaï, Eye, Eye, Eye, Asanie, Asaraie: et in nomine Adonaï, Dei Israël, qui creavit luminaria magna, ad distinguendum diem a nocte: et per nomen omnium angelorum, deservientium in exercitu secundo coram terra angelo majori, atque forti et potenti: et per nomen stellæ, quæ est Mercurius: et per nomen sigilli, quæ sigillatur a Deo fortissimo et honorato: per omnia prædicta super te, Raphaël angele magne, conjuro, qui es præpositus die quartæ: et per nomen sanctum, quod erat scriptum in fronte Aaron, sacerdotis altissimi Creatoris: et per nomina angelorum, qui in gratiam Salvatoris confirmati sunt, et per nomen sedis animalium habentium senas alas, quod pro me labores,etc. *(continue as on Sunday)*."

Translation*: I conjure and call upon you, ye strong and holy Angels, good and powerful, in a strong name of fear and praise, Yah, Adonaï, Elohim, Shaddaï, Shaddaï, Shaddaï; Eye, Eye, Eye; Asamie, Asamie; and in the name of Adonaï, the God of Israel, Who hath made the two great lights to distinguish the day from the night for the benefit of His creatures; and by the names of all the Angels which serve in Second Legion before the thrice-great Angel, strong and powerful, and by the name of his star which is Mercury; and by his sacred and revered seal, by all those previously announced, I call upon thee, O great angel Raphael, thou great angel who presidest over the Fourth Legion: and by the holy name which is written in the forehead of Aaron, priest to the Most High Creator, and by the names of all the angels who are constant in the grace of the Savior, and finally by those of the Throne* *of the Animals who have six wings, to come and assist me in my labors to accomplish my will.*

Their power is to give all sorts of metal, to reveal hidden treasures, to pacify judges, to give victory in battle, to procure knowledge, to change the elements of things, to give or remove good health, to raise the poor, to bring down the rich.

Regular form of the Spirits of Mercury or Wednesday

Their bodies are normally of medium height, cold and damp, however, quite handsome, their demeanor is affable, their form is human and the figure that of an armed man; they have a transparent color. Their movement is like a silver cloud, and their sign is to inspire terror in those who invoke them.

Their particular forms are:

A king riding a bear; a fair man; a woman holding a strainer; a dog: a magpie; a multicolored habit; a wand; a staff.

Conjuration for Thursday

"Conjuro et confirmo super vos, Angeli sancti, per nomen, Kadosh, Kadosh, Kadosh, Eschereie, Eschereie, Eschereie, Hatim, Hatim, Ya, fortis firmator seculorum, Cantine, Jaym, Janie, Anie, Calbar, Sabbat, Berisay, Alnaym, et per nomen Adonaï, qui creavit pisces, reptilia in aquis, et aves super faciem terræ, volantes versus cœlos die quinto: et per nomina Angelorum servantium in sexto exercitu coram pastore Angelo sancto et magno et potenti principe: et per nomen stellæ quæ est Jupiter: et per nomen sigilli sui: et per nomen Adonaï, summi Dei omnium creatoris: et per vim et virtutem carum: et per nomina prædicta, conjuro te Sachiel, Angele magne, qui es præpositus diei Jovis, et pro me labores, etc. *(continue as on Sunday)*."

Translation: *I conjure and confirm upon you, ye holy angels, by the names Kadosh, Kadosh, Kadosh, Eschereie, Eschereie, Eschereie, Hatim, Hatim, Ya, strong founder of the worlds; Cantine, Jaym, Janie, Anie, Calbar, Sabbat, Berisay, Alnaym; and by the name Adonai, who created fishes and reptiles in the waters, and birds upon the face of the earth, flying towards heaven, in the Fifth Legion; and by the Angels serving in the Sixth Legion, in presence of the Holy Angel, their chief, the great and powerful Prince and by the name of the star of Jupiter, and by his sea; by Adonai, the supreme Creator of all things, and by the name of all the stars, and by their* *powers and virtues, and by all the names aforesaid, I conjure thee, O Great Sachiel, who rules over the day of Thursday, etc.*

Their power is to reconcile the love of women, to make men happy, to end legal proceedings, to soften enemies, to heal sickness, in a word, to make good from evil.

Regular form of the Spirits of Jupiter or Thursday

Their bodies are the color of blood, they look bilious and melancholic, their movements are frightening, but their countenance is gentle, their demeanor pleasant, their color is that of fire. Their movement is lightning followed by thunder, and their sign is of men appearing to be devoured by lions.

Their particular forms are:

A King, sword in hand, riding a stag; a mitered man dressed in long robes; a girl with a laurel crown decorated with flowers; a stag; a peacock; an azure habit; a sword; a flute.

Conjuration for Friday

"Conjuro et confirmo super vos Angeli fortes, sancti atque potentes, in nomine On, Hey, Heya, Ia, Ie, Adonaï, Shaddaï, et in nomine Shaddaï, qui creavit quadrupedia et animalia reptilia, et homines in sexto die, et Adamæ dedit potestatem super omnia animalia: un de benedictum sit nomen creatoris in loco suo: et per nomina Angelorum servientium in tertio exercitu, coram Agiel Angelo magno, principe forti atque potenti: et per nomen stellæ quæ est Venus: et per Sigillum ejus, quod quidem est sanctum, et per nomina prædicta super, conjuro te Anael, qui es præpositus diei sextæ, ut pro me labores, etc. *(continue as on Sunday).*"

Translation*: I conjure you, ye strong and holy Angels, by the names On, Hey, Heya, Ia, Ie, Adonai, Shaddaï, and in the name Shaddaï, who on the sixth day created four-footed beasts and creeping things and men, and gave to Adam all power over all creatures; wherefore blessed be the name of the Lord, by the name of the Angels serving in the Third Legion, in the presence of the great angel Agiel, strong and powerful Prince, and by the name of the star Venus, and by his holy seal and by the aforesaid names, I conjure thee, Anael, great Angel, who presides over the sixth day, etc.*

Their power is to give silver, to make men more luxurious, to approach their enemies through luxury, to make marriages, to excite the love of women in the hearts of men, to heal ailments.

Regular form of the Spirits of Venus or Friday

Their bodies are beautiful, of middling height, their countenance is gracious, affable, their color is white or green. Their coming is announced by a brilliant star, their sign is some young girls who are playing, and who try to engage those who are in the Circle to take part in their games.

Their particular forms are:

A King holding a scepter, riding a camel; a superbly dressed girl; a naked girl; a dove; a she-goat; flowers; savine.

Conjuration for Saturday

"Conjuro et confirmo super vos, Caphriel vel Cassiel, Machatori, et Seraquiel, Angeli fortes et potentes: et per nomen Adonaï, Adonaï, Eie, Eie, Eie, Acim, Acim, Acin, Kadosh, Kadosh, Ina vel Ima, Ima, Shaddaï, Ia, Sar, Domini formatoris seculorum, qui in septimo die quievit: et per illum qui in beneplacito suo filiis Israël in hereditatem observandum dedit, ut eum firmiter custodirent et sanctificarent, ad habendem inde bonam in alio sæculo remunerationem: et per nomina Angelorum servientium in exercitu septimo Booel Angelo, magno et potenti principi, et per nomen stellæ, quæ est Saturnus: et per sanctum sigillum ejus, et per nomina prædicta super, conjuro te, Caphriel, qui præpositus es diei septimo, quæ est dies Sabbati, quòd pro me labores, etc. *(continue as on Sunday).*""

Translation: *I conjure and confirm upon you, Caphriel or Cassiel, Machatori, and Seraquiel, strong and powerful Angels; and by the name Adonaï, Adonaï, Adonaï, Eye, Eye, Eye, Acim, Acim, Acim; Kadosh, Kadosh, Kadosh, Ina vel Ima, Ima; Shaddaï, Ia, Sar, Lord and maker of the world, who rested on the Seventh Day, Who wished His people of Israël, that they should keep and sanctify the same, to have thereby a good reward in the world to come; and by the names of the Angels who serve in the seventh Legion, before Booel, a great and powerful Angel; by star of Saturn; by his holy seal, and by the names before spoken, I conjure thee, Caphriel, who presides over this day.*

Their power is to sow discord, the give birth to hate, to incite evil thoughts, to give lead, to kill, to mutilate.

Regular form of the Spirits of Saturn or Saturday

Their body is normally long and thin; they have a furious and angry air. They have four faces, one in the front, the other behind, the third and fourth on either side, and each face has a long beak; their color is black and shines like jet. Their movement is like the agitation of winds which seems to be accompanied by an earthquake; and their sign is to make the earth whiter than snow.

Their particular forms are:

A King with a long beard, riding a dragon; a old man with a long beard; a old woman leaning on a staff; a pig; a dragon; an owl; a black habit; a scythe; a juniper tree.

Declarations and Submission of the Spirits

We predominating Spirits, that is: Kings, Emperors, Princes, Dukes, Counts, Marquesses, Barons, Governors-General, Captains, Ministers, Lords and others, we subject Spirits recognize, certify, attest, swear and vow on the most high and holy Names of God, the Conjurations and Exorcisms contained in this Book, as also our characters belonging to us, to merit and serve in general all those who avail themselves of the present Book in all their needs and whatever general necessities, and without exception, following the power we have received from God, and we confirm all the following things:

FIRSTLY, We undertake and submit ourselves to faithfully serve all those who will require us to do so by these presents, following our declaration, and to make or cause by means of our subject every desire and will, and that never will a mortal have knowledge of what will be operated and executed by our ministration, and that no Spirits will be able to give knowledge to anybody that they were invoked for this purpose. We also promise to bring them or have brought or carried everything that they require of us, without deception or fraud, and that all will be good and loyal to their will, and without that we cannot continue either during their life, nor after their death, and that we can expect no reward for the services that we provide them.

Item: We agree to appear to all those who call us by our names enclosed within this Book, in a kindly human form, without any ugliness or deformity, every time and whenever we will be called, without doing any wrong to those who have been received of God, nor to their five senses of Nature, not to those who will be in their company, nor to the place or house where they may call us, and that without making any noise, nor thunderclaps, nor thundering, nor lightning, nor disturbance, nor rupture, nor fracture, nor racket, in any manner whatsoever, and no living creature will see our coming, except those who call upon us and their companions, if commanded of us; we also agree to reply to all their questions and demands made of us, and or replies will be true, without ambiguity, nor double sense; on the contrary, we will speak well in the language of the Operator[222], precisely and intelligibly; and having satisfied what is required of us, we will retire in peace and without tumult, observing the same conditions in coming as in going, when they pronounce the License to Depart.

Item: To execute all the aforesaid conditions, we oblige and engage ourselves, under pain of augmentation of increasing our torments a hundredfold, from moment to moment, and the privation of our duties, honors and dignities; by virtue of which we have attached our seals, stamps and characters, and signed the present Book, to serve all those who will invoke us, and will immediately do that which will be required of use without any delay.

*
* *

In this chapter, we didn't intend to create a completely new work. We have simply sought to clarify and put together a host of details which are either confused or contradictory in most of the Grimoires. You can review the manuscripts in the libraries, to see if we have succeeded.

But these details only have any value if they allow the possibility of *obtaining a practical result.*

Now, we only began to set up the following experiments on these phenomena in 1891, and from the first attempts we obtained such results that we could affirm the POSSIBILITY OF SUCCESS.

Here, some additional details are needed.

---

[222]Naturally, the original says: 'in French'.

THE MAGICAL EXPERIMENTS OF THE INDEPENDENT GROUP FOR ESOTERIC STUDIES

In 1889, we founded the *Independent Group for Esoteric Studies* in Paris, intended to run experiments concerning those forces whose actions on man and Nature are still unknown.

The first months were devoted to propaganda[223], and the works could be fruitfully pursued from the beginning of 1891. At this time the group was divided into technical sections, with one pursuing Practical Magic. We personally conducted several experiments with success, as did our friend, François-Charles Barlet: but these experiments needed a control, which only subsequent studies could provide. The year of 1891 was dedicated to initial studies, and at the beginning of 1892 several attempts, accompanied by a Vegetarian diet and a focus on seeing Elementals, were undertaken and crowned with success, principally with regard to the experiments of Delfosse. In the middle of the year, facts reported in the Grimoires were submitted to experimental control, and Michelet, one of the managers, was even able to certify that a diamond prevented magnetic activity from passing through it. This fact, reported by Agrippa and unknown to modern physicists is familiar to diamond merchants, exactly as it was verified. At the same time, an experiment with *conscious evocation* was attempted by H. and, despite many oversights and faults, this experiment produced most interesting and instructive results. We will report the main findings according to the Operators themselves.

In the month of March 1892, during the period of the crescent moon, H. and K., members of a commission of inquiry into magical phenomena, attempted the following experiment which was conducted in the most absolute secrecy.

After 12 days of threefold training: Vegetarian from the physical aspect, purifying from the moral aspect, and ritual from the psychic aspect, a preparatory Magic Ceremony of consecration of the locale was performed on the eve of the day of Operation.

"Following this preparatory consecration", says the report before me, "we felt such a sadness and sense of dejection, that we hesitated to continue the following day, seized with a kind of dread in our weakness. The astral doesn't like the man who looks through a chink in the door."

---

[223] In Papus' time, the term 'propaganda' still meant nothing more than the dissemination of information. It didn't take on its largely negative connotation until later, in the 20th Century.

Despite this, the experiment was attempted the following day. The Operators decided to see the effect of a Pentagram drawn with their blood and projected into the astral by fire.

This was, as they realized later, a deplorable basis for an experiment and outside of all normal conditions. Blood projected into the astral could only attract a crowd of larvae, and it wasn't this aim that the practitioners were pursuing.

But for now, we should return to the facts. "The following morning", said the report, "with the requisite conditions for the magical words completed, the Circle drawn, the mirror, the censer and the lights set out, two Operators, one with a sword and the other with the trident of Paracelsus (in tin, because the day of Operation was Thursday), dressed in robes and embellishments in the corresponding planetary color and the magic signs engraved in accordance with the ritual, entered the Circle; and the evocation began at 11:30 am."

This evocation was said, or rather chanted slowly in a sonorous manner, during which incense was burned. At the end of this evocation, the Operators said: "We felt *cold breaths of wind*, like those felt in most séances involving the materialization of spirits. These breaths of wind were objective, since the leaves of oaks and poplars were stirring. At the same time, very unusual *grey vapors* traced the contours of the apparition, passing and turning before the magic mirror which both of us were watching."

Now, according to the practitioners, "the aim of the work was to restore the blood used to draw the Pentagram, and which belonged to the two Operators, to its original fluid state. This was the great fault", they added. We have just said why.

In sum, after this clear outline of the apparition, after this sensation of a cold breath of wind and the object's movements, accompanied by characteristic cracking sounds throughout the bedroom, the Operators thought that everything was over, and carefully put away all the objects which they had used during the Operation.

The experiment had been performed in a large apartment in Paris, and this bedroom was situated at the back of the right wing of this apartment. The left wing was occupied by the brother of one of the Operators, a man of mature age and teacher of mathematics in a large public educational establishment. At that time, this man had gone to bed early, not suspecting anything of the studies his brother was pursuing, and in any case having no belief in Magic or any of its corollary teachings.

At the moment the practitioners, isolated and safe from any surprise in their Circle, attracted a shower of larvae into the apartment without being aware of it, the teacher was sleeping like a log quite far from all this.

Now, at the exact moment of the evocation, he was woken by the violent blow of a fist on his shoulder, and experienced a sharp kind of pain, due no doubt to this brusque awakening. Believing he was being attacked by an evildoer, he stood up on his bed and took his revolver which was to hand, then lit his candle, and realized with stupefaction that nothing odd was going on in the apartment he occupied. He went back to bed, but the sharp pain continued for a long time afterwards.

(Comparing this experiment to the facts of Cideville, we can already see on a small scale the reproduction of the same Law.)

This sensation of the punch disturbed the teacher so much, that the following morning he described it to his young brother, who carefully recorded the facts and the time of the phenomenon, while being careful not to speak about his experiment.

But the manifestations didn't stop there. Everything had been tidied up in the bedroom which had been used for the Operation, and there was nothing abnormal to see in this room. At nine o'clock in the morning, the practitioner having left to attend to his medical pursuits, the housekeeper came as usual to do her work. But when she opened the bedroom door, the woman was suddenly affected by a kind of panic, a great dread, and ran out of the apartment.

Interrogated by the practitioner's brother about the cause of this dread, she couldn't specify anything in particular, and said: "It affected me like that, but I don't know why."

Finally, on one of the following nights, while the Operator was asleep in his bedroom, a superb crystal inkpot broke in two as if with a saw, something which would be almost impossible to reproduce experimentally.

Now, this was an experiment performed by young and inexperienced Operators which is very eloquent from the theoretical point of view of an experiment in evocation having succeeded completely. Since then, other interesting experiments have been attempted and succeeded, but we selected that one as being typical, not wanting to describe one of our own attempts which wouldn't be as convincing for the reader as facts described by others.

However, we will transcribe this report, coming from the same practitioner, which he sent to us in a letter dated January 5th:

"Alone, the same ritual as usual, without including a consecration, and fixing the will upon the astral.

"To the preceding transparency I added an impression in wax of a Pentagram seal, during which, following the system you taught me, I burned the piece of paper on which was written what I desired. The result was satisfactory, for despite all the odds, what I had asked for was granted."

If we add that the attempts at psychometry pursued by the same group were very successful, we will have shown what can be accomplished in one year by works followed methodically, from the point of view of this type of study.

But at that time, we were very poorly organized, and since 1893 our abilities to act have considerably increased, and the group now possesses a laboratory for Practical Magic in Paris, which has been placed at the disposition of the members who have been specially charged with this study, and nobody doubts that, very shortly, still more important results will be obtained here. We also have another laboratory in Province where there is a foundry and machine tools, which will allow us to create all the metallic objects we will need for planetary correspondences.

*
* *

THE EXTERNALIZATION OF THE ASTRAL BODY

In these last few years, the scientific world has been somewhat astonished to learn of the number of authentic observations made by Gurney and Myers[224] concerning *splitting of the human being in two*, either while alive, or immediately after death. In France, Prof. Richet of the School of Medicine in Paris has bravely taken the lead in studies of this kind, and inspired a magazine devoted to these questions. Now, these facts agree with the teachings of Occult

---

[224] Edward Gurney (1847 – 1888) and Frederick W. H. Myers (1843 – 1901) were founders of the English Society for Paranormal Research (SPR) in 1883. Following a number of investigations into mediums in the 1870s, and the discovery of much fraudulent practice, they had hoped to establish a society where more rigorous scientific methods would be upheld. However, some historians have also seen the founding of the SPR as a reaction to Darwinism, and an outlet for those scientists – and others – who had somewhat lost their faith in Christianity and Judaism as a result, to find another means of seeking reassurance of life after death. Unfortunately, much of their early work was marred by the fact that they used two subjects for much of their investigations into telepathy and other hypnotically-induced paranormal phenomena, namely George Albert Smith and Douglas Blackburn, who themselves turned out to be charlatans. Some even suggest Gurney took his own life as a result, when he overdosed on chloroform in Brighton in 1888. Even the papers they produced around the 1880s and 1890s were subject to considerable controversy among more 'orthodox' scientists. Given this, Papus' breathless praise of them in 1893 is therefore a little odd, especially in a section devoted to scientific methodology.

Science connected with the *astral body* and its possible externalization outside the physical body. One school, called Theosophical, remarkable for the imperturbable self-assurance with which its members, claiming to be experts, answer the questions about which they are most ignorant, has the whole of Magic consisting of creating a double of the human being which is accomplished through a Vegetarian diet followed for a period of time. Regarding their magical success, we have already spoken about the physiological errors committed by these types of sect followers. Therefore, it seems pointless to us to dwell further on this subject.

The actions of the will upon the astral body is intimately linked to the study of respiration and its mysteries; but what is important to know, is that the conscious manifestation of action at a distance of this astral body is preceded by certain unconscious phenomena, which have been studied little up to this time, though often described. Thus, there are three possible ways an individual can act completely at a distance over another:

1. The other person being conscious of this action, without the Operator being himself aware of it;
2. The other person not being aware of the action to which he submits, but the Operator being aware of the actions he is producing;
3. Both individuals being aware of the phenomena produced.

A series of observations corresponds to each of these classifications, which will clarify completely the sense of our divisions, and which will allow the Magister to easily deduce the theory and practice of these types of phenomena.

FIRST CASE

Receiver aware, Operator unaware at the moment of the phenomenon's production.

Miss de T., who for a long time had studied and practiced spiritualistic phenomena, having heard talk concerning the possibility of eternalizing the psychic force and of creating a double, wanted to try a decisive experiment on this subject.

She was in Paris at that time, having just left some good friends in a large town in South America. She decided to appear there to one of her friends, and focused her will strongly on this subject for several days. On the day of the experiment itself, she gave herself over to very tiring work, even going to dig up potatoes in a field for several hours, all this to break any possible resistance from the physical body by means of exhaustion.

That evening, around 9:00 in the evening, she went to bed after having concentrated all her will on the appearance she wanted to manifest in Latin America. It didn't take her long to fall into a deep sleep.

The following morning on waking up, she hadn't preserved any consciousness of anything having taken place, and absolutely didn't know if the experiment had succeeded or not.

Only one month later, she received by regular mail a letter from the person on whom she had wanted to act. This person wrote that, finding himself one evening (on the date of the experiment), around 10:00 and 10:30pm at a very lively ball, he retired on his own for a moment to a casement window. It was at that moment, that to his great astonishment, he saw Miss de T. in the opening of the window, dressed all in white and smiling. The letter contained all the details concerning this subject. Here, too, is the report of the facts by the practitioners themselves:

January 30th, 1893

I am sending you a copy of part of the letter I spoke to you about. The friend who wrote it was unaware that I had wanted to appear to him, and believed he was having a hallucination. I have the original letter in my possession, and at your disposal.

As for the other letter of the same kind, I still haven't been able to find it. It came from my mother who, being in St. Petersburg, while I myself was in Buenos Aires, saw me in her bedroom one night, and had been so afraid, she begged me not to do the same thing to her again.

I have in fact performed ten attempts at producing a double: these two succeeded.

J. de T.

Febrero 1887, Puerto-Cabello.

Sueno o alucinacion ? No puedo explicar lo que me sucedio, pero se lo voy à contar pidiendo no se burle de su pobre amigo ! A las diez del dia de ayer me dirégi al baile del senor E.., saludé à la novia que me parecio muy triste, y, de repente, hubo un instante en que, encontrandome rodeando de senoras en una pequena sala, oï su voz de V^e muy conocida y agradable, que me decia, « Yo tambien estoy aqui, Senor B. » – Me volvi con presetza, latiendo mi corazon, y la vi, amiga mia, recostada en el alfeisar de una ventana y souriendome con dulzura y picardia. Vestia V. un traje blanco. – Oh ! la vi, crealo V… no es una historia, se lo aseguro, y, mi sorpresa fué tan grande que una senora me pregunto : « qu le pasa à V. ? Le ha sucedido algo ? » – La vision fué rapida, huyo con presteza de mis ojos pero no de mi alma y durante toda aquella noche fué V. la companera de mi silencio. – Si para créer en esa vision, necesita V. mi palabra de honor, se la doy.[225]

SECOND CASE

Operator aware; Subject of Operation unaware.

One of our friends in Lyon who is very advanced in the study of meditation and its practice, V., had a considerable battle going on while conducting some very important business at one time. Every probability indicated total defeat in a lawsuit someone was trying to file against our friend, yet he didn't lose his courage.

Profiting from the fact that the person he wished to change completely despite their viewpoint went to bed early, V… concentrated all his psychic powers during the first two hours of sleep on him on whom he wanted to act. He transported himself mentally to the sleeping person, and there, little by little, and with extreme gentleness, pleaded his case and defended his point of view.

More of these experiments followed, and then the ideas of the person on whom he was acting began to change, despite himself. At the end of some time,

---

February 1887, Puerto-Cabello: Dream or hallucination? I can't explain what happened to me, but I know what I'm going to be asking you, so don't make fun of your poor friend! At ten o'clock yesterday I went to the dance of Señor E., greeted the bride who appeared to me to be very sad, and, suddenly, there was a moment when, surrounded by ladies in a small room, I heard your voice which is very well known and pleasant, which said to me, "I am here too, Mr B." – I turned quickly, my heart beating, and I saw you my friend, standing in the gap of a window and smiling at me with sweetness and mischief. You wore a white dress. – Oh! I saw you there, believe it… It is not a story, I assure you, and, my surprise was so great that a lady asked me: "What happened to you? Has something happened?" – The vision was quick, and fled swiftly from my eyes but not from my soul; and during the entire night you were the companion of my silence. – If believing in that vision requires you to have my word of honor, I give it.

NOTE: the Spanish is unusual – whether due to it being old or a dialect of Argentina, accents and phrases are different. V. appears to be the old form of Ud. signifying *Usted*, or the formal version of 'You'.

it was by his own volition that he wanted to execute an action which was completely the reverse of his initial viewpoint.

Bringing this case to the attention of Desbeaux and Hennique, they saw its great importance.

Here we're talking about an action suggested consciously and at a distance from an individual who submitted unconsciously to the order given mentally. The report on this event had no other purpose than to expand on the explanation of this action.

V. whom we are discussing, has often manifested surprising proofs of exceptional psychic powers. This is how on many occasions he has predicted – before witnesses and in a precise manner – political events prior to their happening six months later, and with the exact date when the events would take place. He has also frequently been able to verify prophetic scenes and make known a great number of other facts, strange to anyone who did not possess the key. Yet, V. has only been pursuing such studies for barely four years, and before that he had been a positivist.[226]

THIRD CASE

Both individuals aware of the phenomena being produced.

Experiments by Émile Desbeaux with G...[227]

On May 23rd, 1891, I had G..., a professor of physical science, for whom these kinds of experiments were completely unknown, sit in a dark corner of the room. It was nine o-clock in the evening. G... was blindfolded, with his face turned towards the wall.

I stood four meters away from him, in front of a small table on which there were two lamps.

---

[226] Positivism asserts that all knowledge can only be firmly based on the sensory perception of natural phenomena, interpreted through logic and reason; and therefore, nothing which cannot be empirically observed can exist. Despite the growth of antipositivism, much of science is still based on this premise, which puts it in direct opposition both to religion and to any esoteric doctrine.

[227] We have extracted this series of experiments from the *Annales des Sciences psychiques* ('Annals of Psychic Sciences'), a publication appearing every two months in pamphlets for 2F 50, from Alcan, Editor, 108 Boulevard Saint-Germain, Paris. [PAPUS]

FIRST EXPERIMENT

Without any noise, and without the knowledge of G…, I took an object and hold it up in the light. I focused my gaze upon it and wished G… to see this object.

After 30 minutes, G… told me that he saw a *round metallic object*.

Now, the object was a *silver spoon* (a small coffee spoon) whose handle was hidden in my hand, and on which I only focused on the paddle which was of an *elongated oval shape*.

SECOND EXPERIMENT

G… saw a *brilliant rectangle*.
I was holding a *silver snuff-box*.

THIRD EXPERIMENT

G… saw a *triangle*.
I had drawn with bold lines, on a cardboard box, a *triangle*.

FOURTH EXPERIMENT

G… saw a square with *luminous ridges*, with *brilliant pearls*; sometimes he only saw two pearls, sometimes he saw many.

I was holding an object whose presence it was hardly possible for him to guess: it was a large die in white card, and the light brightly lit its *ridges* and the engraved points on the top the brilliant reflections of black *pearls*.

FIFTH EXPERIMENT

G… saw a *transparent object with a luminous net forming an oval at the base*.

I was holding a *cut crystal beer tankard with an oval base*.

There, I thought, were five experiments done in excellent conditions of control and sincerity, which could be considered as having succeeded.

In turn, I became the *receiver*, taking the place of G… who became the *transmitter*.

FIRST EXPERIMENT

I saw a *small, very brilliant oval.*
G… was holding a gold wedding-ring.

SECOND EXPERIMENT

I saw two *arcs of a circle* separated from one another, and making a vertical counterpart.

G… was holding a Japanese vase whose contours recalled what I had seen. However, I considered the result of this experiment as a failure, and only attributed the preceding one the value of being half successful.

EMILE DESBEAUX

Experiments by Émile Desbeaux with Léon Hennique

With my friend Léon Hennique, I tried to perform telepathy at a great distance: Hennique was on vacation in Ribemont (Aisne), while I remained in Paris, so we were separated by 171 kilometers. It had been agreed that Hennique would be, or rather, would focus on being the transmitter, and that our first attempt would take place the night of June 11th to 12th, at half past midnight.

I can do no better than to transcribe the letters we exchanged concerning these experiments.

FIRST EXPERIMENT

Paris, night of June 11th to 12th, 1891

My Dear HENNIQUE,

It is fifty-five minutes past midnight, and I will let you know what I have just seen. At thirty minutes past midnight, I sat down in an armchair facing as closely as possible the direction of Ribemont. I had covered my eyes with a blindfold, and the lamp was behind me on the table.

At the end of a period of time I saw a brilliant 'V', then thin clouds, like scintillating phosphorescence, appearing, disappearing, reappearing without a discernible form; an interruption; then suddenly, very brilliant, very visible but scarcely remaining for two seconds, I saw a bouquet, a *bunch of flowers.*

I waited in the same position for a period of time, but nothing else showed itself. I decided to remove my blindfold: it was then fifty-five minutes past twelve. I am rather curious to know you wanted to transmit to me.

Emile DESBEAUX

Ribemont, June 13th, 1891

My Dear DESBEAUX,

I took a book and waited for the time for communication. The book was boring, and I was drowsy. At forty minutes past midnight, I had a brusque awakening for no reason. I decided that you would see my *lamp*, and, turned towards Paris, I wished it to appear to you where my thoughts were directed. My lamp had a Japanese lampshade which was painted, on one side, with a kingfisher on a stake, and on the other a *bunch of flowers*. The lamp was extinguished, but a nightlight almost underneath it made the *flowers* appear through it. I willed this for around six minutes, then my will was exhausted.

The psychic being and the Spirit crossing the Astral Plane
(The Realm of the Elementals).

I received your letter. According to what took place, there has been a beginning to the phenomena, a partial success. I would add that in the oval cage of the lamp glass, I verified that the nightlight reflected itself in a 'V' shape.

Léon HENNIQUE

SECOND EXPERIMENT

Paris, June 18th, 1891, 11:30pm

My Dear HENNIQUE,

I don't know if you got my letter in time, and if you were able to "do the telepathy" with me?

For my part, at eleven o'clock, seated in my armchair and turned to your direction, eyes blindfolded, holding your last letter in my hands, I soon saw a small phial of water with a very clear design; then thin clouds followed, trying to take form. Finally, a last phosphorescent cloud condensed into *a ball, a sphere, full and luminous*.

After a time during which I evaluated this for six to ten minutes, with my eyes still bandaged, I saw nothing more. I still waited, and when I removed the blindfold, the pendulum marked twenty minutes past eleven. I remained ten or fourteen minutes more without seeing anything further.

AFTER DEATH

I'm interested in knowing: 1. If you performed the experiment; 2. If you did it during this period of time, between eleven and six or ten minutes past eleven. I await your reply.

Emile DESBEAUX

Ribemont, June 19th, 1891

My Dear DESBEAUX,

This evening, June 18th, the clock rang eleven. This was the hour agreed on. I took a glass lamp *globe* and set it down *in full light* on my table, under my lampshade. I immediately began to think of you. Turning towards Paris I imagined passing through the various stations which separate us: Saint-Quentin, Terguier, Chauny, Compiègne, Creil, Chantilly, Paris. I came to your road and my thoughts went to your house, to your room. There, I began to wish for my *globe* to be seen by you. For at least ten minutes I maintained this wish.

On June 19th, I received your letter. The experiment succeeded perfectly, since you told me that you saw a *ball*, a *sphere, full and luminous*. That is extraordinary!

Léon HENNIQUE

THIRD EXPERIMENT

Paris, July 6th, 1891, 11:30pm

My Dear HENNIQUE,

This was a truly special effect. It came from you in "pushes", in successive waves. I seemed to see the results of each of your efforts, with a maximum intensity on the final jolts. These are the phosphorescent images which succeeded one another suddenly and very quickly, seeming to seek to a form which was increasingly clear: then suddenly nothing, and one might say your effort was exhausted.

Finally, here is what I saw: in the first clouds, a very rough form of a copper circle from which metallic rays were escaping. Then it became more brilliant while still preserving its stellar shape; one might say the space between the rays was decorated with diamonds. Then I had the confused impression of a jewel, a woman's brooch decorated with precious stones, but I didn't still have a sensation which was alive or perceptible as an idea (ἐδιωλον) seeming to seek to come to me.

Emile DESBEAUX

Ribemont, July 7th, 1891

My Dear DESBEAUX,

We have completely missed on our little Operation. I have attached the word which I tried to have you see.[228] So, we can try again one of these days. You appear to have felt my efforts, but we should consider this third attempt as a failure. The atmospheric conditions were poor[229], perhaps, and it must be very difficult in these conditions to dispatch four letters. I will try something simpler the next time.

Léon HENNIQUE

While waiting to resume our experiments, I am sending you the results of our first three attempts, without adding any commentary.[230]

Emile DESBEAUX

EXPERIMENT OF SEPTEMBER 2ND, 1891

Paris, September 2nd, 1891

My Dear HENNIQUE,

It is 11:30pm. I took off the blindfold. The bedroom is black, and since eleven o'clock I have been waiting for a telepathic image, but none has come! I only see black. I have only seen black. Am I no longer receptive enough? Did you forget? Let me know.

Emile DESBEAUX

Ribemont, September 4th, 1891

My Dear DESBEAUX,

My experiment succeeded completely.
I needed to know if telepathic images were being sent to you against my will. I decided to isolate you, that is, to free you of ambient preoccupations, and I *wished* you to be alone, completely alone, mentally. You saw nothing. So, this

---

[228] This word was *Dieu* ('God') drawn in large thick black lines. [PAPUS]
[229] July 6th, new moon, stormy. [PAPUS]
[230] This letter was clearly to Papus from Desbeaux, enclosing the previous correspondence.

proves that my will, suggesting the images in the preceding experiments appears to me close to having taken place.

Léon HENNIQUE

CONCLUSION

We have defined Magic as:

The action of the human will on the rapid evolution of the living forces of Nature, and our book's only purpose has been to justify and develop this definition.

We hope we have succeeded in setting out, according to the ideas of contemporary physiology and by applying these ideas, the psychological constitution of man formerly published by Plato and later taken up by Fabre d'Olivet. This work was essential for all those who seriously want to concern themselves with these questions.

Besides, several chapters in this treatise have been devoted to the study of the living forces of Nature, their astral origin, and their correspondences in the sublunary world.

These are points which are almost always neglected by those who want to study Magic without resorting to the immutable principles fixed by tradition for the general divisions of Esotericism.

Finally, many seekers want to own a complete summary of all those Grimoires, all those Clavicles, all those ritual manuscripts which, despite the naiveties they contain, and the gross errors multiplied there, still allow for the discovery of points about the Practical Kabbalah which are hardly known in our times.

To satisfy this legitimate curiosity, and to avoid true seekers having to spend considerable sums of money, in this last section we've brought together everything which is most interesting in the various practical anthologies.

We had to refrain from discussing the truly personal part of our work, which would have been very useful for the aspirations of all serious people and supporters of our principles, and which are more than just vulgar achievements: but it is our express opinion that the writer who wishes to examine a question from all aspects hasn't taken into account the rejudices or slander it would stir up. This book also ends with an cation which strictly follows Traditional Magic.

When you have understood the theory of Magic, you can certainly move beyond these words and prayers, and your immortal soul, which is so important to your integrity, will know how to help you find the terms adequate to your intellectual worth.

But this is your personal work: for us, our duty consists in showing you the path and to turn away the incompetent and profane by certain means.

Prayers! Conjurations! Mysterious prayers! And all this presented to the 19th Century by an author who claims to be serious, who invites his readers to distrust clericalism as much as materialism. Isn't it ridiculous to attract the attention of these "Sons of progress" and these "Illustrious children of the century of railroads and telephones"?

Would it take anything more to have this book thrown on the fire by worldly skeptics, vain and incompetent, impatient to perform an evocation in five minutes flat?

Nowadays, when it's fashionable to be in possession of such studies, when Magic, great Initiates, teachers of Occultism and Enchantment are on every street corner, and brashly assail editors and magazines with their indigestible lucubrations, a beacon of light is indispensable. We must put every intelligent reader in a position to be able to judge the true worth of these prematurely great men, and if our book accomplishes this end, we will be completely recompensed for our efforts; and as a result, open ourselves up to be disdained by the perfidious spite of those malcontents, envious in essence and intellectually impotent by temperament.

As for the men who are sincerely convinced of the greatness of contemporary science, and those who think that the study of Magic is simply an empty dream or amateurish imagination, flawed in its sentimental fervor, we would ask them whether the Law of Evolution can't be applied to physical forces just as it is to all of Nature, and it we have the right to set limits to energy, in whatever way it manifests?

Isn't the folly of today the wisdom of tomorrow? Doesn't analogy allow us to state that what is illogical in appearance is, in fact, simply the logical manifestation of causes still unknown?

Logic is seen in the action of an electrical machine, insulated by its glass feet, transforming mechanical work into electrical energy expended in order to put the glass into motion, and condensing the power produced in its copper balls.

Yet the action of the Magician isolated in his circle of charcoal, transforming the work of training to which he has submitted his body into astral energy, and condensing the power which is produced into the magnetic ball at the end of his wooden wand, covered in insulating varnish, is considered *a priori* absurd and folly.

There is logic and reason in the action of a lightning-conductor which draws off and tames the electrical energy of a cloud, or the action of a metallic point which allows electricity to dissolve in a Ramsden machine[231].

But when a Magician, armed with a metallic point called a magic sword, draws off the energy condensed in an agglomeration of astral power, immediately all the so-called men of science cry: madness, hallucination, or charlatanism.

One again, the powers on which the Magister acts are of the same order as all the possible forces of Nature, and obey the same Laws. Only these are generated, thanks to the transformation of so-called physical forces, by a living environment, and participate to some extent in their origination, by manifesting proofs of intelligence.

Clerics, ignorant and sectarian by nature, see the devil in it. The contemporary scholar, disturbed from his meticulous additions to the list of microbes, can only see alienation in those who dare to focus on these issues, which aren't be found in any university examination. The independent seeker should make his own inquiry into this subject, and not fear words.

Believing that something happens "by chance" or "by an odd coincidence", is to give proof of intellectual laziness and scientific cowardice.

Believing that something "supernatural" exists in the universe is to wrong those creative forces whose Laws are immutable and analogically correspondent throughout.

---

[231] A Ramsden Machine was an electrostatic generator invented by Jesse Ramsden in 1768. This stood on four glass insulating feet, and glass plate was turned by a cranking handle (hence the comment about mechanical work being required to put the glass in motion, mentioned two paragraphs earlier) creating the friction necessary to generate electricity, and collecting it in copper electrodes (or metallic points) to be discharged.

Therefore, we cannot think of a better way to end this treatise on Magic, than with the dual affirmation which should guide every Magister worthy of that name:

CHANCE DOESN'T EXIST   –   THE SUPERNATURAL DOESN'T EXIST

APPENDIX

APPENDIX

CHAPTER I – CEREMONIAL MAGIC

A Historical Look

The Magical Ceremony, as we have been able to see it by what has come before, is the result of a series of theoretical principles forming the very basis of the whole of Occult knowledge.

The principle preparations to observe in all experiments are of two orders:

1. One must act consciously upon the astral forces and direct them towards the end desired;
2. One must also be sufficiently insulated to avoid dangerous reactions, and even be read to avert these reactions if they are produced.

Let us see how the Operator accomplishes these two first conditions of all magical experimentation.

After the personal training which is required, the Operator begins by setting up his field of isolation by tracing the Circle.

The Circle is the personal signature of the Operator's will, allied to the astral influences. Also, clairvoyant subjects describe a circle of flames and columns of scintillating lights, there where our physical senses only perceive a charcoal line and Hebrew names.

The Circle is to the Magister what a fortress is to the man of war. It is within the shelter of this protective rampart that the experiments are going to follow their course.

When this first line of defense is constituted, the Operator sets out the substances which should attract the astral forces. These substances are either vegetable or animal, whose astral body is going to be used in the experiment, and will serve as the means of fixation and material manifestation of the psychic realities which have been evoked.

Finally, the Magister adds to this first means of attraction the personal dynamism of his will, by condensing the nervous power into the magnetic wand of Operations which serves to direct the forces emitted towards the goal, and which allows the creation of more or less considerable astral light.

But the magic sword is also at the service of the practitioner, and if, once the conjuration has been done, reactions are produced which are excessively violent, drawing off the superfluous quantity of astral power with the metallic point of the sword will remove from those psychic entities their material implement of materialization.

The Magical Operation is truly a combination of effort and knowledge, and the Operator possesses both the poles of all action: the pole of attack or projection by means of the magnetic wand with its round end, and the pole of defense and dissolution by means of the magic sword with the pointed end.

We can summarize what we have just said concerning the Magical Ceremony in three rules:

1. Construction of a line of defense (training, personal circle and mystical names);
2. Attraction of astral forms (vegetable, animal, blood, etc., etc.);
3. Conscious action over astral forms evoked (wand and sword).

Now, we are going to see how the traditional rules have been profaned by the ignorant and the incapable, and how this Operation has descended from the level of a scientific experiment based on immutable principles, to the blind and superstitious practices in use in most of the mystical groups of our times. Nevertheless, we can confirm that the whole Ceremony has been preserved intact across the Centuries by Occult Fraternities, and we will follow them from Homer to the 19th Century. After reviewing these historical points, we will study the degeneration of Magical Evocation.

HOMER

"Here, Perimedes and Eurylochus held the victims, while I drew my sword and dug the trench a cubit each way. I made a drink-offering to all the dead, first with honey and milk, then with wine, and thirdly with water, and I sprinkled white barley meal over the whole, praying earnestly to the poor feckless ghosts, and promising them that when I got back to Ithaca I would sacrifice a barren heifer for them, the best I had, and would load the pyre with good things. I also particularly promised that Tiresias should have a black sheep to himself, the best in all my flocks.

"When I had prayed sufficiently to the dead, I cut the throats of the two sheep and let the blood run into the trench, whereon the ghosts came trooping up from Erebus – brides, young bachelors, old men worn out with toil, maids who had been crossed in love, and brave men who had been killed in battle, with their armor still smirched with blood; they came from every quarter and flitted round the trench with a strange kind of screaming sound that made me turn pale with fear.

"When I saw them coming I told the men to be quick and flay the carcasses of the two dead sheep and make burnt offerings of them, and at the same time to repeat prayers to Hades and to Proserpine; but I sat where I was with my sword drawn and would not let the poor feckless ghosts come near the blood till Teiresias should have answered my questions."

HOMER: Odyssey, Book XI, trans. Samuel Butler

In this evocation we can see the essential points that we have mentioned, which are:

1. PREPARATION – Conjuration – Ditch.
2. ATTRACTION – Blood.
3. RADIATION – Use of the sword – Distancing of spirits, except those one wants to interrogate.

THE THOUSAND AND ONE NIGHTS

Historians particularly concerned about the date they should attribute to the Arabic stories, translated by Galland under the title *Thousand and One Nights*, are in general agreement about dividing these stories into two parts; one very ancient and probably of Hindu origin, and the other written in the 13th Century and of Arab origin. Avoiding any discussion by adopting the latter epoch, in this collection we can follow certain details of Ceremonial Magic among which we will particularly emphasize the following account:

"The Princess Lady of Beauty went to her chamber, from which she fetched a knife with some Hebrew words engraved on the blade. She then asked the Sultan, the chief of the eunuchs, the little slave, and myself to descend into a secret court of the palace; and there, leaving us beneath a gallery which ran all round, she went to the center of the court, where she traced a large Circle and in it wrote several words in it in Arabic, ancient and other characters which are called characters of Cleopatra.

"When she had finished and prepared the Circle in the manner she desired, she went and stood in the middle of it, where she made some abjurations and repeated some verses from the Koran. Imperceptibly the air grew dark, as if it appeared to be night and the earth was about to crumble away. We were seized with extreme fear; and this fear increased further, when we saw the genie, the son of the daughter of Eblis, suddenly appear under the form of a colossal lion."

(80th night)

MARTINES DE PASQUALLIS

(18th Century)

Louis-Claude de Saint-Martin was "illuminated" by his Master in practice: Martines de Pasquallis.

According to the writings of Saint-Martin himself, the Master brought his Disciples together in some room, not doubt purified by a few prior Operations. Martines then traced a Circle in the middle of the room and wrote in Hebrew the requisite names of angels and Divine names in the Circle. These preparations astonished the young Disciple so much that at one point he cried out: "What? Are all these things necessary to communicate with Heaven?" However, he had no good reason to regret these preparations, for once the conjurations had been performed, the "Psychic Beings" appeared and gave striking proof of the reality of their existence in the invisible world.

Those who were present at such experiments became "illuminated," that is to say, that for them the existence of the invisible world and the immortality of the soul became realities even more certain than the existence of matter in the physical world. And these "illuminated ones", scorning death, were ready to do anything to spread and to defend the doctrines which were so dear to them.[232]

*
* *

(19th Century)

We now come to modern experiments and we are going to quote the evocation practiced in 1854 by Eliphas Lévi. In this you may find the complete ritual of Ceremonial Magic.

---

[232] During the printing of this treatise, we have been alerted by our friends in Lyon, Vitte and Elie Steel to take note of many manuscripts by Martines de Pasquallis and Louis-Claude de Saint-Martin, whose conservation we owe to Cavarnier. These manuscripts throw a completely new light on the Ritual Magic of Martinists. We are moreover preparing a special work on this subject. [PAPUS]

THE EVOCATION OF APOLLONIUS DE TYANA

The preliminaries terminated on the 24th of July: it was proposed to evoke the phantom of the divine Apollonius and interrogate it upon two secrets, one which concerned myself and one which interested the lady. She had counted on taking part in the evocation with a trustworthy person, who, however, proved nervous at the last moment, and, as the triad or unity is indispensable for Magical Rites, I was left to my own resources. The cabinet prepared for the evocation was situated in a turret; it contained four concave mirrors and a species of altar having a white marble top, encircled by a chain of magnetized iron. The Sign of the Pentagram, as given in the fifth chapter of this work, was graven and gilded on the white marble surface; it was inscribed also in various colors upon a new white lambskin stretched beneath the altar. In the middle of the marble table there was a small copper chafing-dish, containing charcoal of alder and laurel wood; another chafing-dish was set before me on a tripod. I was clothed in a white garment, very similar to the alb of our catholic priests, but longer and wider, and I wore upon my head a crown of vervain leaves, intertwined with a golden chain. I held a new sword in one hand, and in the other the Ritual. I kindled two fires with the requisite prepared substances, and began reading the evocations of the Ritual in a voice at first low, but rising by degrees.

The smoke spread, the flame caused the objects upon which it fell to waver, then it went out.

The smoke still floating white and slow about the marble altar; I seemed to feel a quaking of the earth, my ears tingled, my heart beat quickly. I heaped more twigs and perfumes on the chafing-dishes, and as the flame again burst up, I beheld distinctly, before the altar, the figure of a man of more than normal size, which dissolved and vanished away. I recommenced the evocations and placed myself within a Circle which I had drawn previously between the tripod and the altar. Thereupon the mirror which was behind the altar seemed to brighten in its depth, a wan form was outlined therein, which increased and seemed to approach by degrees. Three times, and with closed eyes, I invoked Apollonius. When I again looked forth there was a man in front of me, wrapped from head to foot in a species of shroud, which seemed more grey than white. He was lean, melancholy and beardless, and did not altogether correspond to my preconceived notion of Apollonius.

I experienced an abnormally cold sensation, and when I endeavored to question the phantom I could not articulate a syllable. I therefore placed my hand upon the Sign of the Pentagram, and pointed the sword at the figure, commanding it mentally to obey and not alarm me, in virtue of the said sign. The form thereupon became vague, and suddenly disappeared. I directed it to return, and presently felt, as it were, a breath close by me; something touched my hand which was holding the sword, and the arm became immediately benumbed as far as the elbow. I divined that the sword displeased the spirit, and I therefore placed its point downwards, close by me, within the Circle. The human figure reappeared immediately, but I experienced such an intense weakness in all my limbs, and a swooning sensation came so quickly over me, that I made two steps to sit down.

Whereupon I fell into a profound lethargy, accompanied by dreams, of which I had only a confused recollection when I came again to myself.

For several subsequent days my arm remained benumbed and painful. The apparition did not speak to me, but it seemed that the questions I had designed to ask answered themselves in my mind.

To that of the lady an interior voice replied – Death! – it was concerning a man about whom she desired information. As for myself, I sought to know whether reconciliation and forgiveness were possible between two persons who occupied my thoughts, and the same inexorable echo within me answered – Dead.

I am stating facts as they occurred, but I would impose faith on no one. The consequence of this experience on myself must be called inexplicable. I was no longer the same man; something of another world had passed into me; I was no longer either sad or cheerful, but I felt a singular attraction towards death, unaccompanied, however, by any suicidal tendency. I analyzed my experience carefully, and, notwithstanding a lively nervous repugnance, I repeated the same experiment on two further occasions, allowing some days to elapse between each. There was not, however, sufficient difference between the phenomena to warrant me in protracting a narrative which is perhaps already too long. But the net result of these two additional evocations was for me the revelation of two kabalistic secrets which might change, in a short space of time, the foundations and laws of society at large, if they came to be known generally.

ELIPHAS LÉVI, *Dogma*, trans. Arthur Edward Waite

*
* *

It is to continue these experiment that we founded the *Independent Group for Esoteric Studies*, which has its headquarters at 29 rue de Trévise, in Paris, and where some members have already been able to obtain important results.

Such is the Magical Ceremony worked *consciously*, and while taking all the precautions necessary to ensure avoidance of the dangers inherent in such experiments. Let's see the transformations effected by this Ceremony across the ages.

While we won't discuss the experiments of those witches who, during the Middle Ages, replaced training by pomades with an opium base, retaining the Circle but making an appalling use of blood, we will say a few words about the modern experiments of spiritualism, with which certain Adepts claim to make an experimental synthesis.

1. The Degeneration of Magical Evocation

In spiritualist evocations, one finds some of the elements of magical evocation, but distorted in a strange manner. Besides, everything which would allow the practitioner to defend himself against pernicious influences are pitilessly suppressed under the pretext of "superstition"! Also, a spiritualist practitioner is never sure what he is going to produce, and chance guides everything, and the excellent experiments of the previous evening can be transformed the following morning into a foolish or pornographic communication. It's the triumph of the unconscious and the unexpected; it's also the triumph of the ignorant vanity of mediums and cult followers, and one can truly understand the haughty indifference with which a true Adept of the Science of the Mages tries to keep this demagoguery of psychic phenomena distanced from his Oratories and his Sacred Laboratories. The spiritualist doctrine can be recommended in its elementary teachings, for it summarizes a few points of the Esoteric Tradition concerning reincarnation and astral evolution; but the practice of spiritualism takes the mediums into neurasthenia passing through hysteria, and the adherents to skepticism or cultism. But let us leave this pointless discussion and return to the facts, that is, to the degeneration of magical experiments into spiritualist experiments.

The Magister condenses his will firstly around his center of action by creating the Circle; than on the magnetic wand of Operations.

In spiritualism the Circle, when it exists, is transformed into a mass of hands belonging to beings who are not in the least trained, and whose disparate fluids could only put up the weakest barrier against pernicious manifestations. Moreover, the invisible beings who do manifest and who control everything, instead of being controlled, are careful to push their "dear proteges", little by little, to do away with this final rampart which is not very troublesome in any case. Thus, many séances are conducted without the Chain whose origin is the Magic Circle.

As for the implement to condense the astral fluid, the wand of the ancient Operators is transformed into a simple wooden table on which the psychic forces emanated from mediums apply themselves to acrobatics which are more or less enjoyable.

The Magister makes use of plants or animals from Nature whose astral fluids are used as the starting point of the condensation required to manifest the being's evocation. Thus, it's by evolving natural forces up towards humanity that the Magister accomplishes his experiment. The smoke of incense completes the active elements necessary to the being which is going to manifest itself.

It's from a human being who has degenerated into a mode of animality under the influence of hypnosis; from a medium rendered unconscious from actions he produces (when it isn't trickery), gasping from the expropriation of his vital power by the astral beings, that the spiritualist group borrows the force necessary to produce the phenomena called materializations.

Finally, conjurations are replaced by popular refrains or songs, when they aren't omitted completely, and all the means of defense have disappeared: no more metal, no more points, no more swords; no more anything which would prevent obsession, nervous anemia, and even more serious accidents.

We personally possess a most instructive series of letters, which come from unfortunate mediums who gave themselves over with all their strength to experimentation, and who are today dangerously obsessed by the beings who came to them under false names and who assumed the personalities of their deceased parents.

Our readers also know, we are certain, the teachings of Dr. Paul Gibier on this subject. We have included the following fact from his latest work which will suffice to instruct incautious people.

"Three *gentlemen*, desirous of finding out whether certain spiritualistic allegations were true, locked themselves up one evening without a light, in one of the rooms of an uninhabited house, having agreed previously through honor and oath to be perfectly serious and to act in good faith.

"The room purposely was absolutely bare, save three chairs and a table. Around the latter they took their seats.

"It was agreed that as soon as anything unusual occurred the first one in readiness was to light a wax taper with which they were provided. They had remained motionless and quiet for some time, mindful of the least noise, or the slightest movement which might take place at the table upon which their joined hands were resting. No sound could he heard; the darkness was appalling, Suddenly, a strident cry of distress burst upon the silence of the night. Immediately after, a fearful noise was heard and a hail of projectiles fell upon the floor, table and observers.

"Filled with terror, one of those present lighted a taper, as had been agreed upon, and as soon as the darkness had given place to light, two of them saw that their companion was missing, and his chair upset at the end of the room.

"As soon as they had recovered from their astonishment, they found their missing friend under the table, inanimate, with his face and head covered with blood.

"What had taken place?

"It was seen that the marble mantel piece, broken in pieces, had been torn from the wall and cast at the unfortunate man's head.

"The victim of this accident remained in an unconscious state for nearly ten days, wavering between life and death, and but slowly recovered from the terrible cerebral shock which he had sustained."[233]

Dr. Paul Gibier (*Analysis of Things Existing*, from *Psychism*, pub. Bulletin Pub. Co. NY)

All experiments concerning the astral are extremely dangerous, and they are even more dangerous when one is unconscious and unarmed.

Now, experiments in magical evocation take place in the light (albeit colored to avoid the dissolution of the astral fluid), while nine-tenths of experiments in spiritualist manifestations take place in complete darkness. In a magical experiment, the Operator is conscious and armed against discharges of Odic electricity; in spiritualist experiments the Operator is unconscious of what is being produced, and unarmed. We leave to the reader the work of concluding and judging between the "claimed superstitions" of the ancient Magicians, and the research called "scientific" in the modern circles of democratic spiritualism.

And we weren't seeking to compare the successes produced in the two types of evocation; for the fact of materialization is extremely rare in spiritualism, and even after ten years they have simply been republishing the same phenomena studied by three of four serious practitioners. In Paris, among six leaders in spiritualism, just over half have even been present at a seriously confirmable phenomenon of materialization.

---

[233] This extract is taken directly from the 1899 version of this book, which is in English, being published in New York. Dr. Paul Gibier was born in France in 1851, before moving to New York in 1889, and founding the Pasteur Institute there, using Pasteur's techniques to inoculate people against rabies, eventually settling on a large farm near Nyack, NY, where he established a hospital to treat tuberculosis. He was also greatly interested in psychic phenomena and spiritualism, writing several books on the subject, including the one cited by Papus.

The question is therefore in abeyance, and the future alone will show how this can reach a conclusion. Up till now, we have judged it sensible not to summon all the seekers of knowledge away from magical experimentation. Here we have strived to atone for the reasons for this exclusivity, and we dare to hope that, very soon, new facts will come to expand our dossier and proclaim the guarantees which our approach offers.

For now, let us stop this discussion and take a look at the bibliography of magical phenomena.

2. Summarized Bibliography

Our intention isn't to provide a complete bibliography on this topic. Far from that. You will find in our work on the *Kabbalah* (Paris, 8° format, 1,200 p., 1892) and in our work on *Occult Science* (Paris, 8° format, 1,200 p., 1891) a general bibliography which will allow serious seekers to expand on their studies completely.

We wish simply to provide a quick review of some of the works which particularly interest the Magister, be they Grimoires which he should beware of, or useful books which he should consult.

In the Kabbalistic tradition, Magic takes its place in the theoretical treatises such as the *Zohar* or the *Sepher Yetzirah*, and above all is represented in Hebrew manuscripts, of which only a few poor translations exist in our libraries. These manuscripts are known by the name of "Clavicles of Solomon" or the "Shemhamphorasch", and are linked to the exercise of prophecy in Israel.

From this source are derived a host of treatises on sorcery, books on hucksterism, creations of false and bizarre pontifications which, for the common man, constitute the "cream of occult knowledge."

We are going to consider in turn:

1. The most well-known treatises on practice which can be read or studied: "The Grand Albert – The Little Albert – the Enchiridion – The Grimoire of Honorius – The True Keys (or *Clavicles of Solomon*)."
2. Books on hucksterism, comprising a disordered collection of ridiculous recipes and forming the basis of the naïve or pious practices of Folk Magic.
3. The ancient and modern didactic treatises about the magical phenomenon: AGRIPPA – ELIPHAS LÉVI – DU POTET – DE GUAITA – etc.).

3. Treatises in Current Use

Clavicles

THE ADMIRABLE SECRETS OF THE GRAND ALBERT – *Lyon*, the inheritors of the Brothers Beringos, according to the teachings of Agrippa – 1791.

This small treatise, as found in the editions of the Brothers Beringos of Lyon, contain certain teachings which one can use mixed in with bizarre recipes and magical tradition of the country.

The 'Grand Albert' includes:

1. A treatise on embryology following the prevailing beliefs of the 16th Century. One will notice a curious study on astral influences which we have reproduced in our Chapter on Astrology.
2. A treatise on magical correspondences devoted to a study on the virtues of herbs, stones and animals – with a table of planetary influences.
3. A book of "secrets" relating more to the practices of witchcraft than to those of magic.
4. Finally, an Appendix containing elementary ideas of physiognomy.[234]

As one can see, only the second part is worthy of study by the Magister.

THE MARVELOUS SECRETS OF NATURAL AND KABBALISTIC MAGIC OF THE LITTLE ALBERT – *Lyon*, the inheritors of the Brothers Beringos – 1758.

The "Little Albert" is principally devoted to popular traditions in Magic. In it one can find whole pages inspired by the "Occult Philosophy" of Agrippa; but

---

[234] Physiognomy is the assessment of a person's character from external traits, particularly the face. More scientifically it is also used to indicate the general appearance of terrain, object or plants, as in the 'physiognomy of plants'. Though popular in the 15th Century, by the 16th Century Leonardo da Vinci – among other – a proclaimed it to have no merit. However, he did believe that a study of the lines of the face, caused over time by repeated facial expressions, could give an indication of personality. While the study has long been discredited, at least one aspect has remained in the study of non-verbal communication, or 'body language', where fleeting facial expressions or tics, and body movements are interpreted as signs of internal emotional state, whether the person is lying, etc.

one will mainly find naïve or interesting recipes used by witches to inspire or increase love.

A first series of recipes on this subject are described from pages 10 to 24 (We have reproduced some in our study on "Love Potions" later in this Chapter), not forgetting the means to tie and untie "a lanyard" and a means of "protection from becoming a cuckold" (page 35).

Love topics being ended, the book starts on satisfying interests in and resolving questions concerning money. Here we find more or less infantile procedures for seeking treasure (page 124). This final chapter is only of interest because of the theoretical study which discusses the subject of "spirits of the dead" on the one hand, and the gnomes which guard the aforesaid treasures, on the other hand.

We will point out "domestic secrets" (pages 52 – 71) and a study on "Talismans" (pages 72 to 108), followed by a work on magic perfumes (page 108 to 140), before beginning on the question of treasures. It is in this part of the work that we find a rare plate which reproduces the obverse of the planetary talismans. This plate, pointed out by Eliphas Lévi, has been reproduced in our book.

Finally, we should note, in particular, the indignation which seized the author at the thought that there were "charlatans" who exploited popular credulity regarding magic and unworthily deceived the public concerning the issue of *the Mandragore*. A Grimoire from the 16th Century drawing attention to fraud with regard to phenomena – isn't that amazing!

This little book ends, like all similar works, with a host of more or less precious "secrets" and which fill pages 140 to 300, followed by a very short chapter dedicated to the connections between the hours and the planets.

Such is the layout of this treatise, considered to be the *ultimate* in magical revelations by our practitioners of Folk Magic.

ENCHIRIDION LEONIS PAPÆ SERENISSIMO IMPERATORI CAROLO MIGNO IN MUNUS PRETIOSUM DATUM NUPERRIME MENDES OMNIBUS PARAGATUM – *Rome*, 1660.

This edition is complete and allows us to understand the character of this work. It contains a series of prayers and psalms with their magical characteristics, as well as a series of *oraisons* (p. 10 et seq.), which have made the fortune of this little book across the ages. In this book you will find the Seven Mysterious Prayers for the seven days of the week reproduced (see the section on Meditation). In addition, there are prayers for everything, to make a woman faithful (p. 65), for human weakness (p. 51), for travel (p. 55). We also find some interesting figures in the Enchiridion, among others the Labarum of Constantine with its consecration. In certain cases, one can appeal to experiment, as the following title demonstrates (p 90):

Prayer against arrows, so that they will fly against a dog or other beasts, rather than the one who wears this orison, or the other which follows, about his neck.

From pages 121 to 123 we find several "secrets:" of interest to shepherds then, suddenly, after page 123, a treatise on Practical Magic commences, containing exorcisms, conjurations and prayers to say over implements and parchment. This is the *Key* of the orisons mentioned above. Also, on page 103, it gives the means to make use of the Seven Mysterious Prayers:

"To make use of these prayers, on the first Tuesday of the Moon, before the sun rises, you must give alms to the first pauper you will find in church where you have gone to hear Mass. Then, when you return home, write the aforesaid prayers on virgin parchment. The crosses you find there should be drawn in blood drawn from the middle finger of the left hand, and each cross you come across, you should make one on yourself, after which you should bless and cense these aforesaid prayers, and carry them upon yourself, and you will be protected against all the snares of your enemies."

Finally, from page 131 is found the key of all these prayers and the true means of using them. This continues to page 152, which is the beginning of the inevitable "mystical secrets" which end the volume on page 168.

In sum, the "Enchiridion" is an excellent little treatise about the Magic of human speech, and because of this, it merits the full attention of the connoisseur.

THE MAGICAL WORKS OF HENRY CORNELIUS AGRIPPA, *by Peter Albano,* **in Latin and French with Occult Secrets –** *Liège,* **1798. (The back of the volume contains the HEPTAMERON or the magical elements of PETER ALBANO, philosopher and disciple of HENRY CORNELIUS AGRIPPA).**

This little volume is one of the most useful the Magister can have, on condition that one makes a few corrections to the Hebrew names given. One can find a very complete list of magical and kabbalistic correspondences concerning the septenary[235], as well as Conjurations and the technical details we have already reproduced to a great extent in our Chapter on the Great Operation.

---

[235] Pertaining to the number '7', such as: days of the week, number of ancient planets, the seven lower Sephiroth, etc.

From page 104 to 138 we find a host of "secrets" as in the majority of treatises of the same kind. We don't recommend dwelling on this second part.

THE CLAVICLES OF SOLOMON. *A copy contains: a translation from Hebrew into the Latin language by Rabbi Abognazar, and rendered in the common tongue by Monseigneur Barault, Archbishop of Arles.*

We saw in the last Chapter on Adaptation, that every practitioner should himself create a manuscript book which he will use in his evocations.

This tradition explains the many copy manuscripts in circulation of the *Clavicles of Solomon*, which can be found from time to time in circulation, and whose price varies from 100 francs to 10 francs, depending on the case.

The National Library in Paris possesses some of these manuscripts, classed respectively under the numbers 14.785, 14.786, 14.787 in one location, 25.314 in another location, and finally 24.244 and 24.245.

The manuscript titled the *Clavicles of Solomon* has been photocopied and the 143 proof pages obtained have been bound in a volume whose few rare copies have each been sold for 100 Francs.

We possess two manuscript copies, one in octavo on vellum, the most complete of the manuscripts we have seen; and the other in quarto is similar to the photocopied version, but containing a very interesting second part, too.

In general, each of these manuscripts is divided into three parts:

1. A part devoted to astrological correspondences and Operational implements, as well as prayers and conjurations;
2. A part devoted to "occult secrets";
3. A part devoted to talismans and rings and containing a host of figures.

One will find everything of special interest in the *Clavicles of Solomon* in this book

4. Grimoires – Hucksterism

THE TRUE CLAVICLES OF SOLOMON – **Treasure of occult knowledge followed by a large number of secrets, and notably the magic of the Green Butterfly –** *Memphis, pub. Alibeck the Egyptian, approved by Agalcarept.* – **On the frontispiece, an engraving representing the following subject:** *"Solomon explains how and when one should use his Clavicles."*

Solomon is seated in a Renaissance armchair. He is clothed in a mantle covered in 'fleurs-de-lys' and is explaining his secrets to two people, one dressed in Renaissance clothing, the other dressed as a Knight Templar. Eclectic archeologists wouldn't be too happy!

A bad book on sorcery in sum. Numerous demonic signatures. A few pages drawn from the "Clavicles", between others concerning the magic mirror and divination by the word of Uriel.

This ends with more or less fantastic "Secrets" without much value.

GRIMOIRUM VERUM, **vel probatissime "salomonis Claviculæ – Translation from the Hebrew by** *Plaingière*, **a Jesuit Dominican (sic.), with a summary of curious secrets. –** *Memphis, pub. Alibeck the Egyptian, 1517.*

Another vulgar Grimoire of sorcery containing 18 authentic demonic signatures and destined to alienate the unfortunate reader who follows the rites indicated to summon Lucifer or Luciferge. The suggestions concerning the consecration of salt, water, etc., are taken from the "True Clavicles." – But it contains reference to a certain goat kid which seems to me to be terribly tinged with black magic. – Eliphas Lévi also provided the key to this enigma. The "Secrets" are similar to those of the *True Clavicles* of the preceding Grimoire, printed by the same publisher.

THE RED DRAGON **or the Art of Commanding the Celestial, Arial and Infernal Spirits. –** *Milan, pub. Gaspardo Buffanelli.*

The masterpiece of Grimoires. – One of the rare treatises which details how to enter into pacts. – It is from this that Eliphas Lévi drew the origin of his indignant protestation against the evocation of the dead by the process written on page 94. – This process can only be executed by a dangerous madman or a criminal. – It is followed by a recipe for a horrible venereal mix called *Composition of the Dead – or the Philosophical Stone* (page 102 et seq.).

The copy sent to us by V. de Lyn is authentic and of great bibliographic rarity.

THE MAGICAL WORKS OF HENRY CORNELIUS AGRIPPA, translated into French by *Peter Albano*, with occult secrets, notably that of the Queen of Hairy Flies[236] **- Approved by me, Sargatas (with the signature of this honorable demon). – Rome, 1744.**

This date and this city indicate the origin of all the preceding Grimoires, since the "Queen of Hairy Flies" must be the antecedent of the "Green Butterfly", and the Demon "Sargantes" closely linked to "Agalcarept." In sum, the publishing house which produced these falsifications is indeed Rome, their date of publication is the 18th Century, and the authors are those good Reverend Fathers who one always finds behind this kind of forgery. And our opinion is confirmed by a small list placed at the end of the volume. This list is exquisite, and reveals the existence of other Grimoires whose titles would singularly attract the minds of naïve village sorcerers.

From this list were have extracted the following:

TRUE BLACK MAGIC OR THE SECRET OF SECRETS, a manuscript found in Jerusalem in Solomon's Sepulcher containing 45 talismans with their engravings, as well as the manner of using them and their marvelous properties and all the magical characters known up to this day, 1750 edition.

RED MAGIC, cream of the occult, natural or divinatory sciences.

TREASURE OF THE ANCIENT OF THE PYRAMIDS, true knowledge of talismans, followed by the *Black Owl*.

SECRETS OF THE OLD DRUID OF THE MENAPIAN FOREST, preceded by the Precepts of John of Milan.

To these we should add the following reprints.

From the **ENCHIRIDION** *of Pope Leon* (1740) to the **GRIMOIRE** *of Pope Honorius* (1760) to have the complete catalog of books which we strongly counsel our reader to leave to one side, unless their spleen can take it.[237]

---

[236] Bizarrely enough this is not a mistranslation: the book indeed contains instructions on how to train hairy flies to find treasure!

[237] Note that the 'original' Enchiridion of 1660 *is* recommended: it is only this later and adulterated version – and a part of the series of books published by the Vatican between 1740 and 1760 in order to muddy the water, according to Papus – which is not.

THE TRUE RED DRAGON, and *The Black Pullet*, edition augmented by the secrets of Queen Cleopatra, secrets to make oneself invisible, the secrets of Artephius[238], etc., etc.

This treatise is a reedition of the original from 1521, printed very recently in Paris (pub. Victor Goupy, rue Garancière, 5th Arrondissement). It is a poor Grimoire which contains nothing of interest, and is of no more value than any books on common sorcery, despite its pretentions as an edition for the bibliophile. It contains reprints of old images of black magic.

GRIMOIRE OF POPE HONORIUS, with a summary of the rarest secrets, *Rome*, 1670.

"This Grimoire is not without importance to those curious of the art. In the first place, it simply appears to be a tissue of revolting absurdities; but to Initiates of the signs and secrets of the Kabbalah, it becomes a true monument to human perversity."

ELIPHAS LÉVI (*History of Magic*, p. 307).

This judgement should absolve us from any further commentary on this book on sorcery which is more dangerous for the mind of weak practitioners than for the enemies of witches.

5. Educational Treatises

OCCULT PHILOSOPHY by *Henry Cornelius Agrippa*, counsellor and biographer of Emperor Charles V. – La Haye, 1727 (translation), 2 Volumes.

The work of Agrippa constitutes the first true encyclopedia of occultism.

Occult Philosophy is divided into three books, of which the first is comprised of 74 Chapters, the second of 60 Chapter and the third, of 65 Chapters.

The first book begins with a study of the Elements, and progresses from there to the study of the three worlds and their analogical correspondences, the theoretical foundation of all studies of occult knowledge. The study of sympathy and antipathy is developed at length, which then leads to the first principles of Astrology. Astral influences are described in several Chapters (30 – 38); then Chapter 39 is devoted to the author's theory on the divine world or theurgy, and

---

[238] Artephius was a 12th Century author who is alleged to be the author of a number of alchemical works, notwithstanding the fact that he lived centuries before the majority of such texts. However, his 'Secrets' were reverently referred to by Roger Bacon.

from Chapter 40 onwards the book considers the physical world and the magical use of the substances provided by it. The (theoretical) study of the sciences of divination and procedures for the training of the individual is contained in the next ten Chapters (50 – 60). Finally, the book ends with a description of the patent or occult virtues of the human soul, the means of exalting these virtues and the influence of man's soul over the physical world on the one hand; and the influence of the astral world over the soul on the other.

Here is a complete treatise on Occult Sciences in 74 Chapters. We will now find the technical details in the succeeding books.

*
* *

The second book is particularly devoted to numerical and astrological Kabbalah. Having discussed the nature of numbers both collectively and individually, as well as their analogical correspondences (Chapters 1 – 21), the author considers Astrology itself, after discussing the connection between music and the astral (Chapters 21 – 29). The title of Chapter 28, "*Concerning the Observation of Celestial Things which are Necessary for all Magical Practices*", indicates the utility of this teaching which is so neglected by contemporary so-called 'Mages'. Chapters 30 – 51 go into details about talismanic figures and their characters concerning the planets, and the book ends with a study on the Soul of the World and the connections this Soul has with the human soul. Let us quote in detail the title of Chapter 60, the last of book two:

Containing the fact that human imprecations naturally impress their powers on external things, and teaches how man's mind, through each degree of dependence arrives at the intelligent world, and becomes like the most sublime spirits and intelligences.

*
* *

The third book is almost completely devoted to magical teaching and practice.

The educational preliminaries cover nine Chapters (1 – 9). From Chapter 10, the esoterism of the Kabbalah, the Sephiroth and the Divine World is covered. This study continues from Chapters 10 – 34, where there are a few words about the intermediary intelligences between the Divine and the human on the one hand (the animastical order), and between man and Nature on the other "the gods subject to death", which we call the Elementals. All this leads us to Chapter 37. From, here we return to the human soul, considered to be susceptible to serving the basis of magical realization. Note Chapter 62 is devoted to the obtaining of psychic powers, (prophecy, passion, ecstasy, oracles, etc.)[239] The training of the will is described in Chapter 54 onwards, both in theory and practice (cleanliness – chastity – fasting – solitude – penitence – adoration – sacrifices – consecrations – etc., etc.). Chapters 54 – 65 ends the French translation of *Occult Philosophy*.

We should mention the existence of a fourth book which is generally considered to be apocryphal, and which is concerned with practice in all its details. This book, however, was a great help to Eliphas Lévi, who reproduced it almost completely in his ritual.

It's in the Latin editions of Agrippa that one finds this fourth book which covers magical correspondences, the preparation of the venue for the experiment, consecrations, and in particular that of the magical book of spells, conjunctions and invocations, etc.

In the version given to us by our friend Philophotes, this book is followed by a very interesting series of treatises on practices such as those of Peter Abano, the ARBATEL, Letters on Magic, etc. The Latin edition is, from this point of view, preferable to the French editions. However, there is also a Latin version in octavo which only contains the three books.

*
* *

Here, then is a short analysis of this wonderful work which continues to be one of the best-established monuments erected to the glory of esoteric tradition in the 16th Century.

RITUAL OF HIGH MAGIC, by *Eliphas Lévi*. – 2nd Edition,
Paris, 1861, octavo.

We said in our introduction that our work has no other purpose than to serve as an introduction to the Magical Ritual of Eliphas Lévi. This is sufficient to show the importance we give to this work.

This is not the place to discuss Lévi's work in its entirety. We are only considering magical phenomena, and are focusing our attention solely on the ritual of High Magic.

---

[239] This is not strictly accurate. Chapter 62 talks about Consecration. Yet most of the third book is focused on this kind of topic.

The author manages to solve some of the most complicated problems. Coming to these conclusions alone, without assistance, in an age where such questions were unknown to the educated public, Eliphas Lévi knew how to write a true treatise on Occultism for the true Adepts in a dual sense and so craftily done, that it appeared to the profane to be just an empty and incomprehensible, perhaps spirited and Voltaire-like, book. The influence of this book has been considerable, and the majority of current writings on Magic, be they novels or treatises, simply paraphrase this deeply profound dogma and ritual which Occultism presently possesses. It's even more necessary to draw the reader's attention to this Master, since some contemporary Disciples – certainly the noisiest – focus all their effort to denigrate or even try to suppress the works of Eliphas Lévi.

The book we are discussing here is divided into 22 Chapters, following the Keys of the Tarot, and is followed by an Appendix. Properly speaking, it is composed of three treatises of seven Chapters.

The first septenary mainly covers didactic teachings without going into all the details about practice. The Chapter titles are: *Preparations – Magical Equilibrium – The Triangle of Pentagrams - The Conjuration of the Four – The Blazing Pentagram – The Medium and Mediator – the Septenary of Talismans.*

With the second septenary, we enter into the various divisions of practice: *A Warning to the Imprudent – The Ceremonial of Initiates – The Key of Occultism – The Triple Chain – The Great Work – Necromancy.*

The following septenary talks about negative, or black magic, which we have been careful to avoid in our treatise. These are Chapters 15, 16, and 18. Here are the rest of the titles of all the Chapters in this septenary:

14. *Transmutations* – 15. *The Sabbath of the Sorcerers* – 16. *Witchcraft and Spells* – 17. *The Writing of the Stars* – 18. *Philtres and Magnetism* – 19. *The Mastery of the Sun* – 20. *The Thaumaturge* – 21. *The Science of the Prophets.*

Finally, the conclusion of the entire practice is in Chapter 23, *The Book of Hermes*, which is given over to the Tarot by Eliphas Lévi, which nevertheless doesn't give the complete key (see our work on *The Tarot of the Bohemians*).

*
* *

The practice of Magic, based on the law of universal analogy, can be exercised on several planes. Eliphas Lévi, in order to deflect the curious, described the most fastidious kind of Ceremonial Magic, such as was practiced in the Ancient Mysteries. But we wanted to show that these true teachings could be *adapted* to the limited means available to the modern practitioner: this is the sole purpose of our book. This is also why the work of Eliphas Lévi will always mark the highest point to which one can aspire in the exposition of the theory and practice of High Magic.

MAGIC AND ASTROLOGY, by *Alfred Maury*.

This volume, crowned by the Academy, is very well done both from the critical and the historical point of view. From the dogmatic point of view, the author has neglected to understand all the details of his subject, and confuses Magic with a host of connected arts. Therefore, we have refrained from analyzing this most curious book, which is nevertheless useful to a true Adept of Occultism.

HISTORY OF MAGIC, by *Christian*.

This large volume is very interesting from two points of view. Firstly, as a summary of the magical legends, and secondly, as an analysis of the Grimoires. The history of initiation in antiquity is covered quite well; but it is inferior to that by Delaage (*The Knowledge of Truth*).

As to the astrological part, which in reality is only a particular version of onomancy[240] and numerical Kabbalah, the authors' son personally provided us with the key to the numerous obfuscations it contains.

In fact, there was a miscommunication between Christian and the editors of his work prior to publication, which left the entire part on Astrology incomplete, making it impossible to use in the form found in this book.

Shortly thereafter, Christian's son completed a book on Onomantic Astrology containing all the unpublished documents left among his father's documents.

But, from the strictly magical point of view, Christian's book is only useful for its well-researched analysis of Witchcraft and the Grimoires.

---

[240] Onomancy: divination by using a person's name, and therefore similar to Geomancy. While Hebrew letters correspond directly to numbers, and therefore words with a similar total value were believed in Kabbalistic tradition to be related, this practice was carried across to Latin, Greek and even English, etc. For example, the English language contains 26 letters, and if one assigns a number (a=1... z=26) to each letter, one can obtain a total value for a name. This total can be reduced by theosophical addition to a number between 1 – 9 (for example, 26 = 2 + 6 = 8), and a meaning can be ascribed to this number.

MAGNETIC MAGIC, by *Cahagnet - Paris*, 1858.

This historical and practical treatise discusses fascination, Kabbalistic mirrors, apports, suspensions, pacts, charms, evocations, possession, enchantment, sorcery, the magic of words, sympathetic correspondences and necromancy.

The author, writing from the viewpoint of spiritualist magnetism, has performed very interesting experimental research, particularly concerning magic mirrors. This volume, while weak on the doctrinal part, is particularly interesting in its historical and practical part. The book is very fruitful for the Magister with a good understanding of the theory of phenomena which he is called to study.

STANISLAS DE GUAITA – Essays on Cursed Knowledge – II. *The Serpent of Genesis*, first septenary: The Temple of Satan, Vol I. – *Chamuel*, editor 1891.

Stanislas de Guaita is one of the wisest and most erudite men among contemporary defenders of occultism.

Every volume by this author is a serious work, extensively profound, written in a superb and elevated style. There is none better than Guaita, who could aspire to the direct succession of Eliphas Lévi.

The *Serpent of Genesis* is firstly of interest to the Magister for its theoretical section, and then in particular for its *Evaluation of the Sorcerer's Arsenal*, from page 333 to 382, and is composed of small font, which shows its importance.

Moreover, several experiments of great interest to the Magister are described and analyzed from the esoteric point of view (see in particular the information concerning Cideville, p. 383 et seq., and the studies under hypnosis, p. 417 et seq.) Finally, spiritualism and its practices are reduced to their true worth with regard to the Hermetic tradition (p. 397 et seq.).

All that, together with the explanations and theories connected with black magic, make this work a monument to knowledge and erudition to any conscientious seeker.

HOW TO BECOME A MAGUS, by *Joséphin Péladan*.

Under this title, a few months ago Joséphin Péladan published the first volume of a series intended, according to its author, to revolutionize the world under the title of "Amphitheater of Dead Sciences."

Péladan is a great artist and his definition, or rather his definitions of Magic can be felt from this cerebral exclusivity. Used to creating everything by the wonderful inspiration of his rich imagination, the author strives to recreate Magic, scorning to abase his pride in order to study the Masters. From this comes a special kind of Magic, solely based on the creation of man, and constituted by commentaries on Eliphas Lévi and Favbre d'Olivet (Golden Verses). Péladan, who wrote *Tradition chaldéo-grecque* ('The Chaldean-Greek Tradition') and the scientific axiom that *the preciousness of metals is in direct relationship to their density*, which would make Mercury (13.6 g/cm^3) more precious than Silver (10.5 g/cm^3), is certainly a great story-teller, but too superhuman a being to be bothered with science and, above all, Magic! His books would never be dangerous except for the errors they contain, and this Chaldean wandering among the Positivists of the 19th Century has omitted the study of Astronomy and Astrology, no doubt through his grudge against his country.

We are convinced that, in the next edition of his works, this descendent of the ancient Chaldean Astrologers who emigrated to Lyon will almost certainly change his title and replace *Comment on devient Mage* ('How to become a Magus') to *Le Roman d'un Sâr* ('The Romance of a Sâr').

We apologize for having made such a severe criticism of a work which contains some excellent pages; but the magical tradition doesn't create itself, and pride, even extended to self-deification, cannot replace hard work.[241]

MAGIC UNVEILED, or Principles of the Occult Sciences, by *Du Potet*, 1 Volume in octavo (republished in 1892 for 10 Francs), having been on sale for 100 Francs by the Master exclusively to his Disciples – pub. *Paul Vigot*.

---

[241] It is perhaps surprising to read such a withering description of work of a fellow Martinist and member of the Ordre Kabbalistique de la Rose+Croix (OKRC), given that Péladan and Papus had previously all moved in all the same circles. The sarcastic description of Péladan as a stray Assyrian or Chaldean wandering among contemporary men reflects his taste for outlandish clothes, and using the title 'Sâr' which was an Assyrian title for 'leader'. A brief history behind this is as follows: initially Péladan, de Guaita and Papus has been good friends. However, in 1891 Péladan left the OKRC, and in 1892 he held his first *Salon de la Rose+Croix* in Paris. During that time (and the publication of this book) a very public battle had broken out between the two camps, called the 'War of the Roses' by a bemused press. His exit from these groups was accompanied by the publication of a series of books under the collective title: 'Amphitheater of Dead Sciences', in which he rejected the Ceremonial Magical teachings of bygone ages, with its Magic Circles, magical implements, talismans and incantations, and focused instead on a more spiritual form of theurgy, ironically an approach which more closely matches Martinism. In the first book of the series, *Comment on deviant Mage*, he states: "I must give you a definition of Magic: it is the art of sublimation of man; there is no other formula."

In this work the famous magnetizer regularly confuses Psychurgy with Magic. Simple experiments with magnetism are presented as evidence of Magic, and we are hard pressed to quote the historical research (pages 167 – 201) which is interesting to consult, along with its corollaries (pages 265 – 302) in which the author quotes excerpts from Agrippa's 'Occult Philosophy' (pages 297, 300 and 301) without naming the author, which is rather naughty for such a famous magnetizer.

On the other hand, the Operator who wishes to experiment practically with subjects in a sleeping state should read this book, whose title leaves much to be desired.

PRACTICAL MAGIC, by *Jules Lermina*, 1 volume in octavo,
3.50 Francs, edited by *Kolb*.

We have quoted from this excellent little work many times in our bibliography, above all on the question of Elementals. The theories of the different Occultist Schools concerning the constitution of man and the evolutions of psychic abilities are very well represented in this book. The clarity and solidity of style, and the spirit of synthesis which is characteristic of the talent of Jules Lermina is found on every page of this small manual, which we strongly recommend to every conscientious seeker.

CHAPTER 2 – LOVE POTIONS

(Folk Magic)

Few questions interest the curious as much as "Love Potions." We have shown often enough in the body of our work that the amorous, who are already slave to another will than theirs, cannot magically command the astral forces. But an impulsive being can be affected by magical procedures and as very few individuals know how to resist the impulses of their mortal soul, potions based on sympathetic correspondences often have a great chance of succeeding.

The theory behind the love potion can be compared to that of the "lasso" of the Mexicans. Firstly, the "lasso" needs to be thrown at the target: that is, you must make an impression on the imagination of him or her over whom you want to act. This is the first point.

Then the "lasso" must surround the being you want to capture: that is, you must fix the magnetic fluid of the person over whom you are acting, using substances which condense this fluid such as nails, teeth, hair and above all, blood.

Finally, the person contained in the "lasso" must be drawn to you by breathing in the externalized magnetic fluid. It is here that words and ceremonies take on their importance.

As for love potions created by mixing poisonous substances, these are processes which only evildoers use. In the Magical Dictionary at the end of this book, you will find complementary details on the subject of *love*.

Potions can be categorized in the following manner:

1. Purely astrological potions;
2. Potions which act through suggestion;
3. Potions which act through magnetism and magic (correspondence);
4. Compound procedures which combine several of the preceding processes.

All these categories may be found in the procedures now described.

*
* *

When talking to a young girl whose affection you wish to obtain, pretend to want to cast her horoscope in order to divine, for example, if she will have a happy marriage. During this meeting, which must take place without any witnesses, make sure she looks at you face to face, and, when your eyes are united, say the following resolutely: "*Kaphe, Kasita, non Kapheta et publica filii omnibus suis.*[242]" Don't be surprised by the enigmatic language whose occult sense eludes you; and if you said it with faith, you will immediately be loved.[243]

*
* *

Draw some of your blood on a Friday in Spring, leave it to dry in a small jar, together with the two testicles of a hare and the liver of a dove. Reduce it all to fine powder, and get the person on whom you have designs ingest around half a drachma of it. If it has no effect the first time, repeat up to three times, and you will be loved.

*
* *

If you can paste on the back of a woman or girl's bed, as close as possible to the place where she rests her head, a piece of virgin parchment on which you have written: "*Michael, Gabriel, Raphael, make N... conceive for me a love equal to mine*", that person will be unable to sleep without thinking of you, and soon love will be born in her heart.

*
* *

So that the person you love will remain faithful to you, take a lock of her hair, burn it, and spread the ashes on the wooden frame of her bed after rubbing it with honey. It is easy to repeat this Operation from time to time in order to maintain constancy in love.

Do you want your notes or business letters to successfully accomplish your desires? Take a sheet of virgin parchment and write the following invocation on it on both sides: "*Adama, Heva, as the Almighty Creator united you in earthly Paradise in holy union, together and indissoluble, so may the hearts of those to*

---

[242] It isn't possible to translate this, since country witch spells commonly use bastardized Latin. This spell is also often quoted as a means to make the person see you in their dreams, and in other versions the phrase must be repeated three, six or many times.
[243] This, and the following love spells, are taken from the Little Albert Grimoire.

whom I write be favorable to me and refuse me nothing: Ely + Ely + Ely." Then burn this sheet of parchment, carefully retaining all the ashes. Then take ink which has never been used, put in a new, small earthenware pot, and mix in the ashes together with seven drops of milk from a woman who is suckling her first-born, and add a pinch of lodestone reduced to powder. Then use a new quill pen which you have cut with a new penknife. Everyone to whom you write with the ink so prepared, on reading your letter, will be disposed to grant you anything which is in their power.

*
* *

Take five of your hairs, combine them with three from the person you love, and throw them in the fire, saying: "*Ure, igne Sancti Spiritus, renes nostros et cor nostrum, Domine. Amen.*", and you will succeed in your love.

On the Eve of St. John, before the sun rises, go and harvest the plant called *Œnula compana*[244]. Carry it in a fine linen bag over your heart for nine days; then pulverize this plant and spread the powder on a bouquet or the food of the person whose love you want, and soon your desires will be fulfilled.

*
* *

Psalm 137[245], which begins thus: *Confitebor tibi, Domine, quoniam audisti, etc.*, according to tradition, has the power to excite love in the heart of the person who is the object of your desires. Here is the means to operate:

Place oil from the white lily into a crystal cup, and recite the Psalm over the cup, ending by pronouncing the name of the angel *Anaël* and that of the person whom you love. Then write the angel's name on a fragment of cypress which you plunge into the oil; then gently anoint your eyelids with this oil, and attach the piece of cypress to your right arm. Choose a suitable moment to touch the right hand of the person you wish to love you, and that love will be born in their heart. The Operation is very powerful if you perform it at sunrise, on the Friday following the new moon.

---

[244] *Elecampane*, which is a corruption of its pre-Linnaean name, *Enula campana*. It appears to have been popular in herb gardens and healed many ailments.

[245] Psalm 137 in the Vulgate is in fact Psalm 138 in most bibles, beginning: "I will praise Thee with my whole heart...".

*
* *

Our forebears assure us that the bird called the green woodpecker (Note: *picvert* in French) is a sovereign remedy against Witchcraft using the knotted lanyard[246], if one eats it roasted on an empty stomach with blessed salt... If one inhales the fumes of burned teeth of a man recently dead, one will also be delivered from the charm...

The same effect can be obtained if one puts quicksilver in a torch made of oat straw or wheat straw, and place this torch by the pillow of the one afflicted by this curse... If a man and woman are afflicted by this charm, to be cured, the man must piss through the wedding ring which the woman holds while he does so.

Take a gold ring decorated with a small diamond which has never been worn since it came from the hands of the craftsman, enclose it in a small piece of silk stuff, and carry it for nine days and nine nights between the shirt and the skin, affixed to your heart. On the ninth day, before sunrise, engrave inside the ring with a new awl the word: *Scheva*. Then find some means to obtain three hairs from the person you want to love you, and add three of yours, saying: "*O body, may you love me, and may your intention succeed as ardently as mine by the efficacious virtue of Scheva.*" These hairs must then be knotted into a Lake of Love[247], so that the ring is almost entwined in the knot, and after putting it in the silk stuff, carry it once more upon your heart for a further six days, and on the seventh day remove the ring from the Lake of Love and arrange it so that the person loved receives it. The complete Operation should be performed before sunrise, and while fasting.

---

[246] Binding rituals are common in 'low' magic, and often include tying knots in rope or string, or using a wooden peg. Either way, these spells were the terror of newlyweds, since the intention was usually to render the man impotent! Given this, it is easy to see why the woodpecker was featured in cures, since much herbal and animal magic was sympathetic, so that we find many herbs bearing the name of the part of the body they were expected to cure, such as *lung*wort, *liver*wort, *eye*bright, *heart*sease, etc. Here the idea of the 'pecker's sharp beak drilling into unyielding wood (for that matter, the *pic* of *picvert* in French would convey the same sense) must have struck a similar note with sorcerers. In most cases the simplest solution was to find the offending article and untie the knot, or remove the wooden peg.

[247] The Lake of Love knot is a common feature of magic and also continental Freemasonry. In English it is more commonly known as the Love knot, or Figure of Eight knot.

For love.

On the first Friday of the moon. Buy without haggling a red ribbon ½ ell long, in the name of the person loved.

Make a Lake of Love knot in it but not tightly, and say the *Pater Noster* over it up to *in tentationem*, replacing *sed libera nos a malo* with *ludea-ludei-ludeo*, and at the same time tighten the knot.

Add an extra *Pater Noster* each day until you reach 9, each time making a knot.

Place the ribbon on your left arm against the skin. Then touch the person.[248]

*
* *

What if a man wishes to see an image of the woman he should marry in his dreams? He should take pulverized coral, powdered lodestone, the blood of a white pigeon and create a small piece of paste from them, which he will put into a large fig, then place it in a blue silk square. He will put this beside his neck, and under his pillow he will put a branch of myrtle, and then say this prayer: "*Kyrie clementissime, qui Abraham servo tuo dedisti uxorem Saram, et filio ejus obedientissimo per admirabile signum indicasti Rebeccam uxorem; indica mihi servo tuo quam nupturus sim uxorem, per ministerium tuorum Spirituum Baalibeth, Assaibi, Abumostith. Amen.*"[249]

In the morning he should call to mind the image he saw in the dream. If he saw nothing, he should repeat the magical experiment the three following Fridays; and if, after this third Operation, no vision has been produced, one may surmise that there will be no wedding for him.

If it is a girl who wishes to see in a dream whom she will marry, she should obtain a small branch of poplar, join its arms with a ribbon of white thread, and fasten it under her pillow. Then she should rub her temples with the blood of the

---

[248] With regard t this spell, an *ell* is an old measurement of about a cubit, so half an ell would be 9 inches long, which would be short if one is expected to tie nine knots in it and wraps it around one's left arm. The *Pater Noster* is simply the 'Our Father' in Latin, and the 'but deliver us from evil' is replaced with *ludea-ludei-ludeo*, which sounds like a variation on the Latin *ludo, ludes, ludet,* or I/you/he plays.

[249] There are so many variants on this prayer it is almost impossible to find a completely correct Latin version. Essentially, it reminds the 'Most Clement Lord' of his gift of Sarah to Abraham and of Rebecca to his son, and asks for a wife who is similarly faithful. Some variations include the names of the person and the object of his affection. The version in Papu's book has been tidied up as much as possible.

hoopoe bird before going to bed, and recite the previous prayer, but replacing the words "*servo tuo quam nupturus sim uxorem*" with "*ancillæ tuæ quem sin nuptura virum*".

*

* *

CHAPTER 3 – A WITCH'S GRIMOIRE

COLLECTION OF SECRETS

Drawn from the Five Books of Moses and from several books of the Holy Scriptures.

Against headaches

Write on an olive leaf:
Athena.
Fasten this leaf to the head.

To staunch blood

From Adam's blood death is born.
From Christ's blood life is born.
O blood, stop!

Against firearms

Swallow this, written on a note:
Armisi farisi restingo.
Say these words when in danger.

Against scarcity and famine

It is a very great secret which I tested in the last famine and I had the good fortune to save lives of many people. It is the same one which Elijah and Elisha used; one can also find it in the Gospel which Christians attribute to Jesus Christ when He fed so many people with so little bread, for the all drew from the same foundation, and used the three principal points of Kabbalah.

Pray to the Lord of Lords every morning and evening for 7 days. On the 7th day, after your morning prayers, take the leaf of a plant one commonly eats, such as lettuce, salad (*sic.*), etc. Take the leaf of a tree, and write the following words with honey, dew or rainwater before sunrise, on the top side: "*I will make you rain bread from the highest heaven*", and on the other side: "*Manetur.*" Cense it and eat it.[250] He who eats it will pass 7 days without hunger. This may be continued 7 more times, which is 40 days, but you must not go beyond this. This is the bread which the angel brought to the prophet in the desert.

To break chains or iron bars

Take equal parts of sublimated mercury and arsenic, and a half ounce of ammonia salts, and add to urine, rub it on the iron or wrap it with a cloth steeped in the liquid.

Means to bring forth grain in abundance from soil which has not been manured

Take the seeds you wish to put into the ground, and leave them to soak for six hours in water made putrescent with manure. Remove them at the end of this time without letting them stand any longer, and let them dry thoroughly in the sun. At the end of three days soak them again for three hours. That will suffice. Then sow them.

To stop a serpent

Say this when you see it: *Osi, Osoa, Osia*. It will allow itself to be picked up.

To stop a murderer

Take blood from the deceased while it is still warm, throw it on the fire and let it boil. You will see that the murderer cannot flee, and when he is four leagues distance he will be forced to return to the scene.

To stop one or several people in their tracks

Say:

VEIDE, RONGAN, RADA, BAGABIN.

Kneel on the right knee with the right wrist on the ground, and fall back. Get up again without allowing the left wrist to touch anything.

---

[250] Strangely, nothing is said about the lettuce leaf, unless both are eaten together?

To be happy on a voyage

Carry artemisia and verbena on you.

To subdue a spirited horse

Place a small, round pebble in its ears, and it will stop moving.

Against infected wounds

Put quince juice on the wound, and it will draw out the poison.

To heal deep and mortal wounds

Take some *Vinea purvinea*[251] together with its roots, put it in wine, and give it to the wounded person drink after a few hours. If he finds wood, iron or another substance on the wound's surface, all the poison will come out and the invalid will be healed without any other medicine.

To know whether an invalid will be cured or die

Take a little bacon fat, and rub it on the bottom of the invalid's feet, and then give it to a dog to eat. If the dog eats it, it is a sign of healing; if not, it is a sign of death.

When a woman is in labor with a child

To have the afterbirth and dead child come out of the body, have the woman eat two pieces of root from the white fleur-de-lys, or have her drink the water in which you have boiled 2 eggs. The remedy is infallible.

---

[251] There is no such plant. It is either a fabulous plant, or a poorly rendered spelling on another plant. Given the law of sympathy which is often found in folk remedies, it is likely grape vine, with the idea of placing the raw plant into the fermented produce, as an analogy of the ability of the liquid to draw out the impurities in the body.

To staunch blood

Take in hand the herb known as *bursa pastoris*[252], or *onagollis*[253] if a woman, and hang it for your neck next to the skin.

Real oriental turquoise will have the same effect.

To heal earache

Take a small onion, cook it thoroughly in cinders; then take a fine cloth with some unsalted butter, put the butter and the onion into the cloth, and apply it, as hot as possible, to the affected ear. Hold it there for one minute. Tried and tested.

For corns on the feet

Take the inside of a fig, and place some on the swelling of the corn for several days, and you will be healed.

For toothache

Put some eau-de-vie in the hollow of your hand, and breathe through the nostril on the side where you have the pain.

To pass a stomach ache

Take gum Arabic in milk.

Remedy for burns

1 spoonful of good vinegar.

12 spoonfuls of water.

Beat them together, adding Spanish whiting in powder to form an amalgam which has the consistency of slightly thick cream. Spread it on a cloth and apply it immediately.

---

[252] Shepherd's purse.

[253] *Anagallis*, the best-known variety being the Scarlet Pimpernel. Often used in homeopathy to treat rashes and nervous complaints.

Against the death of animals

Take the yellow spongy excrescences which grow on lime trees, put them in the water you give your animals to drink, and if the animals are attacked by some contagious illness, pulverize them a little and put them in their watering trough.

To know which animals will live or die

Note that all animals which are born when the moon is no longer clear, that is, 3 or 4 days before or after the new moon, die within the year. Those which are born outside of this time are good to raise, but the others should be sold.

To prevent bees from stinging

Take three leaves from the plant called *plantago amita*[254], and keep these in your mouth when approaching them.

To have trees bear a lot of fruit

They should be grafted 3 or 4 days before the new moon.

To make a girl relieve herself

Take 3 small black beans.
Place one between each finger of the right hand, sit on your chair at the level of the heart, attract the girl's attention, and say:

EGO AGO ET SUPERAGO ET CONSUMMATUM EST.

Alternatively:

Take 3 white beans. Say:

ESE, MEBE, MATRISTOPE.

---

[254] This is the plantain.

To avoid being wounded in war

Write the following words on a zinc plate: *"See the sword of Adonaï and Gideon."* This plate should be cut in the form of a seven-sided star. Cense it and place it in the pommel of your sword. You will wound all your adversaries even when they are wearing armor.

Fat to prevent arms from rusting

100 grams of lard.
100 grams of lamb or beef fat.
5 grams of regular candle wax.
5 grams of camphor.
15 grams of zinc oxide.

The fats should be melted and mixed with the wax and camphor, then gently stir with a spatula and add the zinc oxide when it begins to cool and take on a thicker consistency. If the zinc oxide is mixed too quickly, it will precipitate and remain at the bottom, and the mixing will be incomplete. When the arms are dry, rub them with this grease using a hard and very strong brush. It is important to get the grease onto the metal by brushing with a hard brush. The grease doesn't have to be visible.

Lustral water

While fasting, give the person a glass of water to drink, in which a red hot poker has been extinguished.

Over the water, say (the breath penetrating the water): *"By Adonaï, may all passion be extinguished in you as the heat of this iron is extinguished in this water* (5 times).*"

Evocation

For 9 entire days, while the moon is growing after its 5th day, burn incense in honor of the protective powers of suffering souls, each time reciting the *Pater Noster* solely for the repose of these same souls, and burning the incense to this same end a tallow candle in honor of the protective spirits of suffering souls for their proper repose for the intention one has.

From time to time you may burn incense in honor of the geniuses to this end.

The three following evenings, at night (avoid Friday), light fire, and make three circuits to mentally describe a circle. Take incense, and throw it into the fire, thinking or verbally imploring Hecate (goddess of enchantments), then, returning into the circle and standing in the middle, imploring the support of the stars of sight and thought, say:

"O Hecate, goddess in the heavens, goddess on the earth, and Proserpine of Hades, O mother of the shadows, supreme queen of the army of the dead, do not launch your legions against me, O Hecate, but rather have them serve me. O triune Hecate, may your divinity come to me, may your power encompass me, and my Father (the heaven), be not offended!

"By Hecate, O genius of the airs, by Hecate, suffering souls of the dead, by Hecate, O restless souls of the realm below, by Hecate, become my aids, my arms, my army!"

Then, leaving the circle, take the incense to offer to the geniuses, and formulate your request.

Afterwards, burn bread and wine with the intention of suffering souls in general, and when this has been done, you say:

"By Hecate, in the silence of the nights I have called the legions of airs, the favorable army of Obs: to the one I have offered incense which soothes them, to the other the bread for which they hunger. And, while the stars shine brightly, may the Forces called here act, like a sovereign in his purple mantle, your servant, O Hecate, will go to sleep in confidence."

*

* *

Iron repulses occult influences. When you fear sorcery, take an iron rod in your hand.

Wash your head with water over which has been said: *"O Adonaï, deliver and heal your servant"* three times, and once finished, let the water dry on your head.

*

* *

Lectisternia[255], the meal offered to the dead. Invite the dead (by name) to the dinner. Set the table and make a great fire in the hearth. Call them by their names, but serve them and pour out wine for them too, then throw it on the fire for them. Make honey cakes for them to offer them supper, cut them into pieces and throw these on the fire. Speak to them, then ask them what you wish.

Means of drawing power from animals in order to transplant it into men

Take all the semen from a stallion when it is covering a mare, which should be done on the 27th or 28th day of the moon. Put this in fertile soil, and also plant the black chameleon[256], let it grow, then give it to the weak person to eat on the first Friday of the moon. Also take this plant by the neck[257] and have the person live among robust and healthy horses. They will become weak while the person becomes strong and robust. Then transplant this root on the same day into different soil.

This secret is a great hidden mystery.

---

[255] Initially a Roman Festival, normally to thank the gods for being spared from a catastrophe, in which couches and sofas were set up in the street, a banquet laid out, and effigies of the gods placed on the couches and sofas. Later on, the festival was arrogated by the Christians, who held feasts in celebration of the dead.

[256] Sadly, there is no direct translation for this intriguing plant. The best guess would be the *Houttuynia* or 'Chameleon Plant'. However, this is indigenous to Japan, China and the Far East. It is also poisonous!

[257] The test doesn't say what you do with this plant prior to replanting it elsewhere, once the person has regained their strength.

CHAPTER 4 – A LITTLE DICTIONARY OF FOLK MAGIC

SUMMARIZING IN ALPHABETICAL ORDER THE SECRETS AND PRINCIPLE
FORMULAS OF PRACTICE CONCERNING FOLK MAGIC[258]

ALOES	The juice of *aloes* mixed with vinegar prevents hair loss.
ALUM	If one rubs a cloth with the white of an egg mixed with *alum*, after washing it with salt water and lets it dry, it prevents fire from burning (BÉLINUS). If one takes *red arsenic* with *alum* and grinds them together, and mixes them with the sap of *sempervivum* and juniper gum, a man who rubs his hands with it can handle and hold a hot fire without being burned (G. 94).
ANEMIA	See RULES.
ANGELICA	An infusion of *angelica* in wine cures interior ulcerations.
ANISEED	Infused in wine, with saffron, cures *inflammation of the eyes*. Pieces of the same plant, introduced into the nostrils after being macerated in water, heal ulcers of the nose.
ANTS (To chase away)	Crush *wild marjoram* and reduce it to powder on the place they are.
ASTHMA	See PURSLAIN.

---

[258] Each interesting tradition drawn from a Grimoire having been quoted elsewhere, the strictly alphabetical order hasn't been followed, and the same word is sometimes quoted several times under the same letter. The letters which follow each quotation indicate the original Grimoires from which each quote is taken. There is little point in warning the reader about the number of superstitions contained in these traditions of Low Magic. [PAPUS] Also, most of these names are archaic, which further confuses identifying the herbs. Naturally, the alphabetical order has been adjusted to follow the English language, so would be hard to follow against the original book.

BEDBUGS	To kill all the bedbugs in a bed, take a *cucumber* in the form of a serpent, preserve it and soak it in water, then rub it all over your bed.
	Or take the spleen of an ox, mixed and dissolved in vinegar, rub it on the bed and you will see that thereafter there will be no more bedbugs.
	To take them alive without touching them when going to bed, place a large *comfrey* on the pillow. All the bedbugs will gather on in and will not go elsewhere. We have experienced this many times (G. 113).
BEE STINGS	Cow dung applied to the sting immediately relieves the pain.
BEES	Assembling them (see NEPETA); preserving them (see MARSH-MALLOW).
BIRDS	If you want to *have birds in your hand*, take some of any seed and soak them well in *wine lees* with *hemlock*, then throw them onto the ground, and all the bird which eat them won't be able to fly.
	If you want to *understand birdsong*, take two friends with you and go together into a forest on the 5th of the Kalends of November, bringing *dogs* as if you wanted to go hunting. Take back to the house the first animal you catch, which you will eat with the heart of a *fox*; and soon you will understand the singing of birds, and if you want those who are present to understand them as well, you only have to kiss them.[259]
BIRDS (To attract them)	See CHINESE MISTLETOE[260] (see later).
BLADDER (Problems)	*OFFODITIUS.*

---

[259] In the Latin calendar the Kalends were the first of the following month, and days were counted including both ends of the count. In this instance, the date is probably 27th November, being 5 days before 1st December, counting both 27th November and 1st December. Note also the last phrase is ambiguous. Although *baiser* initially meant 'to kiss', its meaning turned far more intimate over time, and now the word *embrasser* is used. Therefore, to have those present understand birdsong, one either had to kiss them, or perhaps get a whole lot more intimate…

[260] *Gui de Chine.*

BREAST	All illnesses of the breast will disappear with the application of sedative poultices composed of *henbane* (CHR. 401). For abscesses, apply flour of large white beans in a compress on the forehead, the temples and the feet with an infusion of myrtle leaves.
CABBAGE	(See ROSE).
CELANDINE	Carry it on yourself with the *heart of a mole* to ward off *enemies*, and also for business and *lawsuits*. Placed on the head of an *invalid*, sing if he should live; cry, if he should die (G. 50).
CINQUEFOIL	(*Pentaphilon*, influence of **Mercury**). The root in a salve works on wounds. Heals *scrofula* if its sap is drunk with water. The sap appeases *toothache* when put in the mouth. Obtains what one desires, when carried upon oneself.
CLEANING	Gravelly ashes.... ½ pound White soap..........2 ounces Gum Arabic........2 ounces Slag of alum.........2 ounces Bird lime...........1 ounce Pasque-flower.....1 ounce Reduce all to a powder, mix – dissolve in limpid water.
COCK	To prevent it from crowing: anoint the head and comb with oil. To prevent it from coupling: anoint its arse with oil (G. 92).
COLIC	Take the root of the White Henbane (Aristotle).
CONCEPTION	(See STERILITY).
CONVULSIONS	Put bracelets of raw silk round the wrists of children, and they will never have convulsions (CHR. 406).
COUGH	Hanging a *pumice-stone* around the neck of a child who has a cough will stop it (G. 93).
COWS	To stop their milk (see LILY) G. 50. (See later).
COWS (To cure bad feet)	Coat the animal's horns with wax, oil and pitch.
CUCUMBER	(See BEDBUGS).

DEVIL	To have the devil appear to a sleeping person, take the blood of a *hoopoe* and rub it on her face. She will imagine that all the devils are around her.
DIVORCES (Preventing)	Two quail hearts, one male and the other female. Have the woman carry the female one, and the man the male one.
DOG'S DUNG	(See DYSENTERY).
DOGS	Various effects on them (see HOUND'S TONGUE).
DRUNKENNESS	If one puts several eels in a pot of wine and leaves them there to die, he who drinks this liquid will hate wine for a year, and will perhaps never drink it again during his lifetime.
DYSENTERY	(See *ORNOGLOSSE*).
	Pebbles from a stream. – Warm them over a strong fire, throw them into a vase full of urine in which has been mixed powdered *dog's dung*. - Give it to be drunk twice a day for three days (proven). (G. 118).
	(See PLANTAIN); (see RAISINS).
ENEMIES	(See CELANDINE).
EPILEPSY	A decoction of *viburnum* leaves in wine cures epilepsy (CHR. 402).
	(See VERBENA).
EROTIC DREAMS (To be delivered from)	Apply a lead blade to the stomach in the form of a cross.
EYES	*Polygonum root*. LIRIOPE (see ANISEED).
FEAR (To inspire)	(See CENTAURY).
FIRE	(See ALUM).
FIREWATER	Take wine which isn't heavy, strong and old. Mix it with a quart of quicklime and powdered sulfur. Add tartar and kitchen salt. Put everything in a well-stoppered bottle with an alembic above it, into which you will distil this water, which you must keep in a glass flask.
FISH (To catch them by hand)	(See NETTLE; see PERIWINKLE).
FISH BONE	If a fish bone is stuck in your throat, put a foot in cold water (CHR. 405).

FLEAS	To get rid of fleas from a bedroom, sprinkle it with a decoction of *rue* and urine from a brood-mare, and they won't remain there (Pliny).
FRECKLES	Cow's spleen mixed with eggshells from a hen, dissolved in vinegar (applied to the skin).
FUTURE	Take the curdled blood of an *ass* with the fat and lungs of a *lynx*, in equal amounts, and make pellet of them with which you perfume the house. Then you will see someone during sleep who will tell everything which will happen (G. 103).
GLANDS	A goat's head hung from the neck of a person who has scrofulous glands, will heal him perfectly (G. 92).[261]
GOUT	HENBANE ROOT.
GRAPES	Grape pips, cooked, pulverized and applied as a poultice to the stomach, heals dysentery.
GREAT COMFREY	(See BEDBUGS).
GREEK FIRE	Natural sulfur, tartar, sarcocolla, picolle (?)[262], cooked salt, common oil, petrol, boil all together.
GUESTS	If you want to give joy and entertainment to a company during a meal, take four leaves of *verbena* which are steeped in wine, then sprinkle the place where the meal is to take place; all those who are invited will appear happy and joyful.
HAIR	*To make hair grow*, burn some bees, mix their ashes with mouse droppings and infuse this mixture in roseate oil; add the ashes of burned chestnuts or beans, and hair will grow on any part of the body that you anoint with this oil.
HAIR (Falling out)	(See ALOES).
HALLUCINATIONS	(See KNAP-WEED; see LAMP; see DEVIL).
HARES (To attract them)	(See HENBANE).
HEAD (Aches)	*ORNOGLOSSE* ROOT. (See LAMP).
HEART (Ailments of)	KNOT-GRASS.

261

[262] Most of these ingredients are not easy to find in dictionaries. Some can be guessed at, but the nearest to *picolle* is perhaps *picot*, meaning 'splinter', which might suggest adding splintered wood to the mixture?

HE-GOAT	Take droppings from a he-goat and mix with wheat flour. Dry the mixture, then crush it and let it warm with oil only. After that, rub it all over the prepuce immediately prior to copulation, and it is certain that your wife will only love you alone.
	The same thing can also be accomplished by using the tallow of a he-goat.
HELIOTROPE	Gather the plant in the month of August, when the sun is in the sign of Leo.
	Wrap it in a laurel leaf with a wolf's tooth and carry it with you against *slander*. Put under the head during the night allow you to see those who would *rob* the owner of the herb.
	Put in a church prevents *women unfaithful to their husbands* from leaving until it has been removed. (G. 49).
HEMORRHAGING (Uterus)	To heal hemorrhaging of the uterus, take *seven oranges*, cook their peels in three pints of water until reduced to a third of the volume.
	Add sugar and make her take a dozen spoonfuls three or four times a day.
HEMORRHOIDS	(See VERBENA). – To heal them sit on a lion's skin (Aristotle; G. 92).
HENBANE	Its sap will break a silver cup in which it is placed. Mixed with the blood of a young hare, and put on its skin, will attract *all the hares* to the place where one has placed it. (See later).
	(Influence of **Jupiter**). Its root prevents *ulcers* and removes them. Pounded, it prevents pain from *gout*. Its sap drunk with honey works against illnesses of the *liver*. Carried on yourself makes women love you. (See later).
HENBANE (Cure poisoning by)	Drink sap of *purslain* mixed with sweet wine.
HOUND'S TONGUE	Placed in a spot with the heart and womb of a frog will make *dogs* assemble there.
	Carried on the big toe prevents dogs from barking. Put on a dog's neck will make him roll over and die (G. 51).
HUSBAND	(See WOMAN).

HYDROPSY	(See PLANTAIN). You will surely cure a person with hydropsy if you make him swallow for 9 days any drink containing the dung of an unweaned pup, dried and pulverized; but the invalid must be unaware of the nature of this remedy (CHR. 405).
IMPOTENT (To make)	To make a man impotent, one only has to have him swallow one of those worms which glow in summer.[263]
INCOMBUSTIBLE (To render)	(See ALUM).
INFIDELITY	(See WOMAN).
INSOMNIA	Stems of *fennel* cooked in oil and applied to the head.
INTERIOR ULCERATIONS	(See ANGELICA).
INVALID (To know if he will die)	CELANDINE. (See also SICKNESS).
INVISIBLE (To become)	In the nest of the hoopoe one may find a certain stone of diverse colors, and he who carries on himself will become invisible.
JAUNDICE	Make the invalid drink each morning for eight days, before eating, five small pieces of goat dung in white wine.
KIDNEYS	(PAINS, *OFFODITIUS*, LIRIOPE).
KNAPWEED	Mixed with the blood of a *female hoopoe*, and put into a lamp with the oil produces *hallucinations* in those present. Throw into the fire when the stars are shining, they appear to chase each other. Put under someone's nose, makes him afraid.
KNOT-GRASS	(Influence of the **Sun**). Cures *heart* and *stomach problems* (G. 56). Drunk, it excites one to love. The root carried on oneself heals *eye problems*.
LAMP	If you want everything in a palace to appear black, take care to soak the wick of the *lamp* or candle one is going to light in well-beaten meerschaum.

---

[263] *Un ver luisant* – a 'glowworm'.

To make everyone in a room appear not to have heads, throw yellow sulfur mixed with honey into a lamp, then after lighting it, place it in the middle of the assembly.

If you make a wick out of a winding sheet or a black sheet, and light the lamp in the middle of a room, you will see wonderful things.

Take a green *frog* and decapitate it on a mortuary sheet, soak it in *elder-tree* oil make a wick out of it which you light in a green lamp, and you will see a black man who holds a lamp in his hand, and several other interesting things (G. 105).

If you want to make a chamber full of *serpents* appear, take the fat of a serpent and mix is with a little salt. Then take a piece of mortuary sheet which you will cut in four, in each of which put some of this fat. Make four wicks from these, and light them in the four corners of the room, with *elder-tree oil* in a new lamp, and you will see the effect described.

LAWSUIT	(See CELANDINE).
LEG (Ailments of)	*OFFODITIUS.*
LETHARGY	A strong decoction of *monk's pepper, wild celery* and *sage* in *salted water*, used as a friction rub on the back of the head, brings invalids fallen into lethargy back to life.
LILY	Harvested in August and mixed with the sap of *laurel*, then put for some time beneath a pile of dung, this plant will generate worms. Their powder prevents a person sleeping or gives a fever.
	Put in a vase in which there is cow's milk, and the vase covered with a cow skin of the same color, all the cows in the region will lose their milk (G. 52).
LIRIOPE	(Influence of the **Moon**). Its flower cures kidney problems.
LIVER (Ailments)	HENBANE.
LOVE	See PERIWINKLE; HENBANE; VERBENA; HE-GOAT; WOMEN; DIVORCE.
LUNGS	(See THISTLES).
MAGICAL HERBS	Only harvest these from the 23rd to the 29th day of the month.

State the use to which it will be put while pulling the herb from the ground. Then put it under wheat or barley up to the moment it will be used. The principle ones are:
Heliotrope – Henbane – Nepeta – Nettle – Mandrake – Celandine – Periwinkle – Hound's Tongue – Lily – Mistletoe – Centaury – Sage – Verbena – Melissa – Snake-wood.

MANDRAKE[264] With the juice of *mandrake*, when given to a bitch makes her pregnant.

MARSH-MALLOW (See WOMB, URINE). Marsh-mallow seeds pulverized and kneaded into the form of an unguent, and rubbed lightly on the face and hands, preserves from wasp and bee stings, etc.

MEAL (See GUESTS).

MELANCHOLY (Treatment for) *OFFODITIUS.*

MELISSA Carried on one makes one pleasant.
Attached to an ox's neck makes him follow the Operator.

MEMORY A *hoopoe's* tongue, hung from the neck, makes the *memory* and judgement return to those who have lost them (G. 95).

MERCURY (Its herb) CINQUEFOIL.

MIGRAINES Inhale warm vapor infused with *myrtle* through the mouth.

MISCARRIAGE See WORMWOOD.

---

[264] *Vierge de Pasteur*, literally 'Pastor's Virgin'. However, it appears that this should be *Verge de Pasteur* (without the 'i'), which coarsely means 'Pastor's Rod'! Under 'Mandrake' or 'Mandragore' it says: 'See Pastor's Rod'. Under 'Pastor's Rod' it says that a mix of Mandrake and Pastor's Rod will render a bitch (female dog) *grosse*, or pregnant. However, it is quite possible the Mandrake and the Pastor's Rod are being conflated, and that is the option selected here. The Mandrake has long been a favorite of Folk Medicine. The apparent similarity of its root to the shape of a man (or woman) has long associated it with procreation, and it was said that, when pulled for the ground, its scream could kill a man, so often a dog was tied to it and meat placed just out of reach, while the harvester blocked his ears with wax and stood far away. Either way, whether e Pastor's Rod is another name of Mandrake or a separate plant, it doesn't ly affect this Dictionary.

MOLE	To capture a mole put an onion, a leek and some garlic bulbs in its burrow, and a short time after it will come out without any strength.
MOON	Its plant is *ORNOGLOSSE*.
MUSHROOMS	For cure (see NETTLE).
(Poisoning by)	Swallow some *saltpeter* mixed with oil.
MYRTLE	(See VOMITING, SLEEP).
NAME	If you want to see your name imprinted or written on a peach-grower's *peach pits* or and almond-grower's *almond kernels*, take a pit from a good peach, put it in the soil at the proper time to plant, and leave it for six to seven days until it is half open, then take it up gently without damaging anything, and with *cinnabar*, write on this *pit* what you want; and when it has dried, put it back into the soil, after closing it up and holding it together with a strong, thin, loosely-tied thread, and without doing anything further to encourage it to grow into a tree, you will see that the fruit it bears will carry the same name written on the *pit*. You can perform the same experiment on the kernel of an *almond*; and that will give fresh proof (G. 115).
NEPETA or **CATMINT**[265]	Makes animals dizzy when placed in the nose. Assembles *bees* and prevents them from leaving. Revives drowned or almost dead bees (G. 51).
NETTLE	Held in the hand with *yarrow* prevents fear of phantoms (harvest them between 19th July and 23rd August). Mix its sap with the juice of the snake-wood, rub it into one's hands and throw the rest into water. Then take out the fish found there with one's hands (G. 50). (See later). The seeds of the *nettle* cooked in wine cures pleurisy and inflammation of the lungs (CHR. 403). The leaves ground up and applied to wounds and *ulcers* prevent gangrene.

---

[265] The word used is *Nepte*, which doesn't appear anywhere. *Nepeta* is Latin for 'Catmint', which is more likely, and has been used here.

	A decoction of the seeds of this plant heals *poisoning by mushrooms or toadstools.*
NIGHT	If you rub your face with bat's blood, you will see and hear at night as well as in the day.
NOSE (Ulcers of)	(See ANISEED).
OFFODITIUS[266]	(Influence of **Saturn**). Herb which heals: *With its sap* – problems with the kidneys and aches of the legs, bladder problems. *With is cooked root* – relieves those possessed or melancholic when carried in a white cloth. The herb chases away *evil spirits* from houses.
ORCHITIS	(See TESTICLES).
ORNOGLOSSE[267]	(Influence of **Mars**). Root works against headaches. Sap works against dysentery.
OX	To make it follow (see MELISSA). An ox whose tongue has been rubbed with garlic allows itself to die more than if one only washes its mouth out with salt and vinegar (G. 92).
PEACHES	(See WORMS).
PERIWINKLE	Reduced to powder with earthworms brings *love* to those who eat this powder on their meat. Mixed with sulfur and thrown into a pond, this compound will make all the *fish* die. Thrown into the fire makes it bluish (G. 51). Given to a *buffalo*, it immediately makes it die.
PHANTOMS (To not be afraid)	(see NETTLE).
PIGEONS (To attract them)	VERBENA. (See later).
	Place a man's skull in a dovecote (G. 90).
PIMPLES (on the skin)	*Sempervivium* ground with barley flour and oil will make scurf and other skin eruptions disappear. A decoction of tobacco leaves, boiled and applied as a lotion, makes pimples and redness of the face disappear.
PLAGUE	Barberry water, half an ounce; theriac, one dram.

---

[266] As stated in footnote 94, it has been impossible to find a translation of this word.
[267] Unable to find a word in English even remotely similar to this, which doesn't exist in French. All one can be certain of is that it is a plant with a significant root.

	Give it to drink to the person afflicted with the ailment, the mixture being warm. Then make the invalid sweat. Chewing the *burnet* in times of epidemic preserves one from the scourge.
PLANTAIN	Boiled leaves applied in poultices heals *ulcers*. The seeds boiled in wine or its leaves stewed in vinegar stop *dysentery*.
PLEURISY	(See NETTLE).
PNEUMONIA	(See NETTLE).
POTIONS	(See LOVE; see HE-GOAT).
PREGNANCY	(See STERILITY). For a woman to conceive, reduce a stag's horn to powder and mix it with cow dung. Then the woman carries it on herself while she is having an affair with a man, and infallibly she will become pregnant. (See VINE). If a woman cannot conceive, make her drink, without her knowing it, the milk of a *brood-mare*, and then a man should *know* her.
PUMICE-STONE	(See COUGH). Put in an ass's ear, he will immediately fall into a faint.
PURSLAIN	(See VISIONS). Cures poisoning by Henbane. (See HENBANE; see later). Its seeds heal *asthmatics* (CHR.403), boiled and eaten with honey.
RABIES	Drink wine in which *verbena* stalks have been boiled; also apply to the wound the crushed leaves of this plant (CHR. 401); the same result can be obtained with *angelica*.
RATS	One can chase *rats* from one's home if one perfumes it with the horn (from the hoof) or a horse or a mule.
REGULATE	To reestablish the coursing of the blood, one must take some infusions of fresh parsley leaves as a tea. Also, good to prevent a pale complexion.
REQUESTS (Success with)	(See CINQUEFOIL).
ROSE	A seed with a mustard seed, and the foot of a weasel hung from a tree, makes it *sterile*.

This composition makes *cabbages* which are nearly dead revive in a day.

Put in a lamp it produces hallucinations.

Mixed with olive oil and natural sulfur and rubbed around a house it seems as if everything is on fire while the sun shines (G. 53).

RUE	(See FLEAS).
SAGE	Rotting on a dung heap, gives birth to a worm (G. 53).
SATURN	Its herb is *OFFODITIUS*.
SCORPIONS	If one applies a rat to a scorpion's bite, it will heal it. To chase away *serpents* and *scorpions* from a house, cense it with the lung of an *ass*.
SCROFULA	(CINQUEFOIL; VERBENA). Place a *barberry* root on the neck (Gallien).
SCURFY	(See PIMPLES).
SEA (Spume)	(See LAMP).
SEE IN THE NIGHT	(See NIGHT).
SERPENTS	If one wants to kill a serpent quickly, let him take a plump snake-root, grind it up well with a frog which you will boil and mix with the snake-root. Then, after grinding everything up in a paper on which you have written the name of the one you love, throw it at the serpents, who will immediately die. (See LAMP; see STRAWBERRY PLANT).
SICKNESS	To know if a person will die from a sickness or if they will recover, go to see them, carrying *verbena* in your hand, and when you are close to the invalid, ask him how he feels; if he says that he feels fine, he will recover.
SLANDER	(See HELIOTROPE).
SLEEP (Deprive of)	(See SNAKE-WOOD). Makes one talk in one's sleep (see WOMAN). If one wants to make a sleeping person afraid, put him upon the skin of an ape.
SNAKE-WOOD	(See NETTLE). Put on the head prevents one from sleeping.
SPECKS IN THE EYES	Decoction of *royal comfrey* in compresses (a kind of chamomile).
STAG (horn)	(see PREGNANCY).

STERILITY	(G. 91). To keep a woman sterile: Set the milk teeth of young children when they fall out, in silver and hang them from the woman's neck. Drink a glass of mule's urine every month. Hang the finger of a dead fetus around the neck (G. 92).
STOMACH (Ache)	POLYGONUM.
STRAWBERRY PLANT	To prevent serpents from doing any harm when you are walking in the countryside, take some *strawberry* leaves and place them around your body.
SUBJUGATION (of animals)	Rub the head of the animal you want to go into its stable with a *squill bulb*[268] (G. 91).
SUN	Its herb is KNOT-GRASS.
TEETH	The tooth of an animal or a yearling hung around a child's neck will make its teeth grow without pain. Rub the gums with the cooked brains of a hare. The teeth will never rot, if every morning you melt three grains of sea salt in your mouth and, with the tongue, spread this solution over the teeth and gums.
TEETH (Ache)	Sap of *cinquefoil*.
TESTICLES	Fresh cow dung fried in a stove with chamomile flowers, roses and sweet clover will cure all testicular inflammations in two days.
THISTLES	An infusion of blessed thistle cures ulcers in the lungs (CHR. 403).
TOBACCO	(See PIMPLES).
TREE	Making sterile (see ROSE); writing a name (see NAME).
TUMORS	*Goat manure* will make them suppurate, when applied in poultices (Gallien).
ULCERS	HENBANE, VERBENA and PLANTAIN roots.
UNFAITHFUL WOMEN	(See HELIOTROPE; see WOMAN).
URINE	MARSH-MALLOW ROOT infused in wine cures urine retention.

---

[268] A 'squill' is a Mediterranean plant, at a best guess for the French term *un ail de squille*. *Ail* is garlic, but the word could possibly be *aile* or wing, in which case *squille* might be the misprinted name of a bird.

VERBENA	Harvest in sunlight in the sign of Aries.
	Mixed with seed from a year-old *peony*, cures epilepsy.
	Put in a dovecote, it brings nearby pigeons together.
	The powder thrown *between two lovers* will make them argue. (See later; see RABIES).
	(Influence of **Venus**). Its root on the neck heals scrofula, ulcers, hemorrhoids.
	Carried on oneself, admirable for love. Chases away evil spirits (see GUESTS).
VIBURNUM	(See EPILEPSY).
VINE	The leaves and filaments of the vine, ground into poultices and applied to the stomach will heal women who, newly-pregnant, are tormented by a disordered appetite (CHR. 402).
VINEGAR	If you throw *peppercorns* into spoiled vinegar, it will regain its strength.
VISIONS	(See LAMP). To prevent them, put *purslain* on the bed.
	If you wish to see what other cannot see, take the dung of a *cat* with the fat of a white *hen*, mix them together in wine and rub it onto your eyes.
VOMITING	The fruit of myrtle, dried, pulverized and mixed with the white of an egg, then applied as a salve on the mouth and stomach, prevents vomiting.
VOYAGES	(See WORMWOOD).
WICK	(See LAMP).
WINE (Revulsion for)	(See DRUNKENNESS).
WOLVES (To frighten them)	Smear the body with hare dung.
WOMAN	It is written in the book of Cleopatra that a woman who isn't happy with her husband as she should be, has only to take the marrowbone from the left foot of a wolf and carry it upon her, and it is certain that she will be satisfied and that she will be the only one he loves.
	To make a woman confess what she has done, take a live frog from the water, remove its tongue and then keep it in water; then place this tongue on the heart

of the woman while she is asleep; and she will reply to all the questions you ask her.

WOMB

The flower of *marsh-mallow*, kneaded with pork fat and turpentine, then applied to the outside of the womb, dissolves any inflammations.

WORMS, MAGGOTS

Peach leaves mixed, with vinegar, and mint and alum, then applied to the navel, is an infallible vermifuge for children (CHR. 401).

WORMWOOD

When one wishes to undertake a voyage easily and without becoming tired, hold the herb called *wormwood*, and make a girdle of it when moving; then one can cook this herb and wash the feet with it, and one will never become tired (G).

Fumigations with boiled *wormwood*, taken in a seated bath, deliver women in confinement from the dead fruit of their womb.

The same plant, cooked in wine and drunk in small but frequent doses, keep a woman from the danger of *abortion* (CHR. 402).

WOUNDS

CINQUEFOIL ROOT.
(See NETTLE).

YARROW

(See NETTLE).

END

CHAPTER 5 - RECOMMENDED BIBLIOGRAPHY

The following books were consulted during the translation of this book, and are highly recommended both as source references and a means of accessing the most up to date information on Solomonic Magic in general. Note that publication dates don't reflect when the book originally appeared: only the publication of the edition I was using.

Since the scientific fields of neurology, neuropathy, psychology, psychiatry and hypnotherapy have advanced so much over the past one hundred twenty years, no books have been recommended for these field, since it would be difficult to find any which still adhere completely to the theories of the 1880s and 1890s.

Agrippa, **Henry Cornelius** (Ed. Donald Tyson). *Three Books of Occult Philosophy*. Llwewllyn, Woodbury, MN. 2014.

Barrett, **Francis**. *The Magus – A Complete System of Occult Philosophy*. Citadel Press, New York, NY. 1995.

Leitch, **Aaron**. *Secrets of the Magical Grimoires*. Llewellyn, Woodbury, MN. 2005.

Lévi, **Eliphas** (trans. John Michael Greer and Mark Anthony Mikituk). *The Doctrine and Ritual of High Magic – A New Translation*. TarcherPerigee, New York, NY.2017.

Lévi, **Eliphas** (trans. Arthur Edward Waite). *The History of Magic*. Samuel Weiser Inc., York Beach, ME. 1999.

Lévi, **Eliphas** (trans. Arthur Edward Waite). *Transcendental Magic*. Bracken Books, London. 1995.

McGregor Mathers & Aleister Crowley. *The Greater and Lesser Keys of Solomon the King*. Mockingbird Press, Bristol. 2016.

Peterson, Joseph H. (ed.). *Grimoirum Verum*. Createspace, US. 2007.

Peterson, Joseph H. (ed.). *The Veritable Clavicles of Solomon.* Accessed Sept – Oct 2017 at (http://esotericarchives.com/solomon/l1203.htm).

Skinner, Stephen. *Techniques of Solomonic Magic.* Golden Hoard, Singapore. 2015.

Warwick, Tarl (ed.). *Heptameron: or Magical Elements.* Createspace, US. 2015.

Warwick, Tarl (ed.). *The Enchiridion of Pope Leo III.* Createspace, US. 2016.

Warwick, Tarl (ed.). *The Grand Grimoire – The Red Dragon.* Createspace, US. 2015.

Warwick, Tarl (ed.). *The Grimoire of Pope Honorius.* Createspace, US. 2015.

I would especially like to thank Joseph Peterson for answering a number of my questions, and clarifying my thinking, while this project was underway.

* *
*